[THE COMPLETE PROSE WORKS OF MATTHEW ARNOLD]

II

Democratic Education

MATTHEW ARNOLD

DEMOCRATIC EDUCATION

Edited by R. H. Super

ANN ARBOR THE UNIVERSITY OF MICHIGAN PRESS

Second printing 1963
Published in the United States of America by
The University of Michigan Press and simultaneously
in Toronto, Canada, by Ambassador Books Limited
Library of Congress Catalog Card No. 60-5018

Manufactured in the United States of America

Editor's Preface

This volume is one of two in the present edition of Arnold's prose that is to be devoted almost entirely to works on education. It contains two of his books, *The Popular Education of France* and *A French Eton;* one pamphlet, *The Twice-Revised Code,* and four articles—all published anonymously or pseudonymously—from the daily or weekly press. Three of these last, "The Code out of Danger," "Ordnance Maps," and "Mr. Walter and Schoolmasters' Certificates" were first traced by the present editor from clues in Arnold's quarterly accounts.

Since the principles upon which this volume is edited are those which governed the first volume, there is no need to repeat here the former Preface. The text is the latest which could have had Arnold's attention, and variants in the language of earlier texts (if any) are recorded in the Textual Notes. Manifest misprints are corrected, but if there is any reasonable suspicion that they were errors of the author rather than the typesetter the fact of the correction is recorded. Notes at the bottom of the page are Arnold's own, but the editor has occasionally amplified them (in square brackets).

Both this volume and the third were prepared for the press before Volume I of this edition received the benefit of much serious criticism. Since two reviewers have expressed regret that the publisher is giving each volume a title of its own that is not Arnold's, the editor should like to concur in these scruples. Unfortunately, most volumes of this edition will not be strictly identifiable by one, or even two, of the titles Arnold himself gave to his collections of essays; the chronological principle of arrangement will even require that the articles once gathered as *Essays in Criticism,* Second Series, be scattered among the three final volumes. The editor can only suggest that perhaps an author whose books include *Mixed Essays* and *Irish Essays and Others* was less interested in his titles than in getting his work before the public and that therefore he might forgive the editorial presumption. Nonetheless, the presumption is there, and when (as will happen) a single work of Arnold's nearly coincides with a volume of this edition, Arnold's title will be used.

The Critical and Explanatory Notes are meant to be useful to general readers and to scholars; the editor is aware of many of their shortcomings and his critics will be aware of many more. It is to be hoped that future students will be saved a few steps in their work with Arnold, but the editor's principal expectation is that the provision of a complete and accurate text will make critical study of Arnold easier.

It is a pleasure to acknowledge the friendliness with which Arnold's grandson, Mr. Arnold Whitridge, greeted the first volume and the generosity of his assistance with the project. Professor Arthur Kyle Davis, Jr., has continued his previous kindness. Mr. John R. Atkin, Mr. Rolland C. Stewart, and Professor Paul M. Spurlin have been helpful consultants on many matters. Mr. Morris Finder has sent me an index he made for Whitridge's *Unpublished Letters of Matthew Arnold.* A dissertation from the Ohio State University, R. C. Tobias' *Matthew Arnold and Edmund Burke* (Ann Arbor: University Microfilms, 1958), has proved most useful in tracing some of Arnold's references and will doubtless continue to assist these editorial labors. William B. Guthrie's valuable edition of *Matthew Arnold's Diaries, The Unpublished Items* has now been published (Ann Arbor: University Microfilms, 1959).

The volume was entirely prepared during a year's leave of absence from teaching made possible by a fellowship from the American Council of Learned Societies. The Horace H. Rackham School of Graduate Studies at The University of Michigan has provided funds for expenses incurred in its preparation and has advanced the cost of its publication. The editor is most grateful for the generous confidence of these two bodies

Ann Arbor, Michigan

Contents

The Popular Education of France

INTRODUCTION Democracy 3

CHAPTER I Objects and Means of Inquiry 30

II Organisation of Modern France 33

III Popular Education in France before the Revolution 35

IV Popular Education in France under the Revolution 46

V Popular Education in France under the First Empire 53

VI Popular Education in France under the Restoration 61

VII Popular Education in France under the Monarchy of July, 1830.—Law of 1833 67

VIII Popular Education in France under the Revolution of 1848 and the Second Empire.—Legislation of 1850, 1853, and 1854 76

IX Present Material and Financial Condition of Popular Education in France 92

X Present Intellectual and Moral Condition of Popular Education in France.—Schools in Paris 105

CHAPTER XI Present Intellectual and Moral Condition of Popular Education in France.—Schools in the Provinces 123

XII Present Intellectual and Moral Condition of Popular Education in France.—Normal Schools 134

XIII The Popular Education of France and England Compared.—Legislation 142

XIV The Popular Education of France and England Compared.—Results on the People 150

Popular Education of Switzerland

XV Popular Education in French Switzerland 166

Popular Education of Holland

XVI Popular Education in Holland under the Law of 1806.—Reports of M. Cuvier and M. Cousin 179

XVII Present School Legislation of Holland.—Law of 1857 189

XVIII Present Condition of Popular Education in Holland 204

The Twice-Revised Code 212

The "Principle of Examination" 244

The Code out of Danger 247

Ordnance Maps 252

Mr. Walter and Schoolmasters' Certificates 257

A French Eton 262

Critical and Explanatory Notes 327

Textual Notes 382

Index 401

The Popular Education of France

Introduction: Democracy

I know that, since the Revolution, along with many dangerous, many useful powers of Government have been weakened.

BURKE (1770)

In giving an account of education in certain countries of the Continent, I have often spoken of the State and its action in such a way as to offend, I fear, some of my readers, and to surprise others. With many Englishmen, perhaps with the majority, it is a maxim that the State, the executive power, ought to be entrusted with no more means of action than those which it is impossible to withhold from it; that the State neither would nor could make a safe use of any more extended liberty; would not, because it has in itself a natural instinct of despotism, which, if not jealously checked, would become outrageous; could not, because it is, in truth, not at all more enlightened, or fit to assume a lead, than the mass of this enlightened community.

No sensible man will lightly go counter to an opinion firmly held by a great body of his countrymen. He will take for granted, that for any opinion which has struck deep root among a people so powerful, so successful, and so well worthy of respect as the people of this country, there certainly either are, or have been, good and sound reasons. He will venture to impugn such an opinion with real hesitation, and only when he thinks he perceives that the reasons which once supported it exist no longer, or at any rate seem about to disappear very soon. For undoubtedly there arrive periods, when, the circumstances and conditions of government having changed, the guiding maxims of government ought to change also. *J'ai dit souvent*, says Mirabeau,[1] admonishing the Court of France in 1790, *qu'on devait changer de manière de gouverner, lorsque le gouvernement n'est plus le même*. And these decisive changes in the political situa-

[1] *Correspondance entre le Comte de Mirabeau et le Comte de la Marck*, publiée par M. [Adolphe] de Bacourt, Paris, 1851, vol. ii. p. 143.

tion of a people happen gradually as well as violently. "In the silent lapse of events," says Burke,[1] writing in England twenty years before the French Revolution, "as material alterations have been insensibly brought about in the policy and character of governments and nations, as those which have been marked by the tumult of public revolutions."

I propose to submit to those who have been accustomed to regard all State-action with jealousy, some reasons for thinking that the circumstances which once made that jealousy prudent and natural have undergone an essential change. I desire to lead them to consider with me, whether, in the present altered conjuncture, that State-action, which was once dangerous, may not become, not only without danger in itself, but the means of helping us against dangers from another quarter. To combine and present the considerations upon which these two propositions are based, is a task of some difficulty and delicacy. My aim is to invite impartial reflection upon the subject, not to make a hostile attack against old opinions, still less to set on foot and fully equip a new theory. In offering, therefore, the thoughts which have suggested themselves to me, I shall studiously avoid all particular applications of them likely to give offence, and shall use no more illustration and development than may be indispensable to enable the reader to seize and appreciate them.

The dissolution of the old political parties which have governed this country since the Revolution of 1688 has long been remarked. It was repeatedly declared to be happening long before it actually took place, while the vital energy of these parties still subsisted in full vigour, and was threatened only by some temporary obstruction. It has been eagerly deprecated long after it had actually begun to take place, when it was in full progress, and inevitable. These parties, differing in so much else, were yet alike in this, that they were both, in a certain broad sense, *aristocratical* parties. They were combinations of persons considerable, either by great family and estate, or by Court favour, or lastly, by eminent abilities and popularity; this last body, however, attaining participation in public affairs only through a conjunction with one or other of the former. These

[1] Burke's *Works* (edit. of 1852), vol. iii. p. 115.

connections, though they contained men of very various degrees of birth and property, were still wholly leavened with the feelings and habits of the upper class of the nation. They had the bond of a common culture; and, however their political opinions and acts might differ, what they said and did had the stamp and style imparted by this culture, and by a common and elevated social condition.

Aristocratical bodies have no taste for a very imposing executive, or for a very active and penetrating domestic administration. They have a sense of equality among themselves, and of constituting in themselves what is greatest and most dignified in the realm, which makes their pride revolt against the overshadowing greatness and dignity of a commanding executive. They have a temper of independence, and a habit of uncontrolled action, which makes them impatient of encountering, in the management of the interior concerns of the country, the machinery and regulations of a superior and peremptory power. The different parties amongst them, as they successively get possession of the government, respect this jealous disposition in their opponents, because they share it themselves. It is a disposition proper to them as great personages, not as ministers; and as they are great personages for their whole life, while they may probably be ministers but for a very short time, the instinct of their social condition avails more with them than the instinct of their official function. To administer as little as possible, to make its weight felt in foreign affairs rather than in domestic, to see in ministerial station rather the means of power and dignity than a means of searching and useful administrative activity, is the natural tendency of an aristocratic executive. It is a tendency which is creditable to the good sense of aristocracies, honourable to their moderation, and at the same time fortunate for their country, of whose internal development they are not fitted to have the full direction.

One strong and beneficial influence, however, the administration of a vigorous and high-minded aristocracy is calculated to exert upon a robust and sound people. I have had occasion, in speaking of Homer, to say very often, and with much emphasis, that he is *in the grand style*. It is the chief virtue of a healthy and uncorrupted aristocracy, that it is, in general, in this grand style. That elevation of character, that noble way of thinking and behaving, which is an eminent gift of nature to some individuals, is also often generated in whole classes of men (at least when these come of a strong and good race) by the possession of power, by the importance and responsibility of high station, by habitual dealing with great things, by being placed above the necessity of constantly struggling for little things. And it is the source of great virtues. It may go along with a not very quick or open intelligence; but it cannot well go along with a conduct vulgar and ignoble. A governing class imbued with it may not be capable of intelligently leading the masses of a people to the highest pitch of welfare for them; but it sets them an invaluable example of qualities without which no really high welfare can exist. This has been done for their nation by the best aristocracies. The Roman aristocracy did it; the English aristocracy has done it. They each fostered in the mass of the peoples they governed,—peoples of sturdy moral constitution and apt to learn such lessons,—a greatness of spirit, the natural growth of the condition of magnates and rulers, but not the natural growth of the condition of the common people. They made, the one of the Roman, the other of the English people, in spite of all the shortcomings of each, great peoples, peoples *in the grand style*. And this they did, while wielding the people according to their own notions, and in the direction which seemed good to them; not as servants and instruments of the people, but as its commanders and heads; solicitous for the good of their country, indeed, but taking for granted that of that good they themselves were the supreme judges, and were to fix the conditions.

The time has arrived, however, when it is becoming impossible for the aristocracy of England to conduct and wield the English nation any longer. It still, indeed, administers public affairs; and it is a great error to suppose, as many persons in England suppose, that it administers but does not govern. He who administers, governs,[1] because he infixes his own mark and

[1] *Administrer, c'est gouverner*, says Mirabeau; *gouverner, c'est régner; tout se réduit là.*

stamps his own character on all public affairs as they pass through his hands; and, therefore, so long as the English aristocracy administers the commonwealth, it still governs it. But signs not to be mistaken show that its headship and leadership of the nation, by virtue of the substantial acquiescence of the body of the nation in its predominance and right to lead, is nearly over. That acquiescence was the tenure by which it held its power; and it is fast giving way. The superiority of the upper class over all others is no longer so great; the willingness of the others to recognise that superiority is no longer so ready.

This change has been brought about by natural and inevitable causes, and neither the great nor the multitude are to be blamed for it. The growing demands and audaciousness of the latter, the encroaching spirit of democracy, are, indeed, matters of loud complaint with some persons. But these persons are complaining of human nature itself, when they thus complain of a manifestation of its native and ineradicable impulse. Life itself consists, say the philosophers, in the effort *to affirm one's own essence;* meaning by this, to develop one's own existence fully and freely, to have ample light and air, to be neither cramped nor overshadowed. Democracy is trying *to affirm its own essence;* to live, to enjoy, to possess the world, as aristocracy has tried, and successfully tried, before it. Ever since Europe emerged from barbarism, ever since the condition of the common people began a little to improve, ever since their minds began to stir, this effort of democracy has been gaining strength; and the more their condition improves, the more strength this effort gains. So potent is the charm of life and expansion upon the living; the moment men are aware of them, they begin to desire them, and the more they have of them, the more they crave.

This movement of democracy, like other operations of nature, merits properly neither blame nor praise. Its partisans are apt to give it credit which it does not deserve, while its enemies are apt to upbraid it unjustly. Its friends celebrate it as the author of all freedom. But political freedom may very well be established by aristocratic founders; and, certainly, the political freedom of England owes more to the grasping English barons than to democracy. Social freedom,—equality,—that is rather the field of the conquests of democracy. And here what I must call the injustice of its enemies comes in. For its seeking after equality, democracy is often, in this country above all, vehemently and scornfully blamed; its temper contrasted with that worthier temper which can magnanimously endure social distinctions; its operations all referred, as of course, to the stirrings of a base and malignant envy. No doubt there is a gross and vulgar spirit of envy, prompting the hearts of many of those who cry for equality. No doubt there are ignoble natures which prefer equality to liberty. But what we have to ask is, when the life of democracy is admitted as something natural and inevitable, whether this or that product of democracy is a necessary growth from its parent stock, or merely an excrescence upon it. If it be the latter, certainly it may be due to the meanest and most culpable passions. But if it be the former, then this product, however base and blameworthy the passions which it may sometimes be made to serve, can in itself be no more reprehensible than the vital impulse of democracy is in itself reprehensible; and this impulse is, as has been shown, identical with the ceaseless vital effort of human nature itself.

Now, can it be denied, that a certain approach to equality, at any rate a certain reduction of signal inequalities, is a natural, instinctive demand of that impulse which drives society as a whole,—no longer individuals and limited classes only, but the mass of a community,—to develop itself with the utmost possible fulness and freedom? Can it be denied, that to live in a society of equals tends in general to make a man's spirits expand, and his faculties work easily and actively; while, to live in a society of superiors, although it may occasionally be a very good discipline, yet in general tends to tame the spirits and to make the play of the faculties less secure and active? Can it be denied, that to be heavily overshadowed, to be profoundly insignificant, has, on the whole, a depressing and benumbing effect on the character? I know that some individuals react against the strongest impediments, and owe success and greatness to the efforts which they are thus forced to make. But the question is not about individuals. The question is about the common bulk of mankind, persons without extraordinary gifts or exceptional energy, and who will ever require, in order to make the best of themselves, encouragement and directly favouring circumstances. Can any one deny, that for these the spectacle, when they would rise, of a condition of splendour, grandeur, and culture, which they cannot possibly reach, has the effect of making them flag in spirit, and of disposing them to sink despondingly back into their own condition? Can any one deny, that the knowledge how poor and insignificant the best condition of improvement and culture attainable by them must be esteemed by a class incomparably richer-endowed, tends to cheapen this modest possible amelioration in the account of those classes also for whom it would be relatively a real progress, and to disenchant their imaginations with it? It seems to me impossible to deny this. And therefore a philosophic observer,[1] with no love for democracy, but rather with a terror of it, has been constrained to remark, that "the common people is more uncivilised in aristocratic countries than in any others;" because there "the lowly and the poor feel themselves, as it were, overwhelmed with the weight of their own inferiority." He has been constrained to remark,[2] that "there is such a thing as a manly and legitimate passion for equality, prompting men to desire to be, *all* of them, in the enjoyment of power and consideration." And, in France, that very equality, which is by us so impetuously decried, while it has by no means improved (it is said) the upper classes of French society, has undoubtedly given to the lower classes, to the body of the common people, a self-respect, an enlargement of spirit, a consciousness of counting for something in their country's action, which has raised them in the scale of humanity. The common people, in France, seems to me the

[1] M. [Alexis] de Tocqueville. See his *Démocratie en Amérique* (edit. of 1835), vol. i. p. 11. "Le peuple est plus grossier dans les pays aristocratiques que partout ailleurs. Dans ces lieux, où se rencontrent des hommes si forts et si riches, les faibles et les pauvres se sentent comme accablés de leur bassesse; ne découvrant aucun point par lequel ils puissent regagner l'égalité, ils désespèrent entièrement d'eux-mêmes, et se laissent tomber au-dessous de la dignité humaine."

[2] *Démocratie en Amérique*, vol. i. p. 60.

soundest part of the French nation. They seem to me more free from the two opposite degradations of multitudes, brutality and servility, to have a more developed human life, more of what distinguishes elsewhere the cultured classes from the vulgar, than the common people in any other country with which I am acquainted.

I do not say that grandeur and prosperity may not be attained by a nation divided into the most widely distinct classes, and presenting the most signal inequalities of rank and fortune. I do not say that great national virtues may not be developed in it. I do not even say that a popular order, accepting this demarcation of classes as an eternal providential arrangement, not questioning the natural right of a superior order to lead it, content within its own sphere, admiring the grandeur and high-mindedness of its ruling class, and catching on its own spirit some reflex of what it thus admires, may not be a happier body, as to the eye of the imagination it is certainly a more beautiful body, than a popular order, pushing, excited, and presumptuous; a popular order, jealous of recognising fixed superiorities, petulantly claiming to be as good as its betters, and tastelessly attiring itself with the fashions and designations which have become unalterably associated with a wealthy and refined class, and which, tricking out those who have neither wealth nor refinement, are ridiculous. But a popular order of that old-fashioned stamp exists now only for the imagination. It is not the force with which modern society has to reckon. Such a body may be a sturdy, honest, and sound-hearted lower class; but it is not a democratic people. It is not that power, which at the present day in all nations is to be found existing; in some, has obtained the mastery; in others, is yet in a state of expectation and preparation.

The power of France in Europe is at this day mainly owing to the completeness with which she has organised democratic institutions. The action of the French State is excessive; but it is too little understood in England that the French people has adopted this action for its own purposes, has in great measure attained those purposes by it, and owes to its having done so the chief part of its influence in Europe. The growing power in Europe is democracy; and France has organised democracy with a certain indisputable grandeur and success. The ideas of 1789 were working everywhere in the eighteenth century; but it was because in France the State adopted them that the French Revolution became an historic epoch for the world, and France the lode-star of Continental democracy. Her airs of superiority and her overweening pretensions come from her sense of the power which she derives from this cause. Every one knows how Frenchmen proclaim France to be at the head of civilisation, the French army to be the soldier of God, Paris to be the brain of Europe, and so on. All this is, no doubt, in a vein of sufficient fatuity and bad taste; but it means, at bottom, that France believes she has so organised herself as to facilitate for all members of her society full and free expansion; that she believes herself to have remodelled her institutions with an eye to reason rather than custom, and to right rather than fact; it means, that she believes the other peoples of Europe to be preparing themselves, more or less rapidly, for a like achievement, and that she is conscious of her power and influence upon them as an initiatress and example. In this belief there is a part of truth and a part of delusion. I think it is more profitable for a Frenchman to consider the part of delusion contained in it; for an Englishman, the part of truth.

It is because aristocracies almost inevitably fail to appreciate justly, or even to take into their mind, the instinct pushing the masses towards expansion and fuller life, that they lose their hold over them. It is the old story of the incapacity of aristocracies for ideas,—the secret of their want of success in modern epochs. The people treats them with flagrant injustice, when it denies all obligation to them. They can, and often do, impart a high spirit, a fine ideal of grandeur, to the people; thus they lay the foundations of a great nation. But they leave the people still the multitude, the crowd; they have small belief in the power of the ideas which are its life. Themselves a power reposing on all which is most solid, material, and visible, they are slow to attach any great importance to influences impalpable, spiritual, and viewless. Although, therefore, a disinterested looker-on might often be disposed, seeing what has actually been achieved by aristocracies, to wish to retain or replace them in their preponderance, rather than commit a nation to the hazards of a new and untried future; yet the masses instinctively feel that they can never consent to this without renouncing the inmost impulse of their being; and that they should make such a renunciation cannot seriously be expected of them. Except on conditions which make its expansion, in the sense understood by itself, fully possible, democracy will never frankly ally itself with aristocracy; and on these conditions perhaps no aristocracy will ever frankly ally itself with it. Even the English aristocracy, so politic, so capable of compromises, has shown no signs of being able so to transform itself as to render such an alliance possible. The reception given by the Peers to the bill for establishing life-peerages was, in this respect, of ill omen. The separation between aristocracy and democracy will probably, therefore, go on still widening.

And it must in fairness be added, that as in one most important part of general human culture,—openness to ideas and ardour for them,—aristocracy is less advanced than democracy, to replace or keep the latter under the tutelage of the former would in some respects be actually unfavourable to the progress of the world. At epochs when new ideas are powerfully fermenting in a society, and profoundly changing its spirit, aristocracies, as they are in general not long suffered to guide it without question, so are they by nature not well fitted to guide it intelligently.

In England, democracy has been slow in developing itself, having met with much to withstand it, not only in the worth of the aristocracy, but also in the fine qualities of the common people. The aristocracy has been more in sympathy with the common people than perhaps any other aristocracy. It has rarely given them great umbrage; it has neither been frivolous, so as to provoke their contempt, nor impertinent, so as to provoke their irritation. Above all, it has in general meant to act with justice, according to its own notions of justice. Therefore the feeling of admiring deference to such a class was more deep-rooted in the people of this country, more cordial, and more persistent, than in any people of the Continent. But, besides this, the vigour and high spirit of the English common people bred in them a self-reliance which disposed each man to act individually and independently; and so long as this disposition prevails through a nation divided into classes, the predominance of an aristocracy, of the class containing the greatest and strongest individuals of the nation, is secure. Democracy is a force in which the concert of a great number of men makes up for the weakness of each man taken by himself; democracy accepts a certain relative rise in their condition, obtainable by this concert for a great number, as something desirable in itself, because though this is undoubtedly far below grandeur, it is yet a good deal above insignificance. A very strong, self-reliant people neither easily learns to act in concert, nor easily brings itself to regard any middling good, any good short of the best, as an object ardently to be coveted and striven for. It keeps its eye on the grand prizes, and these are to be won only by distancing competitors, by getting before one's comrades, by succeeding all by one's self; and so long as a people works thus individually, it does not work democratically. The English people has all the qualities which dispose a people to work individually; may it never lose them! A people without the salt of these qualities, relying wholly on mutual co-operation, and proposing to itself second-rate ideals, would arrive at the pettiness and stationariness of China. But the English people is no longer so entirely ruled by them as not to show visible beginnings of democratic action; it becomes more and more sensible to the irresistible seduction of democratic ideas, promising to each individual of the multitude increased self-respect and expansion with the increased importance and authority of the multitude to which he belongs, with the diminished preponderance of the aristocratic class above him.

While the habit and disposition of deference are thus dying out among the lower classes of the English nation, it seems to me indisputable that the advantages which command deference, that eminent superiority in high feeling, dignity, and culture, tend to diminish among the highest class. I shall not be suspected of any inclination to underrate the aristocracy of this country. I regard it as the worthiest, as it certainly has been the most successful, aristocracy of which history makes record. If it has not been able to develop excellences which do not belong to the nature of an aristocracy, yet it has been able to avoid defects to which the nature of an aristocracy is peculiarly prone. But I cannot read the history of the flowering time of the English aristocracy, the eighteenth century, and then look at this aristocracy in our own century, without feeling that there has been a change. I am not now thinking of private and domestic virtues, of morality, of decorum. Perhaps with respect to these there has in this class, as in society at large, been a change for the better. I am thinking of those public and conspicuous virtues by which the multitude is captivated and led,—lofty spirit, commanding character, exquisite culture. It is true that the advance of all classes in culture and refinement may make the culture of one class, which, isolated, appeared remarkable, appear so no longer; but exquisite culture and great dignity are always something rare and striking, and it is the distinction of the English aristocracy, in the eighteenth century, that not only was their culture something rare by comparison with the rawness of the masses, it was something rare and admirable in itself. It is rather that this rare culture of the highest class has actually somewhat declined,[1] than that it has come to look less by juxtaposition with the augmented culture of other classes.

Probably democracy has something to answer for in this falling off of her rival. To feel itself raised on high, venerated, followed, no doubt stimulates a fine nature to keep itself worthy to be followed, venerated, raised on high; hence that lofty maxim, *noblesse oblige*. To feel its culture something precious and singular, makes such a nature zealous to retain and extend it. The elation and energy thus fostered by the sense of its advantages, certainly enhances the worth, strengthens the behav-

[1] This will appear doubtful to no one well acquainted with the literature and memoirs of the last century. To give but two illustrations out of a thousand. Let the reader refer to the anecdote told by Robert Wood in his *Essay on the Genius of Homer* (London, 1775), p. vii. and to Lord Chesterfield's *Letters* (edit. of 1845), vol. i. pp. 115, 143; vol. ii. p. 54; and then say, whether the culture there indicated as the culture of a *class* has maintained itself at that level.

iour, and quickens all the active powers of the class enjoying it. *Possunt quia posse videntur*. The removal of the stimulus a little relaxes their energy. It is not so much that they sink to be somewhat less than themselves, as that they cease to be somewhat more than themselves. But, however this may be, whencesoever the change may proceed, I cannot doubt that in the aristocratic virtue, in the intrinsic commanding force of the English upper class, there is a diminution. Relics of a great generation are still, perhaps, to be seen amongst them, surviving exemplars of noble manners and consummate culture; but they disappear one after the other, and no one of their kind takes their place. At the very moment when democracy becomes less and less disposed to follow and to admire, aristocracy becomes less and less qualified to command and to captivate.

On the one hand, then, the masses of the people in this country are preparing to take a much more active part than formerly in controlling its destinies; on the other hand, the aristocracy (using this word in the widest sense, to include not only the nobility and landed gentry, but also those reinforcements from the classes bordering upon itself, which this class constantly attracts and assimilates), while it is threatened with losing its hold on the rudder of government, its power to give to public affairs its own bias and direction, is losing also that influence on the spirit and character of the people which it long exercised.

I know that this will be warmly denied by some persons. Those who have grown up amidst a certain state of things, those whose habits, and interests, and affections, are closely concerned with its continuance, are slow to believe that it is not a part of the order of nature, or that it can ever come to an end. But I think that what I have here laid down will not appear doubtful either to the most competent and friendly foreign observers of this country, or to those Englishmen who, clear of all influences of class or party, have applied themselves steadily to see the tendencies of their nation as they really are. Assuming it to be true, a great number of considerations are suggested by it; but it is my purpose here to insist upon one only.

That one consideration is: On what action may we rely to replace, for some time at any rate, that action of the aristocracy upon the people of this country, which we have seen exercise an influence in many respects elevating and beneficial, but which is rapidly, and from inevitable causes, ceasing? In other words, and to use a short and significant modern expression which every one understands, what influence may help us to prevent the English people from becoming, with the growth of democracy, *Americanised?* I confess I am disposed to answer: On the action of the State.

I know what a chorus of objectors will be ready. One will say: Rather repair and restore the influence of aristocracy. Another will say: It is not a bad thing, but a good thing, that the English people should be Americanised. But the most formidable and the most widely entertained objection, by far, will be that which founds itself upon the present actual state of things in another country; which says: Look at France! there you have a signal example of the alliance of democracy with a powerful State-action, and see how it works.

This last and principal objection I will notice at once. I have had occasion to touch upon the first already, and upon the second I shall touch presently. It seems to me, then, that one may save one's self from much idle terror at names and shadows if one will be at the pains to remember what different conditions the different character of two nations must necessarily impose on the operation of any principle. That which operates noxiously in one, may operate wholesomely in the other; because the unsound part of the one's character may be yet further inflamed and enlarged by it, the unsound part of the other's may find in it a corrective and an abatement. This is the great use which two unlike characters may find in observing each other. Neither is likely to have the other's faults, so each may safely adopt as much as suits him of the other's qualities. If I were a Frenchman I should never be weary of admiring the independent, individual, local habits of action in England, of directing attention to the evils occasioned in France by the excessive action of the State; for I should be very sure that, say what I might, the part of the State would never be too small in France, nor that of the individual too large. Being an Englishman, I see nothing but good in freely recognising the coherence, rationality, and efficaciousness which characterise the strong State-action of France, of acknowledging the want of method, reason, and result which attend the feeble State-action of England; because I am very sure that, strengthen in England the action of the State as one may, it will always find itself sufficiently controlled. But when either the *Constitutionnel* sneers at the do-little talkativeness of parliamentary government, or when the *Morning Star* inveighs against the despotism of a centralised administration, it seems to me that they lose their labour, because they are hardening themselves against dangers to which they are neither of them liable. Both the one and the other, in plain truth,

> "Compound for sins they are inclined to,
> By damning those they have no mind to."

They should rather exchange doctrines one with the other, and each might thus, perhaps, be profited.

So that the exaggeration of the action of the State, in France, furnishes no reason for absolutely refusing to enlarge the action of the State in England; because the genius and temper of the people of this country are such as to render impossible that exaggeration which the genius and temper of the French rendered easy. There is no danger at all that the native independence and individualism of the English character will ever belie itself, and become either weakly prone to lean on others, or blindly confiding in them.

English democracy runs no risk of being overmastered by the State; it is almost certain that it will throw off the tutelage of aristocracy. Its real danger is, that it will have far too much its own way, and be left far too much to itself. "What harm will there be in that?" say some; "are we not a self-governing people?" I answer: "We have never yet been a *self-governing democracy*, or anything like it." The difficulty for democracy is, how to find and keep high ideals. The individuals who compose it are, the bulk of them, persons who need to follow an ideal, not to set one; and one ideal of greatness, high feeling, and fine culture, which an aristocracy once supplied to them, they lose by the very fact of ceasing to be a lower order and becoming a democracy. Nations are not truly great solely because the individuals composing them are numerous, free, and active; but they are great when these numbers, this freedom, and this activity are employed in the service of an ideal higher than that of an ordinary man, taken by himself. Our society is probably destined to become much more democratic; who or what will give a high tone to the nation then? That is the grave question.

The greatest men of America, her Washingtons, Hamiltons, Madisons, well understanding that aristocratical institutions are not in all times and places possible; well perceiving that in their Republic there was no place for these; comprehending, therefore, that from these that security for national dignity and greatness, an ideal commanding popular reverence, was not to be obtained, but knowing that this ideal was indispensable, would have been rejoiced to found a substitute for it in the dignity and authority of the State. They deplored the weakness and insignificance of the executive power as a calamity. When the inevitable course of events has made our self-government something really like that of America, when it has removed or weakened that security for national dignity, which we possessed in *aristocracy*, will the substitute of the *State* be equally wanting to us? If it is, then the dangers of America will really be ours; the dangers which come from the multitude being in power, with no adequate ideal to elevate or guide the multitude.

It would really be wasting time to contend at length, that to give more prominence to the idea of the State is now possible in this country, without endangering liberty. In other countries the habits and dispositions of the people may be such that the State, if once it acts, may be easily suffered to usurp exorbitantly; here they certainly are not. Here the people will always sufficiently keep in mind that any public authority is a trust delegated by themselves, for certain purposes, and with certain limits; and if that authority pretends to an absolute, independent character, they will soon enough (and very rightly) remind it of its error. Here there can be no question of a paternal government, of an irresponsible executive power, professing to act for the people's good, but without the people's consent, and, if necessary, against the people's wishes; here no one dreams of removing a single constitutional control, of abolishing a single safeguard for securing a correspondence between the acts of government and the will of the nation. The question is, whether, retaining all its power of control over a government which should abuse its trust, the nation may not now find advantage in voluntarily allowing to it purposes somewhat ampler, and limits somewhat wider within which to execute them, than formerly; whether the nation may not thus acquire in the State an ideal of high reason and right feeling, representing its best self, commanding general respect, and forming a rallying-point for the intelligence and for the worthiest instincts of the community, which will herein find a true bond of union.

I am convinced that if the worst mischiefs of democracy ever happen in England, it will be, not because a new condition of things has come upon us unforeseen, but because, though we all foresaw it, our efforts to deal with it were in the wrong direction. At the present time, almost every one believes in the growth of democracy, almost every one talks of it, almost every one laments it; but the last thing people can be brought to do is to make timely preparation for it. Many of those who, if they would, could do most to forward this work of preparation, are made slack and hesitating by the belief that, after all, in England, things may probably never go very far; that it will be possible to keep much more of the past than speculators say. Others, with a more robust faith, think that all democracy wants is vigorous putting-down; and that, with a good will and strong hand, it is perfectly possible to retain or restore the whole system of the Middle Ages. Others, free from the prejudices of class and position which warp the judgment of these, and who would, I believe, be the first and greatest gainers by strengthening the hands of the State, are averse from doing so by reason of suspicions and fears, once perfectly well-grounded, but, in this age and in the present circumstances, well-grounded no longer.

I speak of the middle classes. I have already shown how it is the natural disposition of an aristocratical class to view with jealousy the development of a considerable State-power. But this disposition has in England found extraordinary favour and support in regions not aristocratical,—from the middle classes;

and, above all, from the kernel of these classes, the Protestant Dissenters. And for a very good reason. In times when passions ran high, even an aristocratical executive was easily stimulated into using, for the gratification of its friends and the abasement of its enemies, those administrative engines which, the moment it chose to stretch its hand forth, stood ready for its grasp. Matters of domestic concern, matters of religious profession and religious exercise, offered a peculiar field for an intervention gainful and agreeable to friends, injurious and irritating to enemies. Such an intervention was attempted and practised. Government lent its machinery and authority to the aristocratical and ecclesiastical party, which it regarded as its best support. The party which suffered comprised the flower and strength of that middle class of society, always very flourishing and robust in this country. That powerful class, from this specimen of the administrative activity of government, conceived a strong antipathy against all intervention of the State in certain spheres. An active, stringent administration in those spheres, meant at that time a High Church and Prelatic administration in them, an administration galling to the Puritan party and to the middle class; and this aggrieved class had naturally no proneness to draw nice philosophical distinctions between State-action in these spheres, as a thing for abstract consideration, and State-action in them as they practically felt it and supposed themselves likely long to feel it, guided by their adversaries. In the minds of the English middle class, therefore, State-action in social and domestic concerns became inextricably associated with the idea of a Conventicle Act, a Five-Mile Act, an Act of Uniformity. Their abhorrence of such a State-action as this they extended to State-action in general; and, having never known a beneficent and just State-power, they enlarged their hatred of a cruel and partial State-power, the only one they had ever known, into a maxim that no State-power was to be trusted, that the least action, in certain provinces, was rigorously to be denied to the State, whenever this denial was possible.

Thus that jealousy of an important, sedulous, energetic executive, natural to grandees unwilling to suffer their personal authority to be circumscribed, their individual grandeur to be eclipsed, by the authority and grandeur of the State, became reinforced in this country by a like sentiment among the middle classes, who had no such authority or grandeur to lose, but who, by a hasty reasoning, had theoretically condemned for ever an agency which they had practically found at times oppressive. *Leave us to ourselves!* magnates and middle classes alike cried to the State. Not only from those who were full and abounded went up this prayer, but also from those whose condition admitted of great amelioration. Not only did the whole repudiate the physician, but also those who were sick.

For it is evident, that the action of a diligent, an impartial, and a national government, while it can do little to better the condition, already fortunate enough, of the highest and richest class of its people, can really do much, by institution and regulation, to better that of the middle and lower classes. The State can bestow certain broad collective benefits, which are indeed not much if compared with the advantages already possessed by individual grandeur, but which are rich and valuable if compared with the make-shifts of mediocrity and poverty. A good thing meant for the many cannot well be so exquisite as the good things of the few; but it can easily, if it comes from a donor of great resources and wide power, be incomparably better than what the many could, unaided, provide for themselves.

In all the remarks which I have been making, I have hitherto abstained from any attempt to suggest a positive application of them. I have limited myself to simply pointing out in how changed a world of ideas we are living; I have not sought to go further, and to discuss in what particular manner the world of facts is to adapt itself to this changed world of ideas. This has been my rule so far; but from this rule I shall here venture to depart, in order to dwell for a moment on a matter of practical institution, designed to meet new social exigencies: on the intervention of the State in public education.

The public secondary schools of France, decreed by the Revolution and established under the Consulate, are said by many good judges to be inferior to the old colleges. By means of the old colleges and of private tutors, the French aristocracy could procure for its children (so it is said, and very likely with truth) a better training than that which is now given in the lyceums. Yes; but the boon conferred by the State, when it founded the lyceums, was not for the aristocracy; it was for the vast middle class of Frenchmen. This class, certainly, had not already the means of a better training for its children, before the State interfered. This class, certainly, would not have succeeded in procuring by its own efforts a better training for its children, if the State had not interfered. Through the intervention of the State this class enjoys better schools for its children, not than the great and rich enjoy (that is not the question), but than the same class enjoys in any country where the State has not interfered to found them. The lyceums may not be so good as Eton or Harrow; but they are a great deal better than a *Classical and Commercial Academy*.

The aristocratic classes in England may, perhaps, be well content to rest satisfied with their Eton and Harrow. The State is not likely to do better for them. Nay, the superior confidence, spirit, and style, engendered by a training in the great public schools, constitute for these classes a real privilege, a real engine of command, which they might, if they were selfish, be sorry to lose by the establishment of schools great enough to beget a like spirit in the classes below them. But the middle classes in England have every reason not to rest content with their private schools; the State can do a great deal better for them. By giving to schools for these classes a public character, it can bring the instruction in them under a criticism which the stock of knowledge and judgment in our middle classes is not of itself at present able to supply. By giving to them a national character, it can confer on them a greatness and a noble spirit, which the tone of these classes is not of itself at present adequate to impart. Such schools would soon prove notable competitors with the existing public schools; they would do these a great service by stimulating them, and making them look into their own weak points more closely. Economical, because with charges uniform and under severe revision, they would do a great service to that large body of persons who, at present, seeing that on the whole the best secondary instruction to be found is that of the existing public schools, obtain it for their children from a sense of duty, although they can ill afford it, and although its cost is certainly exorbitant. Thus the middle classes might, by the aid of the State, better their instruction, while still keeping its cost moderate. This in itself would be a gain; but this gain would be slight in comparison with that of acquiring the sense of belonging to great and honourable seats of learning, and of breathing in their youth the air of the best culture of their nation. This sense would be an educational influence for them of the highest value. It would really augment their self-respect and moral force; it would truly fuse them with the class above, and tend to bring about for them the equality which they are entitled to desire.

So it is not State-action in itself which the middle and lower classes of a nation ought to deprecate; it is State-action exercised by a hostile class, and for their oppression. From a State-action reasonably, equitably, and nationally exercised, they may derive great benefit; greater, by the very nature and necessity of things, than can be derived from this source by the class above them. For the middle or lower classes to obstruct such a State-action, to repel its benefits, is to play the game of their enemies, and to prolong for themselves a condition of real inferiority.

This, I know, is rather dangerous ground to tread upon. The great middle classes of this country are conscious of no weakness, no inferiority; they do not want any one to provide anything for them. Such as they are, they believe that the freedom and prosperity of England are their work, and that the future belongs to them. No one esteems them more than I do; but those who esteem them most, and who most believe in their capabilities, can render them no better service than by pointing out in what they underrate their deficiencies, and how their deficiencies, if unremedied, may impair their future. They want culture and dignity; they want ideas. Aristocracy has culture and dignity; democracy has readiness for new ideas, and ardour for what ideas it possesses. Of these, our middle class has the last only: ardour for the ideas it already possesses. It believes ardently in liberty, it believes ardently in industry; and, by its zealous belief in these two ideas, it has accomplished great things. What it has accomplished by its belief in industry is patent to all the world. The liberties of England are less its exclusive work than it supposes; for these, aristocracy has achieved nearly as much. Still, of one inestimable part of liberty, liberty of thought, the middle class has been (without precisely intending it) the principal champion. The intellectual action of the Church of England upon the nation has been insignificant; its social action has been great. The social action of Protestant Dissent, that genuine product of the English middle class, has not been civilising; its positive intellectual action has been insignificant; its negative intellectual action,—in so far as by strenuously maintaining for itself, against persecution, liberty of conscience and the right of free opinion, it at the same time maintained and established this right as a universal principle,—has been invaluable. But the actual results of this negative intellectual service rendered by Protestant Dissent,—by the middle class,—to the whole community, great as they undoubtedly are, must not be taken for something which they are not. It is a very great thing to be able to think as you like; but, after all, an important question remains: *what* you think. It is a fine thing to secure a free stage and no favour; but, after all, the part which you play on that stage will have to be criticised. Now, all the liberty and industry in the world will not ensure these two things: a high reason and a fine culture. They may favour them, but they will not of themselves produce them; they may exist without them. But it is by the appearance of these two things, in some shape or other, in the life of a nation, that it becomes something more than an independent, an energetic, a successful nation,—that it becomes a *great* nation.

In modern epochs the part of a high reason, of ideas, acquires constantly increasing importance in the conduct of the world's affairs. A fine culture is the complement of a high reason, and it is in the conjunction of both with character, with energy, that the ideal for men and nations is to be placed. It is common to hear remarks on the frequent divorce between culture and character, and to infer from this that culture is a mere varnish, and that character only deserves any serious attention. No error can be more fatal. Culture without character is, no doubt, something frivolous, vain, and weak; but character without culture is, on the other hand, something raw, blind, and dangerous. The most interesting, the most truly glorious peoples, are those in which the alliance of the two has been effected most successfully, and its result spread most widely. This is why the spectacle of ancient Athens has such profound interest for a rational man; that it is the spectacle of the culture of a *people*. It is not an aristocracy, leavening with its own high spirit the multitude which it wields, but leaving it the unformed multitude still; it is not a democracy, acute and energetic, but tasteless, narrow-minded, and ignoble; it is the middle and lower classes in the highest development of their humanity that these classes have yet reached. It was the *many* who relished those arts, who were not satisfied with less than those monuments. In the conversations recorded by Plato, or even by the matter-of-fact Xenophon, which for the free yet refined discussion of ideas have set the tone for the whole cultivated world, shopkeepers and tradesmen of Athens mingle as speakers. For any one but a pedant, this is why a handful of Athenians of two thousand years ago are more interesting than the millions of most nations our contemporaries. Surely, if they knew this, those friends of progress, who have confidently pronounced the remains of the ancient world to be so much lumber, and a classical education an aristocratic impertinence, might be inclined to reconsider their sentence.

The course taken in the next fifty years by the middle classes of this nation will probably give a decisive turn to its history. If they will not seek the alliance of the State for their own elevation, if they go on exaggerating their spirit of individualism, if they persist in their jealousy of all governmental action, if they cannot learn that the antipathies and the shibboleths of a past age are now an anachronism for them—that will not prevent them, probably, from getting the rule of their country for a season, but they will certainly *Americanise* it. They will rule it by their energy, but they will deteriorate it by their low ideals and want of culture. In the decline of the aristocratical element, which in some sort supplied an ideal to ennoble the spirit of the nation and to keep it together, there will be no other element present to perform this service. It is of itself a serious calamity for a nation that its tone of feeling and grandeur of spirit should be lowered or dulled. But the calamity appears far more serious still when we consider that the middle classes, remaining as they are now, with their narrow, harsh, unintelligent, and unattractive spirit and culture, will almost certainly fail to mould or assimilate the masses below them, whose sympathies are at the present moment actually wider and more liberal than theirs. They arrive, these masses, eager to enter into possession of the world, to gain a more vivid sense of their own life and activity. In this their irrepressible development, their natural educators and initiators are those immediately above them, the middle classes. If these classes cannot win their sympathy or give them their direction, society is in danger of falling into anarchy.

Therefore, with all the force I can, I wish to urge upon the middle classes of this country, both that they might be very greatly profited by the action of the State, and also that they are continuing their opposition to such action out of an unfounded fear. But at the same time I say that the middle classes have the right, in admitting the action of government, to make the condition that this government shall be one of their own adoption, one that they can trust. To ensure this is now in their own power. If they do not as yet ensure this, they ought to do so, they have the means of doing so. Two centuries ago they had not; now they have. Having this security, let them now show themselves jealous to keep the action of the State equitable and rational, rather than to exclude the action of the State altogether. If the State acts amiss, let them check it, but let them no longer take it for granted that the State cannot possibly act usefully.

The State—but what is *the State?* cry many. Speculations on the idea of a State abound, but these do not satisfy them; of that which is to have practical effect and power they require a plain account. The full force of the term, *the State*, as the full force of any other important term, no one will master without going a little deeply, without resolutely entering the world of ideas; but it is possible to give in very plain language an account of it sufficient for all practical purposes. The State is properly just what Burke called it—*the nation in its collective and corporate character*. The State is the representative acting-power of the nation; the action of the State is the representative action of the nation. Nominally emanating from the Crown, as the ideal unity in which the nation concentrates itself, this action, by the constitution of our country, really emanates from the ministers of the Crown. It is common to hear the depreciators of State-action run through a string of ministers' names, and then say: "Here is really your *State;* would you accept the action of these men as your own representative action? In what respect is their judgment on national affairs likely to be any better than that of the rest of the world?" In the first place I answer: Even supposing them to be originally no better or wiser than the rest of the world, they have two great advantages from their position: access to almost boundless means of information, and the enlargement of mind which the habit of dealing with great affairs tends to produce. Their position itself, therefore, if they are men of only average honesty and capacity, tends to give them a fitness for acting on behalf of the nation superior to that of other men of equal honesty and capacity who are not in the same position. This fitness may be yet further increased by treating them as persons on whom, indeed, a very grave responsibility has fallen, and from whom very much will be expected;—nothing less than the representing, each of them in his own department, under the control of Parliament, and aided by the suggestions of public opinion, the collective energy and intelligence of his nation. By treating them as men on whom all this devolves to do, to their honour if they do it well, to their shame if they do it ill, one probably augments their faculty of well-doing; as it is excellently said: "To treat men as if they were better than they are, is the surest way to *make* them better than they are." But to treat them as if they had been shuffled into their places by a lucky accident, were most likely soon to be shuffled out of them again, and meanwhile ought to magnify themselves and their office as little as possible; to treat them as if they and their functions could without much inconvenience be quite dispensed with, and they ought perpetually to be admiring their own inconceivable good fortune in being permitted to discharge them; —this is the way to paralyse all high effort in the executive government, to extinguish all lofty sense of responsibility; to make its members either merely solicitous for the gross advantages, the emolument and self-importance, which they derive from their offices, or else timid, apologetic, and self-mistrustful in filling them; in either case, formal and inefficient.

But in the second place I answer: If the executive government is really in the hands of men no wiser than the bulk of mankind, of men whose action an intelligent man would be unwilling to accept as representative of his own action, whose fault is that? It is the fault of the nation itself, which, not being in the hands of a despot or an oligarchy, being free to control the choice of those who are to sum up and concentrate its action, controls it in such a manner that it allows to be chosen agents so little in its confidence, or so mediocre, or so incompetent, that it thinks the best thing to be done with them is to reduce their action as near as possible to a nullity. Hesitating, blundering, unintelligent, inefficacious, the action of the State may be; but, such as it is, it is the collective action of the nation itself, and the nation is responsible for it. It is our own action which we suffer to be thus unsatisfactory. Nothing can free us from this responsibility. The conduct of our affairs is in our own power. To carry on into its executive proceedings the indecision, conflict, and discordance of its parliamentary debates, may be a natural defect of a free nation, but it is certainly a defect; it is a dangerous error to call it, as some do, a perfection. The want of concert, reason, and organisation in the State, is the want of concert, reason, and organisation in the collective nation.

Inasmuch, therefore, as collective action is more efficacious than isolated individual efforts, a nation having great and complicated matters to deal with must greatly gain by employing the action of the State. Only, the State-power which it employs should be a power which really represents its best self, and whose action its intelligence and justice can heartily avow and adopt; not a power which reflects its inferior self, and of whose action, as of its own second-rate action, it has perpetually to be ashamed. To offer a worthy initiative, and to set a standard of rational and equitable action,—this is what the nation should expect of the State; and the more the State fulfils this expectation, the more will it be accepted in practice for what in idea it must always be. People will not then ask the State, what title it has to commend or reward genius and merit, since commendation and reward imply an attitude of superiority, for it will then be felt that the State truly acts for the English nation; and the genius of the English nation is greater than the genius of any individual, greater even than Shakspeare's genius, for it includes the genius of Newton also.

I will not deny that to give a more prominent part to the State would be a considerable change in this country; that maxims once very sound, and habits once very salutary, may be appealed to against it. The sole question is, whether those maxims and habits are sound and salutary at this moment. A yet graver and more difficult change,—to reduce the all-effacing prominence of the State, to give a more prominent part to the individual,—is imperiously presenting itself to other countries. Both are the suggestions of one irresistible force, which is gradually making its way everywhere, removing old conditions and imposing new, altering long-fixed habits, undermining venerable institutions, even modifying national character: *the modern spirit.*

Undoubtedly we are drawing on towards great changes; and for every nation the thing most needful is to discern clearly its own condition, in order to know in what particular way it may best meet them. Openness and flexibility of mind are at such a time the first of virtues. *Be ye perfect*, said the Founder of Christianity; *I count not myself to have apprehended*, said its greatest Apostle. Perfection will never be reached; but to recognise a period of transformation when it comes, and to adapt themselves honestly and rationally to its laws, is perhaps the nearest approach to perfection of which men and nations are capable. No habits or attachments should prevent their trying to do this; nor indeed, in the long run, can they. Human thought, which made all institutions, inevitably saps them, resting only in that which is absolute and eternal.

CHAPTER I

Objects and Means of Inquiry

Having been entrusted by the Royal Commissioners, appointed to inquire into the state of popular education in England, with the charge of reporting to them on the systems of popular education in use in France, Holland, and the French Cantons of Switzerland, I proceeded to Paris on the 15th of March, 1859.

The British Ambassador at Paris, Earl Cowley, to whom my warmest acknowledgments are due for the prompt kindness with which he gave me his assistance on every occasion when I appealed to him for it, introduced me to M. Rouland, the Minister of Public Instruction, who furnished me with all facilities for prosecuting my inquiry. Not only did M. Rouland obligingly place at my disposal the aid, in Paris, of those officers of his department who could best guide me, but he also supplied me with letters to the Prefects and Rectors, by which I was enabled, after leaving Paris, to extend my researches to the provinces, and to visit schools in every part of France.

From every functionary of the French Government with whom I was placed in relation, I experienced uniform courtesy, attention, and assistance. My thanks are due to them all; but I must be allowed to mention by name two gentlemen, whom I had the advantage of consulting constantly, and to whom my obligations are unbounded—M. Magin and M. Rapet.

M. Magin, now Inspector-General of primary instruction, and formerly Rector of the Academy of Nancy, the metropolis of one of the best educated districts in France, has peculiar qualifications, in his wide experience, his thorough mastery of the whole system of French education, his perfect disinterestedness, and his singular clearness of judgment, for guiding an inquirer charged with such an errand as mine. If I have not wholly failed in finding my way through the complicated general question which in France I had to study, it is M. Magin whom I have had, almost always, to thank for my clue.

Recommended by Lord Granville's kindness to the notice of M. Guizot, (whose service in the cause of popular education is one of his many distinctions), I was introduced by M. Guizot to a Primary Inspector, who was, he said, of all men the best qualified to inform me respecting the French schools and the practical working of their system—M. Rapet. This testimony borne by M. Guizot to M. Rapet's excellence I soon found that every other voice—official and unofficial, clerical and lay—cordially confirmed. Indeed, I could not but be astonished to find one, whom all thus united in deservedly praising, placed in the official hierarchy of public instruction so far below his merits. M. Rapet's guidance and information were invaluable to me in prosecuting my visits to schools.

I afterwards visited Holland and the French Cantons of Switzerland. In these countries, also, I received every assistance, both from the British Legation and from the officers of Government. But the time which I was able to pass in Holland and Switzerland was very limited; it was to France that I principally directed my attention. M. Cousin's report on Public Instruction in Holland is in every one's hands; the state of things which it describes is to this day little changed. In Switzerland, the German Cantons, the Cantons most interesting to the student of public education, (Canton Aargau is said to possess the best primary schools in Europe), were beyond the province assigned to me by my instructions. Even had they fallen within it, I should have hesitated, though their schools are undoubtedly superior to the French schools, to shorten my inquiry in France in order to visit them.

The day has gone by, when the actual mechanism of primary schools formed the principal object of inquiries upon public education. Rival school-methods have fought their fight; and at the present day we in England, at any rate, think that we know pretty well in what good school-keeping consists. It was not to arbitrate between the monitorial and simultaneous systems, or to give the palm to the best plan for fitting and furnishing schools, that the Education Commission was appointed. That appetite for school-details must indeed be voracious, which at the present day can make its possessor forget, in the spectacle of highly perfected schools, that the vital question is no longer the perfection of elementary schools, but their creation; their creation, and upon what scale this is accomplished, and under what conditions.

France is a country, in population, in extent, in resources, not ill-matched with our own country. In France, therefore, the problem of popular education is presented in nearly the same terms as to ourselves. How is it solved? What does this great agent of popular education do for this great French people, so like to us in its numbers, so like to us in its power, so like to us in its difficulties? This question, I confess, had invincible attractions for me. Moreover, while the popular education of Holland and Germany has had its historians, that of France has hitherto remained undescribed.*

I begin, therefore, with France; and my notices of primary instruction in Holland and Switzerland will be but supplementary.

* I speak of special works, composed in the English language, or of which English translations exist. But for general works noticing French education along with that of other countries, see Mr. [Joseph] Kay's interesting book, *The Education of the Poor in England and Europe*, London, 1846; and also *National Education in Europe*, by Henry Barnard, Superintendent of Common Schools in Connecticut; Hartford, U.S., 1854.

CHAPTER II

Organisation of Modern France

France contains, according to the last census, a population of 36,039,364 inhabitants. Its 86 departments have, for administrative purposes, a division which it will often be necessary, in reading what follows, to bear in mind. Each *department* is divided into *arrondissements;* each *arrondissement* is subdivided into *cantons* and *communes*. There are 363 arrondissements in France, 2850 cantons, 36,826 communes. The department, the arrondissement, and the commune have each a special civil administration. At the head of the department is the prefect, assisted by a "prefect's council" (*conseil de préfecture*), a judicial body charged with the settlement of legal disputes arising out of the administration of the department; and by an elective council-general, a deliberative body which assigns to the several arrondissements the share to be contributed by each to the State-taxation of the department, and votes the funds employed by the departmental executive. At the head of the arrondissement is the sub-prefect, assisted by another deliberative body, the *conseil d'arrondissement*, which performs for the communes and the arrondissements the same functions which the council-general performs for the arrondissements and the department. Lastly, at the head of the commune is the mayor, assisted by a third deliberative body, the municipal council. The representatives of the executive power in each of the three stages of this hierarchy—the prefects, the sub-prefects, and the mayors—are nominated by the central executive power, the State; the deliberative and tax-voting assemblies are elected by the tax-paying bodies whom they respectively represent.* This organi-

* It is to be noted, however, that the prefect has the power to dissolve any municipal council of his department, and to replace it by a

sation was established in 1800, under the government of the First Consul.

The mayors and the municipal councils in France, (with whom popular education is chiefly concerned), form a machinery for local self-government which we do not possess. The commune does not correspond to our parish, (a word still used in France, but as an ecclesiastical term only,) because the commune, even in the largest French town, is but one, while the parishes in most English towns of importance are many. But if we imagine every English borough retaining its unity of municipal organisation, and this organisation extended to every town not a borough, and above all to every country parish; if we imagine, in every small town, in every considerable village of England, an elective local council, answerable for the police, the sanitary condition, the roads, the public buildings, the public schools of their locality, we shall be able to conceive the completeness of the municipal organisation which actually exists in France.

Three forms of religious worship are recognised by the law: the Roman Catholic, the Protestant, and the Jewish.* The ministers of these three communions are alike salaried by the State. The Roman Catholic religion is truly, as designated in the Concordat, (the instrument which fixes the modern legal constitution of the French Church), "the religion of the great majority of the French people." It is professed by more than thirteen-fifteenths of the population. There are about five millions † of Protestants, divided between the Lutheran and Calvinist communions. The Calvinists are the more numerous, having 510 salaried ministers, while the Lutherans have but 255. The Jews are in number about 70,000.

---

municipal commission of his own naming. At Paris and in all the great towns this has been done; but it is, also, often done in the country. About 2,000 municipal councils have been thus dissolved since 1851.

* In France always called *Israélite*, the terms *Jew, Jewish*, being considered somewhat opprobrious.

† I quote from the latest information, a work by M. [Alfred] Magin, *Cours de Géographie Moderne*, Paris, 1858, authorised by the French Government for use in the public schools. But on this subject of the numbers of the French Protestants there is the most astonishing diversity of assertion. The lowest estimate which I have seen puts them at one million; the highest at six millions.

CHAPTER III

Popular Education in France Before the Revolution

In France, as in other countries, the Christian Church has from the earliest times recognised the duty, and asserted the right, of organising and controlling public education. Besides the monastery-schools, besides the ecclesiastical or episcopal schools, the church professed the obligation to provide schools of a humbler order, schools for the poor laity, *les pauvres laïques*. The capitularies of Theodulf, appointed bishop of Orleans by Charlemagne, direct his clergy to open, in the towns and villages of his diocese, schools where the children of the faithful might receive, free of cost, the elements of instruction.* From the fourth century to the sixteenth, canons and decrees enjoined even the village priest to collect at the ecclesiastical dwelling (*pastophorium*) a certain number of readers, and to train them to the study of letters as well as to the ministry of the altar. The Lateran Council of 1179 gave injunctions, renewed by the Lateran Council of 1215, that a prebend in every cathedral should be devoted to the maintenance of a preceptor charged to instruct, without fee, the young. This instruction, like that of the higher schools, was under the superintendence of an ecclesiastical functionary delegated for the purpose by the bishop. He bore the title of *écolâtre*, or master of the schools, and generally filled at the same time the office of *chantre*, or master of the choir.

But, if the Church arrogated to herself the right of governing public education, the State, in France, arrogated it yet more

* See p. 90 of *Histoire de l'Instruction Publique en Europe, et principalement en France*, par [Auguste] Vallet de Viriville, professeur auxiliaire à l'École [Nationale] des Chartes, 4to, Paris, 1849; a work to which, both here and in what follows, I am much indebted.

imperiously. This power, which, though maintaining Roman Catholicism, opposed to ecclesiastical encroachment the Propositions of Bossuet in 1682, the Organic Articles of the Concordat in 1802, inherits from the Roman Empire, and has never ceased to put in practice, the loftiest idea of State attributions and State authority. It has maintained this idea against the Pope; it has maintained it against its own subjects. Charlemagne assumed the right of subjecting his bishops to his own examination, in order to assure himself that, amid the distractions of their benefices, they had not let their learning grow rusty. Henry the Fourth, in his Statutes of Reformation for the University of Paris, issued in 1598, takes it upon him to ordain, that no boy who has passed the age of nine years shall be allowed to be educated at home.* Napoleon, after establishing his University, decrees, that after a certain day every educational establishment in France which is not provided with an express authorisation from his Grand-Master, shall cease to exist.† The French State may refuse to concede to the Church the control of public instruction, but it agrees with the Church in holding that public instruction must be in the hands of an authorised body. *Collegia illicita dissolvantur*, said the Roman law; unauthorised associations are to be dissolved. The greatest of French jurists, the friend of Pascal ‡, enforces the same maxim: "The first rule for all associations," he says, "is that they be established for some public advantage *and by the order or permission of the Sovereign;* for all assemblages of more than one or two persons without this order or permission would be unlawful." "Every one knows," says another great lawyer §, "that no assembly of persons may take place in the realm unless with the authorisation of the Sovereign." Finally, the same principle is consecrated by the existing law of France, by the Penal Code ||, which declares

* Art. 4. "Nullus in privatis ædibus pueros, qui nonum annum excesserint, instituat et doceat."

† Decree of 11 September 1808.

‡ [Jean] Domat, the author of *Les Lois civiles dans leur Ordre naturel.* He died in 1696.

§ Rousseaud de Lacombe, author of the *Recueil de Jurisprudence civile,* and of the *Recueil de Jurisprudence canonique.* He died in 1749.

|| *Code Pénal,* art. 291.

that "no association of more than twenty persons, whose object shall be to assemble daily or at certain fixed times in order to occupy themselves with religious, literary, political, or other matters, may be formed unless with the consent of the Government, and under such conditions as it shall please the public authorities to impose." Theocracy in France, with M. de Bonald for its organ *, may desire to intrust education to a clerical corporation; modern society in France, with the first Napoleon for its organ, may desire to intrust it to a lay corporation; but both are agreed not to intrust it to itself. Liberty of instruction, such as we conceive it, appears in French legislation once, and once only; it appears there in 1793, under the Reign of Terror.

The high Roman and Imperial theory as to the duties and powers of the State has never obtained in England. It would be vain to seek to introduce it; but it is also vain, in a country where this theory is powerless, to waste time in decrying it. I believe, as every Englishman believes, that *over-government* is pernicious and dangerous; that the State cannot safely be trusted to undertake everything, to superintend everywhere. But, having once made this profession of faith, I shall proceed to point out as may be necessary, without perpetually repeating it, some inconveniences of *under-government;* to call attention to certain important particulars, in which, within the domain of a single great question, that of public education, the direct action of the State has produced salutary and enviable results.

From the fifth to the fifteenth century the institutions founded for popular instruction bore little or no fruit, because instruction in Europe was up to that time nearly confined to one class of society, the clergy. From the very earliest times, indeed, a simple shepherd boy, like Saint Patroclus of Berry, might enter a monastery-school and become one of the learned men of his epoch; but it was on condition of embracing the ecclesiastical profession. The urban and rural free schools, of which mention has been made, served chiefly to train boys designed for the service of the choir, like the schools for choristers which still survive; or, like the lesser seminaries, of which they were probably the germ, to give the first teaching to boys designed for

* See his *Théorie du Pouvoir politique et religieux*, published in 1796.

the ministry. The collectors of autographs, in their quest of the handwriting of noble and distinguished persons, do not mount beyond the fourteenth century, because up to that time even great personages seldom knew how to write. When such was the school-learning of the rich and noble, it may be imagined what was that of the poor and lowly. It was confined to a little instruction in the catechism and the rudiments of religion, given, where it was given at all, to the children of both sexes alike.

In the fifteenth century there are signs in the laity of France both of a growing demand for school instruction and of a sense that the Church inefficiently performed her duty of supplying it. In 1412, the inhabitants of Saint Martin de Villers, in the diocese of Evreux, founded a school for their own parish. The bishop complained of an encroachment on his privilege. The new school, he said, injured his own school at Touque. The dispute was settled by the consent of the lay founders of the new school to vest in the bishop the appointment of their teacher. On other occasions the dispute was carried into the courts of law; the courts of law upheld the exclusive privilege of the ecclesiastical authority, and the lay school was closed. But while thus maintaining her school rights, the Church failed to amend her discharge of her school duties.* A canon of Notre-Dame, Claude Joly, master of the choir and master of the schools in the metropolitan cathedral, who himself exercised in the seventeenth century the superintendence of the ecclesiastical schools of Paris, and who has left an historical account † of them, avows the obligation of the Church and confesses her failure. This confession is made in 1678; not twenty years later ‡ every parish in Scotland had its school.

It is well known how prodigious an impulse the Reformation gave in Protestant countries to the education of the people. The

* The great Chancellor of the University of Paris, Jean Gerson, (born 1363, died 1429), was in advance of his order and his age in his zeal for popular education, as in other matters. In his retirement at Lyons, at the end of his life, he himself taught the children of the poor; and his is the remarkable saying, "The Reformation of the Church must be commenced with the young children."

† *Traité historique des Écoles épiscopales et ecclésiastiques*, Paris, 1678.

‡ In 1696.

primary instruction of Holland, of Scotland, of Protestant Germany, dates from that event. In France, the ferment of mind, which in England and Germany produced the Reformation, existed; but it took a different course. Yet everywhere the new spirit showed solicitude for popular education, although it could not everywhere found it. In the meetings of the States-General held at Orleans and at Blois in 1560, 1576, and 1588, the Estates called the attention of the sovereign to the want of elementary schools. The nobles proposed to make church benefices contribute yearly a certain sum, to be employed in maintaining schoolmasters and literate persons (*pédagogues et gens lettrés*) in all towns and villages, "for the instruction of the children of the poor in the Christian religion and other needful learning, and in sound morality." The Third Estate insisted on the obligation of the clergy to "instruct or cause to be instructed the children of the poor in all good learning, according to their capacity, even from their earliest years, *not delaying or excusing themselves on pretext of the negligence of parents and sponsors.*" The nobles even demanded that "parents who neglected to send their children to school should be subjected to compulsion and fine." Little was done, however. The ordinance of Orleans, designed to meet the wishes of the Estates of 1560, attempted to revive the ancient prescription of the Councils, by directing that in "every cathedral or collegiate church one prebend, or the revenues of the same, should be permanently devoted to maintain a preceptor, and to give free schooling to the children of the place." It added a provision unknown to Councils, that this preceptor should be appointed *by the ecclesiastical and municipal authorities conjointly*. In 1563, Charles IX. attempted by letters patent to put this ordinance into execution at Paris; the ecclesiastical authority, the master of the schools, resisted, complaining that his privilege was infringed; and the king gave way.

The Church owed to the laity some compensation for her obstructiveness, and she paid her debt in a certain measure. Civilisation owes much to the great religious orders which laboured in the work of teaching; to the Dominicans, the Franciscans, the Benedictines, the Oratorians, the Jesuits. These, however, busied themselves with the education of the rich; but humbler efforts were not wanting, devoted to the service of the poor. A member of the severest of religious communities, a Minim of the Order of St. Francis of Paola, the Père Barré, founded in 1671 an association of teachers for the instruction of poor children of both sexes. The association took the title of "Brothers and Sisters of the Christian and Charitable Schools of the Child Jesus." Towards 1700 the Ursulines and other sisterhoods, by the establishment of their schools for girls, carried onward this effort. In 1789 the religious societies engaged in teaching the poor of France were twenty in number; but the religious society which has prosecuted this work most effectually, which has most merited gratitude by its labours for the education of the poor, and which, at the present day, most claims attention from its numbers and from its influence, is undoubtedly the society of the "Brethren of the Christian Schools." *

It dates from 1679. In that year it was founded by Jean Baptiste de Lasalle, a canon of the cathedral church of Rheims and a man of apostolic piety and zeal, in Rheims, his native town. He resigned his canonry in order to be able to tend his infant institution more assiduously. He drew up for it statutes which are a model of sagacity and moderation, and by which it is still governed. He composed for his schools a handbook of method †, of which later works on the same subject have little improved the precepts, while they entirely lack the unction. He lived long enough to see the fruit of his labours. In 1688 he established at Paris a colony of his *teaching brethren*.‡ In 1705 he fixed the head-quarters of his institute in Rouen, at the house of Saint Yon, from which his community took one of the titles by which it long was familiarly known.§ When he died in 1719, with the title of Superior-General of the Brethren of the Christian

* Institut des Frères des Écoles Chrétiennes.

† *Conduite des Écoles Chrétiennes.*

‡ Frères enseignants.

§ The brethren have gone by the names of Frères de Saint Yon, Frères Ignorantins, and Frères des Écoles Chrétiennes. They are now almost universally called by the latter title.

Schools, his order was established in eight dioceses. In 1724, when the society received a bull of confirmation and approbation from Pope Benedict XIII., it possessed 23 houses in France. In 1785, the number of children taught by the brethren was reckoned at 30,000. Dispersed at the Revolution, they were re-established under the reign of Napoleon, and in 1825, during the Restoration, the number of their houses was 210. In 1848 they had in France 19,414 schools, and taught 1,354,056 children.* Their central house is now at Paris.

The brethren are enjoined by their statutes to devote themselves to the instruction of boys in all things that pertain to an honest and Christian life. They are not forbidden to receive the rich into their schools, but their principal business is to be with the poor, and to their poorer scholars they are to extend a special affection. They are to obey a Superior-General, who, with two assistants, is to be elected by the assembled directors of the principal houses. The Superior-General is chosen for life, the assistants for ten years. The separate houses are to be governed by directors, chosen for three years. No brother is to take holy orders. Their vows, which are for three years only, are the three regular vows of chastity, poverty, and obedience, with another of stability, and of teaching without fee or reward. Even these three-year vows they are not permitted to make until they have been members of the institute two years, one of which is passed in the noviciate, the other in a school. They are always to go in company with others of their order; at first they went in parties of two, now they must be at least three. Together with religious knowledge they are to teach their scholars reading, writing, and arithmetic. They are to have in each of their houses a store of school-books and school-material, which they are to sell to their scholars at the cost price. They are not to talk or gossip with their scholars, or to hear any

* I quote from returns supplied by the Superior of the brethren, the Frère Philippe, to M. Vallet de Viriville for his *Histoire de l'Instruction Publique en Europe*, and published in that work. But the above numbers seem to me, I confess, hard to reconcile with those which, taken from official returns, will be given hereafter.

news from them. They are to be sparing of punishments. The director of each house is to have the inspection of the schools in connection with it.

Such are the rules to which this remarkable association owes its vitality. The pious founder, to whose thoughts the misery flowing from the debasement and ignorance of the poor and working classes was perpetually present *, and with whom its relief was a passion, took every precaution not to found, instead of an order of schoolmasters, an order of monks. He proscribed bodily mortification: he strictly limited the number of fasts to be observed by his brethren; he tried to dissuade them from perpetual vows. "He was fearful," says his biographer, "to see his disciples bind themselves too hastily." At first he allowed them to engage themselves for but a single year; then he fixed three years as their term of service; finally, and against his will, he consented to admit to perpetual vows some of the most fervent among his followers. The weakness of the disciples was not long in justifying the master's hesitation.

A similar community, established some years later on a much smaller scale, deserves notice, because in connection with its operations we have one of the few facts, testifying to fruit borne by popular instruction, which are to be met with before the Revolution. In the most populous quarter of Paris, the Faubourg St. Antoine, a society for the education of the poor had been founded under the title of "Brethren of the Christian Schools of the Faubourg St. Antoine," by an ecclesiastic, the Abbé Tabourin. In 1738, this society had established seventeen schools. The functionary at the head of the police of Paris declared that the police of the quarter cost, since the establishment of these schools, 30,000f. less than it cost before.

The labours of these religious societies were, however, principally confined to the towns. To their diffusion through the

* He established his institute, says Pope Benedict XIII., in his bull of approbation, "piè considerans innumera quæ ex ignorantiâ, omnium origine malorum, proveniunt scandala, præsertim in illis, qui, vel egestate oppressi, vel fabrili operi unde vitam eliciunt operam dantes, quarumvis scientiarum humanarum, *ex defectu æris impendendi*, non solùm penitus rudes, sed, quod magis dolendum est, elementa religionis Christianæ persæpè ignorant."

rural districts was opposed the serious obstacle of their expensiveness—an obstacle pointed out in 1818 by the Education Minister of that day, the excellent and admirable M. Royer-Collard.* "The brethren," said M. Royer-Collard, "are undoubtedly highly useful and highly to be respected; they do good service in the towns: *it would not be easy to introduce them into the rural districts, because they cost so much more than the ordinary schoolmasters.*" The rule which forbids the brethren to serve in parties of less than three, excellent in many respects, has the inconvenience of rendering difficult their employment in a poor country village where there are not funds for the payment of three teachers. To spread instruction through the length and breadth of the country was out of their power; and the State continued to find this service undischarged.

The century which saw the brotherhood founded did not close without seeing an effort of the State to undertake the task which for the brotherhood was impossible. But to this effort the State was prompted by a spirit wholly unlike to that which inspired M. de Lasalle, and it reaped from it no more success than it deserved. After the revocation of the Edict of Nantes, the persecuting government of Louis XIV. bethought itself of the village schoolmaster as a useful agent in its work of forcible conversion. A royal edict of December 13th, 1698, gave orders to take the children of heretics from their families at five years old, in order to bring them up, by compulsion, in Catholic schools. But these Catholic schools did not yet exist. The edict, therefore, went on to provide that "there should be established, so far as it was possible, schoolmasters and schoolmistresses in every parish which was without them, in order to instruct the children of both sexes in the principal mysteries of the Catholic,

* In a debate on a proposal to exempt the brethren from military service. The whole debate, which is very interesting, is to be found (copied from the *Moniteur*) in M. Ambroise Rendu's *Essai sur l'Instruction publique*, Paris, 1819, vol. ii. p. 581. M. Ambroise Rendu, Inspector-General and afterwards Councillor of the University, distinguished himself by his labours in the cause of public education. His son, M. Eugène Rendu, now employed in the Department of Public Instruction at Paris, has published interesting reports on popular education in Germany and England.

Apostolic, and Roman religion . . . in order, likewise, to teach reading, *and even writing*, to all who might need them." "To this end, it is our pleasure," the edict continues, "that, in places where there are no other funds, there shall be a power of taxing all the inhabitants to raise stipends for the said schoolmasters and schoolmistresses, up to a sum of 150 livres a year for a master, and of 100 for a mistress." * But the arbitrary and violent provisions of this edict made it inexecutable. The village children of France remained free from forcible initiation into the mysteries of the Catholic, Apostolic, and Roman religion. They remained, also, without learning how to read and write.

The era approached from which dates a wholly new history for France; and it is impossible to determine accurately in what state the Revolution of 1789 found the instruction of those masses, on whom it was to confer such unbounded power. Statistics on this point almost entirely fail us. In a list of the establishments of public instruction which the Revolution found existing in France—a list given by M. Villemain in a most interesting report on secondary instruction †—there is indeed the entry, "*Écoles cantonales, écoles de village*," but opposite to this entry, where the eye looks for figures, it finds a blank, and in a foot-note the words, "The elements for this calculation are wanting." The poor of the towns had the schools of the religious congregations. It appears, too, that in the want of good elementary schools, the colleges, or grammar-schools for the middle and upper classes, to a very limited extent supplied the deficiency, by admitting to some of the numerous scholarships with which they were endowed a certain number of children from the lower classes. To this cause it is said to be attributable that, in 1789, 1 in every 31 boys of from 8 to 18 years of age was receiving in France secondary instruction, while in 1843 the proportion was but 1 in 35.‡ In the country, village schools existed here and there. In these no teacher could be appointed unless approved by the ecclesiastical authority; most often he

* Art. 9.

† [Abel François Villemain,] *Rapport au Roi sur l'Instruction secondaire*, Paris, 1843.

‡ *Ibid.* p. 56.

was directly named by the curé. In France, as in other countries, popular tradition represents the incumbent as usually nominating to the post of schoolmaster either his sacristan or the cripple of the village. In the case of foundation schools, the founder or his representatives nominated the teacher; but here, too, the concurrence of the ecclesiastical authority was always required.* The instruction of the mass of the poor remained very nearly what it had been in the middle ages. In conversing with middle-aged working men in the French provinces, I found almost invariably that my informant himself had attended school; more rarely, that his father had attended it; that his grandfather had attended it, never.

* An edict of Louis XIV. (dated April 1695) says, "Les régents, précepteurs, maîtres et maîtresses d'écoles des petits villages seront approuvés par les curés des paroisses ou autres personnes ecclésiastiques qui ont droit de le faire."—Art. 25.

CHAPTER IV

Popular Education in France Under the Revolution

The Revolution presented itself with magnificent promises of universal education. Already, in 1775, Turgot, in his celebrated programme, had drawn the outlines of a uniform and national system, to be superintended by a Royal Council. The instructions of all three orders of the States-General loudly called for it. The clergy, while demanding a national system, insisted above all on the necessity of executing with more strictness "the regulations which tend to maintain and fortify the precious influence of the curés upon education." The nobles declared simply that "the time was come for propagating through the country districts the means of instruction for those who lived there, and for extending this instruction even to the poor." The Third Estate demanded that "public education should be so modified as to be adapted to the wants of all orders in the State; that it might form good and useful men in all classes of society." With the precision of a power which had already discerned its future means of strength, and was determined to use them, this formidable claimant suggested that the municipal and lay authorities should in future share with the Church the appointment and control of public teachers. The Constituent Assembly hastened to respond to the national wishes. A commission was appointed, which after two years of laborious inquiry appeared with a report and the project of a law. By a singular chance, as if no great public question, however alien to him, was to escape this most versatile of statesmen, the reporter of the commission was M. de Talleyrand. The Constituent Assembly received the report on the eve of its separation. It voted no plan of public instruction; but it consecrated in a single famous article the principle upon which such a plan was to repose. It decreed *: "There shall be created and organised a public instruction, common to all citizens, gratuitous in respect of those branches of tuition which are indispensable for all men. Its establishments shall be distributed gradually, in a proportion combined with the division of the kingdom."

On the 1st of October the Legislative Assembly met, and six months afterwards † it received from Condorcet another report on national education—another proposed law. But the time was no longer favourable for founding. The Convention replaced the Legislative Assembly ‡; the revolutionary decrees flew thick and fast, and nearly every one of them struck down an institution without giving to it a successor. On the 8th of March, 1793, it was decreed that the property of all endowed seats of education in France should be sold, and that the proceeds should go to the State. On the 18th of August in the same year, the religious corporations devoted to teaching, along with all other corporations, religious and secular, were suppressed, on the ground that "a truly free state must not tolerate within itself any corporate body whatever, not even those which, having devoted themselves to public instruction, have deserved well of their country." § A little later, on the 15th of September, the abolition of all existing colleges and faculties was pronounced, and the renowned University of Paris, with a host of less distinguished institutions, fell in a common ruin. So complete was the destruction, that in the next year a warm friend of education, Fourcroy, afterwards the chief agent of the First Consul in reviving and reorganising public instruction, declared to the Convention that France was fast relapsing into barbarism. To this had come the demands of 1789, and the promises of the Constituent Assembly.

* In the *Fundamental Dispositions* of the Constitution of September 3rd, 1791. "Il sera créé et organisé une instruction publique, commune à tous les citoyens, gratuite à l'égard des parties d'enseignement indispensables pour tous les hommes, et dont les établissemens seront distribués graduellement, dans un rapport combiné avec la division du royaume."

† April 20th, 1792. ‡ September 21st, 1792.

§ "Considérant qu'un état vraiment libre ne doit souffrir dans son sein aucune corporation, pas même celles qui, vouées à l'enseignement public, ont bien mérité de la patrie," &c.

The Convention had unquestionably a sincere zeal for popular instruction, and even an exaggerated faith in it. One of its members proposed that no less than three sittings of the Assembly in every ten days should be devoted to this subject alone. It was the Convention which endowed France with two admirable institutions, of which the vitality has proved not less great than the usefulness—the Normal School and the Polytechnic School. But it would have been powerless to carry any organised instruction, even a humble one, into a region of society not then prepared to receive it; and the instruction which it dreamed of was by no means humble. By decrees of the 12th of December, 1792, and of the 30th of May, 1793, it ordered the establishment of primary schools. By a decree of the 21st of October, 1793, it gave development to its plan. The primary schools were to be proportioned in number to the population. There was to be one for every 1500 inhabitants; but no place with more than 400 inhabitants was to be left without a school. The children of all classes were to receive in these schools "that first education, physical, moral, and intellectual, the best adapted to develope in them republican manners, patriotism, and the love of labour." They were to learn "those traits of virtue which most honour freemen, and particularly those traits of the French Revolution, the best adapted to elevate the soul and to render men worthy of liberty and equality." They were to be taught to speak, read, and write correctly the French language; they were to learn "some notions of the geography of France; the rights and duties of men and citizens; the first notions of natural and familiar objects; the use of numbers, the compass, the level, weights and measures, the lever, the pulley, and the measurement of time. They were to be often taken into the fields and workshops where they might see agricultural and industrial work going on, and they were to take part in it so far as their age would allow." In this manner the Convention filled up the outline traced by the Constituent Assembly. These were the "branches of tuition" which the French Revolution held to be "indispensable for all men."

A few days afterwards * it proceeded to organise the instruc-

* Decree of October 29th, 1793.

tion decreed. A "commission of enlightened patriots and moral persons" was to be established in every district, in order to determine where the new schools should be placed, and to "*examine all citizens who proposed to devote themselves to the work of national education in the primary schools.*" The commission was to examine candidates as to their acquirements, their aptitude for teaching, their morals, and their patriotism. The examination was to be public. The commission was to form a list of the candidates who had satisfied them, and this list was to be published in each school district. On the *décadi* following its publication, such inhabitants as were parents and guardians were to meet and choose a teacher from it. Vacancies were to be filled up in the same manner. The decree was to apply to schoolmistresses as well as schoolmasters, and for the salaries of both it fixed a mimimum of 1200 francs (48*l.*). But no woman of noble family, no woman who had formerly belonged to a religious order, no woman who had formerly been named to the post of teacher by a noble or by an ecclesiastic, was to be eligible for the office of schoolmistress. There was no fear that men thus circumstanced would be chosen by the local authorities; their compassion or their embarrassment might dispose them to be less severe in excluding resourceless women.

The Convention could furnish a programme of instruction, but it could not furnish schools. In despair it renounced the attempt, and addressed itself to private enterprise. On the 19th of December, 1793, appeared the startling decree which abandons abruptly the consecrated traditions of public instruction in France, and which, in the eyes of every orthodox functionary of that instruction, stands as the abomination of desolation, witnessing that the end of the world is come. *L'enseignement est libre*, begins this new voice;—"Teaching is free—it shall be public; citizens and citizenesses who desire to avail themselves of their liberty to teach" shall merely be required to inform the municipal authority of their intention to open a school, and of the matters which they propose to teach, and shall produce, besides, a "certificate of civism and good morals." Thus fortified, a teacher might open his school, and the Republic undertook to pay his scholars' fees. There was no fear lest these should be wanting; for the law provided that parents should be compelled, under pain of fine, to send their children to school, thus transferring to the scholar the control from which it exempted the teacher.

Such liberty was too novel to last; and a decree of the next year restricted it.* Freedom of instruction was maintained, in so far as it was still left to the individual to place a school where he would, without first asking the State's leave; but the teacher was subjected to a more exact superintendence. Even his charter of liberty, the decree of December, 1793, had committed him to the watchfulness "of the municipality or section, of parents and guardians, and of society at large;" any of whom might denounce him if he taught anything "contrary to the laws and to republican morality." The law of 1794 placed him in the hands of a "jury of instruction," to be chosen by the district administration from among fathers of families. This jury was to examine and elect the teacher; he had then to be approved by the district administration; afterwards he was to be superintended in the management of his school by the jury. To quicken the zeal of those parents whom the penalties of the decree of 1793 had failed to move, the new law ordered that "those young citizens who have not attended school shall be examined, in the presence of the people, at the Feast of the Young, and, if they shall then be found not to have the acquirements necessary for French citizens, shall be excluded from all public functions until they have attained them." The law fixed a minimum for the salaries of teachers, and for the proportion of schools to population, nearly at the same rate as preceding laws, but somewhat more liberally. It provided that in every commune where the clergyman's house had not been already sold for the benefit of the republic, this house should be given up to the schoolmaster for a dwelling and for a school.† It maintained the former programme of instruction, and even amplified it, adding to the course gymnastics, military exercises, and swimming. The revolutionary theory of the "acquirements indispensable for all men" here reached its fullest efflorescence.

* Decree of November 17th, 1794.

† This provision was repealed by a decree of August 31st, 1797.

In a year all was changed. On the 25th of October, 1795, appeared the most memorable of the revolutionary laws of public instruction, the law (as it is still called) of the 3rd of Brumaire, year IV.* This law, founded on a remarkable report by Daunou, organised the whole of instruction; it embraced primary schools, central schools, special schools, public museums, public libraries, the Institute. For primary schools it established a state of things which endured, with little change, till 1833. But at what a sacrifice! To effect the practical foundation of a very little, the Revolution had to renounce almost all its illusions. Popular education, which had had laws upon laws to itself, was confined, in the law of 1795, to the limits of one short chapter. The "acquirements indispensable for all men" had dwindled to reading, writing, ciphering, and the elements of republican morality. The State, which was once to give everything, was now to give nothing but a schoolhouse. The schoolmaster's salary of from 1200 to 1500 francs a year out of the public purse, descended to a salary such as he could extract out of "the local authorities." The free schooling promised to all scholars came down to a schooling which all but one-fourth of the scholars were to pay for. In compensation the youth of France might attend school or not, as they and their parents pleased. Guarantees for the efficiency of the schoolmaster were still maintained. He was still to be examined by a jury of instruction; the municipal authorities presented him for examination; the departmental authorities nominated him when examined. He was thenceforward under the superintendence of the municipal administration. The concurrence of the jury, the municipality, and the department was necessary for his dismissal. Thus the Convention atoned for its first extravagance. The day after the passing of this law, it separated.†

"What," I ventured to ask M. Guizot, "did the French Revolution contribute to the cause of popular education?" "Un déluge de mots," replied M. Guizot, "rien de plus." As regards

* The first chapter of this law, which alone relates to primary instruction, is printed textually at the end of this volume. [The appendices are not printed in this edition.]

† On the 26th of October, 1795.

the material establishment of popular instruction, this is unquestionably true. Yet on its future character and regulation the Revolution, as unquestionably, exercised an influence which every Frenchman takes it for granted that an inquirer understands, and which we in England must not overlook. It established certain conditions under which any future system of popular education must inevitably constitute itself. It made it impossible for any government of France to found a system which was not *lay*, and which was not *national.*

CHAPTER V

Popular Education in France Under the First Empire

The weak government and the exhausting wars of the Directory left, as is well known, the whole of the internal administration of France in neglect and confusion. Public instruction suffered with everything else. In 1799 Napoleon began the task, his efforts in which have shed an imperishable glory on the Consulate, and which it would have been well for him never to have forsaken for any task less pacific and less noble—the task, to use his own words, of "founding a new society, free alike from the injustice of feudalism and from the confusion of anarchy." Of his labours, modern French administration, the Concordat, the public schools for the middle and upper classes, the Legion of Honour, the Code, the University, are monuments. Primary schools did not escape his attention. But the urgent business of the moment was to deal with secondary schools; to rescue the education of the richer classes themselves, those classes in whose hands the immediate destinies of a civilised and regular society are placed, from the state of ruin into which it had fallen. To this the First Consul addressed himself. The law of the 1st of May, 1802, founded secondary instruction in France as it at this day exists. For the feeble and decaying central schools of the Convention *—mere courses of lectures, without hold on their pupils, without discipline, and without study—the new law substituted the communal colleges and the lyceums, with boarders, with a rigid discipline, and with a sustained course of study; institutions which do not, indeed, give an education equal to that of our best public schools, but which extend to all the middle

* The law of the 3rd Brumaire, year IV., had decreed one for each department. In 1802 only thirty-two were found to have had any success. These thirty-two were the first *Lycées* under the new law.

classes of France an education which our public schools give to the upper classes only. For the exclusively mathematical and scientific course of the revolutionary theorists, it substituted, but with proper enlargement, that bracing classical course which the experience of generations has consecrated, and which Napoleon, though he had not himself undergone it, had the power of mind to appreciate. Finally, by the establishment of 6400 scholarships, fairly distributed, it opened an access as wide as was possible, or even desirable, to the schools which it created.

Only the first chapter of the law of 1802 related to primary schools. This merely repeated the humble provisions of the last law of the Convention. The commune was to furnish a school-house to the teacher, who still, after this was supplied to him, had to depend for his support upon the payments of his scholars. The number of these to be exempted, on the ground of poverty, from the school-fee, was reduced from a fourth to a fifth. The superintendence of the teacher by the municipal authorities was confirmed. Finally, the schools were placed under the supreme charge of the newly created departmental executive, the sub-prefects and the prefects.

Small as was the attention then bestowed on schools for the poor, in comparison with that which at a later time they received, it is curious to remark how strongly the inconvenience of their total disorganisation was felt in the French provinces, as long ago as the beginning of this century. It seems as if, rude and illiterate as was the village-school of France before the Revolution, its disappearance could leave a blank as serious as the blank which the disappearance of the village-school would leave now. In its endeavour to bring order out of the chaos which the Revolution had left, the Consular government invited in 1801 the practical suggestions of the council-general of each department upon the wants of the locality. The councils-general, in their replies, expressed, among other things, the greatest dissatisfaction at the state of the primary schools, and the greatest desire to see it improved. Many of them called for the re-establishment of the religious orders devoted to teaching. "The Brethren of the Christian Doctrine, the Ursulines, and the rest, are much regretted here," says the council-general of the Côte d'Or. That of the Pas de Calais begs the government "again to employ in the instruction of boys and girls the *Frères ignorantins*, and the Daughters of Charity, and of Providence." That of the Pyrénées Orientales says, "People here regret the religious associations which busied themselves in teaching the children of the poor." That of the Aisne asks, like that of the Pas de Calais, for the "reorganisation of the religious communities devoted to the elementary instruction of children of each sex." To commit the primary instruction of France to religious corporations was at no time the intention of Napoleon. To avail himself of the services of these corporations, under the control of a lay body, modern in its spirit, and national in its composition, he was abundantly willing. Such a body he designed to establish in his new University.

By a short law of the 10th of May, 1806, the University of France was called into existence. "There shall be formed," says the law, "under the name of *Imperial University*, a body with the exclusive charge of tuition and of public education throughout the empire. The members of the teaching body shall contract civil obligations of a special and temporary character." The new University was organised by a decree of the 17th of March, 1808. Under a hierarchy of grand-master, councillors, inspectors-general, and rectors, was placed the whole instruction of France. The faculties, the lyceums and communal colleges, the primary schools, were alike made subject. "No school, no establishment of instruction whatsoever, can be formed outside the pale of the University, and without the authorisation of its chief." * By the imposition of dues on examinations, dues on degrees, dues on the fees paid by boarders and day scholars in grammar-schools, superior and secondary education became tributary to the new power. It was also endowed with a sum of 400,000 francs charged on the State, and with all the property of the old educational bodies of France which the Revolution had not yet alienated. It became a great civil corporation, with the power of acquiring, inheriting, and transmitting. The Grand-Master and his council represented it in the capital; twenty-six Academies, each governed by its Rector, corre-

* Decree of March 17th, 1808, art. 2.

sponding in their districts with the ancient Courts of Appeal, represented it in the provinces.

Such was the Imperial University created by Napoleon. The powers which he conferred on it did not, at that period of disorganisation and of demand for effective government, appear exorbitant. It had at a later time no fiercer enemies than the clergy; yet in 1808 a bishop writes to the Chancellor of the new University that he is rejoiced at its establishment; for "education," he says, "is at the present day in the hands of the first comer, and one has the pain of seeing it conducted by men who have neither acquirements nor principles." Created an endowed corporation, not a mere department of state, it wore a character of independence which all modern governments in France are apt to regard with suspicion, and which Napoleon himself was the last man to confer hastily. His reasons assigned for this unusual distinction are judicious, and even noble. "His Majesty," he says, in his instructions to the University Council at its first formation,—"his Majesty has organised the University as a corporate body, because a corporate body never dies, and because, in such a body, there is a perpetual transmission of organisation and spirit. It has been his Majesty's desire to realise, in a state of forty millions of people, what Sparta and Athens accomplished, what the religious orders attempted in our own day, and failed in accomplishing because they lacked unity. His Majesty wants a body whose teaching may be free from the influence of the passing gusts of fashion; a body that may keep moving, even though Government be lethargic; whose administration and statutes may be made so thoroughly national, that no one shall lightly lay his hands upon them."

These wishes have not been wholly frustrated. Disliked as a Napoleonist creation by the Bourbons, hated by the clergy, decried by the friends of liberty of instruction, ill supported by successive ministries incapable of Napoleon's elevation of views, the University of France has been unable to maintain its exclusive privileges and its corporate character. In 1824 it became a ministerial department *; in 1833 its special budget was sup-

* The Ministry of Public Instruction was created by an ordinance of the 26th of August, 1824.

pressed; in 1850 its property was annexed to the State.* But the Minister of Public Instruction is still, at the same time, Rector of the Academy of Paris, and head of the University; his chief functionaries are functionaries of the University, graduated in its faculties and inspired by its traditions. That transmission of a corporate spirit, which Napoleon wished for, has been accomplished, while the exclusive privileges which the tendencies of the age would not tolerate have been withdrawn; and from this corporate spirit the members of the University derive an independence, a self-respect, and a disinterestedness, which distinguishes them from the whole body of French officials. The University of France has not the attributes of ancient universities; it has neither great estates, nor august associations, nor historic grandeur. But it has attributes, the first to which modern institutions have to aspire, and the possession of which may perhaps compensate for the absence of all others; it has intelligence, and it has equity.

Of the decree organising the University, only four articles related expressly to primary schools. The first of the four † specifies among the schools of which the twenty-six new Academies were to take charge, the schools for the poor, primary schools, in which are taught reading, writing, and the first notions of arithmetic. These Napoleon, like the authors of the law of 1795, pronounces to be the "elementary acquirements necessary for all men." He naturally omits from his programme the republican morality of the Convention. No special mention is made of religious instruction for the primary schools; but the decree proclaims that the whole teaching of the University is to be based upon the precepts of religion, of loyalty, and of obedience. Another article ‡ directs the University to take care that the persons who give elementary instruction be persons capable of giving it properly. Another § prescribes the formation, in the lyceums and grammar-schools, of normal classes destined to form masters for the primary schools. In these classes are to be taught the "best methods for bringing to perfection the art of teaching children to read, write, and cipher." Finally, the

* By a vote of the Legislative Assembly, August 22nd, 1850.

† Decree of March 17th, 1808, art. 5. ‡ Art. 107. § Art. 108.

decree mentions by name the religious order most concerned in popular education, the Brethren of the Christian Schools. The brethren were to be certificated by the Grand-Master, admitted to take the University oath, and specially encouraged. The Grand-Master was to examine their statutes, and to superintend their schools.

The operation of the law of 1802 had wrought little change in the primary schools. In a statistical report on the Department of Vaucluse, published in 1808 by authority of the prefect, nearly the same picture is drawn of their condition as the councils-general had drawn in 1801. Nearly one-half of the communes are without any school at all. Where schools exist, they are often under the care of teachers now old and infirm; when these teachers are gone, there is no one to take their place. Both the "Ignorantine Friars" and the old village pedagogues are greatly regretted in the country. Napoleon sincerely desired the spread of elementary instruction, although he meant to keep it within strict limits.* In establishing the University, he conceived that he established a body in whose hands the future destinies of popular education rested. The University accepted the charge. Its Grand-Master, M. de Fontanes, a man of letters, and a proficient in that florid declamation which often passes for eloquence, sincerely addressed himself to learn the facts of a system of instruction in which there was nothing academic. He directed his inspectors-general, sent in 1809 into the departments to inspect superior and secondary instruction, to examine, so far as they could, into the state of primary instruction, and to report to him on it. They reported a state of languor, degradation, death. But the establishments of the Congregation of the Christian Schools were beginning to reappear. M. de Fontanes issued a general diploma † to the brethren, authorising them to hold schools; he revised and approved their statutes; he offered to them pecuniary aid; he exerted himself to rescue them and other teachers from the conscription. He wrote to

* By a decree of November 15th, 1811, the University was ordered to see that "les maîtres ne portassent point leur enseignement au-dessus de la lecture, l'écriture, et l'arithmétique."

† August 4th, 1810. The diploma was delivered to the Superior-General.

the bishops and prefects, requesting information about village schools and schoolmasters, to guide him in continuing or dismissing the latter. In one letter, written by him to a prefect in 1809, there is a passage which is valuable as showing how teachers were at that time appointed:—"The modes in which primary teachers are nominated," he says, "are extremely various; in some cantons they have to be examined before a jury; in others, the municipal council expresses its wishes; in others, again, the teacher is empowered to open school on his mere personal request, accompanied by the consent of the inhabitants, who enter into no engagement to maintain him." M. de Fontanes soon became convinced of his want of materials for immediately reconstructing primary education. He tried to use the old materials where he could. By a circular addressed in 1810 to his rectors he desired them to send him lists, for every department, of the existing schools and schoolmasters, specifying those of the latter who, in the opinion of the rector and in that of the local authorities, merited to be confirmed in their office. To these he undertook to send certificates. Meanwhile, he promised, at no distant period, a comprehensive plan of popular education.

The best criticism on the actual performance of the University is to be found in the tables of its expenditure. All that primary instruction, during the Empire, received from the public purse, was a sum of 170*l.** Even this was not contributed from the funds of the University, but from those of the Minister of the Interior. The enemies of the University were in the habit of saying that it did little for primary instruction, because from primary instruction it could draw no revenue. This was unjust. The University had, in truth, no funds and no staff for dealing with popular education. The primary schools were in too suffering a condition to be restored by the occasional efforts of rectors and inspectors-general. The country districts of France,

* 4250 fr. See *Le Budget de l'Instruction Publique,* par M. Charles Jourdain, Paris, 1857, p. 175. M. Charles Jourdain, (himself distinguished in the world of letters, to which his father rendered a signal service), is at the head of the financial department of the Ministry of Public Instruction. His work is invaluable for all that relates to the finance not only of primary, but also of superior and secondary instruction.

swept by the conscription, were too harassed and exhausted to care whether their schools were suffering or not. In more than one case the University offered funds for the assistance of such schools, and could find no one to receive and administer them. One remarkable effort in the cause of popular education, and one only, dates from the Empire. In 1810 the first normal school in France for primary teachers was founded at Strasbourg, by a prefect whose intelligent beneficence is still remembered in Alsace—M. Lezay de Marnésia. But the time for educating the French people was not yet come. Napoleon was conscious both that the work remained undone, and that it was indispensable to accomplish it. In decreeing, on the report of Carnot, the establishment of a model school, he expresses his dissatisfaction that the people should be so ill educated, his conviction that it was possible to educate them better.* But this decree dates from the very last days of his power, after his return from Elba, and six weeks before Waterloo.

* *Moniteur* of April 30th, 1815:—"Considérant l'importance de l'éducation primaire pour l'amélioration du sort de la société; considérant que les méthodes jusqu' aujourd'hui usitées en France n'ont pas rempli le but de perfectionnement qu'il est possible d'atteindre; désirant porter cette partie de nos institutions à la hauteur des lumières du siècle," &c.

CHAPTER VI

Popular Education in France Under the Restoration

To the Restoration is due the credit of having first perceived, that, in order to carry on the war with ignorance, the sinews of war were necessary. Other governments had decreed systems for the education of the people; the government of the Restoration decreed funds. An ordinance of the 29th of February 1816 charged the treasury with an annual grant of 2000*l.* for the provision of school-books and model schools, and of recompenses for deserving teachers. The sum was small; but it was the first. The same ordinance prescribed the formation of cantonal committees, to watch over the disicipline, morality, and religious instruction of primary schools. These committees (which were to be unpaid) were to consist of the curé, two local officials of the government, and four notables of the canton to be nominated by the rector to whose academy the school belonged, and approved by the prefect. Above all, this ordinance instituted a certificate of three degrees, to be obtained by examination before the rector's deputy. It made special provision for the independence of Protestant schools. It may truly be said that this ordinance of 1816 presents, in germ, several of the best provisions of the law of 1833.

But in its government of public instruction, as in its government of other public interests, the Restoration was not happy. It laboured under the incurable weakness of being a traditionary monarchy working with revolutionary tools; it was placed as Charles II. would have been placed had he returned to England bound by the Commonwealth-laws instead of the Declaration of Breda. The legislation of the English Republic disappeared from the statute-book; that of the French Republic survived to hamper the Restoration. In its treatment of public instruction, as of other questions, the monarchy was perpetually striving to assert its own traditions in face of a legal situation of which it was not master, and perpetually failing. One of its first acts was to strike a blow at the University. A royal ordinance of February 17th, 1815, announced the intention of taking public instruction out of the hands of an authority "whose absolutism was incompatible with the paternal intentions and liberal spirit" of the Restoration, and which "reposed on institutions framed rather to serve the political views of the former government, than to spread among the people the benefits of a moral and useful education." Napoleon reappeared, and the University was respited. At its second return, the monarchy, more moderate or more timid, maintained provisionally a system for which it had no substitute ready.* The Grand-Master and council were replaced by a Commission of Public Instruction †; but the University was left in possession of its dues, its academies, and its exclusive privileges, of which the ordinance of February had deprived it. The friends of the monarchy urged it to decentralise as much as possible ‡; to foster institutions which, by their local strength, independent permanence, and conservative spirit, might serve in the country as points of support to the government. M. de Tocqueville has pointed out how, even before the Revolution, it was the constant effort of French government to overbear such institutions, because all independence was distasteful to it. But, in spite of Government, they existed in the ancient France in great numbers. They were the necessary result of the isolation of provinces, the variety of jurisdictions, the multitude of corporations. The humble Institute of the Christian Schools offered to the Restoration an opportunity of

* By an ordinance of August 15th, 1815.

† This Commission consisted at first of five, afterwards of seven, members. M. Royer-Collard was its first president.

‡ "En France, aujourd'hui, les lois tendent à la démocratie, et l'administration tend au despotisme.—Voulez-vous ouvrir une école? prenez un diplôme.—L'Université ne demande qu'une chose aux Frères, c'est de dissoudre leur congrégation, pour devenir de simples instituteurs primaires dont elle disposera souverainement.—L'Université s'occupera de vous fournir le savoir, et les tribunaux s'occuperont de vos mœurs."—*Conservateur* of November, 1818.

reverting to the old order of things. The moment this congregation was relieved from the Empire, it attempted to shake off the yoke of the Imperial University. The occasion was the certificate prescribed by the ordinance of 1816, and which the rectors endeavoured to enforce. The Superior-General directed the brethren to refuse to be examined. The individual certificate was calculated, he said, "to weaken the dependence of the members on their chief, and to destroy their congregation." * He boldly maintained, in defiance of the revolutionary legislation, that as his community had never ceased to have a legal existence, it ought to continue in the enjoyment of its ancient civil rights. His adversaries retorted that if the corporation of the Christian Schools had not been suppressed by the revolution, then neither had the most absurd and obsolete corporations, whom to name was to provoke a smile, been suppressed, and they were still legally existing. We in England, with our judicious contempt of logic, should probably have contented ourselves with ignoring the monstrous decree of 1792, when a useful institution was at stake, while we left useless institutions to its operation. The government of the Restoration thought it convenient to keep the religious societies dependent on it for their existence, but it freely conceded to them exemptions and privileges. That is to say, it denied to these bodies the power of aiding it as independent forces, while it gained for itself the odium of an unjust favouritism. In July, 1818, the Commission of Public Instruction decided that the brethren of the Christian Schools should be exempted from examination, and should receive their certificates on presenting their letters of obedience. In 1824 † the Minister of Public Instruction, M. de Frayssinous, remodelled the cantonal committees, so as to give the entire command of the Catholic primary schools to the bishops and clergy. Whether the Restoration was a just or an unjust steward to the French people, it cannot, at any rate, be commended for having done wisely. Without strengthening itself, it managed to offend every liberal sentiment, and to unite against its own existence the most moderate friends of liberty with the most reckless anarchists.

* The Frère Gerbaud to the Minister of the Interior, July 7th, 1818.
† By an ordinance dated April 8th.

It reimposed Latin as the language of college lectures, while it continued to refuse to fathers of families the power of disposing of their property as they pleased. It abandoned the primary schools to the clergy, while it continued to keep the Church the salaried servant of the State.

Yet, in respect to popular education, it showed uniform solicitude and occasional glimpses of liberalism. In 1828 * a new Minister of Instruction, M. de Vatimesnil, restored to the cantonal committee its lay element, and to the University its control of the primary schools. He gave, for the first time, to dismissed teachers an appeal from the rector and his academic council to the Royal Council of Public Instruction at Paris. He extended the cantonal committee's right of inspection to girls' schools, which an ordinance of the 3rd of April, 1820, had subjected to the prefect alone. In 1830 † M. Guernon de Ranville, one of the ministers who signed the fatal ordinances of July, again abrogated this latter provision. The superintendence of girls' schools under sisters of the religious communities he took away from the cantonal committees, and assigned to the bishops alone. Yet this same M. Guernon de Ranville called ‡ the municipal councils to deliberate on the immediate establishment of a system of communal schools which prefigures the system founded in 1833. In 1829 the State doubled the sum which since 1816 it had annually allotted to primary instruction; in 1830, on the eve of the Revolution, it increased it sixfold.§ The primary normal schools, of which the Empire had bequeathed but one to the Restoration, were thirteen in number in 1830. In more than 20,000 of the communes of France a school of some sort or other was established. Yet the reporter || of the law of 1833 could say with truth that the monarchy of July had received popular education in a deplorable state from its predecessor.

In fact, the situation of primary instruction in 1830, far from

* By an ordinance dated April 21st.

† Ordinance of January 6th, 1830.

‡ Ordinance of February 14th, 1830.

§ The grant in 1829 was 100,000 fr. (4000*l.*), in 1830 it was 300,000 fr. (12,000*l.*).

|| M. Cousin, in the *Moniteur* of May 22nd, 1833.

brilliant as it appeared, was yet externally more specious than internally sound. The ordinance of 1816 imposed on teachers the necessity of being examined and certificated; it thus established the best and only guarantee for the efficiency of that agent on whom a school's whole fortune hangs: but the guarantee was illusory. The reader has seen how the religious corporations were allowed to evade it, by presenting their letters of obedience in lieu of a certificate. There remained the lay teachers. They had to undergo an examination before the rector's delegate. But the rector had at his disposal no proper staff to which to commit such functions. Inspection did not then exist. In nine cases out of ten the rector named as his delegate the curé of the parish for which a schoolmaster was required; the curé named the man of his own choice with or without examination; and the rector bestowed the certificate which his delegate demanded. Even the legal power of control over the choice of incompetent teachers the University lost in 1824. Catholics themselves confessed the injury which Catholic schools had suffered by the exemption of their teachers from the most salutary of tests.* Nor was the communal school in many cases more of a reality than the schoolmaster's certificate. Of the 20,000 communes provided with schools barely one half possessed, even in 1834, school-premises of their own; in the other half the school was held in a barn, in a cellar, in a stable, in the church-porch, in the open air, in a room which served at the same time as the sole dwelling-place of the schoolmaster and his family, where his meals were cooked and his children born.† Where school-premises existed, they were often no better than their less pretentious substitutes: they were often hovels, dilapidated, windowless, fireless, reeking with damp; where, in a space of twelve feet square, eighty children were crowded together; where the ravages of an epidemic swept the school every year.‡ The state of things reported by the inspectors, nearly 500 in

* *Rapport au Roi*, by the Duke of Broglie, October 16th, 1830, in the *Bulletin Universitaire*, vol. ii. p. 174.

† *Tableau de l'Instruction primaire en France*, par M. [Paul] Lorain, Paris, 1837, p. 3.

‡ *Ibid.* p. 3, 162.

number, whom M. Guizot, at the end of 1833, sent through the length and breadth of France to determine accurately the condition of elementary schools with which the law of 1833 at the outset had to deal, is probably the same state of things which a similar inquest, had the happy thought of making it arisen, would have revealed in every country in Europe when popular instruction first began to be closely scanned. Here the teacher was a petty tradesman, leaving his class every moment to sell tobacco to a customer; there he was a drunkard; in another place he was a cripple. The clergy were often found at war with the schoolmaster; but then the schoolmaster was often such that this state of war was not wonderful. "In what condition is the moral and religious instruction in your school?" one of M. Guizot's inspectors asked a schoolmaster. "*Je n'enseigne pas ces bêtises-là*," was the answer. Another inspector found the schoolmaster parading, at the head of his school, the town where he lived; drums beating, the scholars singing the Marseillaise; and the procession halting before the clergyman's house to shout at the top of their lungs, "Down with the Jesuits!" * The apathy of the local authorities, too, was disheartening. "We counted on meeting with gratitude," said the inspectors; "instead of that, we have met, almost everywhere, with resistance." An inspector arrived on a November evening, wet and tired, at a remote commune, to which he brought the promise of a school; he sought out the mayor, on whose hospitality, (for there was no inn,) he reckoned; instead of hospitality he received from the mayor this greeting:—"You would have done a great deal better, Sir, if you had brought us money to mend our roads; as for schools, we don't want them;"—and, late as it was, the unfortunate inspector had to cross a ford, and seek refuge in another village.†

* *Tableau de l'Instruction primaire en France*, p. 131.

† *Ibid.* p. 15. M. Lorain, distinguished in the service of public instruction in France, was one of the agents employed by M. Guizot in the inspection of 1833; his most interesting book is a summary of the results of the whole inspection.

CHAPTER VII

Popular Education in France Under the Monarchy of July, 1830.—Law of 1833

The monarchy of July contained among its chief supporters men who had long revolved the problem of popular education, and who were determined to try to work it out. Brought up in the nurture of the University and imbued with its spirit, they soon made it manifest that education was to be seriously superintended by an educational authority. An ordinance of October 16th, 1830, had finally destroyed ecclesiastical preponderance in the local committees; an ordinance of April 18th, 1831, did away with all exemptions from the certificate. In the two years from 1831 to 1833 thirty new normal schools were created. An order from the Royal Council of Public Instruction minutely regulated them.* The grant for primary education rose in 1831 to 28,000*l.*, in 1832 to 40,000*l.* Meanwhile a great and comprehensive measure was maturing. It was brought before the Chambers in the spring of 1833. The reporter of the commission which examined it was M. Cousin; the Minister of Public Instruction who proposed it was M. Guizot. It became law on the 28th of June, 1833.

This law of 1833 is so important, it is so truly the root of the present system of primary instruction in France, that I have thought it desirable to reprint it in the original at the end of this report.† It had the great merit of being full of good sense, full of fruitful ideas, full of toleration, full of equity; but it had the still greater merit of attaining the object which it had in view. It founded in France for the first time a national elementary education. Succeeding legislation has subverted many important provisions of it; but its all-important provisions remain standing.

* December 14th, 1832.

† [The appendices are not printed in this edition.]

What was previously, to use a French expression, *facultative* to the communes, what the law only recommended to them, and they did or not as they liked, this measure made *obligatory;* and it provided means for the fulfilment of this obligation. I proceed to give a short sketch of it.

The first chapter of the law determined the objects which primary instruction was to embrace. The second and third determined the nature of the schools which were to give this instruction. The fourth and last established the authorities who were to govern it. A fifth chapter had extended to girls' schools the provisions of the law; but it was found premature to deal at that moment with girls' schools; they were first regulated by legislation in 1836.*

The Convention had at first exaggerated what was indispensable in primary instruction; it had afterwards too much reduced it. Napoleon had maintained the reduction. In consequence, a numerous class, needing something more than reading, writing, and arithmetic, but not needing Greek and Latin, was left unprovided for. It remained uneducated, or it was driven into the communal colleges, where it received an education which it did not want, and which left it unfitted for its position in life. For this class the law of 1833 created a *superior* primary instruction, not properly embracing foreign languages, ancient or modern, but embracing all that constitutes what may be called a good French education. For the immense class below, for the mass of the French people, it established an *elementary* primary instruction.

This instruction, the indispensable minimum of knowledge, the "bare debt of a country towards all its offspring," "sufficient to make him who receives it a human being, and at the same time so limited that it may be everywhere realised," † added something to the scanty programme of 1795 and 1802. In the first place it was religious. "Moral and religious teaching" formed a part of it. It added, besides, the elements of French

* By an ordinance dated June 23rd.

† *Exposé des Motifs de la Loi du* 28 *Juin* 1833, by M. [François P. G.] Guizot, Jan. 2nd, 1833.

grammar; and, for a purpose of national convenience, the legal but imperfectly received system of weights and measures.

The Charter had proclaimed liberty of teaching; private schools, therefore, were free to compete with public schools in giving this primary instruction. To establish them there was no longer needed, as heretofore, the authorisation of a rector. The only guarantee which the State demanded of them was the possession by the teacher of a certificate of morality, and of a certificate of capacity. Liberty of teaching was thus secured to all competent persons who claimed it. Liberty to incompetence is not an article of faith with French liberalism.

But by far the greatest part of primary instruction must of necessity be given in public schools. "The principle of liberty, admitted as an only principle, would be," says M. Cousin, "an invincible obstacle to the *universality* of instruction, since it is precisely the most necessitous districts that private adventure visits least." * Every commune, therefore, either by itself or in conjunction with adjacent communes, was to maintain at least one elementary school.† To this school all the indigent children of the commune, no longer a fourth of them or a fifth, but *all*, were to be admitted without fee. These national schools must respect that religious liberty which the nation professed. The wishes of parents were to be ascertained and followed in all that concerned their children's attendance at the religious instruction.‡

The elementary schools were to respect religious liberty, and they were to be planted in every commune; but how were they to be planted? Preceding laws had not answered this question, and they had remained a dead letter. The law of 1833 answered it thus:—*By a joint action of the commune, the department, and the State.*

* See M. Cousin's report in the *Moniteur* of May 22nd, 1833. M. Guizot, in his *Exposé des Motifs*, speaks to the same effect: "Les lieux où l'instruction primaire serait le plus nécessaire sont précisément ceux qui tentent le moins l'industrie."

† *Loi sur l'Instruction primaire*, June 28th, 1833, Art. 9.

‡ *Ibid.* Art. 2.

If the commune possessed sufficient resources of its own to maintain its elementary school, well and good. Some had foundations, gifts, and legacies, for the maintenance of schools; some had large communal property. In the Vosges, for instance, there are communes possessing great tracts of the beech forests with which those mountains are clothed, whose annual income amounts to several thousand pounds sterling. Where the existing resources of the commune were insufficient, it was to tax itself to an amount not exceeding three centimes in addition to its ordinary direct taxation. If this was insufficient, the department was to tax itself, in order to aid this and similarly placed schools, to an amount not exceeding two centimes in addition to its ordinary direct taxation. If this was still insufficient, the Minister of Public Instruction was to supply the deficiency out of funds annually voted by the Chambers for the support of education.[*]

A machinery for providing schools was thus established. It remained to provide for these schools proper teachers. A master's house and a fixed salary for him of not less than 8*l.* a year the commune was bound to supply. The residue of his income was to proceed from school fees. The rate of these was to be determined by the municipal council of the commune. They were to be charged for monthly periods, and to be collected, like other public dues, by the ordinary tax-gatherer. A fund for retiring pensions for teachers was to be formed by a yearly drawback on their fixed salaries.[†] Their maintenance was thus provided for; to provide them with a proper intellectual and moral training every department was bound to furnish a normal school. Certificates of capacity and morality were exacted from them, with precautions to render that of capacity no longer illusory.[‡]

* *Loi sur l'Instruction primaire*, &c., Art. 13. An ordinance of July 16th, 1833, provided that where a commune or department neglected to provide for charges which the law imposed on them, the amount due should be levied by royal ordinance.

† In consequence of the law of June 9th, 1853, regulating civil pensions, the schoolmaster's pension, like that of all other civil servants in France, is now paid by the Treasury from the general funds of the State.

‡ *Loi sur l'Instruction primaire*, &c., Art. 25.

It remained to appoint the authorities with whom was to rest the supervision of the school. They were two, a parish committee and a district committee; the first supplied by the commune, the second by the arrondissement. In both, the chief authorities of the locality, clerical as well as lay, were members by virtue of their office; but in both there was a decided preponderance of the lay element. These committees were to meet once a month. The immediate inspection and superintendence of the schools rested with the communal committee. But the Chamber of Deputies, more zealous than the minister for the action of the Executive, had refused to this committee all voice in the nomination of the teacher. He was presented by the municipal council, nominated, on this presentation, by the district committee *, instituted by the Minister of Public Instruction. The district committee not only nominated the teacher, but also dismissed him; he had, however, an appeal to the Minister in Council.

Such was the law of 1833, not more remarkable for the judgment with which it was framed than for the energy with which it was executed. As if he had foreseen the weak point of his law, the inadequacy of the local authorities to discharge the trust committed to their hands, M. Guizot multiplied his efforts to stimulate and to enlighten them. In successive circulars to prefects, to rectors, to directors of normal schools, to inspectors, he endeavoured to procure the active co-operation of all his agents in the designs of the Government, and to inspire in all of them the zeal with which he himself was animated. On behalf of the elementary schools, he strove to awaken that spirit of local interest and independent activity which he and his friends have never ceased to invoke for their country, and the want of which has, since the Revolution, been the great want of France. He succeeded imperfectly in inspiring his countrymen with a faith in habits of local exertion; and the elementary schools of France have suffered from his want of success. But he succeeded in founding the schools; and he succeeded in inspiring faith in his own zeal for them. In the chamber of the Frère Philippe or of the Père Étienne, as among the Protestant populations of Nismes

* Comité d'arrondissement.

and of Strasbourg; in the palaces of bishops and in the manses of pastors; in the villages of Brittany and in the villages of the Cevennes—everywhere I found M. Guizot's name held in honour for the justice and wisdom of his direction of popular education when it was in fashion, for his fidelity to it now that it is no longer talked of. Singular confidence inspired in quarters the most various upon the most delicate of questions! which insincere ability can never conciliate, which even sincere ability cannot always conciliate; only ability united with that heartfelt devotion to a great cause, which friends of the cause instinctively recognise, and warm towards it because they share it.

The results of the law of 1833 were prodigious. The thirteen normal schools of 1830 had grown in 1838 to seventy-six; more than 2,500 students were, in the latter year, under training in them. In the four years from 1834 to 1838, 4,557 public schools, the property of the communes, had been added to the 10,316 which existed in 1834. In 1847 the number of elementary schools for boys had risen from 33,695, which it reached in 1834, to 43,514; the number of scholars attending them from 1,654,828 to 2,176,079.* In 1849, the elementary schools were giving instruction to 3,530,135 children of the two sexes.† In 1851, out of the 37,000 communes of France, 2,500 only were without schools; through the remainder there were distributed primary schools of all kinds, to the number of 61,481.‡ The charge borne by the communes in the support of their schools was nearly 300,000*l.* in 1834, the first year after the passing of the new law. In 1849 it had risen to nearly 400,000*l.* The charge borne by the departments was in 1835 nearly 111,000*l.*; in 1847 it was more than 180,000*l.* The sum contributed by the State, only 2,000*l.* in 1816, 4,000*l.* in 1829, 40,000*l.* in 1830, had risen in 1847 to 96,000*l.*§ The great inspection of 1834 had been a special effort. But in 1835, primary inspectors, those "sinews of public instruction," were permanently established, one for each department,

* *Mémoires pour servir à l'Histoire de mon Temps,* par M. Guizot, vol. iii. p. 84.

† President's message of June 6th, 1849.

‡ President's message of November 4th, 1851.

§ [Jourdain], *Budget de l'Instruction Publique,* pp. 181–2.

by royal ordinance.* In 1847 two inspectors-general and 153 inspectors and sub-inspectors had been already appointed. An ordinance of June the 23rd, 1836, extended to girls' schools, so far as was possible, the provisions of the law of 1833. It did not impose on the communes the obligation of raising funds for their support; but it subjected them all alike to the authority of the communal and district committees †, who were to delegate inspectresses to visit them; and it required from their teachers the certificate of capacity. From members of the female religious orders, however, their letters of obedience were still accepted as a substitute for the certificate. Normal schools for the training of lay schoolmistresses were at the same time formed. A year and a half afterwards ‡ a similar ordinance regulated infant schools, which ever since 1827, when M. Cochin, the benevolent mayor of the twelfth arrondissement of Paris, founded a model infant school in his own district, had attracted interest and found voluntary supporters. The pecuniary aid given by the State to these institutions was small; the first grant, in 1840, a grant which they had to share with girls' schools, was but 2,000*l.* They multiplied, nevertheless; their number rose from 555 in 1840 to 1,489 in 1843, and to 1,861 in 1848. Primary teachers had been empowered § to establish classes for adults in connection with their schools. In 1837 there existed 1,856 of these classes, giving instruction to 36,965 working people. In 1843 there were 6434 of them, with an attendance of 95,064 pupils; in 1848 the classes were 6877 in number, the pupils 115,164. Public instruction was not only founded, it was in operation.

Two defects in the system soon became visible. One was in the authorities charged to superintend it. Neither the communal committee nor that of the district performed its functions satisfactorily. The communal or parish committee, composed of the

* February 26th.

† Ever since the ordinance of February 9th, 1830, schools under mistresses who belonged to religious communities had been exempted from all supervision but that of the ecclesiastical authority and the prefect.

‡ December 22nd, 1837.

§ By a *Règlement sur les Classes d'Adultes,* issued by the Royal Council of Public Instruction, March 22nd, 1836.

mayor, the clergyman, and one or more principal inhabitants nominated by the district committee, was not disinclined to meddle in the management of the school, but neither its fairness nor its intelligence could be safely trusted. So strongly had this been felt, that the Chamber of Deputies in 1833 had refused to intrust to this committee the powers which the Minister, in his zeal for local action, had destined for it, and had insisted on giving to the Minister the power of dissolving it on the report of the district committee. The district committee, composed of the principal personages, ecclesiastical and civil, of each sub-prefecture, was generally deficient neither in fairness nor in intelligence; but it was distant, it was hard to set in motion, it was disinclined to decisive measures. In truth, a due supply of zealous and respectable persons, both able and willing to superintend primary schools, is wanting in the country districts of France. It was to form such a class that M. Guizot had framed measures and written circulars; for this he had solicited prefects and rectors; for this he had directed every inspector to forego, at first, his right of inspecting schools without notice, to convoke committees and municipalities to meet him, to multiply his communications with them, to invite their confidence and to keep them informed of the views of the government, to make his inspections fully and patiently, not to neglect his rural schools, however humble or however remote, in order that the rural population might itself learn to take interest in its schools, when it saw that "neither distance, nor hardship of season, nor difficulty of access, prevented the government from bestowing active care on them." * He had not succeeded. In England such persons exist in almost every locality; the one thing needful is to choose them.

The other defect was in the position of the teachers. The miserable fixed salary of 8*l.* a year, supplemented by the small fees of the scholars, was wholly insufficient for their maintenance. Fully indoctrinated with a sense of the magnitude of their office, they were transferred from the normal school, where

* See M. Guizot's circular to the inspectors on their appointment, August 13th, 1835, in the *Bulletin Universitaire*, vol. iv. p. 275. The whole circular is well worth reading.

their life was one of comfort; they were planted in a village where they were considerable personages, in constant relations with the mayor and the curé, and obliged to keep up a certain appearance; and there they were left to exist on a pittance which just kept them from starvation. Their position was one of cruel suffering, and their discontent was extreme.

The Government determined to relieve them. In 1847, a measure was introduced by M. de Salvandy, then Minister of Instruction, which fixed three classes of teachers and a minimum of salary for each class: for the lowest class, 24*l.* a year; for the second, 36*l.*; for the highest, 48*l.* In Paris itself the lowest salary of a teacher of the first class was to be 60*l.*

To English schoolmasters in 1860 these salaries will appear despicable; to the French schoolmaster in 1847 they would have been a great boon. But the Revolution of 1848 arrested the measure which promised them.

CHAPTER VIII

Popular Education in France Under the Revolution of 1848 and the Second Empire.—Legislation of 1850, 1853, and 1854

The Revolution of 1848, however, had great designs for the primary teachers. They were to be the agents to popularise and consolidate it. The portentous circular * by which M. Carnot exhorted the schoolmasters of France, on the eve of the elections, to use all their influence to promote the return of sincere republicans, and to combat the popular prejudice which preferred the "rich and lettered citizen, a stranger to the peasant's life, and blinded by interests at variance with the peasant's interests," to the "honest peasant endowed with natural good sense, and whose practical experience of life was better than all the book-learning in the world," is still in every one's memory. The schoolmasters of the department of the Seine had not waited for M. Carnot's invitation to open gratuitous evening classes for the instruction of adults in the "rights and duties of citizens." The Minister applauded their zeal. But satisfactions more solid than applause were due to a class from which so much was expected. The grant of the State for primary education rose in the year after the Revolution to 5,920,000 francs. In 1847 it had been but 2,399,808 francs. The whole addition was destined to augment the salaries of primary teachers.

The Revolution fell; and its conquerors did not forget that it had made the schoolmasters its missionaries. A commission was appointed † to report on the state of primary instruction throughout the country, and on the operation of the law of

* March 9th, 1848.

† When M. de Falloux became Minister of Public Instruction, December 20th, 1848. The commission which reported on primary instruction was a sub-commission of that which, under the presidency of M. Thiers, inquired into the whole public education of France.

1833. Upon its report the main law which now governs public instruction in France, the law of March 15th, 1850, was founded. This commission judged the primary teachers very severely. It condemned their training as ill-planned, their teaching as over-ambitious, their conduct to spiritual and temporal authorities as disrespectful.* A disclosure which took place about this time in the Nièvre, one of the most ignorant and backward departments of France, shook esteem for their morality. Every voice was raised for a repression of their pretensions, and a strict control of their conduct. The religious congregations devoted to teaching were visited by a great increase of public favour. The heads of the principal communities of each sex, the Superior-General of the Brethren of the Christian Schools, the Superior-General of the Lazarists, were examined before the commission as to the operations and wishes of their societies. They were consulted as to the requirement from teachers belonging to religious orders of the certificate of capacity. For reasons which speak with equal eloquence for his own serenity of judgment and for the usefulness of the certificate test, the Frère Philippe desired for the brethren its continuance. For reasons which prevailed with the commission, which he did me the honour to repeat to me, and which seem to me full of weight, the Père Étienne deprecated for the sisterhoods its imposition. One of the most eminent liberals in France told me that, for his part, ever since 1848 he had wished to confide the whole primary instruction of the country to the religious communities. It was declared that the public morals were proved by the statistics of crime not to have improved since the law of 1833, but on the contrary to have deteriorated †, and that recourse must be had to religion to cure a state of disorder which mere instruction had perhaps aggravated, certainly not corrected. Sentences

* *Rapport fait au nom de la Sous-Commission chargée par M. le Ministre de l'Instruction Publique de préparer un Projet de Loi sur l'Instruction primaire;* Paris, April, 1849, pp. 2, 6, 8, 10, 18, 20.

† *Rapport fait au nom de la Sous-Commission*, &c., p. 8. But on this question of the increase of crime, see the interesting criminal statistics at the end of this volume. [The appendices are not printed in this edition.]

of suspension and dismissal were launched by the prefects right and left against the lay primary teachers. But the misdeeds of these functionaries were extravagantly exaggerated. The alarm and irritation of the revolutionary year made their accusers intemperate and unjust. In every quarter of France which I visited, rectors and inspectors united to assure me that grounds for serious complaint against the lay teachers had been very scarce indeed; that the foolish profession of strong republican opinions (to which, besides, the circular of the Minister directly called them) had been the sole fault of the great majority of those who offended; that it was astonishing that a class, so poor and so stimulated, should have, on the whole, behaved so well. On dispassionate inquiry, made at the instance of the University functionaries, a great number of teachers who had been summarily dismissed were reinstated. The loud complaints against their overtraining and against the normal schools gradually died away, and a few years afterwards the Government itself proclaimed how unjust had been the imputations against these latter. "For a time," says the minister, M. Fortoul, in 1854, "people may have made the normal schools responsible for the faults of a few young men whose errors were caused far more by the culpable promptings addressed to them than by the education received in these schools; but on all sides people are now beginning to appreciate them more justly." Under the hostile impressions of 1849, however, the law of March 15th, 1850, was conceived and promulgated.

This law, with the organic decree of March 9th, 1852, and the law of June the 14th, 1854, forms the body of legislation now actually in force in France on the subject of public instruction. The design of the two last-named acts is to complete and to make more stringent the main law of 1850.

The new legislation swept away much of the law of 1833. It changed the authorities in whom the control of primary instruction was vested. It abolished the communal committee and the district committee. In the bodies which it substituted it eradicated the elective principle. It gave to the mayor and the minister of religion in every commune the supervision and moral direction of primary instruction.* The old committees were replaced, as to some of their functions, by delegates from each canton. The canton is a division larger than the commune, smaller than the arrondissement. But these cantonal delegates are the nominees of the departmental council. They inspect the primary schools of their canton; but their powers only enable them to address representations on the results of their inspection to the departmental council or the inspector, and they have no real authority over the schools or teachers. The departmental council meets twice a month at the chief town of the department. It consists of thirteen members, presided over by the prefect. At first a majority of the members proceeded from election. At present every member, except the prefect, the procureur-général, the bishop, and an ecclesiastical nominee of the bishop, who sit of right, is nominated by the Minister. This council has very extensive powers. It nominates the cantonal delegates and the commissions charged with the examination for certificates. It has the regulation of the public primary schools, fixes the rate of school fees to be paid in them, draws up the list of teachers admissible to the office of communal teacher in the department, is the judge of teachers in matters of discipline, can even interdict them for ever from the exercise of their profession, subject to an appeal to the Imperial Council of Public Instruction in Paris. It can refuse to any teacher, without right to appeal †, that permission to open a private primary school which the law of 1833 accorded to all teachers provided with certificates of morality and capacity. But it cannot nominate, suspend, or dismiss a teacher. This power, after some fluctuation, has been confided to the promptest, the sternest, the strongest of public functionaries—the functionary on whose firm hand the Chamber of Deputies, in 1833, in its zeal for a more stringent control of public instruction, had in vain cast longing eyes—the prefect. Even the ministerial institution is no longer necessary for the teacher. The prefect names, changes, reprimands, suspends, and dismisses all public primary

* Law of March 15th, 1850, Art. 44.

† Law of March 15th, 1850, Art. 28.

teachers of every grade.* To interdict them absolutely and for ever from the exercise of their profession is alone beyond his power. It has even been decided that a clause in the decree of 1852 †, giving to municipal councils the right to be heard respecting the nomination of their communal teacher, means merely that they are at liberty to inform the prefect whether they prefer a layman or a member of a religious association.

But the prefect exercises his authority "on the report of the Academy-Inspector."

This introduces us to a new wheel in the machinery of French public instruction. The academies of France, the constituent members of the University, have been at different times twenty-six, twenty-seven, and eighty-six in number. They are now but sixteen. Each academy has a district embracing several departments. The rectors of academies, who under the first Empire and the Restoration were the rulers of primary instruction, have now in their charge only its normal schools, and in elementary schools the methods of teaching and course of study. But attached to every rector, for each of the departments composing his district, is a functionary called an academy-inspector.‡ This official's chief concern is with secondary instruction, but he has also the general supervision of primary instruction; it is to him that the primary inspector makes his reports, and by his representations the prefect, in dealing with the primary teachers, is mainly guided.

One other authority remains to be noticed. It is the Imperial Council of Public Instruction. This council is the latest development of the Council of the University, of the Commission, Council Royal, and Superior Council of Public Instruction. Its composition has undergone many changes. The Minister has always presided at it; but of its members the majority were formerly chosen by the great ecclesiastical, judicial, or learned bodies whom they respectively represented, and it had a permanent section composed of members named for life. Every member is now named by the Emperor; the permanent section is abolished, and members are appointed for one year only. Before

* Law of June 14th, 1854, Art. 8. † Art. 4.

‡ Inspecteur d'Académie.

this council the Minister, if he thinks fit, brings for discussion projected laws and decrees on public education. He is bound to consult it respecting the programmes of study, methods, and books, to be adopted in public schools. To watch in the provinces over the due observance of its regulations on these matters is the business of the rectors and their academic councils. Finally, the Imperial Council has to hear and judge the appeals of teachers on whom departmental councils have laid their interdict.

Thus the French public teacher, in place of the general supervision of the communal council, in which the prepossessions of one member often neutralised those of another, is now put under the individual supervision of two persons, the mayor and the curé. These watch over the morality and religion of his school; the cantonal delegates watch over its instruction. Above these, in place of the easy district-committee, armed with power indeed to reprimand, suspend, or dismiss him, but slow to exercise this power, and liable to have its extreme sentence, that of dismissal, reversed by an appeal to a higher authority *, he has the ever-wakeful executive, the prefect himself, armed with powers which he is prepared to use, and against which there is no appeal. Finally, his scholastic career may be closed altogether by the departmental council.†

But the new legislation, though thus tightening the reins of control for the teacher, could not possibly leave his salary unimproved. His pecuniary condition was so lamentable as to call pity even from his enemies; many thought, indeed, that to the misery of this condition were due nearly all the faults which had made enemies for him. The fixed salary of 8*l.* a year was retained; but it was provided that where the school fees added to this did not make up an income of 24*l.* a year, what was wanted to complete this sum should be paid by the public. This was, in fact, to increase the charges of the State; for no additional taxation was imposed on the commune or the department. With so vast an army of public teachers, to increase the pittance of

* The Minister in Council Royal.—*Loi sur l'Instruction primaire,* 28 Juin 1833, Art. 23.

† But with appeal to the Imperial Council. See above.

each even a little was formidably expensive. A new law * provided a class of "supplying teachers," *instituteurs suppléants*, less costly than the regular communal teacher. In future no one could be appointed communal teacher who had not served for three years since his twenty-first year as an assistant (*adjoint*) or as a supplying teacher. The same decree permitted public mixed schools, where the scholars were not more than forty in number, to be placed under the charge of women, whose salary was to be that of supplying masters. These new teachers were divided into two classes; the minimum of salary for the first was fixed at 20*l.* a year, for the second at 16*l.* a year. They were only to be employed in communes where the number of inhabitants did not exceed 500, or temporarily to fill vacancies in larger places. But, on one pretence or other, large as well as small communes in considerable numbers soon managed to confide their schools to these cheaper teachers. The sufferings which the law of 1850 had sought to alleviate reappeared. By a decree † due to the present Minister of Public Instruction, M. Rouland, the lower class of *suppléants* was abolished, and there is now but one class of supplying teachers, and one minimum of salary for them, 20*l.*

This is grievously insufficient; but the reader is not to suppose that all the public schools of France are starving their teachers on 20*l.* or 24*l.* a year. These are *minima* of salary, frequently exceeded by the free will of communes, and for which no good and experienced teacher can be obtained. The law permits a commune, if it pleases, to establish schools entirely gratuitous; only it must support these schools out of its own resources. In all the principal towns of France this is done, as there is not one communal school in Paris, for instance, in which a scholar pays anything. The teachers of these schools have therefore no school-fees to trust to; but they receive from the municipality salaries far exceeding the bare legal rate, salaries which, though not equal to those of similar teachers in England or Holland, are sufficient to maintain them in comfort. It is in the villages and hamlets of France that the privations of underpaid schoolmasters are to be witnessed.

* Decree of December 31st, 1853.

† Decree of July 20th, 1858.

The new legislation has thus altered the law of 1833 in all which concerns the supervision of primary schools. It has attempted, not very successfully, to amend the pecuniary situation which M. Guizot's law created for the primary teacher. But the grand and fruitful provision of M. Guizot's law, the money clause, the happy distribution of the cost of public schools between the commune, the department, and the State, victoriously endured the test of hostile criticism. It remained unassailed and unassailable, modified only in an insignificant point of detail.

Another important provision of M. Guizot's law remained untouched, that which guaranteed religious liberty in public schools. It is the happiness of France, indeed, that this liberty is so firmly established that no legislation is likely to try to shake it. Among the many interesting instructions written by M. Guizot between 1833 and 1837, none are more interesting than those which relate to this vital question. The text of the law of 1833, and the tolerant disposition of M. Guizot himself, tended to make denominational schools, as we should call them, the exception, and common schools the rule. "In certain cases," says the law *, "the Minister of Public Instruction may authorise as communal schools, schools more particularly appropriated to one of the religious denominations recognised by the State." "It is in general desirable," writes M. Guizot †, "that children whose families do not profess the same creed should early contract, by frequenting the same schools, those habits of reciprocal friendship and mutual tolerance which may ripen later, when they live together as grown-up citizens, into justice and harmony." But the dangers to which religious liberty was sometimes exposed in these common schools did not escape him. He wished the religious instruction to be, above all things, real; not "a series of lessons and practices apparently capable of being used by all denominations in common." ‡ Such vague abstrac-

* *Loi sur l'Instruction primaire*, 28 Juin 1833, Art. 9.

† In a circular to the prefects, July 24th, 1833. See *Bulletin Universitaire*, vol. iii. p. 293.

‡ See his excellent circular to the rectors, November 12th, 1835. *Bulletin Universitaire*, vol. iv. p. 388.

tions, he said, "satisfied the requirements neither of parents nor of the law; they tended to banish all positive and efficacious religious teaching from the schools." But, the more the religion of the majority is taught positively and really in a school, the more it becomes necessary to guard the liberty of the minority. There is danger either that the minority will be made to participate in the religious instruction of the majority, or else that its own religious instruction will be left uncared for. Against both dangers M. Guizot endeavoured to provide. Rectors were charged to see that in public schools no child of a different religious profession from that of the majority was constrained to take part in the religious teaching and observances of his fellow-scholars. They were to permit and to request the parents of such children to cause them to receive suitable religious instruction from a minister of their own communion, or from a layman regularly appointed for the purpose. They were to take care that in every week, at fixed hours to be agreed upon between the minister of religion, the parents, and the local committee, such children were conducted from the school to the Protestant temple, or any other edifice frequented by members of their communion, there to take part in the lessons and practices of the faith in which they had been brought up. Inspectors and local committees were strictly enjoined to see these regulations observed. Similar provision was made for religious instruction and religious freedom in the normal schools. Finally, where the minority had cause to desire a school to itself, and reasonable numbers to fill it, the authorities were to be very heedful that its demand was not unjustly refused by the municipal councils.

The event proved that religious instruction in common schools presented grave practical difficulties. The new law profited by the lessons of experience. Under the dominion of the new law denominational schools are the rule, common schools are the exception. In those communes where more than one of the forms of worship recognised by the State is publicly professed, each form is to have its separate school.* But the departmental council has power to authorise the union, in a

* *Loi du* 15 *Mars* 1850, Art. 36.

common school, of children belonging to different communions.* Of children thus united, however, the religious liberty is sedulously guarded. It is provided that ministers of each communion shall have free and equal access to the school, at separate times, in order to watch over the religious instruction of members of their own flock.† Where the school is appropriated to one denomination, no child of another denomination is admitted except at the express demand of his parents or guardians, signified in writing to the teacher. Of such demands the teacher is bound to keep a register, to be produced to all the school authorities. I confidently affirm, in contradiction to much ignorant assertion, that the liberty thus proclaimed by the law is maintained in practice. The venerable chiefs of the principal Protestant communities of the French provinces—the president of the Consistory of Nismes, the president of the Consistory of Strasbourg—individually assured me, that, as regarded the treatment of their schools by the authorities, they had nothing whatever to complain of; that Protestant schools came into collision with the authorities no otherwise than as Catholic schools came; that such collision, when it happened, was, in nine cases out of ten, on matters wholly unconnected with religion. In Languedoc, indeed, the embers of religious animosities still smoulder; but it is among the lower orders of the population. It is not that the State persecutes the Protestants; it is that the Protestant and Catholic mobs have still sometimes the impulse to persecute each other, and that the State has hard work to keep the peace between them.

The law of 1833 had proclaimed the right of all indigent children to free instruction. Many who were not indigent had usurped this boon designed only for the poor. The law of 1850, to prevent this abuse, directed the mayor and the ministers of religion to draw up yearly, for each commune, a list of children having a real claim to the privilege; but it was soon found that the mayor and the ministers were far too easy. In fact, the moment a commune had levied its three centimes, all motive for economy on the part of the communal authorities ceased; all

* *Loi du* 15 *Mars* 1850, Art. 15.

† *Loi du* 15 *Mars* 1850, Art. 44; *Décret du* 7 *Octobre* 1850, Art. 11.

further school expenses must be at the charge of the department or the State. At the expense of the department and the State, therefore, the parish authorities freely enlarged their list of claimants for free schooling. As a last resource, the never-failing prefect * has been charged to determine annually, for every public school of his department, the highest number of free scholars to be admitted into that school; the free admissions granted by the mayor and his colleagues must in no case exceed this number. Nor can any free scholar be admitted into a communal school unless he brings with him a ticket for free admission granted by the mayor: this last provision applies even to schools entirely gratuitous.

Finally, the law of 1833 had attempted to establish for the benefit of the lower middling classes of France a superior grade of primary instruction, which, without assuming a classical and scientific character, might yet carry its recipients much beyond the instruction of the elementary schools. It had imposed upon every urban commune, which either was the chief town of a department, or contained more than 6,000 inhabitants, the obligation of establishing, besides its elementary schools, a "superior primary school." † It had instituted two grades of certificates, corresponding to the two grades of instruction. M. Guizot desired ‡ that "as there was to be no commune without its primary school, and no department without its normal school, so there might be no town of 8000 or 10,000 inhabitants without its 'middle school' to crown the edifice of public instruction, and to stop only where the learned studies of classical schools commence." He provided that in these middle schools a certain number of free admissions should be reserved for the best scholars of the elementary school, to be presented, after a competitive examination, by the communal committee. § The design seemed admirable, yet it had not well succeeded. Not that the obligation of the law was eluded: in 1843, out of 290 communes bound

* *Décret du* 31 *Décembre* 1853, Art. 13.

† *Loi sur l'Instruction primaire*, 28 Juin 1833, Art. 10.

‡ See his circular to the rectors on his appointment, October 17th, 1832; *Bulletin Universitaire*, vol. iii. p. 97.

§ *Loi sur l'Instruction primaire*, 28 Juin 1833, Art. 14.

to establish superior primary schools, 222 possessed them; 103 communes, not bound to provide such schools, had voluntarily established them; but they did not much attract the population. In 1837, the average attendance of scholars in the whole number of superior primary schools, public and private, then existing in France, did not exceed twenty-eight in each school.* The lower class of the population remained satisfied with the primary schools; the class above them continued, where the primary schools did not satisfy it, to struggle into the communal colleges.

My limits forbid me to do more than touch on this great subject of secondary instruction; yet to touch on it for one moment in passing I cannot forbear. I saw something of it; I inquired much about it; had I not done so, I should have comprehended the subject of French primary instruction very imperfectly. Let me, then, be permitted to call the English reader's attention to the advantage France possesses in its vast system of public secondary instruction; in its 63 lyceums and 244 communal colleges, inspected by the State, aided by the State †, drawing from this connection with the State both efficiency and dignity; and to which, in concert with the State, the departments, the communes, private benevolence, all co-operate to provide free admission for poor and deserving scholars. M. de Talleyrand truly said that the education of the great English public schools was the best in the world. He added, to be sure, that even this was detestable. But allowing it all its merits, how small a portion of the population does it embrace! It embraces the aristocratic class; it embraces the higher professional class; it embraces a few of the richest and most successful of the commercial class; of the great body of the commercial class and of the immense middle classes of this country, it embraces not one. They are left to an education which, though among its

* *Manuel Législatif et Administratif de l'Instruction primaire,* par M. [Étienne] Kilian, chef de bureau au Ministère de l'Instruction Publique; Paris, 1838–39, p. 116.

† In 1855 the grant from the State to the lyceums was 1,300,000 fr.; to the communal colleges, 98,080 fr. 86 c.—[Jourdain], *Budget de l'Instruction Publique,* pp. 164, 167.

professors are many excellent and honourable men, is deplorable. Our middle classes are nearly the worst educated in the world. But it is not this only; although, when I consider this, all the French commonplaces about the duty of the State to protect its children from the charlatanism and cupidity of individual speculation seem to me to be justified. It is far more that a great opportunity is missed of fusing all the upper and middle classes into one powerful whole, elevating and refining the middle classes by the contact, and stimulating the upper. In France this is what the system of public education effects; it effaces between the middle and upper classes the sense of social alienation; it raises the middle without dragging down the upper; it gives to the boy of the middle class the studies, the superior teaching, the proud sense of belonging to a great school, which the Eton or Harrow boy has with us; it tends to give to the middle classes precisely what they most want, and their want of which is the great gulf between them and the upper; it tends to give them personal dignity. The power of such an education is seen in what it has done for the professional classes in England. The clergy and barristers, who are generally educated in the great public schools, are nearly identified in thought, feeling, and manners with the aristocratic class. They have not been unmixed gainers by this identification; it has too much isolated them from a class to which by income and social position they, after all, naturally belong, while towards the highest class it has made them, not vulgarly servile certainly, but intellectually too deferential—too little apt to maintain perfect mental independence on questions where the prepossessions of that class are concerned. Nevertheless, they have, as a class, acquired the unspeakable benefit of that elevation of the mind and feelings which it is the best office of superior education to confer. But they have bought this elevation at an immense money-price—at a price which they can no better than the commercial classes afford to pay; which they who have paid it long, and who know what it has bought for them, will continue to pay while they must, but which the middle classes will never even begin to pay. When I told the French University authorities of the amount paid for a boy's education at the great English schools, and paid often out of very moderate incomes, they exclaimed with one voice that to demand such sacrifices of French parents would be vain. It would be equally vain to demand them of the English middle classes. Either their education must remain what it is, vulgar and unsound; or the State must create by its authorisation, its aid—above all, by its inspection—institutions honourable because of their public character, and cheap because nationally frequented, in which they may receive a better. If the former happens, then this great English middle class, growing wealthier, more powerful, more stirring every year, will every year grow more and more isolated in sentiment from the professional and aristocratic classes. If the latter, then not only will the whole richer part of our rich community be united by the strong bond of a common culture, but the establishment of a national system of instruction for the poorer part of the community will have been rendered infinitely easier. In fact, the French middle classes may well submit to be taxed for the education of the poor, for the State has already provided for their own. But already there are loud complaints among the lower middling classes of this country that the Committee of Council is providing the poor with better schools than those to which they themselves have access; and we may be very sure that any new measure which proposes to do much for the instruction of the poor, and nothing for that of the middling classes, will meet with discontent and opposition from the latter. It is impossible to overrate the magnitude of this question. English superior instruction is perhaps intelligent enough to be left to take care of itself. Oxford and Cambridge are popularising themselves: with little noise and in the shade, the London University is performing a work of great national benefit. At any rate, superior instruction is the efflorescence and luxury of education; it is comparatively of limited importance. Secondary instruction, on the other hand, is of the widest importance; and it is neither organised enough nor intelligent enough to take care of itself. The Education Commissioners would excite, I am convinced, in thousands of hearts a gratitude of which they little dream, if, in presenting the result of their labours on primary instruction, they were at the same time to say to the Government, "Regard the necessities of a not distant future, and *organise your secondary instruction.*"

The new French legislation recognised the visible fact that the superior primary school was an unprosperous invention. With much good result, with some inconveniences, the communal colleges continued to attract those for whom M. Guizot had destined his middle schools. These schools, therefore, are no longer maintained. But the new law retains the old programme of superior primary instruction, and has introduced it into the elementary schools *, where the instruction certainly needed raising. This superior programme, however, is but *facultative* in the primary schools, and the old elementary programme is alone obligatory. But any commune may, with the authorisation of the departmental council, insist that the whole or part of the *facultative matters*, as they are called, shall be taught in its school.†

For girls' schools the new legislation continued the provisions of 1836 nearly unchanged. For girls the two grades of primary instruction were still maintained, because for girls there was no secondary instruction, like that of the communal colleges, to compete with the superior primary school.‡ All public schools for girls, whether kept by lay teachers or by sisters of some religious order, and all private schools not being boarding-schools, were subjected to the supervision of the authorities charged with that of boys' schools. Lay boarding-schools are inspected by ladies delegated by the prefect; boarding-schools belonging to religious associations by ecclesiastics nominated, on the presentation of the bishop of the diocese, by the Minister

* *Loi du* 15 *Mars* 1850, Art. 23.

† *Loi du* 15 *Mars* 1850, Art. 36. The *matières facultatives* are as follows:—L'arithmétique appliquée aux opérations pratiques; les éléments de l'histoire et de la géographie; des notions des sciences physiques et de l'histoire naturelle applicables aux usages de la vie; des instructions élémentaires sur l'agriculture, l'industrie, et l'hygiène; l'arpentage, le nivellement, le dessin linéaire; le chant, et la gymnastique.

‡ Called by the new law *école de premier ordre,* not *école primaire supérieure.—Décret du* 31 *Décembre* 1853, Art. 6.

of Public Instruction. The certificate of capacity must, as before, be obtained by lay schoolmistresses; and, for the sisters, their letters of obedience still suffice. Such, in its main provisions, is the legislation by which primary instruction in France is at this moment regulated.

CHAPTER IX

Present Material and Financial Condition of Popular Education in France

The reader will desire to know what result is produced by this legislation. I will endeavour to show both the material and the moral result produced. The material result in money raised, schools founded, scholars under instruction; the moral result in the quality of the instruction, the proficiency of the scholars, the effect, so far as that can be ascertained, on the nation. I begin with the former.

The task is not easy. For the last eight years no report on the state of primary instruction has been published by the French Government. In the financial report yearly issued by the Department of Public Instruction, the sums raised for primary schools by their most important contributor, the communes, are not returned. Vast preparations were made in 1858 for a detailed report, to be accompanied by full statistics. At the last moment the Government recoiled before the expense of its publication. The invaluable materials collected for it, and still lying in the archives of the Ministry of Public Instruction, I have had, thanks to M. Magin's kindness, an opportunity of examining. But I owe to M. Rapet the following statistics for the years 1856 and 1857, compiled with great labour from the original returns, many of which are unpublished, and supplying information which no printed official documents contain.* The returns relating to the number of schools and scholars are given in round numbers. I should premise that schools belonging to religious associations are designated by the title of Congreganist Schools—*Écoles Congréganistes.*

* But see also Tables I., II., III., and IV., at the end of this volume. [Not printed in this edition.]

Total number of primary schools existing in France in 1857	65,100

Number of boys' or mixed schools - - - -	39,600
" girls' schools - - - - -	25,500
	65,100

These numbers are divided as follows:—

Public boys' schools - - - - -	36,200	
Private boys' schools - - - -	3,400	
		39,600
Public girls' schools - - - - -	13,900	
Private girls' schools - - - - -	11,600	
		25,500
		65,100

Among the 39,600 public boys' schools, 17,000 are mixed, that is, they admit girls as well as boys. The number of mixed schools tends continually to diminish, by the creation of separate schools for girls. Although M. Cousin, in his report * of 1833, calls the objection to mixed schools a "wide-spread error which makes female education on a great scale an almost insoluble problem," and directs against it the whole weight of his authority, the objection has not ceased to gain strength, and is at the present day, in France, almost universal. Upon no point, I am bound to say, have I found all those connected with education in that country more unanimous. In Holland, on the other hand, there prevails an equal unanimity in favour of mixed schools.

Of the 17,000 mixed schools of France, 2250 are taught by women, of whom the greater number belong to religious orders. The remaining mixed schools are under masters.

Dividing the primary schools of France according to the lay or ecclesiastical character of their teachers, we have the following numbers:—

Public lay boys' schools - - -	34,100	
" Congreganist " - - -	2,100	
		36,200

* *Moniteur*, May 22nd, 1833.

Private lay boys' schools	2,900		
" Congreganist "	500		
		3,400	
			39,600
Public lay girls' schools	4,700		
" Congreganist "	9,200		
		13,900	
Private lay girls' schools	3,200		
" Congreganist "	8,400		
		11,600	
			25,500
			65,100

The number of children under instruction in these schools is 3,850,000, divided as follows:—

Boys, in boys' or mixed schools	2,150,000
Girls, in girls' schools	1,450,000
Girls, in mixed schools	250,000
	3,850,000

Of these children, 2,600,000 paid for their schooling; 1,250,000 were free scholars.

I now come to the chapter of expense.

The total expense of primary instruction in France for the year 1856 was 42,506,012*f.* 46 *c.* This is, in round numbers, 1,700,000*l.*

The items of this expenditure are in part *ordinary* and *obligatory*, (as they are called,) recurring every year; in part *extraordinary* and *facultative.*

	f.	*c.*
Total ordinary and obligatory expenditure	29,202,243	52
" extraordinary and facultative expenditure	12,581,591	61
" cost of inspection	722,177	33
	42,506,012	46

Certain obligatory charges the law regards as belonging properly to the commune, and the families which compose the commune; others as belonging to the department; others to the State.

Obligatory Charges properly belonging to the Communes and Families.

	f.	c.	f.	c.
Teachers' salaries - -	26,197,503	53		
Rent of school-houses - -	1,488,307	51		
Printing forms for the collection of the school-fee - -	107,741	30		
			27,793,552	34

Obligatory Charges properly belonging to the Department and State.

	f.	c.	f.	c.
Ordinary expenses of normal schools - - -	1,360,155	87		
Expenses of examination commissions and cantonal delegacies - - - -	48,535	31		
Inspection (paid by the State)	722,177	33		
			2,130,868	51
			29,924,420	85

The total obligatory expenditure, therefore, for the year 1856, amounted in round numbers to 1,197,000*l.*

The *facultative* or optional expenditure is shared as follows:—

Charges borne by the Communes.

	f.	f.	c.
Maintenance of girls' schools and infants' schools (not obligatory by law) -	4,600,000		
Building, purchasing, and repairing school-houses - - - -	3,800,000		
Expenses for classes of adults, books, and rewards - - - -	1,500,000		
		9,900,000	00

Charges borne by the Department and State.

	f.	c.
Normal schools for young women, and extraordinary expenses for normal schools - - - -	391,321	85

Charges borne by the Department of State.	f.	c.	f.	c.
Grants to communes for the erection, purchase, and repair of school-houses and fittings - - -	961,412	42		
Books for poor scholars - -	32,444	53		
Special grants for girls' instruction	319,919	57		
Grants for classes of adults and apprentices - - - - -	68,486	25		
Grants for infants' schools and needlework - - - - -	472,620	74		
Rewards and relief to teachers -	206,613	36		
Grants to private schools and charitable establishments - -	61,369	00		
Printing and sundries - - -	167,209	89		
			2,681,397	61
			12,581,397	61

Making, in the year 1856, a total extraordinary expenditure, in round numbers, of 503,000*l*. The items of this expenditure vary from year to year, but its general amount remains much the same.

To meet this expenditure, the following sums were received:—

	f.	c.	f.	c.
From donations and legacies - - -			184,320	86
From families:—				
By fees from scholars - -	9,301,552	56		
By payments from normal school students for board, &c. -	513,327	38		
			9,814,879	94
From communes:—				
By obligatory school taxation -	11,955,063	15		
By voluntary school taxation -	9,900,000	00		
			21,855,063	15
From departments:—				
For ordinary expenses - -	4,101,213	55		

	f.	c.	f.	c.
From departments:—				
For extraordinary expenses -	1,171,916	59		
			5,273,130	14
From the State:—				
For ordinary expenses - -	3,660,093	40		
For extraordinary expenses -	1,509,844	52		
			5,169,937	92
			42,297,332	01

So that the amount received nearly equalled the amount expended.

It appears from the above figures that had the communes borne the full ordinary expenses of their schools, as well as the extraordinary expenses actually contributed by them, they would have had to find a sum of, in round numbers, 1,507,740*l.* They actually bore a charge of 874,200*l.*; but of this they were legally bound to bear but 478,200*l.* They voluntarily undertook a burden of 396,000*l.* Families and private persons contributed, in school-fees, board, and donations, about 423,900*l.* The departments bore a charge of 210,920*l.*; of this, the obligations of the law imposed on them 164,040*l.*; they voluntarily taxed themselves for 46,880*l.* Finally, the State directly contributed about 206,800*l.* (nearly the same amount as the departments): to defray regular charges which it had undertaken to make good, it paid 146,400*l.*; while for the additional expenses which have been detailed it granted 60,400*l.*

The expenses of primary instruction above enumerated do not include the expense of the central administration in Paris. This, for 1856, was 659,048*f.* 57 *c.**; in round numbers, 26,360*l.* Not more than one-third of this charge, which embraces the services of superior, secondary, and primary instruction, belongs to primary instruction. We must add the salaries of four

* Thus divided:—*Personnel*, 472,237 *f.* 50 *c.*; *Matériel*, 180,711 *f.* 11 *c.*; *Indemnités à des employés supprimés*, 6,099 *f.* 96 *c.* See the *Compte définitif des Dépenses de l'Exercice* 1856 (*Service de l'Instruction publique*); Paris, 1858.

inspectors-general at 8,000*f*. each, 32,000*f*. (1,280*l*.), and their travelling allowances, 10,000*f*. (400*l*.). This will give a total of, in round numbers, 10,470*l*., to be added to the general expense of primary instruction in 1856. The general total will then, instead of 1,700,000*l*., become 1,710,470*l*.; considerably less than one million and three-quarters sterling.*

Public primary instruction in France, then, cost in the year 1856 about 1,710,500*l*.; of this, parish taxation (as we should say) contributed somewhat less than nine-seventeenths; county taxation about two-seventeenths; the consolidated fund about two-seventeenths; and school-fees and private benevolence somewhat more than four-seventeenths. Taxation, obligatory and voluntary, produced altogether nearly 1,295,000*l*.; that is to say, it produced more than three-fourths of the whole amount expended.

What will, I think, most strike the reader in considering these figures will be this—the immense number of schools maintained in proportion to the money spent. France possessed, in 1856, 65,100 primary schools. Of this number all but 15,000 were, not *aided*, but *maintained*, out of an expenditure of considerably less than one million and three-quarters sterling; the 15,000 private schools received amongst them some assistance out of it, but the 50,100 public schools were, I repeat, *maintained*. Nor does the total of 65,000 primary schools include infant schools, numbering 2,684 in 1859 †, and receiving 262,000 infants. Neither does it include adult schools, apprentice schools, needlework schools, educating among them a great number of pupils, and nearly all assisted, some supported, out of this expenditure, but for which, unfortunately, there are no collected statistics of

* The services of rectors and academy-inspectors (taking, under the head of *Administration académique*, a sum of 817,523 *f*. 32 *c*. in the estimates of 1856) are in part given to primary instruction; but as these functionaries strictly belong to superior and secondary instruction, I charge primary instruction with no share in this item.

† Infant schools in France are now regulated by the decree of March the 21st, 1855, which places them under the immediate patronage of the Empress and of a central committee. The decree establishes inspectresses of infant schools, one for each of the sixteen academies of France; these ladies are named by the Minister, and paid by the State; they each receive 80*l*. a year, and allowances for travelling.

as recent a date as 1856.* If added, these would certainly carry the number of places of instruction for the poorer classes in France to 75,000, and the number of learners in them to above four millions. But, omitting these, omitting the private schools, for 1,710,000*l.* a year more than 50,000 schools are entirely maintained, and more than three millions and a half of children are instructed. Assume the whole expenditure to contribute equally to this result; then, to the three-fourths raised by taxation, three-fourths of the school-result effected are due. In other words, for 1,295,000*l.*, more than 37,500 schools are maintained, and more than two millions and a half of children are taught.

In Great Britain, according to the latest returns, the annual expenditure on primary instruction, properly so called, was about 800,000*l.* Putting out of sight, as we have put out of sight in the case of France, the value received for this expenditure in the shape of administration, inspection, &c., let us ask what it achieved for schools and scholars. It *maintained* no schools, but it aided, we will assume, in one way or other, all the schools liable to inspection; and on this estimate, which is exaggerated, it aided 8,461 primary schools, giving instruction to 934,000 scholars; that is to say, it helped, at the outside, 8,461 schools to exist, and it helped 934,040 children to receive instruction. In France, the same grant would have entirely maintained nearly 25,000 schools, and to more than a million and a half of children it would have entirely given instruction.

The reader will also, I think, be interested to observe, that in France taxation for schools does not appear to extinguish voluntary effort for their support. Certainly, in France, the local interest about schools, the local knowledge about school matters, does not approach to that which we find in England. Yet, in spite of this, it appears that the French communes—already compulsorily taxed, whether they send their children to school or not, to the amount of 478,200*l.* for primary instruction—already compulsorily taxed, if they send their children to school, to the amount of 372,000*l.* for school fees—voluntarily impose

* In 1848 there were 6877 adult schools in France, with 115,164 pupils. In 1843 there were 36 apprentice schools, with 1268 scholars; and 145 *ouvroirs*, or needlework schools, with 5908 girls attending them.

on themselves an additional taxation of 396,000*l.* a year, in order to make their boys' schools better, in order to provide themselves with girls' schools and infant schools, the establishment of which the law does not make obligatory. It appears that the departments, having already undergone a compulsory rate of 164,040*l.* for the establishment of the departmental normal schools, and for the assistance of the communal primary schools, voluntarily rate themselves to the amount of 46,880*l.* more, in order to train schoolmistresses, to improve school-buildings, to furnish school-books to the poor, to supply other wants for which the law does not provide. The truth is, that a school system, once established in a locality, inevitably renders school matters a subject of interest and occupation with the inhabitants of that locality, even though they may not all be very ardent or very enlightened school-promoters; and a normal or a village school in France, which local zeal would probably never have been strong enough to found, local attachment is generally strong enough to maintain and improve when founded.

These schools, indeed, would look humble enough beside an Elizabethan normal college in England, or the elaborate Gothic edifice with which the liberality of the Committee of Council enables an English rector to adorn his village. English certificated schoolmasters would reject with disdain the salaries of their teachers. English normal-college students, accustomed each to his separate room, would look with contempt on the vast dormitories, rigidly plain though scrupulously neat, in which French students sleep by companies, under the charge of an overlooker, like the inmates of an hospital or a barrack. The English Privy Council Office would regard with contempt a certificate examination which occupies but a few hours, and which leaves conic sections unexplored. English inspectors would never quit their fellowships for posts the occupant of which has the salary of an exciseman. This service of inspection, indeed, in which I could not but feel a sympathetic and friendly interest, is, of all the cheap services of French public instruction, the very cheapest. Till recently a primary inspector's salary was such as to appear, even to French officials, cruelly insufficient; intolerably out of proportion with the importance of his functions. It was such as to reduce him to live by what he could borrow, not unfrequently having recourse for his loans to the teachers under his inspection.* But even now that their position is improved †, even now that their salary is raised nearly to the highest point which, in 1857, their compassionate friends thought possible, what is it that French inspectors receive? The highest class of them receives 96*l.* a year; the second class 80*l.*; the third, and infinitely the most numerous, 64*l.* They have besides this, while actually engaged, away from home, in the business of inspection, a personal allowance of 5*s.* 6*d.* a day, with 6*d.* (it is almost incredible) for every school which they visit. Out of this allowance they have to defray their own travelling expenses. Compared with this, the incomes of the officials of the central administration are princely. But compared with our standard, they are, with one single exception, very low. The divisional chief, answering to the secretary to our Education Committee, receives, when his salary has reached its highest point, 480*l.* a year; the two *chefs de bureau*, corresponding to our assistant secretaries, receive 240*l.*; the lower officials in a like proportion. The four inspectors-general of primary instruction, the corner-stone of the administrative fabric, and the employment of whom makes it possible to employ with profit an army of inspectors of a lower grade, receive but 320*l.* a year. Vice-president or vice-minister there is none; indeed, the French officials thought the post of this functionary, when I explained it to them, a very curious invention. "Your vice-presidency," they said, "must generally have for its occupant one who would not have been designated chief minister of public instruction; yet it is he who, under the shadow of a nominal chief's authority, will inevitably transact nine-tenths of your educational business, and give the guidance to your system." Such was their criticism, whether it be sound or not; at all events they have not the office.

* [Jourdain,] *Budget de l'Instruction publique*, p. 192.

† By a decree of June 21st, 1858, due to M. Rouland, the present Minister. There are at present 275 primary inspectors; 30 in the highest class, 60 in the second, 185 in the lowest. There is, besides, for Paris, a special class of inspectors, with salaries of 100*l.* a year. The total yearly cost of inspection is 28,887*l.*

Alone, amid his host of inferior functionaries, with unapproachable brilliancy, *velut inter ignes Luna minores*, shines the Minister. He has a salary of 4000*l*. a year, with a house and allowances, which raise the value of his post much higher. This enormous disproportion between the chief's salary and that of even his highest functionaries strikes an English observer as strange. Perhaps French subordinates console themselves with the reflection that in their country any educated man may aspire to be Minister of Public Instruction, as any common soldier may aspire to be a Marshal of France.

The habits of our country are hardly compatible with official salaries so low as those of France; and to have our schoolmasters' means reduced to the French standard would be a serious misfortune. But there can be no doubt that a certain plainness and cheapness is an indispensable element of a plan of education which is to be very widely extended; that a national system is at this price. In operations on a really vast scale, that rigid economy, even in the smallest matters, which in very limited operations may be thought overstrained, becomes an imperious necessity. The department to which I have the honour to belong is perhaps the most rigidly administered of any of the English public departments; it is of very recent date, it has grown up under the broad daylight of publicity. But its habits were formed when the schools under its supervision might be counted on the fingers. *On ne dote pas une armée*, mournfully cries M. Eugène Rendu, contrasting the condition of French inspectors with that of their English brethren; but an army the English school-inspectors must become if they are to meet the exigences of a national school-system. Yet what nation can afford to employ, in such a service, 275 highly-trained diplomatists, selected to conduct delicate negotiations with influential rectors? The thing is impossible; a vast body like that of the French inspectors must necessarily be taken from a larger class, paid at a lower rate, and recruited in part, as the French inspectors are with eminent advantage recruited, from among the masters of elementary schools. "Should you not gain in some respects by having your inspectors drawn from a higher class in society?" I asked M. Magin. He said that the work of primary inspection was perfectly well done by the present staff, and, so far as I had the means of observing, I entirely agree with him; but even had the actual results been less satisfactory, he would not allow that it was possible to entertain the question for a moment. The number, he said, was too overwhelming. Again, with respect to what may seem small matters of expenditure, it is impossible to over-estimate the saving which is effected in France, where administration is on so vast a scale, by a scrupulous economy in respect to these. Royal and imperial ordinances limit the privilege, and guard against the abuse, of official postage. Stationery and printing, those great administrative agents, are under severe control. "*La paperasserie administrative est le fléau de l'administration française*," said a distinguished official one day to me,—"French administration is bepapered to death;"—in English administration, also, paper plays no small part; but on how much more extravagant a scale! I have before me the form of report used by French inspectors when they visit a school. It is a single note-sheet of ordinary paper, containing printed questions, over against which the answers have to be written. Within these iron bounds is the ill-appreciated but irrepressible eloquence of inspectors confined. An English inspector's visit to any elementary school expends six sheets and a half of excellent foolscap. These appear insignificant matters; but when you come to provide for the inspection of 65,000 schools, it makes a difference whether you devote to each six sheets and a half of good foolscap, or a single sheet of very ordinary note-paper. Again, I take the item of certificate examinations. The charge for these in France is borne by the departments; under one sum is included the outlay for these, the outlay for the cantonal delegacies, the outlay for premises for savings-banks; all three being at the charge of the departments. In 1856 this item for the whole of France was under 2000*l*. For this sum, besides the other expenses just mentioned, the certificate examinations requisite to meet the wants of a system of 47,000 schools employing certificated teachers, were provided for. What, in the same year, was the cost of our certificate examinations for a system of some 6000 schools? I am very curious to know, but unfortunately I cannot ascertain. The French, who are the best account-keepers in the world, have an excellent plan of crediting each department with the cost of its own printing. It would be well, perhaps, if we followed their example; at present an English department has its printing executed, its stationery provided, and in its estimates makes no sign. But I remember the five days' paper-work of our examinations—I remember the supplies of stationery—I remember the crowning operations of the Department of Science and Art. Again, with respect to a far greater source of expense, the building and fitting of schools. In Paris are to be seen school-buildings very handsome, very elaborately fitted; but in the country districts they will not bear comparison, for completeness and architectural decoration, with those in the country districts in England. Buildings are very commonly adapted to school purposes instead of being expressly erected for them; but these school-rooms are quite good enough to be exceedingly useful, and by condescending to use them an education system can carry its schools and teachers into poor and remote communes, which must else have remained strangers to them. I am bound to say that great good sense seemed to me to characterise French administration both in its requirements and in its forbearance when dealing with schools: to take the much disputed article of boarded floors for instance; recommended generally in all schools, these have never been inflexibly required but for infant schools. Perhaps we may one day have to take a lesson from France in some of these respects. Not without doing violence to some crotchets, not without lopping off some elegant but superfluous branches of expenditure, will the plaything of philanthropists be converted into the machine of a nation.

CHAPTER X

Present Intellectual and Moral Condition of Popular Education in France.—Schools in Paris

The reader is now informed of the number and cost of the French primary schools. He will naturally ask next: What are these numerous schools of France like? what sort of an education do they give to their scholars? To this question I shall endeavour to reply by giving an account of a few of the schools which I myself visited, and I will select those which may serve as representatives of the class to which they belong.

This is not difficult. M. Rouland, the Minister of Public Instruction, in an interview with which he honoured me while I was in Paris, assured me, on hearing that I proposed to visit schools in all parts of France, that I was giving myself a great deal of very unnecessary trouble; that when I had seen a few schools anywhere, I had seen enough to enable me to judge of all. It would have been improper for me to accept this assurance, even upon such eminent authority, without verifying it by my own experience. I therefore proceeded on my enterprise, for which M. Rouland obligingly furnished me with the most ample facilities; and I visited schools in all quarters of France. I learned much which, without visiting the localities, I never should have known; but I also learned that M. Rouland had good reasons for his assertion, and that schools in France differed one from another much less than schools in England. Having learned this, I am at least enabled to spare the reader repeated descriptions of the same thing.

On the 17th of April I visited, in company with M. Rapet, a public lay school in the Rue du Faubourg Montmartre. It was a good specimen of its class. Held in a large and imposing building, in a good street, it contained a boys' school and a girls' school, with about 200 scholars in each. The schoolrooms are built over each other, the ceilings being, in all the best and newest schools, so constructed that there is no noise. The rooms were less lofty than our best schoolrooms, but quite as well ventilated; in general I found the ventilation of schools better in France than it is in England. Each school had its covered playground as well as its open-air playground. This covered playground, very rare in England, is a noticeable feature of all the best schools in the French towns; it is generally a large room on the same floor with the schoolroom; its use is to afford to the children a place for recreation in bad weather, and for their meals in the middle of every day. The parents are glad of an arrangement which relieves them throughout the day from the charge of their children, who also are thus saved two journeys in the crowded streets. I saw, in the covered playground of this school, the children, after a game of play, ranged at their dinners, which they bring with them from home; an assistant teacher was present, and the greatest order prevailed. The fittings of the schoolrooms were good, much on the same plan as that formerly followed in our British schools, but with better desks; the walls were barer than with us, and, indeed, it is rare to see on the walls of a French schoolroom the abundant supply of maps so common in English schoolrooms; but there is generally to be found the map of France and the map of Europe. Conspicuous were the crucifix and the bust of the Emperor—the indispensable ornaments of French public schoolrooms. The boys' school occupied two good rooms; one under the charge of the master, a well-mannered and intelligent man; the other under the charge of an assistant master, or *adjoint*. These *adjoints* play an important part in French primary instruction; they are young men not yet arrived at the age when they may be full communal teachers *; the law does not oblige them to be certificated, but all those employed in Paris and in the large towns are certificated, because the municipalities of these towns will employ no other; the departmental council decides whether a school needs an *adjoint* or not; the head-

* To be full communal teacher in France one must be 24 years old, and have served three years since the age of 21 as *adjoint* or as *suppléant*. See *Décret du* 31 *Décembre* 1853.

master names him. Monitors were employed in the lower section, which was that under the assistant's care, and much the largest. The appearance of the boys was very much the same as that of the boys whom I see constantly in British and Wesleyan schools; there were very many whom I could not have distinguished from English children. Their instruction *, also, was much on a par with that of the scholars of a good British or Wesleyan school in London; their reading was somewhat better; their writing, to my eye, not so good, but the French style of handwriting is different from ours; their grammar and dictation about equal; their arithmetic better; their history and geography not so good. The same is true, I think, of nearly all the French primary schools; the reading and arithmetic are better than ours, the arithmetic in particular being in general much more intelligently taught by their masters, and much more intelligently apprehended by their children; the information about geography and history is decidedly inferior. I must notice, however, that in the schools of Nancy, and in the excellent Jewish schools of Paris, to which M. Albert Cohn, the president of the Jewish Beneficent Society, kindly conducted me, the boys answered my questions on geography, and, still more, on history, as well as the best instructed scholars whom I have ever found in an English school.

The girls were all collected in one large room. The city of Paris is about to institute *adjointes*, or assistant mistresses, for girls' schools; in the mean time, the schoolmistress here has the aid of fourteen monitresses, who receive a small sum, the highest of them eight francs a month. The order, both here and in the boys' school, was excellent. The instruction in both, as in all the communal schools of Paris and of every large town in France, is entirely gratuitous. Books, as well as schooling, are given gratuitously by the city of Paris, which spends on popular instruction nearly 100,000*l.* a year. Parents, even the well-circumstanced, receive gladly and without a shadow of scruple this boon of free education for their children. The best judges,

* For the present time-table, (by authority,) of the lay public schools of Paris, see the end of this Report. [The appendices are not printed in this edition.]

however, are of opinion that the urban municipalities have not done well in bestowing it so indiscriminately; the law certainly contemplated the exaction of school-fees from those who can afford to pay them; and, it is said, the want of the funds without difficulty thus obtainable prevents the establishment of new schools which are needed.

The law, indeed, prescribes that no child shall be admitted gratuitously into a public school unless he produces a ticket of admission signed by the mayor; and if this ticket of admission were given with proper caution, scholars who can afford to pay for their schooling would, no doubt, be excluded from schools not intended for them. But, in point of fact, this ticket is given at Paris with great laxity; mayors very generally authorise the teachers of well-conducted schools to make out their own lists of candidates for admission, and this list, when presented, is accepted without further inquiry. But in the teachers, both of lay and congreganist schools, there is an invariable tendency to prefer the better trained, better dressed, more creditable child of well-circumstanced parents, to the ill-conditioned offspring of the poor. A teacher's pardonable pride in having his school respectable, and in winning, through his scholars, an influence with their influential parents, explains well enough this tendency, even if it cannot, in the disciples of the Abbé de Lasalle, entirely excuse it. The deserved popularity of the schools of the Brethren, and the undoubted preference for them of the most respectable part of the urban populations, give them ample opportunities of thus offending. To the Sisters they are yet more abundantly offered, and as seldom resistible. There are communes where, out of five Sisters engaged for the service of public education, one Sister alone devotes her labours to the poor. Under this one Sister all the poor children of the parish, of all ages, are taught in a single free class, often numbering as many as eighty scholars. The four remaining Sisters devote themselves to the diversified instruction of two classes of about fifteen girls each, drawn from the well-circumstanced families of the commune, who pay from three to five francs a month for a daughter's schooling. It is undoubtedly true that in this way the instruction of the poor often suffers; sometimes by the actual exclusion of poor children from public schools where their places are improperly occupied by the rich, sometimes by the undue subordination of their instruction to that of richer scholars.

Yet I could not discover that even in the great towns, where population is thickest, masses of poor children anywhere remained without instruction. There are cases of hardship, such as those which I have mentioned; but I should mislead the English reader if I allowed him to think that I found in any French city educational destitution such as that of the 21,025 schoolless children of Glasgow, such as that of the 17,177 schoolless children of Manchester.* I should mislead him if I let him think that I found in France, or that I believe to exist in France, a schoolless multitude like the 2,250,000 of England. I endeavoured without success to obtain returns showing the number of children in France between the ages of five and thirteen years who remain without schooling. Inquiries have been for the last few years in prosecution with a view to obtain accurate information on this matter; but those conducting them avowed to me that they were not yet sufficiently complete to enable them to give me statistics which might be relied on. It would be well, perhaps, if the statisticians of all countries were equally cautious or equally candid. But in all the large towns which I visited, the inspectors united in assuring me that, irregularly as the schools might be frequented, feeble as might be the result which they produced, no considerable class of children remained out of the reach of their operations. In Paris, where I made special inquiries, M. Rapet—whose assurances, in every case where I could verify them, I never failed to find true, who is not inexperienced, who is not of a sanguine temper, who does not by any means see French public education in a rosy light—assured me of the same thing. Other officials unconnected with education, and with the fullest opportunities for learning the habits of the poor, repeated his assurances. My own observation of the

* See *The State of our Educational Enterprises*, by the Rev. Wm. Fraser, Glasgow, 1858, p. 146. I do not agree with Mr. Fraser's conclusions; but it is impossible to value too highly either the information which he has collected, or the spirit in which he writes.

streets and schools in the most destitute and populous quarters of Paris confirmed them. I believe that in the great cities of France industry is organised down to a much lower stage than in those of England; that the number of families without any recognised and regular mode of living is far smaller; that the number of children, therefore, left by parents, who themselves hang loose upon society, to run as wild through the world as themselves, is comparatively restricted.

A few days later I visited a school in the Rue de la Sourdière, kept by the Sisters. There is here a girls' school with 200 scholars, held in three good and well-fitted rooms, each under the care of a Sister; there is also an infant school of 100, under the care of two other Sisters. These Sisters belong to a community of sixteen, who live in the same house under a superior; five are charged with the care of the schools, the remainder devote themselves to visiting the poor, tending the sick, preparing medicaments for them, and similar works of charity. The premises where the school was formerly held were very bad; two years ago the city of Paris bought the present house, and arranged it excellently for its actual purpose. The order in both schools was admirable; the instruction in the girls' school moderate. The arithmetic, however, was good; nearly all the girls in the upper class could work correctly sums in interest and in vulgar and decimal fractions: in a similar school in England this would seldom be the case. On the other hand, few girls in this class could tell how many departments France contained, or had even an elementary knowledge of geography: the upper class of a girls' school in England is generally fairly informed on geography—certainly has almost always learned the number of the English counties. In Paris, the instruction in the schools of the Sisters is commonly inferior, the inspectors told me, to that of the lay girls' schools. In the provinces it is not so; not, perhaps, that the Sisters' schools are there better, but that the lay schools are worse. Apart from the mere instruction, however, there is, even in Paris, something in the Sisters' schools which pleases both the eye and the mind, and which is more rarely found elsewhere. There is the fresh, neat schoolroom, almost always cheerfuller, cleaner, more decorated than a lay schoolroom. There is the orderliness and attachment of the children. Finally, there is the aspect of the Sisters themselves, in general of a refinement beyond that of their rank in life; of a gentleness which even beauty in France mostly lacks; of a tranquillity which is evidence that their blameless lives are not less happy than useful. If ever I have beheld serious yet cheerful benevolence, and the serenity of the mind pictured on the face, it is here. Is it then impossible—I perpetually asked myself in regarding them—is it then impossible for people no longer under the world's charm, or who have never felt it, to associate themselves together, and to work happily, combinedly, and effectually, unless they have first adhered to the doctrines of the Council of Trent?

The law of France does not recognise perpetual vows; but it is extremely rare—it is so rare as to be almost without example, and an indelible stigma—for a Sister to quit the religious life when she has once embraced it. She may quit, indeed—fatigue or ill-health may often compel her to quit—the laborious profession of a teacher; but it is only to engage in some other charitable service of her calling. If she ceases to be a schoolmistress, she becomes a visitress or a nurse, or she gives her labours in the dispensary. To the end of her life she remains the servant of the necessitous and of the afflicted. This sustained religious character secures to her the unfeigned respect of the common people, and enables her to render invaluable services to society.

Attached to the same establishment is an *asile-ouvroir*, or needlework school, which I visited. These schools are open after or between the ordinary school-hours; they are attended by girls from mixed schools under masters, to which they are often annexed; by girls from ordinary girls' schools, of which the teacher is not particularly skilled in needlework; finally, by girls who attend no other school at all. For the benefit of the latter a little instruction in reading, arithmetic, and religious knowledge is added to the lessons in sewing, knitting, and marking. Embroidery and ornamental work are proscribed by law, except in those districts of France where they form an important branch of female industry. As the schools are open only for a few hours in each day, the services of skilful teachers can be secured for a very moderate remuneration. These establishments, which are of great use, and which have had no small share in giving to French needlewomen their superiority, are unknown as a school institution in England.

The next day I visited two establishments kept by Brethren of the Christian Schools. The first, situated in the Rue St. Lazare, contained 250 boys, and was conducted by three of the brethren. It is not a public, but a private school (*école libre*); but it is a private school in a condition in which many private schools in France actually find themselves, and therefore I mention it. It was founded by private subscriptions, and it was intended to be a kind of parochial school, under the superintendence of the local clergy. Subscriptions fell off, and the city of Paris at the present moment pays the rent of the building where the school is held, and will sooner or later end by taking upon itself the whole expense of the institution, and by converting it into a communal school. Hardly anywhere in France, (in this the reports of all the inspectors concur), can the private boys' schools, whether they be lay or congreganist, hold their own in the competition with the public schools. The private girls' schools kept by the Sisters are more fortunate. But for their boys —although even in the private school the teacher has the indispensable guarantee of the certificate of capacity, without which, in France, no man may teach—parents undoubtedly prefer the public school with its additional guarantees of a public character and a more detailed inspection. To State inspection all private schools are subject; but only in what concerns their provision for the bodily health and comfort of the pupils, and their maintenance of due morality. So strongly do these establishments feel the advantage conferred by the publicity and stimulant of thorough inspection, that they constantly request the inspector to extend his examination from their school premises to their school instruction. Generally he refuses, and for reasons which his English brethren would do well to remember. "If I find the instruction ever so bad and injudicious," he says, "I have no power to get it changed; and I am bound to give public service where I know it can have results." Many an English squire, in like manner, wishes for the stimulant of inspection, while he is determined to keep his school entirely independent. In other words, he wishes to have an inspector down from London occasionally, as he would have a landscape-gardener or an architect, to talk to him about his school, to hear his advice, and to be free to dismiss him, as he might dismiss the landscape-gardener or the architect, the moment his advice becomes unpalatable. He wishes to have a public functionary to act as showman to his school once a year. But it is not for this that the State pays its servants. State supervision is useless if it can be rejected the moment it becomes a reality—the moment it tends to enforce general reason against individual caprice. The counsels of inspection, to be of any real worth, must be in some way or other authoritative.

As the school in the Rue St. Lazare presented in other respects little that was remarkable, I shall pass on from it to another school kept by the Brethren, which I saw on the same morning, a public school in the Rue du Rocher. Here not less than four Brethren were employed; one for each of the four classes into which this large school, containing 400 boys, was divided. The Schools of the Brethren have a decided advantage over the lay schools in the number of their teachers. A lay school in Paris has a master and an *adjoint*, two efficient teachers; a school of the Brethren has never less than three; always, when the school is large, a greater number. For the evening or adult school a fresh relay of Brethren is ready, while the lay teacher has the toil of evening and day alike. A sick or overworked Brother is sent to recover, in perfect rest of body and mind, at one of the houses of residence of his order, while another of his community is sent to take his place, without disturbance or detriment to the school. The illness of a lay schoolmaster agitates him with apprehension, mulcts him in salary, and deranges his school. Such are the advantages which a great association like that of the Brethren confers on its members. But even such an association is not numerous enough to supply to elementary schools an adequate force of teaching power. It supplies more than its lay competitors in France; it has thus a great advantage over them. But what were even four teachers among these 400 boys of the Rue du Rocher, with 110 boys to be controlled and taught in a single room by one brother, 80 by a second, the remainder in two other rooms by the third and fourth? I here touch the weak point of the French schools. The Brethren, it is true, do not employ monitors; but the value of monitors is by this time pretty accurately appreciated. Under certain circumstances the employment of them is indispensable. M. de Lasalle, in his *Manual* *, laid down a plan for the division and subdivision of the school-work by means of the use of monitors, and is, in truth, the earliest inventor of the mutual or monitorial system. In the war between the simultaneous and mutual systems, which raged so hotly in France from 1815 to 1830, the Brethren, like the clergy, naturally took part against a system extolled by their enemies and directed against their influence. The brethren were partisans of the simultaneous system, which centred the whole system in the head-teacher, that is, in one of themselves. The French liberals were partisans of the mutual system, which, as they hoped, would substitute innumerable neutral influences for the one influence of the ecclesiastical head-teacher. But all this is past. The battle between lay and clerical influence is no longer fought with the weapons of the mutual and simultaneous systems. Clergy and laymen alike confess the imperfections of both. I talked little to my friends among the French inspectors about the pupil-teachers of Holland and England. I was in France that I might learn what they knew, and not that I might teach them what I knew. But if these lines ever meet the eye of any one of them, let me assure him that popular education in France will gain more by the introduction of pupil-teachers into a single school, than by libraries of discussion upon the mutual and simultaneous systems.

Pupil-teachers—the sinews of English primary instruction, whose institution is the grand merit of our English State system, and its chief title to public respect; this, and, I will boldly say, the honesty with which that system has been administered. Pupil-teachers—the conception, for England, of the founder of English popular education, of the administrator whose conceptions have been as fruitful as his services were unworthily ma-

* See his remarkable words quoted by M. Ambroise Rendu in his *Essai sur l'Instruction publique*, vol. i. p. 81.

ligned, of Sir James Shuttleworth. In naming them, I pause to implore all friends of education to use their best efforts to preserve this institution to us unimpaired. Let them entreat ministerial economy to respect a pensioner who has repaid the outlay upon him a thousand times; let them entreat Chancellors of the Exchequer to lay their retrenching hands anywhere but here; let them entreat the Privy Council Office to propose for sacrifice some less precious victim. Forms less multiplied, examinations less elaborate, inspectors of a lower grade—let all these reductions be endured rather than that the number of pupil-teachers should be lessened. If these are insufficient, a far graver retrenchment, the retrenchment of the grants paid to holders of our certificates of merit, would be yet far less grave than a considerable loss of pupil-teachers. A certificate, indeed, is properly a guarantee of capacity, and not an order for money. There is no more reason that it should entitle its possessor to 20*l.* than that it should entitle him to a box at the opera. Private liberality can repair the salaries of the schoolmasters, but no private liberality can create a body like the pupil-teachers. Neither can a few of them do the work of many. "Classes of twenty-five or thirty, and an efficient teacher to each class:"—that school-system is the best which inscribes these words on its banners.

The overwhelming size of their classes has naturally an exhausting effect on French teachers. In none of them is this effect more apparent than in the Brethren, originally in many cases the feebler and less robust members of a poor family, who have sought in the career of tuition not only a field of pious labour, but an exemption from military service * and from the rude life of a tiller of the ground. They have often, the younger ones more especially, a languid and apathetic air, and go through their work as if they had strength to go through it only by routine. They speak as little as possible, and to save their voices have invented a machine like a rattle, peculiar to the schools of the brethren, with which they give all the signals that another

* Ever since 1818 the engagement to remain for ten years in the service of public instruction frees him who takes it from the obligation of military service.

teacher would give with his voice. They keep their scholars writing, an English teacher would say, perpetually; in all the French schools, indeed, lay as well as congreganist, the written bear to the oral exercises an exorbitant proportion, but in no schools so exorbitant as in those of the brethren. As some compensation, the caligraphy of their pupils is celebrated. But the habit of oral questioning, (and on this point M. Rapet entirely agreed with me,) is far too little practised.

The Brother who has the principal charge of a school must be certificated. On the Brethren who assist him there is imposed no such obligation. One often finds, therefore, in one of these schools, a great difference between the vigour, confidence, and acquirements of the chief teacher, and those of his assistants. But they live very harmoniously together, and the youthful Brother, in time, obtains his certificate, and qualifies himself to take the principal charge of a school. The superior of the house of residence which furnishes teachers to a school exercises very constantly and very thoroughly his right of inspection of it.

In the Schools of the Brethren there is the same want of maps which is observable in the lay schools, but the nakedness of the walls is generally relieved by religious pictures and religious sentences. The instruction differs in no important particular from that of lay schools. That of the best lay schools, however, is unquestionably, on the whole, somewhat more advanced.* In lay and congreganist schools alike, drawing and music are more systematically taught than in our schools, and taught, in general, by special masters. The communities of the Brethren furnish them with a supply of trained labour in all departments of teaching. I was greatly struck with the appearance of the young Brother who taught drawing in the school of the Rue du Rocher; he had a genuine vocation for his art, and his face expressed the animation and happiness which the exercise of a

* As long ago as 1818, the Rector of the Academy of Strasbourg gives as a reason why there were no schools of the brethren in Alsace, then as now one of the best-educated districts in France, that "dans les endroits plus populeux et plus riches, on exige un enseignement supérieur à celui des Frères."—See [A. Rendu,] *Essai sur l'Instruction publique*, vol. iii. p. 243.

genuine vocation always confers. I visited him and his brethren in their house of residence; their chapel had been elaborately decorated by his sole industry: it must have been a labour of months, but a labour of love.

The Brethren are far less constant than the Sisters to the religious life. For the Sisters the religious life is the principal object of their association, the profession of teaching but the accessory: for the Brethren the career of teaching is the principal, the rest the accessory. Their vows as members of their own community are for three or five years; but as public functionaries in the service of public instruction, and, as such, exempt from the conscription, their engagement is for ten years, and for this term they actually serve in schools. At the end of this time it is not unusual for them to depart at once out of the career of teaching and the pale of their community, and to return to the garb and professions of civil life. Some of them marry and become fathers of families. Their association, therefore, is by no means invested in the eyes of the people with the same religious and sacred character as that of the Sisters.

This is true; and it is probably true, also, that the motives which determine their entrance into their order are often not religious. It is probably true that, as the best-informed persons assert, many a young peasant becomes a Brother of the Christian Schools because he can commence his duties and cease to be a charge to his parents two years sooner than if he embrace the career of a lay teacher. He cannot be admitted into a normal school before the age of 18; the fraternity will receive him at 16. If slow at learning, he dreads the certificate-examination; but without the certificate he cannot earn his bread as a lay teacher, while the fraternity can employ him as one of their numerous under-masters though he be uncertificated. Many of the French inspectors, therefore, eye the schools of the Brethren a little severely. They regard them, certainly, with far less indulgence than the schools of the Sisters; they regard their teachers as wearing a character of religious vocation which often really belongs to them no more than to the teacher of a common lay school; they are fond of maintaining that the congreganist boys' schools afford to parents no better guarantee than the lay schools for the religion and morality of their children; they are eager to prove that parents have really no preference for the former over the latter. The Brethren, on the other hand, are not unwilling to have it understood that they suffer from the hands of authority unmerited obstruction; that their Christian devotedness has its difficulties to contend with; that if their success is great, it is because their merits are irresistible.

Conscious, upon this question, of the most absolute impartiality, I shall frankly state the conclusion at which I have arrived. On the one hand, it is unquestionable that the religious associations have hitherto had rather to bless the favour than to complain of the obstruction of the civil authorities. If they sometimes have the primary inspector a little against them, they almost always have had the primary inspector's masters, the prefect and the Minister, on their side. From the day when a Protestant Minister, M. Guizot, offered to the Superior * of the Christian Schools the decoration of the Legion of Honour —a distinction which its proposed object, with a modesty not less prudent than pious, respectfully declined—to the present time, when Ministers say to a functionary, who reports some infraction of school law by the Sisters, *Vous me faites des difficultés: laissez cela*—when inspectors tell me with their own lips, *Si nous avons quelque chose à reprocher aux frères, nous y regardons à deux fois avant de la dire; cela nous attirerait des misères; c'est extrêmement redoutable*—the religious associations have been to all governments an object of favour and respect, sometimes sincere, sometimes interested. Of this there can be no question.

On the other hand I am profoundly convinced that in the quarters where they are numerous, and certain districts which may be called great centres of lay feeling—Normandy, Lorraine, Alsace—being excluded, the population generally prefers the schools of religious associations to lay schools. With respect to girls' schools there cannot be a moment's doubt; the Sisters' advantage is utterly beyond the reach of competition. With

* The Frère Anaclet, in 1833.

respect to the Brethren's schools also, however, I feel entire certainty. In Paris it is even a bad sign of the respectability and religious character of a family when it prefers for its boys a lay school to a congreganist. In the country, wherever I had the means of making personal inquiry, I found the same thing; if a school of the Brethren was accessible, the more decent, the better conducted a family was, the more certainly it sent its boys there. It was commonly thought that there the children would be under a better influence; that the moral tone, as it is called, of such a school was superior.* I add, with some hesitation on this point, which is not so easy of proof, that I believe the common opinion was right.

The reader must recollect, however, that the schools of the Brethren, although constantly on the increase, are not and cannot be very numerous. The Sisters are everywhere, because teaching is with them but one of many functions, for some of which almost every locality desires them. But the Brethren, who perform no function but that of teaching, who go out in parties of not less than three, who cost a commune 1500 or 1600 francs, instead of the 500 or 600 francs which a common lay teacher costs, and whose schools, being inevitably gratuitous, fail to contribute in aid of their teacher's maintenance the resource of school-fees, cannot be generally introduced into small and poor communes. Among the various associations, more than twenty in number, which devote themselves to the instruction

* Comparisons have often been instituted between the lay and congreganist schools as to their success in combating the revolutionary tendency; but it seems impossible to arrive at any clear conclusion. At Bordeaux, in 1848–9, the youth trained in lay, and those trained in congreganist schools, were observed to be equally quiet and well-conducted; at Bazas, Libourne, and Blaye, (in the same academy-district,) where the schools had long been in the hands of the Brethren, the population was turbulent. In the Landes, where few schools are in the hands of the Brethren, the conduct of the population was perfectly orderly. It was thought to be the relations of the rich with the poor in any locality, (at Bordeaux these are particularly good,) which made the difference as to the behaviour of the working people in that locality. In the academy-district of Paris, the Socialist and revolutionary spirit was observed (say the inspectors) to be as rife in quarters where the religious had the schools as in those where they were taught by laymen.

of the poor, there are some indeed which are less costly than the Brethren of the Christian Schools. There are the Brethren of Marie, in the regions about Lyons * and Bordeaux, who go out as teachers in parties of two: there are in Brittany the Brethren of Lamennais, founded by a brother of the celebrated writer of that name, who go out singly. But none of them enjoy the same favour as the Brethren of the Christian Schools, or can compare with them in success. The Bishop of Quimper told me that the Brethren of Lamennais, who are quartered upon the curé of the parish whither they are sent, and who cost very little, were irksome inmates to the curés, and not willingly accepted by them.† In fact, the moment a Brother goes singly, and can therefore be employed by any poor commune, he loses the virtue which religious association confers upon its members, and which is the source of half their strength. How unlike to the lonely teacher, isolated in his labour, isolated in his weariness, isolated in his joy, isolated in his temptation, is the little company of three devised by M. de Lasalle, meeting after the

* Lyons is also the original seat of the *Société d'Instruction élémentaire*, the most considerable lay association which has in France made popular education its object. In 1826 a few persons in Lyons, about 20 in number, who wished to introduce more lay influence into the management of schools for the poor, formed themselves into a society, which in 1829 was authorised by royal ordinance. The society began with eight or nine schools under its direction; it has now 39 in Lyons and the immediate neighbourhood. It has its own inspector and its executive commission, and assembles monthly to meet its teachers, in presence of the inspector, who then makes his report. The society raises about 10,000 fr. a year by private subscription. At first it was quite independent; but as its operations extended, the municipality of Lyons came to its aid, and now pays the difference between the 10,000 fr. which the society annually raises by subscription, and the 80,000 fr. which it actually spends. But this aid makes the schools of the society *public* and *municipal* schools. As such, they now have their teachers appointed by the prefect, and all the authority left to the society is a right of inspection, and of drawing up for their schools a programme of instruction, which, however, cannot be adopted unless approved by the academy-inspector of the district.

† I found in the department of Finistère but twenty-one primary schools conducted by the Brethren of this order; sixteen public schools and five private. This was in 1859. The whole number of primary boys' schools in the department was 265.

toil of the day in their common home, a society for themselves in the most unsocial spots, at once a solace to each other, and a salutary check!

If the English reader must not think that this excellent association can reach all the poor of France, so neither must he think that to put instruction in its hands is, so far as its action extends, to put it entirely in the hands of the clergy. Their schools are public schools, as the lay schools are; they are subjected to the same authorities as the lay schools; the clergyman has no more power to name or dismiss a teacher, or to interfere with the instruction, (except so far as to satisfy himself that the religious instruction is properly cared for,) in the one than in the other. Undoubtedly, the Brethren are felt by the curé to be more akin to him than the lay teacher is; undoubtedly he prefers them to the lay teacher, and procures their introduction into his parish when he can.* But the school is not really under the clergyman's hand, like the National school of an English parish: it is under the hand of the ordinary civil authorities, the mayor, the cantonal delegates, the inspectors, the prefect. What really resembles our National school is the parochial school of France (*école paroissiale*), generally taught by the religious, but a *private* school, founded expressly that it may be in ecclesiastical hands, and not in civil. But these schools are very rare in France, difficult to maintain, not acceptable to the population. The public school taught by the religious is a school under teachers in general sympathy with the clergy, but not clergy themselves, nor able to become so; and, as members of a great association, having a spirit of their own, an independence of their own, and dealing with the curé nearly as equal to equal. If the National schools of England were taught by an order of lay deacons, nearly equal to the clergyman of the parish in their social position, and legally independent of him, they would then be in the position of the public congreganist schools of France. The National schoolmaster would then stand towards the rector, not as now, much on the same footing as his gardener, but on the

* The hostility of the clergy to lay schools for boys is perhaps diminishing; but they use all their efforts to get the education of girls exclusively into the hands of the Sisters.

same footing as a brother clergyman unattached. The English National schools would then be in the hands of a body which, though with strong clerical affinities, would be a body perfectly distinct from the clergy, and incapable of blending with it; a body with a spirit and power of its own; a body by its very essence more scholastic than priestly; whereas a clergy, however admirable, as a body never forgets that it was priest before it was schoolmaster.

It was important to call the reader's attention to this wide difference between a system of private schools in the hands of the parish clergyman, and a system of public schools in the hands of a religious association and of the State. But I hasten to add, that were the religious associations of France a thousand times more devoted to the clergy than they are, the population would still continue to prefer their schools; and yet the clerical influence would not be a whit the gainer. It is to morality and religion that the French people, in sending its children to the congreganist schools, does homage *, not to any ultramontane theories. For the supremacy of a clerical party in the State it has not the slightest favour; nor, indeed, since the Revolution, does it even dream of such supremacy as possible. I have said this elsewhere, when to many it seemed a matter of question; I repeat it more boldly now, when facts have come to give to it their confirmation. The clergy have no deep-rooted influence with the French masses. They may agitate families. They may frighten governments into making concessions to them: they may induce the State (happy result of the fears of rulers!) to rebuild their churches. They may constrain the attendance at church of Voltairian officials. But no priesthood will at the present day rule the French nation.

* "The *religieux* and *religieuses* are the natural people to teach the young;"—I found this sentiment almost everywhere. At the same time the superiority of the lay boys'-schools in secular instruction was generally admitted.

CHAPTER XI

Present Intellectual and Moral Condition of Popular Education in France.—Schools in the Provinces

Mindful of M. Rouland's saying, I must not carry the reader with me to too many schools; but I must still ask him, after seeing the schools of Paris, to accompany me to one or two in the country. On the morning of the 13th of May, I found myself in the office of the academy inspector of the Gironde, M. Dauzat, whose conversation, full of shrewdness and fine remark, I had been enjoying the day before; the primary inspector of the district, M. Benoît, was there to meet me. I said to the two inspectors, that having visited many institutions by official selection, I had a desire to choose a school to visit, and a country school, for myself. A map of the department hung upon the wall, and they told me to choose where I would. I fixed upon Blanquefort, a place six or seven miles from Bordeaux, and recalling by its castle the memory of the mediæval wars and of the Black Prince. They assured me I could not have chosen more happily; that the schools of Blanquefort were neither better nor worse than the schools of most places of the same class; and that they presented an instructive variety. A little after twelve, accordingly, M. Benoît and I set out in an open carriage for Blanquefort. The day was beautiful; our road lay, at first, among gardens and country houses, but after a mile or two passed into a quiet and rural country. The environs of Bordeaux have not the movement of those of Manchester or Lyons; it is a rich and stately, but somewhat stagnant city. As we drove along, M. Benoît told me what his life was, and how a French inspector in the Gironde passed his year. He had served in the army when almost a boy, had been present with his father at the battle of Vimeiro, and had been included in the Convention of Cintra. At the peace of 1815 he found himself a lieutenant on half-pay, with small prospect of military advancement: having some turn for teaching, he had opened a private school, had been tolerably successful, and finally had been made a primary inspector. It is from the functionaries of secondary instruction, from the principals and professors of communal colleges and of private schools, that the majority of the primary inspectors are taken. They must have either the degree of bachelor of arts, or the complete certificate embracing all the subjects, both obligatory and facultative, of primary instruction; they must also have exercised some educational function for two years. Unless this function has been of a certain rank, they have further to undergo, previous to their actual appointment, a special examination in the laws which regulate French primary instruction, and in pedagogy; this examination takes place before a commission nominated by the rector to whose academy the school-district assigned to the new inspector belongs. A certain number of inspectorships is reserved for the most successful of the primary schoolmasters, and of the lecturers in normal schools; the director of a normal school would not accept the office. His post is worth considerably more than that of a primary inspector, and is the highest prize to which a schoolmaster can aspire.* A few of the best of the primary inspectors are advanced to the rank of academy-inspector: it is the academy-inspector who, in each department, is at the head of primary instruction; who receives the reports of the primary inspectors, advises the prefect, receives the inspector-general on his rounds, and communicates with the central authority in Paris. Among the most efficient of these functionaries are those promoted from primary inspectorships. M. Benoît seemed satisfied with his present position; he had, as most Frenchmen have, some little property of his own; and the department of the Gironde, like other rich departments, gives its primary inspectors a yearly allowance †

* The salary of a normal school director of the highest class is from 2800 fr. to 3000 fr. a year; of the lowest class from 2200 fr. to 3000 fr. a year. Lecturers have from 1000 fr. to 1800 fr. See *Décret du 26 Décembre 1855*, Art. 1.

† In the Gironde this allowance is 400 fr. a year. In 1857 a sum of 29,638 fr. 87 c. was thus spent by the departments in gratuities to primary inspectors.

in addition to their salary from the State. He had under his inspection not less than 646 schools, with 38,250 children; but he lived in Bordeaux, and great part of his work was either in the town itself or in the immediate neighbourhood. While M. Benoît was telling me all this, the carriage rolled on, and presently he pointed out to me the church and village of Blanquefort, upon its vine-covered hill. We drove to the boys' school, and reached it just as the children were assembled for their afternoon lessons.

It was the only boys' school of the place, which is a large, well-built village of about 2000 inhabitants. The master told me that he had 60 boys in ordinary attendance; I found present but 43. Many are absent at this season, (just the old story in England), for field labour; but the field labour of Médoc, not of England—to clear the vineyards of snails and caterpillars, and to gather the strawberry harvest. The schoolroom was large, clean, airy, and well lighted; it was fitted with desks on the old British plan, and the children were at work under monitors. On the walls was one large map of France, and several small ones of other countries. The highest class was reading a lesson on the ostrich, similar to the lessons on natural history in the third Irish reading-book; they read well. We sat down among them, and M. Benoît questioned them in a natural kindly manner, which proved his long experience of children. At his request I examined them in grammar; they parsed a sentence well, better than I should expect to find it parsed in a country school in England. Then I questioned them in geography; they could name the capitals of Europe, its principal mountains, its principal lakes, the seas connected by the Straits of Gibraltar, &c. The chief towns of the French departments they also gave with perfect readiness and accuracy. Of history they knew nothing. In arithmetic M. Benoît examined them, setting them problem after problem; and I really hardly knew which most to admire, the goodness of the examination or the quickness of the children. Their writing was such as in an English school an inspector would describe as very fair. All but fourteen of those present were reading in books. The school-books were of the kind ordinarily used in French lay schools; not good, but not, perhaps, worse than ours. The Brethren, who publish their own school-books, and sell them to all but their poorest scholars, who receive them gratuitously, are not more successful. I generally found their classes reading a series of moral lessons, without substance and without style, and repulsive by their sterile monotony. According to strict rule all books used in the French schools ought to be chosen from a list sanctioned by the Minister of Public Instruction; but there is much laxity. In fact, with them, as with us, there exists no thoroughly good school-series to choose.*

The Blanquefort boys were well disciplined, and their appearance was cheerful and healthy. Five or six of them were without shoes and stockings; but M. Benoît told me, (and the look of the children confirmed what he said,) that this was not because these children were poorer than others; many parents in the South of France, he said, the well-circumstanced as well as the poor, let their children go barefoot in the hot weather for the sake of coolness. There was some poverty, however: of the sixty children in ordinary attendance, one-sixth had free schooling because they were poor; they were chosen by the mayor and curé, approved by the municipal council, and their admission finally sanctioned by the prefect. The rest pay a uniform fee of two francs a month. From April to November the attendance is thin, but never falls below forty scholars.

Attached to the school was the master's house. It was, M. Benoît told me, an unusually good one; it had six rooms, all of them well furnished; in one of them were books and a piano: at the back of the house was a large garden, to which the school playground adjoined. The law prescribes for a schoolmaster's accommodation a three-roomed house and a garden. The salary of the master was 1200 francs a year: of this sum 200 francs were furnished by the commune, the school-pence supplied the rest. He was an intelligent, well-mannered man, of about thirty years of age.

From hence we went on to the girls' school, distant but a few paces. The reader will remember that the law does not impose upon communes the obligation of providing girls' schools. The

* The above was written in 1859. Since then, one excellent series of reading books has been published in this country.

one in question was held in a bad, ill-ventilated building, without playground, and was taught by the master's wife. Forty-eight girls had their names on the books; twenty-eight were present. The girls of Blanquefort were distinguished by wearing no covering on their hair; the country girls from the neighbourhood wore a handkerchief. None of them, I was told, (and they themselves confirmed it to me,) were likely to become domestic servants. For service they avowed a great distaste; their ambition was to live by their needle. For this they are well prepared at school, two hours in every afternoon being devoted to needle-work. They read very well indeed, and worked problems in arithmetic with much cleverness and facility. Their stock of general information was small. Fifteen of them were free scholars on the ground of poverty, the rest paid from one to two francs a month. The mistress has a salary of 800 francs a year; 200 francs of this the commune pays—voluntarily, the reader will remember: the school-fees come to 600 francs.

The schoolmaster of Blanquefort, therefore, has from his own and his wife's salary an income of 80*l.* a year. He is besides secretary to the municipality, an office almost always held by the village schoolmaster *, and which the authorities encourage him to accept. This gives him 300 francs (12*l.*) more. He has also a good house and garden.

There is general ease among the population of the Gironde, and its villages and incomes must not be taken as samples of villages and incomes in the Cantal or the Creuse; but Blanquefort is a fair sample of the villages or little towns of its class in any thriving French department, and the reader will, I think, be struck, as I was, to remark how many things practically here come in to ameliorate the meagre part created for the teacher by the law, and in remote and indigent districts † actually sustained by him.

* He is often, besides, clerk and organist. He is thus at once the man of the mayor and the man of the curé. When they get on well together his position is comfortable; when they quarrel, as they often do, it is difficult enough.

† Even in these districts his position is now somewhat better than the law of 1850 made it. On the favourable report of the prefect, the Minister of Public Instruction is now authorised to augment, from the

We had not yet done with Blanquefort. M. Benoît told me that there was a girls' school kept by the Sisters, which I ought to see; and thither, accordingly, we repaired. These Sisters, six in number, belong to a local order; they rent the houses which they occupy. The commune gives them nothing, but the department gives them 100 francs (4*l.*) a year towards the expenses of their infant school. Two Sisters have charge of the infant school, four of the girls' school. The moment I approached the premises, which stood a little out of the main street of the village, I was struck with the air of propriety, neatness, and order which reigned there. We first entered the girls' school. The cleanliness of the room, the discipline of the children, were really beautiful; flowers stood everywhere, and the open windows admitted the sweet air of the country in May. The furniture and school-fittings were as fresh as those of the lay girls' school were shabby and worn. The walls were well furnished with boards and maps. The girls were at their needlework, which M. Benoît told me enjoyed a high reputation; I saw their copy-books, and I heard their reading, and in any English school I should have highly commended both. Forty-three girls were present, seventy-five had their names on the books. Of these, fifteen are admitted free, as indigent children; the rest pay from one to two francs a month. We passed into the infant school; this school-room also was brilliantly clean. The infants, forty-eight in number, (eighty were on the books,) were arranged on the gallery, the girls, even here, being separated from the boys. Boards and Bible-pictures covered the walls as in a well-provided infant school in England. From one of the pictures a Sister was giving a gallery lesson on the story of Joseph. Her little pupils in the gallery looked clean and happy, and the treatment of them was evidently affectionate and even tender. Their instruction did not go far—why, indeed, should it?—but they knew their letters well, they went through their exercises and their singing regularly and prettily, and their discipline was perfect. Playground, passages, and offices were as

public funds, the annual salaries of deserving schoolmasters to 700 fr. after six years' service, and to 800 fr. after ten years' service. See *Décret du* 31 *Décembre* 1853, Art. 5.

neat and as beautifully clean as the schoolrooms themselves.

I have just touched on the religious instruction; I may add that in the French schools generally, lay as well as congreganist, I found the children well instructed in the catechism and well acquainted with Scripture history. Sunday schools teach them these; they teach them little besides, but they teach them these very fairly. I passed an hour or two at Toulouse in going from chapel to chapel in the cathedral church of St. Stephen, to watch the Sunday classes under their priests; they were crowded but orderly, and work was carried on very diligently. These catechism classes in the churches are, in fact, the French Sunday school; the Protestants have carried the institution somewhat further; but, as an instrument of secular as well as of religious instruction, it is not of much importance in France.

I do not know if the reader will think, as I do, that this visit made without notice to the schools of a country place of my own selection was very satisfactory. I would not have exchanged it for a week of visits made at the choice of the local inspectors. It showed me the everyday life of thousands of spots in the many departments of France; in her thriving departments certainly, but not more thriving than Warwickshire and Lincolnshire are thriving. Of this life it left me with a pleasant impression; an impression which, amidst the many mournful sights and mournful stories of the general life of humanity, I shall not easily lose. We left the Sisters, to whose door the schoolmaster, who, like every one else in the place, lived on good terms with them, had come to join us. I entered the church; there, too, were flowers everywhere, and grateful coolness and shade. We sent the carriage round by the road, and the schoolmaster guided us up and down slopes of grass and vineyards, across a clear brook, to the old castle. The masonry of its keep rises still fresh and unworn out of the reed-grown moat; but all within the walls is a ruin, over which cluster the wild roses. A peasant has made his dwelling where once was the grand entrance; but he has nothing to tell of the castle's history and of the Black Prince. The ploughshare of the Revolution has passed over that feudal age; they are gone, the leopards of England from the gateway, the name of the Black Prince from the memories of the population. Even in the reminiscences of the excellent M. Benoît himself, it did not, I think, hold a very prominent place. Through a thicket of brushwood I climbed to the top of the ruin; around me, beneath the luminous air, stretched the pleasant country of southern France; on the horizon were the towers and spires of Bordeaux, and its smoke hanging in the clear sky. We rejoined the carriage, and reached Bordeaux before nightfall.

A few days afterwards, at Toulouse, I expressed to the obliging inspectors who did the honours to me of that city, my wish, after having seen an average specimen of a French country school at Blanquefort, to see a school which was decidedly below the average, a school which was, from whatever cause, in a somewhat suffering condition. They promised to gratify me; and the next day the primary inspector drove with me to the public lay school of St. Martin de Touche, a village of 800 souls, a few miles from Toulouse. As we entered the village I remarked the handsome church, quite new, and was told that it had just been entirely rebuilt. The school had certainly not been rebuilt; it was a poor building, ill ventilated, with an uneven brick floor and no playground. The master looked depressed and without energy to struggle against his difficulties; he was no longer young, and weighed down with the charge of what is less common in France than in England, a very large family. But the moment I came to talk with him I was struck with his superiority; and the inspector told me that he was a man of very considerable cultivation and mental power, who had been educated for the priesthood, but had married and been driven to turn schoolmaster. His salary was 1000 fr. (40*l.*) a year; all the children had free schooling, but bought their own books. It is the city of Toulouse which pays the master's salary and gives to the village a free school; like the other great cities of France, it does the same for all the villages in its environs. Perhaps it would aid the cause of popular education more efficiently if it spent its money upon it in a somewhat different manner *; but its liberality is unquestionable. There were

* The offer of free schooling fills a school, but *l'enseignement en souffre*—this is the nearly universal testimony of the French inspectors. In the Bas Rhin (a very well-educated district) free schooling is being

twenty-eight boys present; forty-five had their names on the books. I was told that there were generally about thirty in attendance through the summer; in winter the school is quite full. All the boys were wearing wooden shoes without stockings, though the children, almost all of them, of small proprietors pretty well off; they wear shoes and stockings on Sundays only. In general, unless their parents are in great destitution, boys here do not begin to work regularly till the age of thirteen, but in summer their occasional help is often wanted by their parents. The instruction in this school was better than I expected from its unpromising aspect; the reading was very fair, though sing-song, like rustic reading in England; there was little geography (though the walls were not ill furnished with maps) and less history; the grammar and arithmetic were good; the handwriting and dictation very good indeed. The latter lesson amused me; the master was dictating to his pupils, from the *Journal des Instituteurs*, M. Rouland's letter to the bishops desiring their prayers for the success of France in the Italian war. This newspaper, published under the auspices of the Minister of Public Instruction, and taken in by almost every schoolmaster in France, by no means confines itself to scholastic information. A copy of it lies before me *: of fourteen pages which, exclusive of those occupied by advertisements and commercial intelligence, it contains, seven are devoted to *Politique*, and seven to *Pédagogie* and *Sciences usuelles*. Politics have naturally the

gradually suppressed, with the acquiescence of the parents; and in this department there were in 1855 but 750 children, of an age to attend school, who did not attend it. In the adjoining department of the Haut Rhin, there were 4000. But in the academy-district of Besançon, (also well-educated,) the inspectors declare that the attendance at schools which have been made free has doubled, tripled, and even quadrupled; and that the scholars are kept at such schools more steadily. At Lyons, again, "free schooling is not disliked by the population," say the inspectors; "it is rather regarded as a debt which the State owes to them;" and at Lyons, as in Paris, all the public schools are free. But the majority of the reports show that, while free schools are generally filled and even over-filled, and often at the expense of paying schools, the poor are careless about their children's attendance and progress in them, and "value little what they pay nothing for."

* The number for July 31st, 1859.

post of honour. The number commences: *On lit dans le* Moniteur, *On cherche en Angleterre à attribuer à la France la cause des charges que l'on impose au peuple Anglais pour les défenses nationales.* Then follows the rest of the well-known article of the *Moniteur.* A little further on England figures once more:—*La Tamise, dit le* Times, *qui baigne les murs du palais de Westminster, est véritablement en décomposition.* The remainder of the first seven pages is full of news from the seat of war, notices of the countries engaged in it, appreciations of their policy; all undeniably interesting, all irreproachably national, but not the least in the world pedagogic.

We smile: it is thus that M. Rouland fulfils the duty of government to "enlighten public opinion, and not to leave it at the mercy of personal passions and party hatreds." * Yet, perhaps, nothing is wholly ridiculous, which tends to foster that admirable unity of patriotic spirit which pervades France from one end to the other, and which is the great force of the nation.

The master's wife had a class of six little boys in an adjoining room. She had formerly taught the girls of the village, but the Sisters had opened a school, and, as almost always happens, all the girls had been drawn off to them. This school of the Sisters had present, on the day of my visit, forty scholars.

Before quitting elementary schools, I must conduct the reader to a genuine private school. I could not select a better example than the British school in Paris. This is entirely supported by voluntary contributions, and all the State has to do with it is to exercise its legal right of inspection, extending only to matters of what our neighbours call "hygiene, salubrity, and morality." † The boys' school had forty-two children present on the day of my visit; they were very young, the children of British parents, but many of them speaking French better than English; the

* His own words, in a warning to a newspaper: "Éclairer l'opinion "publique, et ne pas la laisser à la merci des passions personnelles et des "haines de parti."

† See *Loi du* 15 *Mars* 1850, Art. 21. "L'inspection des écoles libres "porte sur la moralité, l'hygiène, et la salubrité. Elle ne peut porter "sur l'enseignement que pour vérifier s'il n'est pas contraire à la morale, "à la constitution, et aux lois."

British school-course is followed. The master, a certificated student from the Borough Road Training College, whom I remember to have seen there, is an undoubtedly able and intelligent young man; but he seemed to me to be somewhat out of spirits about his school, and to feel his solitude in Paris a good deal. The girls' school was more thriving. The children were older, the mistress, a former student of the Home and Colonial Institution, appeared sanguine about the success of her school, and in cheerful spirits. In this school I felt myself to be indeed on British ground, for there was a committee. The excellent lady who represented them was there, not in anticipation of my visit, for I had not announced it, but on an habitual errand of kindness to advise and encourage the teacher. Like many British committees in England she seemed to have no ardent fondness for government control; she was somewhat impatient of authoritative visits, even when directed solely to matters of "hygiene, salubrity, and morality;" she lamented that her school should be under the supervision of "bigoted Roman Catholic inspectors." Her fears were vain; for her inspector was M. Rapet, no more a bigoted Roman Catholic than I am. But how many friends of popular education have I seen on British committees in England, during my tours of inspection through nearly all its counties, haunted with the same apprehensions as this benevolent lady; not exactly hostile, but agitated by a susceptibility which never slumbered. *Cœlum non animum mutant:*—it was impossible to forbear smiling.

I had intended to describe a Protestant public school in France; but really such a school differs so little from a Roman Catholic lay school in the same locality, that I forbear. Yet the grown-up Protestant population has certainly throughout France a general superiority over the Roman Catholic, in conduct, industry, and success in life. To what is their superiority owing? It is in great measure, I believe, owing to this, that the French Protestants have the unspeakable advantage, for the character, of finding themselves a small minority in presence of a vast majority; and in order to hold its own and to succeed in life, the minority has to put forth its strength and to do its best.

CHAPTER XII

Present Intellectual and Moral Condition of Popular Education in France.—Normal Schools

From elementary I pass to normal schools *; and before I speak of the ministerial orders which regulate these I will describe what I actually saw in them. Strange to say, in Paris there is no public normal school for primary teachers; there is an institution at Courbevoie for the training of Protestant teachers, and at Versailles there is a departmental normal school; but the capital trusts to the provinces for its supply of teachers, and so powerful are its attractions that it never fails to obtain the best of them. I saw the most efficient, perhaps, of the provincial normal schools; that of Bordeaux, that of Nancy, that of Strasbourg. I will describe that of Bordeaux.

The department of the Gironde and that of the Lot and Garonne unite to maintain this institution, each establishing scholarships in it for its own students. The director has been very successful, and has recently been rewarded with the decoration of the Legion of Honour. In his training school there are fifty-one students. The course is now for three years, having previously to 1851 been for two years only; and considering that the students arrive quite without the previous training of the pupil-teachers by whom our normal schools are peopled, considering that they often have almost everything to learn, three years is not a longer period than is required to form them. The students whom I saw were certainly more rustic and undeveloped than ours; later in life the experience of the world

* In 1859 there were in France seventy normal schools for laymen, with 2,750 students in training in them. There were thirty-four normal institutions for the training of lay schoolmistresses; but the Department of Public Instruction possesses no returns of the present number of students in these. There are, besides, the noviciates in which the religious are trained.

and the natural quickness of their race enable them to present themselves with at least as much advantage as our schoolmasters. Most of them are the sons of country teachers; hardly any of them were town-bred. The class of the third year, consisting of thirteen students, was receiving a mathematical lecture when I visited the institution. They do not go far in mathematics; no student in the institution was advanced as high as quadratic equations, no student was reading Euclid; they were taught, however, the elements of practical geometry. The object is to teach them what is needed for a primary school; the programme of the normal college exactly corresponds to the programme of the primary school; the student is not allowed to pass, at the end of his first year, from the obligatory matters of primary instruction to the facultative, unless he has given proof of his thorough knowledge of the former, and not of his knowledge of them merely, but also of his skill to teach them. The teaching of *method*;—it is on this that circular after circular of the Minister * insists, it is on this that the reports of the commissioners who superintend normal schools perpetually dilate, it is to this that principals and lecturers address all their efforts. Practising schools are annexed to each training college, and in them the French students pass a great deal of their time; much more, in proportion to that spent in the lecture-room, than ours. And with what success? Undoubtedly, a knowledge of method is of the highest importance to the schoolmaster; *donner c'est acquérir*, says a French poet most truly; to teach is to learn; and to give a man, therefore, the power of teaching well is to give him the power of learning much. Undoubtedly, too, the attention to method in the French training schools has resulted in the establishment of improved modes of teaching particular subjects; the teaching of arithmetic, for instance, the teaching

* "Ne les excitez pas à sortir de ce cercle (that of the *obligatory* "part of primary instruction) qui est encore assez vaste, et faites en "sorte que ceux qui le franchiront cèdent à des dispositions véritables, "et non à des prétentions peu justifiées. À vrai dire, ce qui fait le "véritable instituteur, ce n'est pas le brevet, que tout le monde peut "conquérir, c'est l'art de diriger les esprits et la pratique de l'éduca-"tion."—*Instruction générale sur les Attributions des Recteurs concernant l'Instruction primaire*, by M. Fortoul; October 31st, 1854.

of reading, have been facilitated and simplified. Yet I doubt whether, in all this zeal for method, in this exclusive thought for the bare needs of the primary school, in this jealous apprehension lest the normal college pupil should become more of a student than a schoolmaster, the range of study has not been made unduly narrow, and a risk incurred of developing the student's mental power so insufficiently that he will be thoroughly effective neither as student nor schoolmaster. The question is a most difficult one: I have little doubt that we in England have fallen into the contrary extreme; that we crowd so much and so various book-learning into our normal school course that the student, unless a very able man indeed, is left at the end of it stupefied rather than developed; not in the condition of one trained to bring, for all his future work, his faculties into full and easy play, but of one crammed so full and so fast, that, in order to begin his real intellectual life, he must, like Themistocles, seek to learn how to forget. Perhaps, in this matter of normal school training, as in others, common sense, usually the last voice suffered to make itself heard, will be heard at last; will suggest some middle way between the tenuity of the French programme and the extravagance of ours; will devise, for the future masters of our village-schools, some course which neither stints them to the beggarly elements of reading and writing, nor occupies them with the differential calculus and the pedigree of Sesostris.

The staff of a French training school consists of a director, two lecturers, and a chaplain. The director is personally charged with the main part of the tuition. The system of accounts is very exact, and rigidly inspected; so vast and complicated is the machine of public instruction that it can be kept from falling into disorder only by perfect precision on the part of its lower functionaries, and, on the part of the Minister, by unsparing severity to irregularities. The economy of the Bordeaux establishment was austere; the students all slept in one vast common dormitory, but the neatness and cleanliness, in France so far better practised in public establishments than in private, were exemplary. The dietary is regulated by a ministerial decree. Students of the first year pay from their own resources 100 francs, one fourth of the yearly charge of a student here *; after the first year and the examination which follows it the best students complete their training free of charge, the rest continue to pay their fourth. About one-third of the whole number are thus free students. The department supplies the funds for the whole or partial scholarships thus bestowed. A good garden is attached to the establishment; and lessons in horticulture and agriculture, an idle pretence in most of the elementary schools which profess them, are in most of the normal schools of France a reality, and are greatly enjoyed by the students.

Under the legislation of M. Guizot, the admission to normal schools was by competitive examination. In the suspicion which fell on these establishments in 1848, not only the competitive examination, but all examination at entrance, was abolished; and the prefect in departmental council admitted candidates by his own nomination, on their production of certificates of morality and good conduct. It was soon found that candidates who could produce excellent certificates of morality often turned out utterly incapable students.† The normal schools gradually recovered themselves in public estimation, and the jealousy of their over-ambitious studies abated. The Minister, M. Fortoul, found himself constrained to re-establish some examination at entrance ‡; but that which he instituted was no longer competitive, and bore only on the most elementary branches of knowledge. This examination still subsists; it is conducted by the academy-inspector of the district, and excludes from the normal school the utterly incompetent. Those who pass it successfully, who are not less than eighteen years old and not more than twenty-two, who produce certificates of good conduct, and who take an engagement to continue for at least ten years in the service of public primary instruction, are then, as before,

* The annual value of an entire scholarship, or student's fee, is in no French training school higher than 400 fr., in none lower than 300 fr.

† "Beaucoup arrivaient possédant à peine les premiers éléments de l'instruction, et nullement préparés pour suivre avec fruit les cours de l'école. Il en résultait un affaiblissement des études dangereux pour l'avenir de l'instruction primaire." [J.-J. Rapet,] *Manuel de Législation et d'Administration de l'Instruction primaire*, p. 157.

‡ See his circular to the rectors, February 2nd, 1855.

nominated by the prefect if he thinks fit, within the limits of the numbers fixed by the Minister for each normal school. It is the prefect, also, who nominates to scholarships and to portions of scholarships on the favourable report of the *Commission de Surveillance*, which, named by the rector on the proposition of the departmental council, has in each normal school the special charge of the discipline and progress of the students. A student who at the end of the year is judged unfit to pass to the course of the following year, is discharged * from the training school.

The training-school examinations are not those which determine the award of the certificate of capacity. To adjudge this, there sits twice a year, in the chief town of every department, an examination-commission † named by the departmental council, and consisting of seven members, of whom one must be a primary inspector of the department, one a minister of the same religious persuasion as the candidate, and two functionaries of public or private instruction. The examination, like the normal school course, is limited to the programme of primary school instruction. Any person aged not less than eighteen years may appear as a candidate, giving a month's notice of such intention. The examination is oral and written. Exercises in dictation and grammar, handwriting, the four rules of arithmetic (including vulgar and decimal fractions), and in the composition of a narrative or a school-report, are performed by the candidates. For each of these four exercises is allowed a space of time not exceeding three-quarters of an hour. The commission collects and judges these written exercises; the candidate who has failed in them is not allowed to continue his examination any further. Those who have performed them satisfactorily are called up in turn before the commission, and examined orally in reading, religious knowledge, grammar, and arithmetic. The religious examination is always conducted by the minister of the candidate's own persuasion. A quarter of an hour is allowed for each

* The prefect dismisses, *sur l'avis du directeur, la commission de surveillance entendue*. See *Décret du* 26 *Décembre* 1855, Art. 24, 25.

† Law of March 15th, 1850, Art. 46. Regulated by a ministerial circular of February 15th, 1860.

of these oral exercises, and the proper certificate-examination is concluded.*

Those who desire to be examined in all or any of the optional or *facultative* branches of primary instruction, now make known their wishes. A candidate who has passed the obligatory examination with difficulty is not allowed to be examined any further. The others are examined in those subjects which they select. Teachers who have obtained the simple certificate on a former occasion may present themselves for examination in the facultative subjects; but they must take all of them. In each subject the examination is oral, and lasts but a quarter of an hour. When all is concluded, the commissioners draw up a list, in order of merit, of the candidates who have satisfied them; if they differ in opinion respecting a candidate, the majority decides. This list is then forwarded to the rector, who issues the certificate. There is but one grade of certificate; but on the simple instrument is entered a special mention of those facultative subjects in which the candidate may have elected to be examined, and of the degree of satisfaction which he has given to the examiners.

Fortified with this document, the future teacher, if a member of a religious association, awaits his appointment to a public school of his order by the prefect, on the presentation of his superior. If a layman, he has his name entered on the list of admissibility †, drawn up yearly for each department by the departmental council, and from which the prefect makes his nominations to lay schools. This list contains notes respecting each name borne on it, and here the students of normal schools reap the benefit of favourable reports on their ability and conduct by the commission of their normal school.

The legislation of 1850, in its hostility to the normal schools and their high training, provided ‡ that a *certificate of stage*, issued by the departmental council to persons who had taught

* Women-candidates are also examined in needlework by ladies delegated for this office by the rector. The oral examination of men is public, that of women private.

† Decree of October 7th, 1850, Art. 13.

‡ Law of March 15th, 1850, Art. 47.

satisfactorily for three years as assistants in public schools authorised to receive them, might henceforth replace the certificate of capacity. This certificate of stage involved no examination, and its introduction threatened to lower the standard of attainment in public teachers. Happily few departmental councils consented to authorise any *stagiary schools* at all; in the few departments where they were established, they proved failures, and they have now been generally abandoned. At the present moment, for the chief teachers of the public schools in France, the obligation of the certificate may be said to be universal.*

I fear I may have wearied the general reader by these details, but for English inspectors and schoolmasters they will not, I think, be without interest. I will remind these, if they are disposed to make light of such an examination as I have described, that the French certificate is not a prize, but an obligation; that it carries no money with it; that it is a negative not a positive test of merit. I will remind our Privy Council Office that it is greatly to be doubted whether, if the State imposes the certificate-test on the whole body of its schoolmasters, the negative form be not the most advisable, and even the sole possible. When the test is of this kind, it will generally happen, as I found in the French schools, that the pitch of the master's instruction to his best scholars is higher than that of his certificate examination. So too, in England, the pitch of a master's instruction, in the upper forms of Rugby or Harrow, is higher than that of the bare degree examination obligatory upon himself. But in our elementary schools the whole instruction is pitched immeasurably below the scale of attainment demanded as indispensable from our certificated masters; and every stranger who had read our

* In lieu of the regular certificate, the law accepts, besides the certificate of stage above mentioned, the diploma of bachelor of arts, the certificate of entrance from one of the *écoles spéciales*, and the title of actual minister of one of the recognised religious persuasions.—Law of March 15th, 1850. Ministers of religion hardly ever in France become primary schoolmasters; and the degree of bachelor, or the certificate of entrance into an *école spéciale*, involves a much severer examination than the regular certificate of capacity.

teachers' examination questions, would inevitably be disappointed in our elementary schools. In truth, we impose an examination for honours as our schoolmasters' only access to a bare degree.

CHAPTER XIII

The Popular Education of France and England Compared.—Legislation

I have now briefly to sum up the main points of the French system; and I will then in conclusion attempt, although with great diffidence, to give some estimate of its effects upon the French people.

First, then, with respect to a question which meets every system of education upon the threshold—the great question, shall it be secular, or shall it be religious? The French system is religious; not in the sense in which all systems profess to be more or less religious, in inculcating the precepts of a certain universal and indisputable morality: it inculcates the doctrines of morality in the only way in which the masses of mankind ever admit them, in their connection with the doctrines of religion. I believe that the French system is right. When I come to speak of Holland I shall have more to say of this matter, and shall perhaps be able to give some important information concerning it; at present I content myself with saying that this side the French system has chosen. Here it coincides with the systems of England and Germany. Morality—but dignified, but sublimed by being taught in connection with religious sentiment; but legalised, but empowered by being taught in connection with religious dogma—this is what the French system makes the indispensable basis of its primary instruction.

But what dogma? Secular education is one; it would be well if religious education could be one also. It would be well, unquestionably, if there reigned everywhere one truly catholic religious faith, embracing all the faithful in a common bond. But the spirit of sect exists; it has committed its ravages; it is necessary to take account of them. Forcibly to repress it is impossible, except by evoking a spirit more noxious than even the spirit of sect—the spirit of religious persecution. But the French system does not seek divisions; it accepts those that are radical, irreconcilable. All minor shades of division that are not incurably separate, that may without violence to their nature combine, it leaves to combine, it does not deepen by distinguishing them. Protestantism and Roman Catholicism, the great rival systems of authority and inquiry;—Judaism, inveterate in its fated isolation;—these it recognises as necessary, irreconcilable, religious divisions in a modern State of Western Europe. It recognises these, but it recognises no other. In an empire of thirty-six millions it recognises no other.

Here the English system diverges. In Great Britain, in a population of 21,000,000, it recognises no less than seven religious incompatibilities. If it followed the French example, it would accept, as denominations essentially distinct, at most only Anglicanism, non-Anglican Protestantism, Roman Catholicism, Judaism. As it is, it distinguishes Anglican Protestantism, the Biblicalism of the British and Foreign School Society, the Protestantism of Wesleyan Methodism, the Protestantism of the Orthodox Church of Scotland, the Protestantism of the Free Church of Scotland, the Protestantism of the Episcopalian Church of Scotland, and Roman Catholicism.*

But the divergence does not stop here. The French system recognises certain religious divisions in the population; but it does not divide itself in order to meet them. It maintains its own unity, its own impartiality; in their relations with the State, with the civil power, all denominations have to meet upon a common ground; the State does not make itself denominational, they have to make themselves national. When the Concordat was under discussion, neither supplication nor adroitness could prevail with Napoleon to give to the State itself an exclusive denominational character; he steadily refused to call the Roman Catholic religion the religion of the State; he would only consent to call it, what it undoubtedly was, the religion of the majority of the French nation. State-inspection represents the

* We have an eighth class of schools in Poor-law Union Schools; but here the distinction (though perhaps needless), is at any rate based on administrative, not on religious, grounds.

unity of the civil power, not the divisions of rival sects. It takes care that children learn, in the public schools, each the doctrines of his own religion; but it protects each, in learning these, from the intolerance of the other, and itself remains neutral, that it may check intolerance the better. The State, therefore, owes no account to any man of the religious persuasion of its inspectors: for it is not as religious sectaries they have to discharge their duties, but as civil servants; and the moment they begin to discharge them as religious sectaries, they discharge them ill.

In England the State makes itself denominational with the denominations. It offers to them no example of a civil unity in which religious divisions are lost; in which they meet as citizens, though estranged as sectaries. It makes its inspectors Anglican with the Anglicans, Roman Catholic with the Roman Catholics, Orthodox Presbyterian with the Old Church of Scotland, Free Church with the New. It does not hold itself aloof from the religious divisions of the population; it enters into them.

What has been the result? By dint of concession to the denominational spirit, by dint of not maintaining an impartial and unsectarian character, the State, in England, has been betrayed into a thousand anomalies, and has created a system far more irritating to sectarian susceptibilities than if it had regarded none of them. More than four-fifths of the population of France profess Roman Catholicism, and about one-three-hundredth part of French inspection is in the hands of Roman Catholic ecclesiastics. One half of the population of England profess Anglicanism, and more than three-fourths of English inspection is in the hands of Anglican ecclesiastics. I heard the other day of an English National school aided by public money, the only school in the place, which had for one of its regulations that no child of dissenting parents should be admitted unless he consented to be rebaptized. I saw with my own eyes, the other day, in a British school aided by public money, a printed placard stuck up in a conspicuous place in the schoolroom, offering a reward of 10*l.* to any Roman Catholic who could prove, by text, ten propositions; such as, that we ought to adore the Virgin Mary, that we ought to pray for the dead, that St. Peter was unmarried, that he ever was Bishop of Rome, and so on. Is it tolerable that such antics should be played in schools on which the grant of public money confers a public character? Would it be possible that they should be played in a public school in France, where the State permits liberty of conscience, but not liberty of persecution? But it is said that the State, in England, has bound itself not to interfere with the management of the schools which it aids. True; but whom does this answer excuse? It excuses the functionaries who administer the system, not the State which made and maintains it. No State has the right thus to shackle its own reason and its own equity.

The French system, having undertaken to put the means of education within its people's reach, has to provide schools and teachers. Here, again, it altogether diverges from ours, which has by no means undertaken to put the means of education within the people's reach, but only to make the best and richest elementary schools better and richer. Should it ever undertake what the French system has undertaken, perhaps it is in the plan for the provision of schools that it will find its predecessor happiest. Where everything is left to be done by voluntary effort, schools where most needed are not established at all. Where everything, again, is left to be done by the State, there is wasteful extravagance and local apathy. Where everything, finally, is left to be done by the parish, there is niggardly pinching. I read the other day that in Canada the great difficulty in the rating system there followed is that the local boards starve their schools. The French plan places its schools chiefly, but not absolutely, in the hands of local boards; it tempers the parsimony of the parish with the more liberal views of the central power; and between the parish contributor and the State contributor it places a third contributor of less narrow spirit than the first, of more economical spirit than the second,—the Department or County.

I am bound to add, however, that in one most important particular, its provision for teachers, the French system has recoiled, through fear of expense, from making adequate use of the machinery at its disposal. The best authorities are all agreed that the fixed salary of the teacher was put by the law of 1833 too low, and that the law of 1850 ought to have raised it directly, instead of attempting, in a circuitous manner, to provide a palliative for its insufficiency. At present the lay teachers tend to quit their profession as soon as they can for some more profitable career; if it were not for the inducement offered by the exemption from military service, it would be difficult to recruit their ranks. It is in vain that the State offers to them the lure of honourable mentions, medals of bronze and of silver *, and even the rank of academic officer, with the privilege of wearing an official coat with a palm embroidered on the collar †; these public distinctions to the teacher are excellent, but they are of no avail so long as he is utterly underpaid.

The State has provided schools and teachers; under what authority shall it place them? Of inspection, the great guarantee of efficiency, it has abundance; it has first inspectors-general, then rectors and academy-inspectors, then primary inspectors, then cantonal delegates, then the parish authorities, the mayor and the minister of the persuasion followed by the scholars. But what authority shall give effect to the representations of all this inspection? Local school-committees, said the law of 1833; rectors of academies, representing the Department of Public Instruction, said the law of 1852; the prefect, representing the Home Department, says the present law. The local school-committees had undoubtedly performed their work ill. Perhaps in England a well-chosen county committee might safely be intrusted with the functions which in France, under the law of 1833, the district committee performed so unsatisfactorily; but to give them to the more narrowly local body, to the communal committee, to the parish vestry, would be to destroy your school-system, however promising. The Canadian report which I just now quoted says that another of the great difficulties with which the public school-system of Canada has to contend, is the utter unfitness of the local school-commissioners for their functions. To superintend the actual expenditure of money voted, to inspect, and to report to a higher authority, is the proper province of the parochial committee. It cannot safely

* In the year 1857 (the latest for which I have any returns), the sum spent by the State on medals for teachers was 2728 fr. 70 c.

† *Décret du 9 Décembre* 1850.

be trusted with full powers over the teacher. The most liberal persons in France consider it proved, by the working of the law of 1833, that, for public schools, it is expedient to give the ultimate power of confirming or dismissing the teacher to some central authority. With us, indeed, the central Government has no power to get rid of a schoolmaster, the most destructive or the most negligent. It can dismiss a school inspector, but it cannot dismiss a school teacher. Our system provides its chief educational shepherd with abundant resources against his own watch-dogs; with none against the wolf. In France, the local committees no longer retain powers which they showed themselves unfit to exercise. But from the local committees to the prefect is a prodigious step. The prefect and the Home Department, stern authorities of police and public order, are scarcely the proper authorities for dealing with schools and teachers, unless some actual breach of the law has been committed. The Ministry of Public Instruction, with its academies and rectors, is in some sort a literary department of State; and with this character it has something of the humanity of letters. The teachers themselves would prefer the government of the rector to that of the prefect. It is true that the prefect generally acts on the advice of the rector's representative, the academy-inspector; but the rector himself, and the Minister his superior, are much the fittest persons to act upon this advice, and would act upon it with quite sufficient stringency.

The machinery of French inspection is perhaps a little redundant. It is found impossible to obtain from the cantonal delegates, unpaid and with occupations of their own, that regular intervention in the details of primary instruction which the Government solicits from them. Possibly, if they gave it, it might be found to bring with it as many difficulties as advantages. A general supervision, with the office of keeping the higher school-authorities informed, so that the teacher may feel that neither his efforts nor his negligence escape notice,—this is, perhaps, all that can be judiciously asked of the local authorities, or that they can properly give. All above the cantonal delegates is excellent. The primary inspectors are the very life of the school-system; their inspection is a reality, because made when not expected: the Nancy inspector who went round the schools of that town with me, had a pass-key by which he let himself into any one of them when he pleased, and he told me that he entered every public school in the town fifty times in the year. The academy-inspectors, receiving the reports of the primary inspectors, and themselves in connection with the sixteen academies of France, supply local centres for dealing with the mass of details received from the primary inspectors, and thus relieve the central office in Paris. The four inspectors-general, in personal communication with the school-authorities, the primary inspectors, and the Minister, preserve the latter from the danger of falling a victim to the routine of his own bureaux, while he also obtains from four picked and superior men a unity of appreciation of school-matters which he would seek for in vain from the 275 primary inspectors, chosen necessarily with less advantage of selection. If I were asked to name the four deficiencies most unanimously remarked in our system by the most competent foreign judges whom I met, they would be these:—first, the want of district-centres for managing the current details of school business, and the consequent inundation of our London office with the whole of them; secondly, the inconceivable prohibition to our primary inspectors to inspect without previous notice; thirdly, the denial of access into the ranks of the primary inspectors to the most capable public schoolmasters; fourthly, and above all, the want of inspectors-general.

Having established schools with due safeguards, does the French system compel the children of France to enter them? It does not; in France, education is not compulsory. A few advocates for making it so I met with; but, in the opinion of most of those with whom I conversed, the difficulties are insuperable. Perhaps, for a government to be able to force its people to school, that people must either be generally well-off, as in America; or placid and docile, as in Germany; or ardently desirous of knowledge, as in Greece. But the masses in France, like the masses in England, are by no means well-off, are stirring and self-willed, are not the least in the world bookish. The gradual rise in their wealth and comfort is the only obligation which can be safely relied on to draw such people to school. What Government can do, is to provide sufficient and proper schools to receive them as they arrive.

CHAPTER XIV

The Popular Education of France and England Compared.—Results on the People

In what numbers has the population yet, in France, actually arrived in the public schools? What proportion of it remains wholly untaught? What sort of education do those who are taught carry away with them? These are questions which, as I have already said, cannot all of them at present be satisfactorily answered. I believe, however, that the great mass of the population now passes, at some time or other, through the schools. It is an indisputable fact that the attendance in the schools for adults has been for some time falling off, because the actual adult population has grown up in possession of the elementary knowledge which these schools offer. It is a great thing that the primary schools do actually exist almost everywhere in France; they are there, they are always at the population's service, without long journeys, without high fees, without unjust conditions. It is something that the demand for children's labour is as yet considerably less in agricultural France than in manufacturing England. But I should be deceiving the reader if I led him to suppose that the French people exhibits any real ardour in seeking education for its children, or that the bait of the gain to be drawn from his child's labour is, when offered, one whit better resisted by a French than by an English parent. Nay, in the great manufacturing region of France, in the Department of the North *, public opinion and positive law prove far less

* Even from the well-educated Alsace the inspectors report that the mill-schools are far too few in number, and that the manufacturers *exploitent les enfants,* in defiance of the law. But in the Gard I found that the companies carrying on works had very generally established schools for their workmen's children. There are very good schools of this kind at Alais. They are private schools (*écoles libres*), and the schooling is free; none of the children are half-timers, as they do not go to work till they are fourteen. The teachers are well-paid, receiving

powerful than in England to contend with the cupidity of the employer, the necessities of the employed. The French law prescribes that the child's day, in a manufactory, shall be of ten hours; the law is not observed; the child works habitually for twelve. Of these ten hours the law commands that two at least shall be given to schooling; when these two hours are given at all, the master habitually makes the child's day, already of twelve hours in defiance of the law, of fourteen hours, in order not to lose the time taken for schooling. In hardly any of the manufactories is there a school for the children employed.* In the towns without great manufactures, and in the agricultural districts, more children do, I believe, attend school than in similar places in England. But even these attend very irregularly, and are very easily withdrawn; there are just the same complaints from the French inspectors as from the English, of the desertion of schools in summer and autumn. I have looked through the returns, for a number of departments, of the declarations made by conscripts when drawn for the army, as to their own ability to read and write; the number of those declaring themselves unable to do either is remarkable †, and contrasts

---

70*l.* or 80*l.* a year; and the best teachers quit the public schools to take charge of these schools of private companies.

* I have great pleasure in saying that M. Magin mentioned to me, as a signal exception, a manufactory at Coudekerke-Branche, near Dunkirk, belonging to an Englishman, in which there is an excellent school for both the girls and the boys employed on the establishment.

† Even here, however, there is progress. In the Drôme (academy of Grenoble) 42 per cent. of the conscripts drawn in 1842 declared themselves unable to read and write; of those drawn in 1855, only 26 per cent. In the Aube (academy of Dijon) the conscripts declaring themselves unable to read and write were 21 per cent. in 1845, 13 per cent. in 1854. In the Haute Marne (in the same academy-district) they were 27 per cent. in 1828, only 7 per cent. in 1855. In the Doubs (academy of Besançon) they were, even in 1837, but 6 per cent.; in 1855 they were 3 per cent. In the Haute Saône, 21 per cent. in 1835, 9 per cent. in 1855. In the district of the Academy of Paris, there were drawn in 1835, for the department of the Eure and Loir, 738 conscripts unable to read and write; in 1855, 522. For the Seine and Marne, 727 in 1835, 380 in 1855.

Even in the most backward part of the Paris district, the department of the Cher, the number of schools has more than doubled in

strangely with the alleged attendance of the primary schools. It is true that conscripts show almost always an impulse, upon these occasions, to cheapen themselves as much as possible, and to acknowledge nothing which may make them more eligible objects for a service which they try to escape. Officers have assured me that men often turned out to be able to read and write perfectly well, who when drawn had declared themselves incapable of doing either. But it is true, also, that many a peasant-boy does actually lose all his school-learning between the day when he leaves school, and the day when he is drawn for the army; he is not the least studious by nature, and his class are not the least studious; they have an incorrigible preference for the knowledge to be acquired at the cabaret, at the village-ball, in the great world, over that to be acquired in solitude and from books. Even when fully retained, the instruction carried away from a French primary school is also, undoubtedly, most elementary; although, as I have before said, not quite so elementary as one who merely reads the programme in the law would think *, and although not, in my opinion, more elementary than, at present, the instruction offered by a state like France or like England to all its people, ought to be and must be. Still, unquestionably, as regards the actual school-learning of the French peasant, the merit of the French system is more in its probable future than in its actual past or present:—the schools are there.

Yet—and I now come to the last of the topics which I undertook to treat—I am convinced that, small as may be the result yet produced in actual school learning by the school legislation

---

the last twenty years, the number of scholars more than tripled; the number of girl-scholars has sextupled. In the most backward department of all France, the Nièvre, the number of inhabitants able to read and write is declared to have nearly tripled in the twenty years from 1835 to 1855.

* Taking at hazard 42 communal schools in the department of the Haute Garonne, I found that, of the *facultative matters* of primary instruction, history and geography were taught in 37 of them, geometry in 28, drawing in 23, singing in 19, physical science in 1, agriculture in none. Much is said in France about agricultural instruction for the elementary and normal schools; but up to the present time next to nothing has been done.

of France, the result which it has produced upon the temper and intelligence of the population has not been unimportant. But I shall have need of all the reader's indulgence while I attempt to exhibit this important but somewhat impalpable result.

The intelligence of the French people is well known; in spite of their serious faults, in spite of their almost incredible ignorance, it places them among the very foremost of ancient or modern nations. It is the source of their highest virtue, (for the bravery of this people is rather a physical than a moral virtue), of a certain natural equity of spirit in matters where most other nations are intolerant and fanatical. I suppose that this intelligence is a thing not altogether peculiar and innate in the people of France; if it were, the upper classes, adding high culture to this exclusive natural gift, would exhibit over the upper classes of other nations a superiority of which they certainly have not given proof. If it is culture which develops this intelligence in the higher ranks of all nations, then of some culture or other the French masses, in spite of their want of book-learning, must be feeling the beneficent operation, if they show an intelligence which the masses of other nations do not possess. This culture they do actually receive; many influences are at work in France which tend to impart it to them; amongst these influences I number their school-legislation.

This works partly by its form, partly by its spirit. By its form it educates the national intelligence, no otherwise than as all French legislation tends thus to educate it; but even this is worth noticing. It is not a light thing that the law, which speaks to all men, should speak an intelligible human language, and speak it well. Reason delights in rigorous order, lucid clearness, and simple statement. Reason abhors devious intricacy, confused obscurity, and prolix repetition. It is not unimportant to the reason of a nation, whether the form and text of its laws present the characters which reason delights in, or the characters which reason abhors. Certainly the text of an English Act of Parliament never carried to an uneducated English mind anything but bewilderment. I have myself heard a French peasant quote the Code Napoleon; it is in every one's hands; it is its rational form, hardly less than its rational spirit, that the Code has to thank for a popularity which makes half the nations of Europe desirous to adopt it. If English law breathed in its spirit the wisdom of angels, its form would make it to foreign nations inaccessible. The style and diction of all the modern legislation of France are the same as those of the Code. Let the English reader compare, in their style and diction alone, M. Guizot's education-law, printed at the end of this volume *, with the well-known bill of a most sincere and intelligent friend of English education, Sir John Pakington. Certainly neither was the French law drawn by M. Guizot himself, nor the English bill by Sir John Pakington; each speaks the current language of its national legislation. But the French law, (with a little necessary formality, it is true,) speaks the language of modern Europe; the English bill speaks the language of the Middle Ages, and speaks it ill. I assert that the rational intelligible speech of this great public voice of her laws has a directly favourable effect upon the general reason and intelligence of France.

From the form I pass to the spirit. With still more confidence I say—It is not a light thing for the reason and equity of a nation that her laws should boldly utter prescriptions which are reasonable and equitable. It is not a light thing for the spread, among the French masses, of a wise and moderate spirit on the vital and vexed questions of religion and education, that the law of 1833 should say firmly, *Le vœu des pères de famille sera toujours consulté et suivi en ce qui concerne la participation de leurs enfants à l'instruction religieuse*. It is not a light thing that the whole body of modern French legislation on these critical questions should hold a language equally firm, equally liberal. To this it is owing that in a sphere where the popular cry, in other countries, either cannot be relied on or is sure to be wrong, there exists in France a genial current of sound public opinion, blowing steadily in the right quarter. To this it is owing that from dangers which perpetually thwart and threaten intellectual growth in other countries, intellectual growth in France is comparatively secure. To this, finally, it is owing that even on questions beyond this sphere—if they assume a sufficient generality and do not demand a large knowledge of particular facts, of which the mass of Frenchmen is deplorably ignorant—the habit

* [Arnold's appendices are not printed in this edition.]

of intelligence continues in the French people to be active and to enlighten. It is with truth that M. Guizot says in his latest work: "C'est la grandeur de notre pays que *les esprits ont besoin d'être satisfaits en même temps que les intérêts*." *

I wish to make perfectly clear to the reader what I mean. I am by no means praising the whole legislation of the French State. I am by no means praising the general principle of action by which the State, in France, has been guided. There are many points on which it has not informed its people at all; there are many points on which it has informed them ill. It is possible (this is a fair matter for discussion), that, even although on some points it has informed them well, it may have made them pay for that information too high a price. What I say is, that on certain capital points the State in France has by its legislation and administration exercised a directly educative influence upon the reason and equity of its people †, and that of this influence the mental temper of the French people does actually show the fruits.

It would be an interesting, but far too lengthy task, to inquire into the causes which have prevented the State, in England, from performing these educative functions for the intelligence of its people. The State in England has shown neither taste nor aptitude for the practice of government as a profound and elaborate

* *Mémoires*, vol. ii. p. 235.

† To give a curious practical instance. In Corsica, the condition of the woman had for years been that of a mere beast of burden. In order to raise it, the French Government determined to put the elementary schools of the island in her hands. Under M. Fortoul's administration a normal school for young women was established at Ajaccio, and 18,000 francs a year granted for its support. Wherever it was possible, the charge of the primary school was given to a mistress. At first the men strenuously resisted for their children the degradation of being taught by that inferior creature, a woman; but the Government stood firm. Women are now established in charge of a great number of the schools of Corsica, and the consideration and respect paid to the sex has notably increased.

Again: Corsican vengeance is proverbial. In the hope of creating in the young generation a better sentiment, the Government has, in all the schools of the island, covered the walls with texts inculcating forgiveness of injuries, and against private revenge.

art; it has done what was absolutely indispensable, and has left its people to do the rest, if it could, for itself.

Its people has willingly acquiesced in a non-interference agreeable to its independent spirit, and in great measure imposed by its mistrust. Doubtless, the vigour of the national character has under this state of things greatly benefited. Yet it has its inconveniences. The State in England administers so little, so much dreads the suspicion of undue usurpation, that, when occasionally called upon to administer on a great scale, it finds its organism cramped by disuse and apprehension; it moves as a man, whose limbs had been bound for years, would move when first set free and told to walk. The people, with no help from a power greater than its own, with no suggestions from an intelligence higher than its own, fails in functions for which the intelligence and power of an ordinary individual are not sufficient. How often one is forced to say of it, when one sees it attempting these functions, that it seems, *propter* libertatem libertatis *perdere causas;*—to have won the mechanism of free institutions through its energy, to lack the means of turning them to good account through its ignorance! How often may one observe, in any local community in England, that almost everything which individual energy has to do, is well done; almost everything which the collective reason of the community has to do, is ill done! Still, there are some remarkable instances in which, even in England, the national intelligence has been positively influenced by the action of Government. The legislation of free trade—at first established, not in virtue of an irresistible national conviction, but by the initiative of a great Minister and by the exertions of an active party which, though numerous and intelligent, was still a party—has ended by itself creating in its own favour that national sentiment which it did not find, and by educating public opinion on political economy in a sense which the best judges pronounce sound, and to a height to which the public opinion of no other nation has yet been educated. But matters of trade and commerce concern the direct material interests of a nation. With these every government must perforce deal; and here, besides, the English State is on a ground which it imagines solid and secure. With the moral and spiritual interests of a nation, governments find themselves less imperiously called to deal; and here, besides, the English State is on a ground which it imagines shifting and unsafe. It deals with them as little as it can; it sometimes deals with them as if it was the organ of the popular clamour which shouts one thing to-day and another to-morrow; it hardly ever deals with them as if it was *the organ of the national reason.*

It even appears unconscious or incredulous that on these matters a national reason exists. It treats all opinions as of an equal value, and seems to think that the irrational, if expressed as loudly as the rational, must weigh with it as much. It seems not to believe that an opinion has any inherent weakness by virtue of being absurd; or that, in confronting it, the strength of superior reason is really any strength at all. Its proceedings in this respect are in very remarkable contrast with those of the State in France. I will give an example of what I mean, and to find it I will not go beyond the subject of education.

In dealing with education, a government must often meet with questions on which there are two opposite opinions, and both rational. If it is wise, it will invariably treat such opinions with due respect, and will be guided, in deciding between them, by the character of the times, the state of the circumstances, the dispositions of its people. Shall public education be in the hands of the clergy or in the hands of the laity?—shall the instruction given in primary schools be exclusively secular, or shall it be also religious?—here are two questions, upon each of which opposite opinions, both having a ground of reason, may fairly be maintained. In inclining to either, in abandoning its own inclinations on the side of either, a government may be taking a course which reason sanctions; at any rate it is giving victory or defeat to arguments of which reason can take cognisance. The national intelligence can at least follow it in its operations. But a government, in dealing with education, will also sometimes meet with opinions which have no ground in reason, which are mere crotchets, or mere prejudices, or mere passions. Will it have the clearness of vision to discern whether they are such, or the courage, if they are, to treat them as such?—that is the question. Will it encourage and illuminate the national intelligence by firmly treating what is unintelligent as unintelligent, what is fanatical as fanatical, in spite of the loudness with which it may be clamoured? or will it wound and baffle and confuse the national intelligence by treating what is unintelligent as if it were intelligent, as if it were a real power, as respectfully to be parleyed with, as possible to be inclined to, as reason herself? The reader will be conscious that the State has sometimes followed, in England, the latter course.

It will be rejoined, I know, that in France the State is absolute, and can crush alike unreason or reason as it pleases. But this is an error. Among the many remarkable words recorded of the first Napoleon, none are more remarkable than those in which, on more than one occasion, he pointed out the limits to the power of the State in France, the limits even to a power such as his own. Of representative institutions, he said, he might allow as little as he pleased; after the anarchy of the Revolution, the nation was demanding a strong government. With the spirit of revolution, with the spirit of reaction, with all party-spirit, he might, with firmness, deal as he pleased; priestly intolerance, Voltairian intolerance, he was strong enough to disregard; only one force even *he* was not strong enough to disregard, and that was a great force of rational and respectable sentiment in the mass of the French people. Happy for him had he always remembered his own words! Happy if he had not pursued an extravagant and personal policy till he made all the rational sentiment of France warmly hostile to him, or coldly indifferent! But what he said is true; it is impossible for the State, in modern France, to go counter to a great current of rational sentiment. It must, in its acts, have its stand upon some ground of reason, and it can afford to treat cheaply only unreason. When a priest demands to rebaptise dissenters admitted to a public school, when a dissenter demands to be exempted from school-taxation because it hurts his conscience to help to maintain schools in which may be taught a religion which he dislikes, such pretensions as these the French State treats as phantoms which it may confidently disdain—for they are *irrational*.

I say, then, that by its form and by its contents, by its letter and by its spirit, by its treatment of reason and by its treatment of prejudice, in what it respects and in what it does not respect, the school-legislation of modern France fosters, encourages, and educates the popular intelligence and the popular equity.

This is a great national advantage. But there are some national disadvantages which sometimes flow, or seem to flow, from national education; disadvantages which those who never inquire beyond the school itself are apt to overlook, but which all those to whom schools are interesting mainly as instruments of general civilisation, will certainly desire to find noticed by me. Some alleged disadvantages there are, which, in France as in England, hardly merit discussion. Eminent personages complained to me that already popular education in France was carried so far that society began to be dislocated by it; that the labourer would no longer stay in his field, nor the artisan in his workshop; that every labourer would be an artisan, every artisan a clerk. This is the language which we have all heard so often, from those who think that the development of society can be arrested because a farmer's wife finds it hard to get a cookmaid. It is sufficient to say to those who hold it, that it is vain for them to expect that the lower classes will be kind enough to remain ignorant and unbettered merely for the sake of saving them inconvenience. But there are other disadvantages which are more serious. I say boldly, that an English or a French statesman might well hesitate to establish an elaborate system of national education, if it were proved to him that the necessary result of such a system must be to produce certain effects which have accompanied it elsewhere—to Prussianise his people or to Americanise it.

I speak with respect of an important nation, which has done great things with small means, and with which rests the future of Germany. To what I say of it, I cannot here give due development; I must leave it to the judgment of the best European observers. But I say that the Prussian people, under its elaborate system of education, has become a studious people, a docile people, a well-informed people, if you will—but also a somewhat pedantic, a somewhat sophisticated people. I say that this pedantry, this formalism, takes away something from a people's vital strength. I say that a people loses under them much of the genial natural character, much of the rude primitive vigour, which are the great elementary force of nations.

I speak with more than respect, with warm interest, of a great nation of English blood, and with which rests, in large measure, the future of the world. With a boundless energy of character, with a boundless field for adventure, the American people has unquestionably not been enervated by education; but under a universal system of comparatively advanced education, without certain correctives, the American people has become an energetic people, a powerful people, a highly-taught people, if you will—but also an overweening, a self-conceited people. I say that this self-conceit takes away much from a nation's vital worth. The two grand banes of humanity, says Spinoza, are indolence and self-conceit: self-conceit is so noxious because it arrests man in the career of self-improvement; because it vulgarises his character and stops the growth of his intellect. The Greek oracle pronounced wisest of men him who was most convinced of his own ignorance: what, then, can be the wisdom of a nation profoundly convinced of its own attainment? After all that has been said, it remains immutably true that "a little knowledge is a dangerous thing," unless he who possesses it knows that it *is* a little; and that he may know this, it is almost indispensable for him to have before his eyes objects which suggest heights of grandeur, or intellect, or feeling, or refinement, which he has never reached. This is the capital misfortune of the American people, that it is a people which has had to grow up without ideals.

The proud day of priesthoods and aristocracies is over, but in their day they have undoubtedly been, as the law was to the Jews, schoolmasters to the nations of Europe, schoolmasters to bring them to modern society; and so dull a learner is man, so rugged and hard to teach, that perhaps those nations which keep their schoolmasters longest are the most enviable. The great ecclesiastical institutions of Europe, with their stately cathedrals, their imposing ceremonial, their affecting services; the great aristocracies of Europe, with their lustre of descent, their splendour of wealth, their reputation for grace and refinement—have undoubtedly for centuries served as ideals to ennoble and elevate the sentiment of the European masses. Assuredly, churches and aristocracies often lacked the sanctity or the refinement ascribed to them; but their effect as distant ideals was still the same: they remained above the individual, a beacon to the imagination of thousands; they stood, vast and grand objects, ever present before the eyes of masses of men in whose daily avocations there was little which was vast, little which was grand; and they preserved these masses from any danger of overrating with vulgar self-satisfaction an inferior culture, however broadly sown, by the exhibition of a standard of dignity and refinement still far above them.

The masses of the great American people have grown up without this salutary standard. Neither in Church nor in State have they had the spectacle of any august institution before their eyes. The face of the land is covered with a swarm of sects, all of them without dignity, some of them without decency. They have no aristocracy. Accustomed to see nothing grander or more venerable than himself and his fellows, but accustomed to see everywhere a certain mediocre culture diffused with indisputable breadth, the common American, who possesses this, and who sees none higher, grows up with a sense of advantage, which is natural, but also with a sense of perfect self-satisfaction, which is deteriorating. The occasional contact with real superiority finds him half incredulous, half resentful. Thus widely cultured, but thus limited in its culture, and thus unconscious of its limitation, the American people offers a spectacle full of interest, indeed, but inspiring the most grave reflections; —the spectacle of a people which threatens to lose its power of intellectual and moral growth.*

Is it to be apprehended (the question involuntarily arises) that diffused and improved education may possibly make the common people of France and England pedantic like the Prussians, or self-conceited like the Americans? England and France have many safeguards against either danger. Against the first they have ample security in the extraordinary fulness with which both retain, amidst all their civilisation, the activity of

* The above was written at the beginning of last year, when the important events now agitating the American States had not yet occurred.

what the poet calls "the savage virtues of the race." In both, though manifesting itself in very different forms, is stubbornly operant a constitutional preference for the animal over the intellectual life; excessive in one point of view, indeed, requiring greatly to be tempered by education; but, in another point of view, natural and reassuring. In the figured language of which he is a master, M. Michelet said to me of his own people, that it was a *nation de barbares, civilisée par la conscription.* The civilising influence of the conscription may be matter for question; but there can be no question that the masses, both of the French and of the English people, retain a superabundance of the native and barbarous vigour of primitive man, which book-learning may wholesomely temper, but will never vanquish.

Against the second danger the preservatives which England possesses must be evident to every one. The most aristocratic people in the world, as one of the most eloquent of its admirers called it, has naturally the aristocratic virtue of not too easily admiring; it has seen so much which is grand and splendid that it is not likely to be unduly enchanted with a mediocre culture, even when that culture is its own. Democratic France, it might at first sight seem, can have no such safeguards. But it must not be forgotten through what an education of hierarchies and grandeurs the French people has passed. The Revolution is of yesterday; the imagination of the French people was fashioned long before. For more than a thousand years France had the most brilliant aristocracy in Europe; her common people were the countrymen of the Montmorencies, the Birons, the Rohans. She is the eldest child of the Roman Catholic Church, a church magnificent even in its decline. At the present hour, when her feudal magnates are gone, when her ecclesiastical magnates are shorn of their splendour, she has an aristocracy to meet the best demands of the modern spirit—an aristocracy the choicest of its class in the world: she has the Institute. The servility which has degraded the scientific and learned societies of some other nations has, in the French Institute, not been allowed to triumph. It is a true aristocracy of the intellect of France; and, in worthily commanding national respect, where great objects to awaken national respect are rare—in rigidly tempering, in the domain of intellect, science, arts, and letters, the natural self-confidence of a democratic society—in making impossible, for the intelligent French common people, a vulgar and provincial self-satisfaction with a low rate of culture, however general—the blessings which it confers on France are incalculable.

I confess that when I contemplate the probable common immunity of England and France from two of the worst dangers which threaten the future progress of other nations, and when I call to mind other points in which the two peoples have at least an important negative resemblance, the interest with which I regard, in France, the constitution and prospects of a great national agent like popular education, becomes unbounded. The two peoples are alike in this, that they are each greater than all others, each unlike to any other. It is in vain that we call the French Celts, and ourselves Teutons: when nations have attained to the greatness of France and England, their peoples can have no profound identity with any people beyond their own borders. Torrents of pedantry have been poured forth on the subject of our Germanic origin; in real truth, we are at the present day no more Germans than we are Frenchmen. By the mixture of our race, by the Latinisation of our language, by the isolation of our country, by the independence of our history, we have long since severed all vital connection with that great German stem which sixteen centuries ago threw out a shoot in this island. France is equally dissociated, by her own eminence, from her once fellow Celtic or Latin races. It is the same with the greatness of the peoples; each is unique, and has no adequate counterpart but in that of the other. From Messina to Archangel, and from Calais to Moscow, there reigns a universal striving after Parisian civilisation; the ideas which move the masses (I do not speak of aristocratic and learned coteries) are, when ideas reach them at all, French ideas. Cross the Straits and you are in another world: in a world where French ideas have not a breath of influence; in a country assuredly not less powerful than France, assuredly of not less weight among the nations than France, but which owes that power and that weight to a different cause—to its incomparable faculty of extending and of establishing *itself*. Each of the two peoples is alike in its immense national feeling; each is alike, too, in its genuine surprise at the shortcomings of the other. An Englishman is astonished that, in an empire boasting of its civilisation, the newspapers should not be allowed to say, on political matters, what they like; that the private citizen should have no remedy by civil action against the public functionary who exceeds his powers; that he should be without the protection which in England the Habeas Corpus Act affords against arbitrary imprisonment. A Frenchman is astonished that, in an empire boasting of its civilisation, out of funds levied upon the Irish people for the maintenance of religion, the church of the small minority should be endowed, the church of the vast majority receive nothing; that, instead of being equal with the rest of the community before the law, a nobleman who commits a crime is not tried by the same judge as another man; that in the English army an officer, in the nineteenth century, buys his office.

To all these resemblances, which I call negative, the two peoples add the important positive resemblance above mentioned: that of all civilised nations they are incomparably the most natural, while of all unsophisticated nations they are incomparably the most civilised.

Well, then, to two nations thus alike in greatness, and so constituted that education can only augment their power and worth, what system of education do their Governments offer? In France, a national system, which, though very unpretending, is all that a government can prudently attempt to make universal—a system fixing a low level, certainly, of popular instruction, but one which the mounting tide of national wealth and well-being will inevitably push up higher. And this system is so framed as not only not to favour popular unreason or popular intolerance, but positively to encourage and educate popular reason and popular equity. In England, a system not national, which has undoubtedly done much for superior primary instruction, but which for elementary primary instruction has done very little. That it may accomplish something important for the latter, some have conceived the project of making it national. Against this project there are, it seems to me, grave objections. It is a grave objection, that the system is over-centralised—that it is too negligent of local machinery—that it is inordinately expensive. It is a graver, that to make it national would be to make national a system not salutary to the national character in the very points where that character most needs a salutary corrective; a system which, to the loud blasts of unreason and intolerance, sends forth no certain counterblast; which submissively accompanies the hatefulest and most barren of all kinds of dispute, religious dispute, into its smallest channels;—stereotypes every crotchet, every prejudice, every division, by recognising it; and suggests to its recipients no higher rationality than it finds in them.

CHAPTER XV

Popular Education in French Switzerland

I arrived in Switzerland at the end of June, and found the primary schools just closed for the holidays. Holidays are long in Switzerland, and I could not wait there until they should be over. The Normal School at Lausanne—the only normal school in French Switzerland—was also closed. To see the Swiss schools in actual operation, therefore, I found impossible.

I regretted this the less because there is no dispute as to the quality of these schools, which in Geneva, Vaud, and Neufchâtel, are confessedly among the best in Europe. Schools exist everywhere; they are well supplied with efficient teachers and most numerously attended.* As to the actual merit of the schools themselves there exist, therefore, no doubts requiring a personal inspection to resolve them. What I wished to learn was, the system under which these schools were established, the degree of completeness with which that system had fulfilled the designs which its authors had in view, and the influence which this system, combined with the other circumstances of their condition, tends to exercise upon the population.

This I could learn even though the schools were in vacation. Both at Geneva and at Lausanne I had the advantage of consulting persons among the best informed and the most intelligent in Europe, to whom private letters of introduction had given me access. Recommended by the kind offices of the British Minister and the British Consul to the Government authorities, I received from them the most courteous attention, and official information which they alone could command. At Lausanne I had the

* For a view of the present situation of primary instruction in all the principal Cantons, both German and French, of Switzerland, see the Table (compiled from official documents) at the end of this volume. [The appendices are not printed in this edition.]

pleasure of conversing with the President of the Council of State, with the Councillor at the head of the Department of Public Instruction, and with the Director of the Normal School, on the state of popular education in the important Canton of Vaud. At Geneva, M. Piguet, the Councillor of State charged with the Department of Public Instruction, not only gave me oral information of the greatest value, but had the kindness to procure for me the whole body of printed documents relating to public education in the French Cantons. These I have carefully studied, and of that study I now proceed to state very briefly the result, controlled by the explanations with which I was furnished on the spot.

I have to speak of five Cantons;—Geneva, Vaud, Fribourg, Neufchâtel, and the Valais. Of these, Geneva has a population of 66,000; Vaud, of 206,000; Fribourg, of 100,000; Neufchâtel, of 80,000; the Valais, of from 80,000 to 90,000. In Geneva, popular instruction has long prospered, although in the Catholic communes added by the Treaty of Vienna to the territory of the Canton it is more backward than in the rest of the State, where Protestantism, ever since the Reformation, has fostered it. In Vaud, likewise, it has long been well cared for. The industrious and thriving Canton of Neufchâtel, which has redoubled its activity since its separation from Prussia, has lately bestowed zealous care upon its primary instruction, and is at present, of all the French Cantons, that in which it most flourishes. Of Fribourg I shall speak presently. The poverty and wretchedness of the Valaisans, which every traveller has noticed, make their primary schools much inferior to those of the four richer French Cantons. But the school-system of all five was, until very recently, the same in its main outlines; it was, in each, a consequence of the triumph of the democratic and anti-clerical party; it was, in most, a system designed to put public education in harmony with the new democratic constitutions established after the war of the Sonderbund, in 1847. It was founded by law in Vaud in 1846, in Geneva and Fribourg in 1848, in the Valais in 1849, in Neufchâtel in 1850. I shall first notice the points in which these laws mostly agree; special points in which they differ I shall notice afterwards.

It is the general scope of all of them to base Swiss education upon the "principles of Christianity and democracy." * Religious instruction is to be given, but it is regarded as the proper province of the minister of religion, not of the schoolmaster; and it is the only part of the instruction with which the minister is permitted to interfere. Into the ordinary school-lessons the teacher is forbidden to introduce anything of religious dogma; the hours for religious instruction are strictly limited, and, if this instruction is given by the teacher at all, it must be at the request and under the responsibility of the minister of religion whose place he thus consents to fill. This Christian and democratic education is generally, also, compulsory and gratuitous. It embraces all young persons from their eighth to their sixteenth year. If children are privately educated, the State must be satisfied that their education is sufficient. They are liable to be called up for examination with the scholars of the public schools, and to be transferred by authority to a public school if their instruction is found inferior. A certificate of emancipation attests that the obligatory course of learning has been duly fulfilled.

The communes provide and maintain the public schools; but the State assists them when their resources fall short. Every place with more than twenty children of school-age is, as a general rule, bound to have its school. When the number of scholars exceeds fifty or sixty, a second school must be established, a third when the second school has passed this limit, and so on. Boys and girls attend the same school. Infant schools the communes are not compelled to establish; but the State recommends their establishment, and aids it.

It is needless to say that this public school system is under the control of the State. The supreme executive of each Canton, the Council of State, delegates its controlling functions to a board of public instruction, consisting of two or three members, and presided over by a Councillor of State. But on any

* See, for instance, the preamble to the school law of the Canton Vaud:—"Vu l'article de la Constitution, portant: L'enseignement dans les écoles publiques sera conforme aux principes du christianisme et à ceux de la démocratie," &c.

grave matter an appeal lies from this body to the Council of State itself, and it is the Council alone which has the power to dismiss a teacher. Three out of the five Cantons have school-inspectors. Where there are no school-inspectors, their functions are discharged by the members of the board of public instruction, or by a local body, the communal school-committee. This body, consisting generally of from four to seven members, is named by the municipality. The minister of religion is not a member of it, unless the municipality choose to nominate him. The local committee should visit the schools of its commune not less than once a fortnight, besides holding a public general examination of them once a year.

Teachers must be certificated, and their examination for the certificate is conducted by the central board of public instruction. They are afterwards elected to their situations by competition, and have thus a second examination to undergo. This second examination is conducted by the local school-commission. Their salaries are fixed at about 500 francs a year, with a house and garden.

The instruction given in the primary schools has two or even more degrees.* The subjects taught are religion, reading, writing, grammar, arithmetic and book-keeping, geography, Swiss history, and singing. Instruction is of the elementary or superior degree, according as these subjects are taught with more or less extension. Instruction in both degrees may be given in the same school and by the same master.

In thus regulating popular education the five Cantons generally agree. They do not *exactly* agree, however; and, even where there is agreement in their laws, there is sometimes variety in their practice.

In the Canton of Geneva, instruction is not by law compulsory; in the other four Cantons it is. I was anxious to ascertain

* Six in the Canton of Geneva. In this Canton the scholars who have most distinguished themselves in the two highest degrees may be admitted, on the inspector's attestation, into a public secondary school; and, if poor, may there receive free schooling for one year.—*Règlement général des Écoles primaires et des Écoles moyennes du Canton de Genève,* Geneva, 1859, art. 13, 22, 23.

exactly in what this compulsoriness of instruction consisted, and how far it was really made effectual. I read in the law that parents not sending their children to school were to be warned, summoned, sentenced to fine or imprisonment, according to their various degrees of negligence; I found due provision made for the recovery, by means of the ordinary tribunals, of such a fine; for the execution, by their means, of such a sentence of imprisonment. I asked myself, as the English reader will ask himself,—In the Cantons of Vaud, Fribourg, Neufchâtel, and the Valais, must every child between the ages of seven and fifteen actually be at school all the year round, and, if he is not, are his parents actually punished for it?

In the first place I soon discovered that he need not be at school all the year round. To take one of the poorest of the Cantons, a Canton in which it seemed to me incredible that the compulsory principle should be fully carried out; the Canton Valais. The law of the Canton Valais proclaims that education is compulsory. But it also proclaims that the school-year shall not be of less than—what does the reader suppose?—five months.* It is for five months in the year, then, not for ten, that children in the Valais are obliged to go to school. Again, I take the Canton of Fribourg, and I find that there, also, education is obligatory up to the age of fifteen. But the law gives power to the inspector to exempt from this obligation of attendance at school children who are sufficiently advanced, and "children whose labour their parents cannot do without." What a safety-valve to the high pressure of a compulsory system is here! In the Canton of Fribourg, again, the school-vacations, says the law, must not exceed three months in the year.† These are long holidays for primary schools. But I take the largest and richest of all the French Cantons, the Canton of Vaud. In the Canton of Vaud the law makes attendance at school compulsory on all young persons between the ages of seven and sixteen. Are there no exceptions? I go on reading the law, and I find presently that the local school-committee may grant dispensations to all

* *Loi sur l'Instruction publique*, Sion, 1849; art. 6.—*Règlement du* 5 *Septembre* 1849 *sur les Écoles primaires du Canton du Valais;* art. 29.

† *Loi sur l'Instruction publique*, Fribourg, 1848; art. 54, 60, 53.

children above twelve years of age whose labour is necessary to their parents. It is made a condition, however, that these children continue to attend school a certain number of times in a week. But the master may grant a child leave of absence for two days in the week, the president of the school-committee may grant him leave for a week at a time, the school-committee itself for a month at a time.* Children above twelve years of age, then, may in one way or another get their school-time very much abridged; but, on any children at all, or on any parents, is the obligation written in the law ever actually enforced? At Geneva the best-informed persons did not hesitate to assure me that the obligation of school-attendance in the Canton of Vaud was perfectly illusory. When I mentioned this at Lausanne, it was indignantly denied; I was told that the schools of Vaud were excellently attended, its population almost universally instructed. But of this I had no doubt: so they are everywhere in the prosperous Swiss Cantons; so they are in Geneva, where education is not compulsory. What I wanted to find out was, whether the legal obligation was actually put in force to constrain the attendance of children who without such constraint would not have attended; whether in Vaud, where education is compulsory, children went to school, who in Geneva, where it is not compulsory, would have been at home or at work. I could not find that they did. I was told that it was necessary to execute the law with the greatest tact, with the greatest forbearance; but in plain truth I could not discover that it was really executed at all. But perhaps this is because, in Vaud, the children so universally attend school that the executive has no cause of complaint against them, and no infringement of the law ever occurs? By the kindness of the President I was furnished with a copy of the last published Annual Report of the Council of State of Vaud on all the branches of the Cantonal administration. In that part of the Report which relates to schools, I find the following:—"The number of children attending school has somewhat diminished; this diminution is probably caused by the introduction into the Canton of different branches of industry,

* *Loi du* 12 *Novembre* 1846 *sur l'Instruction publique,* Lausanne, 1854; art. 61, 62, 68, 69.

which give employment to the children in their neighbourhood, who are thus drawn off from school. Under these circumstances *the Council of Public Instruction has great difficulty in reconciling the consideration due to the wants of poor families with the demands of the law.*" Returns are then given to show that from 1846, the date of the law, to 1858, the date of the Report, the number of children attending school has steadily diminished.* The Report then continues:—"There is a great number of children who attend no school. Were the Council of Public Instruction more zealously seconded by the prefects, the municipalities, and the local school-committees, the attendance in the primary schools would not exhibit this serious falling-off. With respect to the attendance at school of those children whose names are actually on the books, even this leaves much to be desired, in spite of the efforts of the Council of Public Instruction."

These words are not mine; they are those of the Government of the Canton. And this is in presence of a law of compulsory education! What compulsory education is in America and in Germany I cannot tell; in the only place where I have been able to examine it closely, it is what I have described. Not that primary instruction is unprosperous in the Canton of Vaud; on the contrary, it is most flourishing. What I say is, that the making it compulsory by law has not there added one iota to its prosperity. Its prosperity is due to the general comfort and intelligence of the population; where these are equally present, as in Geneva, the prosperity of education is equal though there is no compulsion; where these fail, the compulsion of the law is powerless to prevent the inevitable check inflicted on education by their absence.

* There were at school in—

1846 .	34,781 children.	1855 .	30,930 children.
1852 .	32,853 "	1856 .	30,717 "
1853 .	32,061 "	1857 .	30,615 "
1854 .	31,720 "	1858 .	30,484 "

See *Compte rendu par le Conseil d'État du Canton de Vaud sur l'Administration pendant l'année* 1858, *seconde partie*, p. 12.

The school-law of French Switzerland generally, prescribes that primary instruction shall be gratuitous; in point of fact it is gratuitous only in Geneva and in the Valais. In Geneva alone are school-books and materials gratuitously supplied to all the scholars. In the other Cantons all but the poor have to purchase these; and in Vaud, Neufchâtel, and Fribourg, the communes are authorised to exact school-fees from all who can afford to pay them, the poor alone having free admission. It must be remembered, however, that in a communal school supported by communal taxation, every family, however poor, contributes something to its support. Where nearly all are poor, as in the Valais, the bare maintenance thus obtained for the school and its teacher must be accepted as sufficient. Where there is wealth, there is a desire to raise the condition of the school and teacher somewhat above this bare maintenance-point. This is effected in Vaud, Neufchâtel, and Fribourg, by levying school fees upon those scholars who can afford to pay them; it is effected in Geneva by direct grant from the State. The direct State-expenditure on education in the little Canton of Geneva, is on this account much greater than the direct State-expenditure on education in the large Canton of Vaud. In Geneva, in 1859, it was 113,450 francs; in Vaud, in 1858, the last year for which I have any account, it was only 93,002 fr. 50 c.

Perhaps the Canton of Neufchâtel adopts the best course, by leaving those who can afford it to pay their school-fees, while it reserves its own liberality to augment the salaries of the teachers, generally far too low in French Switzerland as in France. In Geneva, indeed, these are much better than in Vaud, Fribourg, or the Valais. In Vaud, where the salaries of teachers have lately been raised, the legal *minimum* of a master's salary is even now fixed at 20*l.* a year, that of a mistress's at 12*l.* a year, the salaries of both rising 2*l.* a year after ten years' service, 4*l.* a year after twenty years' service. In Geneva, a master (or *regent* as he is called in Switzerland) has in the town of Geneva itself a fixed salary of 56*l.* a year, in the other communes of 40*l.* a year; a mistress (or *regentess*) has 36*l.* a year in the town, 28*l.* in the country. Besides this all teachers in the Canton of Geneva have a *casual*, paid by the State, of threepence a month for every child present in school up to the number of 50 children; twopence a month for every child above that number.* But in Neufchâtel the State does much more. Municipalities and their school-committees fix the teachers' salaries †; but these salaries the State, on certain conditions, and in a certain combined proportion with the commune, increases as high as 80*l.* a year. This is the salary of a teacher of the highest class, but all teachers, even those of the *Écoles d'hiver* ‡, have their proportionate augmentation. By this means Neufchâtel, though without a normal school of its own, easily procures as its primary teachers the best of the students trained at Lausanne.

This normal school of Lausanne is the only normal school in French Switzerland. It was attended in 1859 by 94 students, 57 of them being young men, 37 young women. It is conducted by a director, to whom I had the pleasure of paying a long visit, and by 11 masters. There is a lady-superintendent, with an assistant, to take general charge of the young women, and to teach them needlework and domestic economy. The training school is held in a building which furnishes only lecture rooms and an office for the director; the students board in the town, at boarding-houses approved and inspected by the director. The course for young men lasts three years, for young women two years. There are no practising schools. The expense of a young man's training is about 14*l.* a year, that of a young woman's about 12*l.* For the last six years the State has on an average allowed to each student 6*l.* a year towards the expense of his or her training, the rest is paid by the students themselves. From 25 to 30 students go out every year to take charge of schools. The best go to Neufchâtel and Geneva, where the teachers are best paid. Fribourg will probably soon establish a training school of its own; at present it trains its French teachers in private establishments,

* *Loi générale sur l'Instruction publique*, Geneva, 1848; art. 101, 102.

† But for the *minimum* which they propose they must obtain the sanction of the Council of State.—*Loi sur l'Instruction primaire*, Neufchâtel, 1850; art. 59.

‡ Schools open during the winter months only; an institution common in Switzerland, and particularly successful in the Canton of Neufchâtel.

its German teachers in the training schools of German Switzerland.*

The school-law of every Canton requires the teacher to possess a certificate of capacity. But this requirement is not always enforced. In Vaud, for instance, five years' service in a public school legally exempts a teacher from the obligation of the certificate. But this is not all. I have said that teachers are appointed to schools after a competitive examination held by the local school-committee. To this examination no candidate can properly be admitted unless entitled by the certificate of capacity, or by the five years' service. But, where no such candidates present themselves, the law allows school-committees to examine and elect other persons, who may be provisionally continued without a certificate from year to year for five years, at the end of which term they are exempt, as I have mentioned, from the obligation of the certificate. Nor is the examination held by the school-committee any effectual substitute for the certificate-examination held by the Central Education Department. The inefficiency of the examinations conducted by the local school-committees I found generally complained of; on the other hand, the certificates granted by the Central Education Department are real guarantees of capacity. The examination for them extends, as in France, only to the subjects taught in the primary schools, and to the art of teaching; but it is serious, and it is conducted by duly qualified persons.

In Vaud and in Neufchâtel the local school-committees are left to fulfil also the functions elsewhere discharged by inspectors: but they supply the want of State-inspection as inefficiently as they supply the want of State-examination. Geneva, Fribourg, and the Valais have inspectors. There are not two opinions as to the value of the services which may be rendered by these functionaries; and they will probably soon be employed by the two Cantons which are now without them.

The school-laws of Geneva and of Neufchâtel appear to me to be superior to those of Vaud and of Fribourg in this,—that their framers had a more single regard to the welfare of primary

* See *Règlement pour les Écoles Normales du Canton de Vaud*, Lausanne, 1849.

instruction and to that only, than the framers of the others. The framers of the others undoubtedly had zeal for primary instruction; but zeal for the ascendancy of the democratic party was too strongly present to their minds at the same time. They have, therefore, omitted provisions for the welfare of the schools which were of great importance; they have introduced provisions to bind the individual, which on educational grounds have no necessity, and which sometimes defeat their own object, by making the law which sanctions them intolerable.

This has been the case in Fribourg. Fribourg is a very powerful canton; its population, though fanatical, is exceedingly vigorous. Until the war of 1847, it was in the hands of the clerical party: the issue of the Sonderbund struggle gave full power to the enemies of the clerical party, to the democrats. The new government, knowing its adversaries' strength, procured its own nomination for a period of nine years, and, in order to indoctrinate the population with liberal ideas, instituted, by the law of 1848, a very developed system of primary instruction. But nine years of Radical government, and the law of 1848, were insufficient to convert the stiff-necked people of Fribourg. At the first elections which took place after the struggle of 1847—the elections of 1856—the clerical party regained its ascendancy, the democratic party fell, and the law of 1848 fell with its authors instead of saving them. When the English reader is informed of some of its provisions, he will not, I think, be much surprised at its fate.* It provided—(in the country of the Père Girard!)—that no religious society, under any denomination whatever, should henceforth be allowed to teach. It provided that, for the future, persons educated by the Jesuits, or by any of the orders affiliated to the Jesuits, should be incapable of holding any office in Church or State. It proclaimed the object of primary schools to be "the development of man's moral and intellectual faculties in conformity with the principles of Christianity and democracy." It imposed a political oath on the schoolmaster. It made instruction obligatory and gratuitous.

* *Loi sur l'Instruction publique,* Fribourg, 1848; art. 8, 9, 41, 82, 6, 54, 5, 104.—*Règlement pour les Écoles primaires du Canton de Fribourg,* Fribourg, 1850; art. 180, 176, 177, 178, 179.

Lest the rising generation should still escape it, it directed, first, that no child living in the Canton should, under any circumstances whatever, be educated at home. Next, that if it was proposed to educate a child in a private school, the parent must first submit the name of the private school to the inspector and to the communal school-committee for their approval. If this was obtained, the pupil was still bound to attend the public half-yearly examinations of the communal school. If he failed to attend, or if he attended and passed a bad examination, the private school which educated him was to be closed. Finally, the resources of the religious, charitable, and grammar-school foundations of communes were henceforth to be made available for the support of primary schools.

This I call the very fanaticism of meddling. But, at the same time, the law instituted an undoubtedly good programme of school-instruction. The reaction swept away both the noxious meddling and the sound programme. By an order dated the 12th of January, 1858, the new Council of State restored foundations to their original uses, relaxed the obligation of attendance at the public schools, gave parents liberty to educate their children at home or in private schools, made the clergyman a necessary member of the local school-committee, freed the teacher from the necessity of taking an oath, raised his salary, and reduced the programme of primary school-instruction.

Reaction and Obscurantism! cry the Liberals. Alas, that reaction and obscurantism should sometimes speak the language of moderation and liberty, and that they should invariably cease to speak it the moment they have the power to use, like their adversaries, that of exaggeration and tyranny! For the clerical party in Fribourg this moment has happily not yet arrived. But the future, in Switzerland at any rate, belongs to democracy; and one would gladly see Swiss democracy more rational and more equitable. It has undoubtedly striven to develope popular education; but the spirit in which it has striven for this object has not been without an unfavourable influence upon education itself.

It is the spirit in which highly-instructed peoples live and work that makes them interesting, not the high instruction itself.

Placed between France and Germany, Switzerland is inevitably exposed to influences which tend to prevent her democracy from exercising, unchecked, the pulverising action which democracy exercises in America. But the dominant tendency of modern Swiss democracy is yet not to be regarded without disquietude. It is socialistic, in the sense in which that word expresses a principle hostile to the interests of true society—*the elimination of superiorities.* The most distinguished, the most capable, the most high-minded persons in French Switzerland, are precisely those most excluded from the present direction of affairs; they are living in retirement. Instruction may spread wide among a people which thus ostracises all its best citizens; but it will with difficulty elevate it.

CHAPTER XVI

Popular Education in Holland under the Law of 1806. Reports of M. Cuvier and M. Cousin

M. Cousin, whose admirable reports on popular instruction in Germany and Holland have made the education of those countries so widely known, was inclined to prefer the school-law of Prussia to the school-law of Holland: but for the Dutch primary schools themselves he expressed the highest admiration. The admiration for them expressed by M. Cuvier, who, in 1811, was deputed by the University of France to visit Holland, and to report on its system of public education, was even warmer. The great naturalist speaks unfavourably of the Grammar-schools and Universities of Holland: these, he said, were in some respects beneath criticism. But of the primary schools he said, that they were above all praise. He has described the emotion of astonishment and delight with which on his first entrance into one of them he was struck *; so unlike was it to any school for the poor which he had ever seen, or which at that time was anywhere to be seen out of Holland. For it was in 1811.

The popular instruction of other countries has grown up since that time; but I have seen no primary schools worthy to be matched, even now, with those of Holland. Other far more competent observers have come to the same judgment. It is the school-law which in 1811 M. Cuvier found in operation, which has produced these results. That school-law has lately been altered; of the alterations made in it I will speak presently. They are important, but they are not of a character materially

* "Nous aurions peine," say M. [Georges] Cuvier and his colleague, M. [François J. M.] Noël, "à rendre l'effet qu'a produit sur nous la première école primaire où nous sommes entrés en Hollande.—La première vue de cette école nous avait causé une surprise agréable; lorsque nous fûmes entrés dans tous les détails, nous ne pûmes nous défendre d'une véritable émotion."

to change the popular education of Holland; even if they were, they are too recent to have yet produced that effect. Up to 1857, the school-law of Holland, the law of 1806, with the four general regulations which accompanied it, subsisted without change. As M. Cuvier found it in 1811, so M. Cousin found it in 1836; the same fruits which it was bearing in 1836, it had been bearing in 1811. How that school-law arose, M. Cuvier's report makes known. This report, which is a perfect model of its kind, and which well deserves reprinting, very few, probably, of my readers have seen; for it is not printed in the collection of M. Cuvier's works, it is not to be found even in the library of the British Museum, and it is almost impossible to procure it. I shall therefore repeat, as briefly as I can, the account which it gives of the foundation of the excellent primary instruction of Holland.

Towards the end of the last century, the Dutch schools for the poor resembled those of all other countries; that is to say, they were exceedingly bad. It is remarkable that even in Holland, even in a stronghold of Protestantism—that Protestantism which is commonly thought to have done so much for the instruction of the people—primary schools should by explicit testimony be declared to have been, eighty years ago, thus inferior. We should probably hear the same of the schools of Scotland at the same period, had there been any capable person to judge and to tell us of them. Not that the credit which Protestantism has received for its zeal in teaching the people is wholly undeserved; Protestantism had, in truth, the zeal to found schools, but it had not the knowledge to make good schools. In Holland, eighty years ago, there were no schools for the poor, except schools in connection with the different religious communions; children whose parents were not enrolled members of some church could attend no school at all. But, at any rate, for the children of its own communion Protestantism built schools; there were Protestant schools in connection with the Protestant churches. In connection with the Roman Catholic churches there were no schools whatever. But the Protestant schools were under the inspection of the church-deacons, who changed continually, and who had no fixed principles of management; there was no provision for the training of fit teachers: the schoolmasters were ignorant, and the instruction beggarly.

Such was the state of things when, in 1784, John Nieuvenhuysen, a Mennonite minister in North Holland, founded, with the assistance of several friends, the Society for the Public Good. This society proposed, first, to prepare and circulate among the common people useful elementary works, not only on religious and moral subjects, but also on matters of every-day life. This first object it accomplished with such success, that in two or three years an improved calendar published by the society beat the popular calendar, a tissue of absurdities and superstitions, the *Moore's Almanack* of Holland, out of the field. The society's second object was to establish model and temporary schools, with libraries, for the use of workpeople who had left school. It proposed, thirdly, to conduct inquiries into the true principles of the physical and moral education of children, and into school-method.

The society prospered. In 1809 it numbered 7000 members, and had spread its operations as far as to the Cape of Good Hope. It formed departments in all the localities where it had subscribers, and to these departments it entrusted the inspection and the management of its schools. The government gradually adopted its plans; in 1797, the magistrates of Amsterdam built their public schools in accordance with the suggestions of the two departments of the society established in their city.

In 1801, the celebrated Orientalist, M. Van der Palm, the agent for public instruction in the Batavian Republic, drew up an education-law, which he further improved in 1803, and which laid the base of the final legislation on this subject. In 1805, M. Schimmelpenninck became Grand Pensionary, and M. Van der Palm retired from public life; but his law was the foundation of the law of 1806, proposed by M. Van den Ende, "the father of public instruction in Holland," who from 1806 till 1833 directed, as Commissioner acting under the authority of the Minister for the Home Department, the popular education of his country.

The law of 1806 was very short and very simple. It adopted the existing schools: but it did two things, which no other school-law had yet done, and which were the foundations of its eminent success;—it established a thorough system of inspection for the schools, a thorough system of examination for the teachers.

To organise inspection:—this is, in fact, the grand object of the law of 1806; with this it begins, and with this it ends. To keep the system of inspection efficient was the central thought, the paramount aim of its author, up to the very last days of his life, when, a venerable old man, he received M. Cousin at Haarlem in 1836, and said to him:—"Take care how you choose your inspectors; they are men whom you ought to look for with a lantern in your hand." * And inspection in Holland was organised with a force and completeness which it has attained nowhere else.

Each province of Holland was formed into a certain number of school-districts, and at the head of each school-district was placed an inspector. The united inspectors of the province formed the provincial commission for primary instruction. This commission met three times a year, and received a report on his district from each inspector who was a member of it. It examined teachers for certificates. It was in communication with the provincial government. Once a year it sent as its deputy one of its members to the Hague, to form with the deputies from other provinces a commission, to discuss and regulate school matters, under the immediate direction of the Minister for the Home Department and his inspector-general. In his own district, by this law, each inspector is supreme; local and municipal school-committees can only be named with his concurrence, and he is the leading member of them all; no teacher, public or private, can be appointed without his authorisation; and he inspects every school in his district twice a year. These powerful functionaries were to be named by the State, on the presentation, for the inspectorships of each province, of the assembled commission of inspectors for that province. They were excellently chosen, amongst the laymen and clergymen who had shown an intelligent interest in popular education. Following a

* *De l'Instruction publique en Hollande,* par M. [Victor] Cousin. Paris, 1837; p. 30.

practice not rare in Holland, where the public service is esteemed highly honourable, and where the number of persons able and willing to take part in it is greater than in any other country, they gave their services nearly gratuitously. They received allowances for their expenses while engaged in the business of inspection, but no salaries. Either they were men with private means, or men exercising at the same time with their inspectorship some other function, which provided them with an income. Their cost to the State was, therefore, very small. There were at first 56 inspectors, whose travelling allowances together amounted to 1,840*l.*; and this sum, with 320*l.* a year for an inspector-general's salary, and with a small charge for the office and travelling expenses of this functionary, was the whole cost to the State of the administration of primary instruction.

Four general regulations accompanied and completed the law of 1806. The provincial and communal administrations were charged to occupy themselves with providing proper means of instruction in their localities, with insuring to the teacher a comfortable subsistence, with obtaining a regular attendance of the children in the schools; but there were no provisions exacting from the communes an obligatory establishment of schools, a legal *minimum* of salary for teachers; none exacting from the children a compulsory school-attendance. Neither did the State enter into any positive undertaking as to its own grants. In general terms, it reserved to itself the right to take such measures as it should think fit, to improve the teacher's position, and to promote the good instruction of the young. It left the rest to the stimulating action of its inspectors upon provincial and communal administrations singularly well disposed to receive it.

Its confidence was justified. The provincial governments fixed the teacher's salary for each province at a rate which made the position of the Dutch schoolmaster superior to that of his class in every other country. Free schools for the poor were provided in all the large towns; in the villages, schools which taught the poor gratuitously, but imposed a small admission-fee on those who could afford to pay it. Ministers of religion and lay authorities combined their efforts to draw the children into the schools. The boards which distributed public relief, imposed on its recipients the condition that they should send their children to school. The result was a popular education, which, for extent and solidity combined, has probably never been equalled. Even in 1811, in the reduced Holland of the French Empire, M. Cuvier found 4451 primary schools, with nearly 200,000 scholars, one in ten of the population being at school. In the province of Groningen the prefect reported, as in 1840 the administration reported in the town of Haarlem, that there was not a child who could not read and write. In Amsterdam there were eleven schools for the poor, so well frequented that candidates for admission to them had to put down their names long beforehand, and scholars who passed out of them were eagerly sought after as servants or apprentices. The deacons' schools, or private parish schools in connection with the churches and under the superintendence of the parish deacons, were gradually giving way before the competition of the public schools. The Lutheran deacons' schools of Amsterdam had recently been closed when M. Cuvier wrote. The village schools were, as at this day, even more prosperous than the poor-schools of the towns; for, being attended by children of a somewhat richer class, they gave a somewhat more advanced instruction; the commune, however, paid for the schooling of the poor, and the school-fee of the rest was only about a penny a week. In the thriving villages of North Holland, M. Cuvier found large schools of 200 or 300 children, exciting his admiration by the same cleanliness, order, and good instruction which he had witnessed in the towns. School was held for two hours in the morning, two hours in the afternoon, two hours in the evening; the evening school was for old scholars who had gone to work, and was most numerously and diligently attended. Finally, and this M. Cuvier justly thought one of the grand causes of the success of the Dutch schools, the position of the schoolmasters was most advantageous. Municipalities and parents were alike favourable to them, and held them and their profession in an honour which then, probably, fell to their lot nowhere else. Hardly a village schoolmaster was to be found with a salary of less than 40*l.* a year; in the towns many had from 120*l.* to 160*l.*, and even more than that sum; all had, besides, a house and garden. The fruits of this comfort and consideration were to be seen, as they are remarkably to be seen even at the present day, in the good manners, the good address, the self-respect without presumption, of the Dutch teachers. They are never servile, and never offensive.

The teacher in Holland, in order to enter his profession, had to obtain a *general admission*. To exercise it, he needed a *special admission*. The general admission was obtained by successfully passing the certificate examination. There were four grades of certificate: to be appointed either a public or a private schoolmaster in the towns it was necessary to hold a certificate of the first or second grade; the first grade could be attained by no one who was not twenty-five years old. The third grade qualified a teacher to hold a village school. The fourth grade was reserved for under-masters and assistants. The examination for the higher grades was considerably higher than the certificate-examination of France, considerably lower than ours, for which, indeed, with its twelve hours of written exercises in mathematics alone *, it would be difficult to find a parallel. But the Dutch regulation, instructing the examiners to admit to the highest grades those candidates only who gave signs of a *distinguished culture*, assigned to the schoolmaster's training a humanising and educating direction, which is precisely what we, with our exaggerated demand for masses of hard information, have completely missed. School-methods, also, and pedagogic aptitude, occupied more space in the Dutch examination than in the French or in ours.

The teacher had now his general admission. If he wished to become a public teacher, he presented himself as a candidate for some vacant public mastership, and underwent a competitive examination. This second examination I found in Switzerland also; it exists neither in France nor amongst ourselves. If successful, the teacher then received his special admission. Of the judges who examined him for this, the law made the inspector of the district necessarily one; if dissatisfied with the decision of his colleagues, the inspector had the right of appealing against it to the Minister. For special admission as a private teacher no

* Lately reduced, I am happy to say, to nine.

second examination was necessary. But the candidate required the authorisation of the municipality; and this authorisation was not granted except with the inspector's concurrence.

The legislation of 1806 did not institute normal schools. How, then, was an efficient body of schoolmasters formed? It was formed by permitting, in the schools of the Society for the Public Good, the best scholars to stay on at school for two or three years longer than usual, without paying, on condition that they acted as teachers: these became, first, assistants; then, under-masters; finally, head-masters. Great eagerness was manifested to be nominated one of these retained scholars. M. Cuvier found this system in operation when he visited Holland, and he speaks warmly of its success. It was the first serious attempt to form a body of regularly trained masters for primary schools. In our eyes it should have a special interest: we owe to it the institution of pupil-teachers.

Finally, under the legislation of 1806 it was not permitted to public schools to be denominational. The law required that the instruction in them should be such as to "train its recipients for the exercise of all social and Christian virtues," but no dogmatic religious instruction was to be given by the teacher, or was to be given in the school. Measures were to be taken, however, said the law, that the scholar should not go without the dogmatic teaching of the communion to which he belonged. Accordingly, the Minister for the Home Department exhorted by circular the ministers of the different communions to co-operate with the government in carrying the new law into execution, by taking upon themselves the religious instruction of the school children belonging to their persuasion. The religious authorities replied favourably to this appeal. They willingly took upon themselves the task required of them; and nowhere, perhaps, has the instruction of the people been more eminently religious than in Holland, while the public schools have remained, by law, unsectarian. M. Cuvier found that the school children, in 1811, were taught the dogmatic part of their religion on Sundays, in church, by their own minister; that on Saturdays, when Jews were absent, they were instructed in school by the schoolmaster in the New Testament and the life of Christ; on other days, in the truths common to all religions. M. Cousin found, in 1836, the same avoidance of dogmatic teaching in the Dutch schools, the same prevalence of sound religious instruction among the Dutch people.

M. Cuvier concludes his report by pointing out the foundation on which the excellent school-system of Holland appeared to him to repose. It reposed, he said, upon three things; the comfort of the schoolmaster, the effectiveness of the inspection, the superiority of the school-methods. To these three advantages the Dutch schools still owe their prosperity.

M. Cousin, in 1836, found two important modifications introduced into the school-system of Holland since the visit of M. Cuvier. M. Cuvier had noticed with approbation the mode of training schoolmasters which I have above described; in truth, this was a more careful mode of training them than any which at that time was pursued elsewhere: but it left something to be desired; it was not yet the training of the Normal School. Normal schools were established in 1816, under the auspices of M. Van den Ende. One was placed at Haarlem, for Holland; another at Lierre, near Antwerp, for the Belgian provinces, at that time united with Holland. These two institutions, however, sufficed but for a select number of students, the most promising subjects among the future schoolmasters of Holland; for the ordinary majority the training which M. Cuvier had praised continued in use. The normal school at Haarlem became justly celebrated for its success, due to the capacity and character of its director, M. Prinsen. M. Prinsen was still at its head when M. Cousin visited Holland. He received M. Cousin at Haarlem; and the vigour of the man, and the personal nature of his influence over his pupils, is sufficiently revealed in his reply to M. Cousin's request for a copy of the regulations of his school: "I am the regulations," was M. Prinsen's answer.*

The other change was in the town schools. In the towns the public schools for the poor, well managed, well taught, regularly inspected, had become very superior to the private schools, the offspring of individual speculation, which received the chil-

* *De l'Instruction publique en Hollande*, p. 34.

dren of the lower middling classes. The requirement of the certificate of indigence, in the public free schools of the towns, excluded these children from benefits which they could enjoy in the public paying schools of the country; and there was danger that their education would sink below that of the class beneath them. To avert this danger, intermediate schools (*tussen-scholen*) were instituted in towns; and in these schools, by payment of a small fee, rarely exceeding 4*d.* a week, children of the middling classes could obtain an instruction invested with a public character and fenced with public guarantees. Above the *tussen-school* was the French school (*Fransche school*), where a still higher education, including the modern languages, but not yet classical, was afforded for a higher fee; above the French school came the classical, the Latin school.

The classical and superior education of Holland M. Cousin judged with not much more favour than M. Cuvier. I have not to deal with this education here; probably it deserved in most respects the strictures passed upon it by its French critics. But it was impossible for me to enter without emotion the halls and lecture-rooms of Leyden and Utrecht, illustrious by the memory of a host of great names, and recalling by their academic costume, their academic language, or their classical predilections, the venerable Universities of our own country. Perhaps the feeling that these, too, long maintained a course which the modern spirit, not altogether without justice, decried as antiquated, but which nevertheless formed generations able to fill, not ignobly, their part in Church and State, inspired me with indulgent tenderness towards their Dutch sisters. Yet this tenderness does not prevent me from acknowledging, with M. Cuvier and M. Cousin, that it is by its primary schools and its popular education that Holland is since 1800 eminently distinguished.

CHAPTER XVII

Present School Legislation of Holland.—Law of 1857

What could have been the inducement to the Dutch Government to alter a legislation which worked so well? Why, when the law of 1806 was there, should the Chambers have been called upon to vote the law of 1857? I proceed to reply very briefly to these questions.

In the first place, in 1848, Holland had the disease from which it seems that, since the French Revolution, no constitutional state on the Continent can escape;—it wrote down its constitution. The Constitution of 1848 proclaimed * liberty of instruction. The legislation of 1806 had fettered this liberty by requiring the private teacher to obtain a special authorisation before he might open school. It was necessary to bring school-legislation on this point into harmony with the new Constitution.

It was asserted, too, that the body of schoolmasters, satisfactory as was their position in general, were yet left too dependent on the will of the local municipality for the amount of their salaries; that there were many cases in which these were quite insufficient; and that it was desirable to establish by law a rate of salary below which local parsimony might not descend.

It was said, also, that the legislation of 1806 had not determined with sufficient strictness the obligation of communes to provide schools, and that in some quarters popular education was in consequence suffering. Returns were quoted to show that the attendance of children in the Dutch schools, satisfactory as compared with that which many countries could boast, was yet unsatisfactory as compared with that which Holland could boast formerly. In 1835 the proportion of the inhabitants of Holland in school was 1 to 8·3; in 1848, when it

* Art. 194.

reached its highest point, it was 1 to 7·78; but in January 1854 it had fallen to 1 to 9·35, and in July of the same year yet lower, to 1 to 9·83. The number of children attending no school, estimated at but 21,000 for 1852, was estimated at 38,000 for 1855. For Holland, this was a suffering state of popular education. Many desired to try whether legislation could not amend it.

Yet, after all, these were light grievances to allege against a law which had in general worked admirably. The special authorisation required for private teachers had never in Holland been felt as a serious grievance, because in Holland it was almost always accorded or refused with fairness. The Dutch schoolmaster had, in general, reason rather for satisfaction than for complaint. The diffusion of instruction among the Dutch people was such as might inspire their rulers with thankfulness rather than disquietude.

Another, a graver embarrassment, placed the legislation of 1806 in question. It arose out of those very provisions of the law which had been supposed essentially to characterise it, and which observers had the most applauded. It arose out of the imposition on the schools of a non-denominational character. M. Cousin's convictions led him to disapprove an instruction for the people which was either purely secular or not directly and dogmatically religious; but he had not been able to refuse his testimony to the success of the non-dogmatic instruction of the primary schools of Holland. He had seen, he declared, in the great schools of Amsterdam, of Rotterdam, of the Hague, Jews, Catholics, and Protestants seated side by side on the same benches, troubled by no religious animosity, receiving harmoniously a common instruction. But what struck him most was that this instruction seemed to him "penetrated with the spirit of Christianity, though not with the spirit of sect;" that it formed men "sincerely religious and in general moral."

This was high praise from such a quarter, and it tended to dissipate the objections most formidable to such a school system as the Dutch. If, in fact, religious training did not suffer in neutral or non-denominational schools, these schools were inevitably to be preferred to all others; for the advantages of their neutrality no one disputes, and the one supposed *dis*advantage of their neutrality was shown not to exist. Precisely on this plea, that, while the Dutch schools were unsectarian, they were yet truly Christian, the venerable M. Van den Ende upheld the system which he had founded. "Yes," he said to M. Cousin in 1836 *, "primary schools ought to be Christian, but neither Protestant nor Catholic. They ought to belong to no one communion in particular, and to teach no positive dogma.—Yes, you are right, the school ought to be Christian, the school must be Christian. Toleration is not indifference.—I cannot approve that the schoolmaster should give any dogmatic religious instruction; such instruction should be given by the ministers of the different denominations, and out of school. I allow that the schoolmaster may in some cases have the catechism said; but even this is not without its inconveniences.—Remember that you are in Holland, where the Christian spirit is very widely spread among the people."

It escaped, I think, M. Van den Ende, it escaped, I think, M. Cousin, that it would have been more strictly to the purpose to say:—"You are in Holland, where the *Protestant* spirit is very widely spread among the people." I think it escaped them, that the religious teaching of the Dutch public schools, a sincere, a substantial religious teaching no doubt, was at the same time substantially a *Protestant* teaching. I think it escaped them, that this Protestant teaching passed without raising difficulties in the Dutch schools, because the religious spirit of the Dutch people in general was a decidedly Protestant spirit, which the Protestant teaching of the public schools of course did not offend. But, in that case, the triumph of the neutral school in Holland was more apparent than real. The Dutch system had not, in that case, yet solved the difficult problem of uniting in a religious instruction genuine Christian teaching with absolute exclusion of dogma.

Events have singularly proved this. In 1848 all religious denominations in Holland were placed by law on a perfect equality. Protestantism lost its exclusive predominance. What was the first step taken by the Catholics in the assertion of their equal

* *De l'Instruction publique en Hollande,* par M. Cousin, Paris, 1837, pp. 28, 29.

rights? It was to claim an exact and literal observance of the law of 1806. "The word *Christian* in the law of 1806," said the Catholics, "had become in practice merely another word for *Protestant;* if possible, banish the word *Christian* altogether, for of that word in a neutral school partisans are sure to take sectarian advantage: but, even if the word remains, the law clearly proscribes all dogmatic teaching, clearly limits the Christianity to be taught to morality only; execute the law, forbid the teacher to give any dogmatic religious instruction whatever, banish from the school the Bible, which contains dogma as well as moral precepts." The law was clearly on the side of the Catholics, and they succeeded in having it strictly put in force. M. Van den Ende's own words to M. Cousin, which I have quoted above, show that probably the Catholics had ground for complaint, show that probably the teacher sometimes actually broke the law by taking part in teaching dogmatic formularies. But even though formularies be excluded, it is hard not to impress a Protestant or Catholic stamp on the religious instruction of a school, if a school admits any religious instruction at all. We have had this difficulty even in the national schools of Ireland, where religious teaching may be supposed to have been reduced to its *minimum.* In the excellent schools of the British and Foreign School Society religious teaching has a more considerable place; it much resembles * the religious teaching of the Dutch schools under the law of 1806. The British schools are unsectarian; they profess themselves, they honestly believe themselves, unsectarian. But if the Catholics in great numbers had to use them, we should soon, I imagine, hear complaints that they were Protestant.

No sooner was the law of 1806 put strictly in force, no sooner did the public schools of Holland become really non-denominational, than the high Protestants began to cry out against them. They discovered that the law of 1806 was vicious in principle. They discovered that the public schools which this law had founded were "godless schools," were "centres of irreligion and immorality."

* The exclusion of dogmatic formularies of religion from the British schools is, however, complete.

The dissatisfaction of this formidable party was the real cause which made the revision of the law of 1806 inevitable. Either the government, while introducing into the school-law of Holland the lesser modifications necessitated by the Constitution of 1848 or by other causes, must obtain from the Chambers a fresh sanction for the important principle of the neutral school, or this principle must be publicly renounced by it. The law of 1857 raised the question.

Never, perhaps, has it been better discussed than in the debates which followed the introduction of that law into the Dutch Chambers. It does honour to Holland that she should have for her representatives men capable of debating this grave question of religious education so admirably. I greatly doubt whether any other parliamentary assembly in the world could have displayed, in treating it, so much knowledge, so much intelligence, so much moderation. These debates prove the truth of what I have before said, that in the upper classes of no country is the education for public affairs so serious or so universal as in Holland; they prove, too, that nowhere does the best thought and information of these classes so well succeed in finding its way into the legislature. A most interesting account * of the discussion has been published in the French language by M. de Laveleye, a Belgian, and a warm partisan of the cause of neutral schools; I strongly recommend the study of his book to all who desire to see the question of religious education fully debated. My space permits me here only to indicate, with the utmost brevity, the parties on each side in this discussion in the Dutch Chambers, and its issue.

Against the neutral school the high Protestant party stood alone; but its strength, though unaided, was great. This party is at the same time the great conservative party of Holland; it was strong by its wealth, by its respectability, by its long preponderance, by the avowed favour of the King. It was strongest of all, perhaps, by the character of its leader, M. Groen van Prinsterer, a man of deep religious convictions, of fervent eloquence, and of pure and noble character. As a pamphleteer and

* *Débats sur l'Enseignement primaire dans les Chambres Hollandaises*, par Émile de Laveleye; Gand, 1858.

as an orator, M. Groen van Prinsterer attacked the neutral school with equal power. "No education without religion!" he exclaimed, "and no religion except in connection with some actual religious communion! else you fall into a vague deism which is but the first step towards atheism and immorality."

If the opponents of the non-denominational school were one, its supporters were many. First of all stood the Roman Catholics; insisting, as in states where they are not in power they always insist, that the State which cannot be of their own religion shall be of no religion at all; that it shall be perfectly neutral between the various sects; that no other sect, at any rate, shall have the benefit of that State-connection which here it cannot itself obtain, but which, when it can obtain it, it has never refused. Next came the Jews and dissenters; accustomed to use the public schools, desiring to make them even more neutral rather than less neutral, apprehensive that of public schools, allotted separately to denominations, their own share might be small. Next came an important section of the Protestant party, the Protestants of the New School, as they are called, who have of late years made much progress, and whose stronghold is in the University of Groningen; who take their theology from the German rationalists, and, while they declare themselves sincerely Christian, incline, in their own words, "to consider Christianity rather by its moral side and its civilising effect, than by its dogmatic side and its regenerating effect." For these persons, the general character of the religious teaching of the Dutch schools under the law of 1806, the "Christianity common to all sects" taught in them, was precisely what they desired. Finally, the neutral schools were upheld by the whole liberal party, bent in Holland, as elsewhere, to apply on every possible occasion their favourite principle of the radical separation of Church and State; bent to exclude religion altogether from schools which belong to the State, because with religion, they said, the State ought to have no concern whatever.

The party which really triumphed was that of the Protestants of the New School. They owed this triumph less to their own numbers and ability than to the conformity of their views with the language of the legislation of 1806. That legislation was dear, and justly dear, to the people of Holland; a school-system had grown up under it of which they might well be proud; they had not generally experienced any serious inconvenience from it. The new law, therefore, while it forbade, more distinctly than the old law, the schoolmaster to take part in dogmatic religious teaching, while it expressly abandoned religious instruction to the ministers of the different religious communions, while it abstained from proclaiming, like the old law, a desire that the dogmatic religious teaching of the young, though not given in the public school, might yet not be neglected,—nevertheless still used, like the old law, the word *Christian*. It still declared that the object of primary education was "to develope the reason of the young, and to train them to the exercise of all *Christian* and social virtues." * This retention of the word *Christian* gave great offence to many members of the majority. It gave offence to the Liberals, because, they said, this word was "in evident opposition with the purely lay character of the State; for the State, as such, has no religion." Yet the Liberals accepted the new law as a compromise, and because, after all, it still repelled the introduction of the denominational school. But the Catholics were less pliant. To the last they insisted on excluding the word *Christian*, because in practice, they said, this word signified *Protestant;* and most of them voted against the law, because this word was retained. The law passed, however, and by a large majority.

Popular instruction in Holland is, therefore, still Christian. But it is Christian in a sense so large, so wide, from which everything distinctive and dogmatic is so rigorously excluded, that it might as well, perhaps, have rested satisfied with calling itself moral. Those who gave it the name of Christian were careful to announce that by Christianity they meant "all those ideas which purify the soul by elevating it, and which prepare the union of citizens in a common sentiment of mutual good will;" not "those theological subtleties which stifle the natural affections, and perpetuate divisions among members of one commonwealth." They announced that the Christianity of the law and of the

* "Christelijke en maatschappelijke deugden."

State was "a social or lay Christianity, gradually transforming society after the model of ideal justice;" not "a dogmatic Christianity, the affair of the individual and the Church." They announced that this Christianity did not even exclude the Jew; for "the Jew himself will admit that the virtues enjoined by the Old Testament are not in opposition with the word of Christ considered as a sage and a philosopher." * The Jews, on their part, announced that this Christianity they accepted. "In a moral point of view," said M. Godefroi, a Jew deputy from Amsterdam, "I believe and hope that there is no member of this Chamber, be he who he may, who is not a Christian. The word Christian, in this sense, I can accept with a safe conscience." †

The Jews might be satisfied, but the orthodox Protestants were not. In a speech of remarkable energy, and which produced a deep impression upon the country, M. Groen van Prinsterer made a final effort against the new law. "If this law passes," he cried, "Christianity itself is henceforth only a sect, and in the sphere of government its name must never more be pronounced. We shall have not only the *ne plus ultra* of the separation of Church and State, but we shall have the separation of State and religion." "But the Constitution," retorted M. Groen's adversaries, "but the Constitution is on our side!" "If the Constitution," replied M. Groen, "makes the irreligious school a necessity, revise the Constitution!" When the law passed, he resigned his seat in the Chamber and retired into private life.

It is too soon yet to pronounce on the working of the law of 1857, for it has been in operation but two years. There seems at first sight no reason why the religious instruction of the Dutch schools should not follow the same course under the law of 1857 as under the law of 1806, for both laws regulate this instruction in nearly the same words. But the question of distinctive religious teaching has been raised; the strict execution of the letter of the law has been enforced; the orthodox Protestants have been made to see that, under that law, a religious

* See the speech of M. Schimmelpenninck, in M. de Laveleye's *Débats sur l'Enseignement primaire*, &c. p. 23.

† *Débats sur l'Enseignement primaire*, &c. p. 53.

instruction such as they wished could be given only whilst their adversaries slumbered—could be withheld the moment their adversaries awoke. The able and experienced inspector who conducted me round the schools of Utrecht, M. van Hoijtema, in pointing out to me a private elementary school, remarked that such schools had a much greater importance in Holland now than a few years ago. I asked him the reason of this; he replied that in the large towns, at any rate, there was an increasing dissatisfaction with the inadequate religious instruction of the public schools, an increasing demand for schools where a real definite religious instruction was given. He added that this was a grave state of things; that in his opinion it was very undesirable that the schools of the State, with their superior means of efficiency, should not retain the education of the people *; that Government would probably be driven to do something in order to try to remove the present objections to them. I was greatly struck by these words of M. van Hoijtema; his testimony is above suspicion; he is a Government official, and a man of great intelligence, experience, and weight. At the same time that he is school-inspector of Utrecht, he is also first judge of the Military Court of the province. But I do not regard his testimony as decisively establishing the failure of the recent school-law of Holland; on the contrary, the hour has not yet come for judging this law decisively. But it is evident, at the same time, that the example of Holland cannot at this moment be appealed to as exhibiting the complete success of the non-denominational principle.

In fact, it may perhaps be doubted, whether any body of public schools anywhere exists, satisfying at the same time the demands of parents for their children's genuine moral and religious training, and the demands of the partisans of a strict religious neutrality. Secular schools exist, but these do not satisfy the

* In Belgium, where the number of children attending some school or other is pretty nearly the same as in Holland, but where, of that number, the proportion attending private, not public schools, is much greater, the instruction is incredibly inferior to that of Holland. See *Débats sur l'Enseignement primaire,* (the author of which is himself a Belgian), p. 7.

great majority of parents. Schools professing neutral religious teaching exist, but these do not satisfy rigid neutrals. They may profess to give "an instruction penetrated with Christianity, yet without any mixture of Christian dogma," * but they have not yet succeeded in giving it. In America the prevalent religious tone of the country is the religious tone of Protestant Dissent, and this, secular as the American school-system may profess itself, becomes the religious tone of the public education of the country, without violence, without opposition. In England, the religious tone of the schools of the British and Foreign School Society is undoubtedly also the religious tone of Protestant Dissent; but in England Protestant Dissent is not all-pervading and supreme. The British schools, therefore, have to try to neutralise their religious tone, so far as they can do this without impairing its religious sincerity; and, precisely because they have to try to do this, precisely because they have to attempt this impossible feat, these excellent schools are not thoroughly succeeding. While they are too biblical for the secularist, they are yet far too latitudinarian for the orthodox. And not the orthodox only, but the great majority of mankind—the undevout, the indifferent, the sceptical—have a deep-seated feeling that religion ought to be blended with the instruction of their children, even though it is never blended with their own lives. They have a feeling equally deep-seated, that no religion has ever yet been impressively and effectively conveyed to ordinary minds, except under the conditions of a dogmatic shape and positive formularies.

The State must not forget this in legislating for public education; if it does, it must expect its legislation to be a failure. The power which has to govern men, must not omit to take account of one of the most powerful motors of men's nature, their religious feeling. It is vain to tell the State that it is of no religion; it is more true to say that the State is of the religion of all its citizens, without the fanaticism of any. It is most of the religion of the majority, in the sense that it justly establishes this the most widely. It deals with all, indeed, as an authority, not as a partisan;

* See the Speech of the Minister of Justice, M. Van der Brugghen, *Débats sur l'Enseignement primaire*, &c. p. 47.

it deals with all lesser bodies contained in itself as possessing a higher reason than any one of them, (for if it has not this, what right has it to govern?); it allows no one religious body to persecute another; it allows none to be irrational at the public expense; it even reserves to itself the right of judging what religious differences are vital and important, and demand a separate establishment *;—but it does not attempt to exclude religion from a sphere which naturally belongs to it; it does not command religion to forego, before it may enter this sphere, the modes of operation which are essential to it; it does not attempt to impose on the masses an eclecticism which may be possible for a few superior minds. It avails itself, to supply a regular known demand of common human nature, of a regular known machinery.

It is not, therefore, unreasonable to ask of those "Religions of the Future" which the present day so prodigally announces, that they will equip themselves with a substantial shape, with a worship, a ministry, and a flock, before we legislate for popular education in accordance with their exigencies. But, when they have done this, their neutralism will be at an end, denominationalism will have made them prisoners; the denominationalism of Groningen or Tübingen, instead of that of Utrecht or Geneva.

The principal change made by the law of 1857 is the establishment of greater liberty of instruction. The certificates of morality and capacity are still demanded of every teacher, public or private: but the special authorisation of the municipality, formerly necessary for every private teacher before he could open school, and not granted except with the district-inspector's

* It is worthy of remark that in France a separate establishment, in virtue of Art. 2 of the law of 1833, was conceded only to schools connecting themselves with one or other of the three *cultes reconnus par l'État,* the Catholic, Protestant, and Jewish. It was not thought expedient to recognise minor divisions as constituting sufficient grounds for separating school-children. The difference between the religious tenets of a Baptist and a Roman Catholic, for instance, would in France be held sufficient to make their claim for separate schools reasonable; not so the difference between a Baptist and a Wesleyan. See an interesting decision of the Council Royal on this subject in M. Kilian's *Manuel* already quoted, p. 72.

sanction, is demanded no longer.* This relaxation makes the establishment of private schools more easy. The programme of primary instruction, and that of the certificate-examination of teachers, remain much the same as they were under the law of 1806. Primary instruction, strictly so called, is pronounced by the law of 1857 to comprehend reading, writing, arithmetic, the elements of geometry, of Dutch grammar, of geography, of history, of the natural sciences, and singing. This is a much fuller programme than the corresponding programme of France or Belgium. The certificate-examination is proportionately fuller also.

The new law expressly prescribes † that primary schools, in each commune, shall be at the commune's charge. The law of 1806 had contained no positive prescription on this point. The schools are to be in sufficient number, and the States' deputies and the supreme government have the right of judging whether in any commune they are in sufficient number or not.‡ School-fees are to be exacted of those who can afford to pay them, but not of "children whose families are receiving public relief, or, though not receiving public relief, are unable to pay for their schooling." § If the charge of its schools is too heavy for a commune, the province and the State aid it by a grant, of which each contributes half.|| The exact amount of charge to be supported by a commune before it can receive aid, is not fixed by the Dutch law; neither is a machinery established for compelling the commune and the province to raise the school-funds required of them. In both these respects the French law is superior. But in the weakest point of the French law, in the establishment of a *minimum* for the teachers' salaries, the Dutch law is com-

* A certificate from the municipality, to the effect that they have seen the private teacher's certificates of morality and capacity, and found them in regular form, is still required. But if the municipality refuse or delay the issue of such certificate, the teacher may appeal to the States' deputies and to the King. See Law of August 13th, 1857; Art. 37, 38. A translation of the whole of this important law (for which I am indebted to the kindness of Mr. Ward, the British Secretary of Legation in Holland), will be found at the end of this volume. [The appendices are not printed in this edition.]

† Art. 31. ‡ Art. 17. § Art. 33. || Art. 36.

mendably liberal. The *minimum* of a schoolmaster's fixed salary, placed at 8*l.* a year by the Belgian and by the French law, the Dutch law places at nearly 34*l.** I need not remind the reader that the sum actually received by a schoolmaster in Holland is much greater. An undermaster's salary is fixed at a minimum of 200 florins; one-half of the salary fixed for head-masters.

Under the law of 1857 the public schoolmaster is still appointed by competitive examination. The district-inspector retains his influence over this examination. After it has taken place, he and a select body of the municipality draw up a list of from three to six names, those of the candidates who have acquitted themselves best. From this list the entire body of the communal council makes its selection. The communal council may also dismiss the teacher, but it must first obtain the concurrence of the inspector. If the communal council refuse to pronounce a dismissal which the inspector thinks advisable, the States' deputies of the province may pronounce it upon the representation of this functionary.†

The law fixes the legal staff of teachers to be allowed to public schools. When the number of scholars exceeds 70, the master is to have the aid of a pupil-teacher (*kweekeling*, from *kweeken*, to foster); when it exceeds 100, of an undermaster; when it exceeds 150, of an undermaster and pupil-teacher; for every 50 scholars above this last number he is allowed another pupil-teacher, for every 100 scholars another undermaster.‡ The head-master receives two guineas a year for each pupil-teacher.

The law of 1857, like that of 1806, has abstained from making education compulsory. But it gives legal sanction to a practice already long followed by many municipalities, and which I have noticed above; it enjoins the municipal council to "provide as far as possible for the attendance at school of all children whose parents are in the receipt of public relief." Great efforts had been made, in the debates on the clauses of the law, to procure a more decided recognition by the State of the principle of compulsory education. It was proposed at least to make the payment of the school-fee obligatory for each child of school-age, if the Chamber would not go so far as to make his actual attendance at

* 400 florins. † Art. 22. ‡ Art. 18.

school obligatory. This obligation of payment (*schoolgeld-pligtigheid*) had already, it was said, been enforced by the governments of three provinces, Groningen, Drenthe, and Overyssel, with excellent effect.* The usual arguments for compulsory education were adduced—that other countries had successfully established it—that ignorance was making rapid strides for want of it—that in China, where it reigns, all the children can read and write. It was replied that compulsory education was altogether against the habits of the Dutch people. Even in the mitigated form of the *schoolgeld-pligtigheid*, a large majority of the Chamber refused to sanction it.

The new legislation organised inspection somewhat differently from the law of 1806. It retained the local school-commissions, and the district-inspectors; but at the head of the inspection of each district it placed a salaried provincial inspector.† It directed that these provincial inspectors should be assembled, once a year, under the presidency of the Minister for the Home Department, to deliberate on the general interests of primary instruction. The Minister for the Home Department, assisted by a Referendary, is the supreme authority for the government of education. Between the provincial inspectors and the Minister, the law of 1857 has omitted to place inspectors-general. M. de Laveleye, in general the warm admirer of the Dutch school-legislation, considers this omission most unfortunate.

The 16th article of the law declares that children are to be admitted into the communal school without distinction of creed. For the much-debated 23rd article the wording finally adopted was as follows:—

"Primary instruction, while it imparts the information necessary, is to tend to develope the reason of the young, and to train them to the exercise of all Christian and social virtues.

"The teacher shall abstain from teaching, doing, or permitting

* In Groningen the number of children attending school had risen from 20,000 to 30,000, in consequence of the adoption in 1839, by the provincial government, of a regulation requiring the payment of the school-fee for every child of from 5 to 12 years of age, whether he attended school or not. See *Débats sur l'Enseignement primaire*, p. 57.

† Art. 58.

anything contrary to the respect due to the convictions of dissenters.

"Religious instruction is left to the different religious communions. The school-room may be put at their disposal for that purpose, for the benefit of children attending the school, out of school-hours."

CHAPTER XVIII

Present Condition of Popular Education in Holland

In Lord Napier's absence, Mr. Ward, the British Chargé d'Affaires at the Hague, to whose kindness I am much indebted, presented me to M. Vollenhoven, the Referendary charged with the department of primary instruction under the authority of the Minister for the Home Department, M. van Tets. M. Vollenhoven not only furnished me with all the official documents which I wished to consult on the subject of primary instruction in Holland, but obligingly placed me in communication with the school-inspectors of the localities which I proposed to visit. My guide at the Hague was M. van Citters, a member of one of the best families in Holland, of good fortune, and a man of letters, but, with the public spirit of which I have before spoken as distinguishing his countrymen, giving his services gratuitously as a school-inspector. Under his guidance I visited one of the public schools of the Hague. It was a mixed school, containing 320 boys and 330 girls; the teaching staff consisted of a head-master, four under-masters, and five pupil-teachers. The head-master has 1000 florins a-year, with a house, fire, and lights; the under-masters have from 350 to 600 florins a-year; the pupil-teachers from 50 to 100, and their instruction. This instruction is organised somewhat differently from that of our pupil-teachers; in each town of Holland the whole body of public school-masters forms one community, jointly giving instruction to the whole body of pupil-teachers, each master taking his own subject. In Holland, as in our own country, there are at the present moment many complaints that pupil-teachers are exceedingly hard to obtain. Those whom I saw appeared to me in general admirably trained; but yet more remarkable was the training of the principal masters. Many of the pupil-teachers spoke a little

French, one or two of them a little English; but among the head-masters it is not rare to find men speaking English or French well, and having a considerable acquaintance with the literature of both languages.

The external appearance of the children, in this school at the Hague, and their discipline, were excellent; yet this was one of the four free schools of the capital; there is also one intermediate or paying school. My imperfect knowledge of the Dutch language prevented me from orally examining the scholars; but I saw enough of their work on their slates and in their copy-books, to convince me of the solidity of their instruction. The school opens daily with general prayer, general enough (it is supposed) for all to join in it; and the head-master teaches scripture history as part of the school-course. Out of school-hours, between 12 and 1 o'clock, special instructors attend, to give, in the school-room, religious instruction to the Protestant scholars; neither the Roman Catholics nor the Jews use the school-room for this purpose, though at liberty to do so. I asked if any inconvenience was experienced from the mixture of boys and girls in one school; I was told, none whatever; the practice is universal in Holland. The three large school-rooms were well lighted and airy; though the weather was hot, and the rooms were somewhat overcrowded, the ventilation was perfectly good. In Holland, as in France, it is common, when a school is wanted, to adapt existing buildings to the purpose, instead of erecting new; the adaptations which I saw were generally successful, and much expense is thus saved.

I visited Haarlem; but M. Prinsen, the celebrated director of the normal school, is no longer there. The present director is M. Geerligs, who is at the same time the school-inspector of the district. M. Geerligs obligingly conducted me through the primary schools of the town. Here, as at the Hague, the public schools for the poor are four in number. Of two of these which I visited, one had 500 scholars, under a head-master with a yearly salary of 1200 florins, five under-masters, and one pupil-teacher. The other, with a somewhat lower instruction, had a head-master with a salary of 1000 florins, six under-masters, and three pupil-teachers, with an attendance of 600 scholars. Both schools were overcrowded. Of the two other public schools in Haarlem, one has 700 scholars, the other 500. The pupil-teachers here have from 12 to 25 florins a-year; the rate of their payment differs in different places. The order and cleanliness in both the large poor-schools which I visited were quite exemplary.

The law of 1857 is to be completed by regulations reorganising the normal schools of Holland; but these regulations have not yet appeared. Meanwhile the normal school of Haarlem is provisionally continued. It contained, when I visited it, 25 students. They are not boarded in the institution, but lodge in the town; this arrangement is undoubtedly faulty, and the new regulations will change it. The institution is entirely at the charge of the State, which allows 200 florins a-year for the maintenance of each student in it. Admission is eagerly sought for. The course lasts four years. The students attend lectures from 8 to 9 in the morning, and from 5½ to 7½ in the evening: the first-year students attend lectures in the afternoon also. But the mornings of all the students, the mornings and afternoons of students of the second, third, and fourth year, are spent in teaching in the different schools of Haarlem. They are practised in schools of all kinds; schools for the poor, schools for the middle class, schools (without Greek and Latin) for the rich. The children of the latter, at an age when in England they would probably be still at home, almost universally attend school in Holland. A school for the richer class of children is attached to the normal school, and belongs to the present director, M. Geerligs. The students commence in the poor-schools, and go gradually upwards, finishing their practice in schools for the richer class, where the attainment required in the teacher is, of course, more considerable than in the others. In Holland this mode of training the future teacher so as to fit him for any kind of primary school, is found convenient; the superior address and acquirement of the best Dutch teachers is probably to be attributed to it. It is possible that in other countries it might be found to have disadvantages. But, at any rate, the large part assigned in the Dutch system of training to the actual practice of teaching, is excellent. Our normal school authorities would do well to meditate on this great feature of the Haarlam course. The reader will perceive that when I said that, in Holland, the training of the future schoolmaster was much more strictly practical and professional than with us, it was not a vain form of words which I was using.

Holland has at present a population of 3,298,137 inhabitants. For her eleven provinces, she has 11 provincial inspectors and 92 district inspectors. In 1857, her public primary schools were 2,478 in number, with a staff of 2,409 principal masters, 1,587 under-masters, 642 pupil-teachers, 134 schoolmistresses and assistants. In the day and evening schools there were, on the 15th of January, 322,767 scholars. Of these schools 197 were, in 1857, inspected three times; 618, twice; 1,053, once. In 817 of them the instruction is reported as very good; in 1,236 as good; as middling in 367; in 55 as bad. There were, besides, 944 private schools, giving instruction to 83,562 scholars. There were 784 infant schools, receiving 49,873 young children. Boarding-schools, Sunday-schools, and work-schools, with the pupils attending them, are not included in the totals above given.*

The proportion of scholars to the population, not yet so satisfactory as in 1848, was nevertheless in 1857 more satisfactory than in 1854; in January of the latter year, but 1 in every 9·35 inhabitants was in school; in the same month of 1857, 1 in every 8·11 inhabitants. But, in truth, the suffering state of popular education in Holland would be a flourishing state in most other countries. In the debates of 1857 one of the speakers, who complained that popular education in Holland was going back, cited, in proof of the justice of his complaint, returns showing the state of instruction of the conscripts of South Holland in 1856. In this least favoured province, out of 6086 young men drawn for the army, 669 could not read or write. Fortunate country, where such an extent of ignorance is matter of complaint! In the neighbouring country of Belgium in the same year, out of 6617 conscripts in the province of Brabant, 2,254 could not read or write; out of 5910 conscripts in the province of West Flanders, 2088 were in the same condition; out of 7192 in East Flanders, 3153. And, while in East Flanders but 1,820

* See Tables I. and II. (compiled from official sources) at the end of this volume. [Not printed in this edition.]

conscripts out of 7192 could read, write, and cipher correctly, in South Holland, in the worst educated of the Dutch provinces, no less than 5268 out of 6086 possessed this degree of acquirement.*

Such, in Holland, is the present excellent situation of primary instruction. In Prussia it may be even somewhat more widely diffused; but nowhere, probably, has it such thorough soundness and solidity. It is impossible to regard it without admiration. Yet I will freely confess that I do not feel in regarding it that lively interest which I should feel if it were produced under conditions more resembling those which exist, or which are likely to exist, in our own country. The circumstances of Holland, though in some external respects singularly like our own, are yet profoundly and essentially different. They are different both in their defects and in their advantages. Holland differs from us in that which most materially influences the course of a nation's life—in the present temper and genius of her people.

C'est une nation éteinte, a clever Frenchman said to me of the Dutch people. This is too strong; yet this people, undoubtedly, is no longer in the heyday and flush of its national life; it has no longer the enthusiasm and the aspirations of confident youth or powerful maturity. Although very far, assuredly, from the weakness of decrepitude, its genius moves with the mechanic and unelastic march of a spirit whose prime is over. The Dutch people has now, as a people, two strong aspirations only—for the maintenance of its separate nationality, and for the retention of its colonial dominion. These are respectable aspirations certainly; but such aspirations are not the whole enthusiastic life of great peoples. They were not the sole aspirations of the great Holland of the sixteenth century—of the Holland of William the Silent. They are not the sole aspirations of the England, the France, the Russia, the America, of the present day, looking inquisitively and ardently towards an unbounded future. They are not the sole aspirations of a mighty and growing people, full of life, full of movement, full of energy.

But the sober and limited spirit of the Dutch people regulates

* *Débats sur l'Enseignement primaire*, p. 59.

all the positive affairs of life with exemplary precision. It regulates them with a precision difficult of attainment for more impulsive and mobile nations. Above all, it regulates them with a precision which its comparatively small numbers render comparatively easy for it. It is easier to have a model village than a model city; it is easier minutely to provide, watch, and keep in order a mechanism for three millions of men, than for thirty millions. What will it be when the three millions are at the same time individually far more still and tractable than the thirty? I do not think we can hope, in England, for municipalities which, like the Dutch municipalities, can in the main safely be trusted to provide and watch over schools; for a population which, like the Dutch population, can in the main safely be trusted to come to school regularly; for a government which has only to give good advice and good suggestions in order to be promptly obeyed.

Even the Government of Holland, however, has regulated popular education by law; even the school-loving people of Holland, so well taught, so sober-minded, so reasonable, is not abandoned in the matter of its education to its own caprices. The State in Holland, where education is prized by the masses, no more leaves education to itself, than the State in France, where it is little valued by them. It is the same in the other country of which I have described the school-system—in Switzerland. Here and there we may have found, indeed, school-rules in some respects injudicious, in some respects extravagant; but everywhere we have found law, everywhere State-regulation. English readers will judge for themselves, whether there is anything which makes the State, in England, unfit to be trusted with such regulation; whether there is anything which makes the people in England unfit to be subjected to it. They will judge, whether there is any danger in intrusting to a State-authority, the least meddlesome, the least grasping, the least prone to over-government in the world—to a State-authority which, even if it wished to change its nature in these respects, would be powerless against the resistance which would confront it—the superintendence of an important concern which the State superintends in all other countries, and which Burke, no friend to petty governmental meddling, would indisputably have classed with religion among the proper objects of State establishment *, had this question of popular education come to the surface in his day. They will judge, whether there is any inherent quality in the English people, fitting it to regulate well by itself a concern which no other people has by itself well regulated.

For a certain part of its education, undoubtedly, the English people is sufficient to itself. In the air of England, in the commerce of his countrymen, in the long tradition and practice of liberty, there is for every Englishman an education which is without a parallel in the world, and which I am the last to undervalue. If I do not extol it, it is because every one in England appreciates it duly. This education of a people governments neither give nor take away. This it receives, not by the disposition of legislators, but by the essential conditions of its own being. But there are some things which neither in England nor in any other country can the mass of a people have by nature, and these things governments can give it. They can give it those simple, but invaluable and humanising, acquirements, without which the finest race in the world is but a race of splendid barbarians. Above all, governments, in giving these, may at the same time educate a people's reason, a people's equity. These are not the qualities which the masses develope for themselves. Obstinate resistance to oppression, omnipotent industry, heroic valour, all these may come from below upwards; but unprejudiced intelligence, but equitable moderation—never. If, then, the State disbelieves in reason, when will reason reach the mob?

In England the State is perhaps inclined to admit too readily its powerlessness as inevitable. It too easily resigns itself to believe that there exists in the country no such thing as a party of reason, capable of upholding a government which should boldly throw itself upon it for support. Perhaps such a party exists; perhaps it is stronger than governments think. No doubt the State has in this country to confront, when it attempts to act, great suspicion, great jealousy. But in other countries, also, it has had its adversaries to contend with; and it has sometimes,

* See the remarkable passage in *Thoughts and Details on Scarcity*, Burke's *Works*, London, 1852, vol. v. p. 210.

even when most despotic, relied for success not on superior brute force, but on an arm which the most constitutional State might blamelessly wield—on superior reason. The Consular legislation of 1802, which I have already mentioned, supplies a notable instance. In his great work of reorganising French society, Napoleon determined to revive, by the institution of the justest system of public recompenses ever founded—the Legion of Honour—those distinctions of rank which are salutary and necessary to society, but which feudalism had abused and anarchy had abolished. Distinctions are in nature; but there are the essential distinctions of Nature herself, and there are the arbitrary distinctions of accident or favour. The decorations of governments usually follow the latter. The Legion of Honour was instituted to do homage to the former. The fanatics of an impossible equality declaimed violently against the First Consul's project. He persevered and succeeded; but both in the Tribunate and in the Legislative Body his measure encountered strenuous resistance. "We have gone a little too fast," said Napoleon to those about him, when he heard of this opposition; "we have gone a little too fast, that must be allowed. *But we had reason on our side; and, when one has reason on one's side, one should have the courage to run some risks.*" Noble words of a profound and truly creative genius, which employed, in administration, something solider than makeshifts!

The Twice-Revised Code

The Archbishop of Canterbury said a few months ago at Maidstone, that the Revised Code, lately promulgated by the Committee of Council on Education, must at last stand or fall according to the verdict pronounced upon it by the *common sense of the country*. His Grace could not have said a truer thing. But the common sense of the country finds itself at some loss for clear data to guide it in coming to a verdict. The system of our Education Department bristles with details so numerous, so minute, and so intricate, that any one not practically conversant with this system has great difficulty in mastering them, and, by failing to master them, may easily be led into error.* With a certain amount of trouble, however, even the details of our Council Office system may of course be mastered. But such an amount of trouble the general public will not take. From this cause the pamphlet of a master of the subject—of the founder of our public elementary education, Sir James Shuttleworth—fails, it seems to us, perfectly to meet the occasion with which it has to deal. For readers already familiar with the subject, for school-managers, school-teachers, school-inspectors, it is admirable: for the general reader it is somewhat too copious. For this last, it goes too much into detail; it presupposes more acquaintance with the subject than he is likely to possess. Every member of Parliament, every one who has to *discuss* the new Code, should read Sir James Shuttleworth's pamphlet. Every one who

* For want of this practical acquaintance, a writer so able and so exact as Dr. Vaughan bases an argument upon the assertion that a low certificate from the Committee of Council does not at present entitle its holder to any grant of money. The assertion and the argument from it are alike erroneous.

is disposed to go deeply into the subject should read it. For those who are not disposed to do this, who desire only to know the essential facts of the case, so as to be able to form an opinion upon it, a simpler statement is required,—a statement dealing less with the details of the subject and more with its *rationale.*

Such a statement we here propose to attempt. We propose, at this last moment before the Parliamentary discussion comes, to show the general reader—1. What it is that the Revised Code will actually do; 2. Why its authors are trying to do this; 3. What is the merit of their design in itself, and what, moreover, is the prospect of its accomplishing what it intends. And we shall notice, in conclusion, the changes in his original scheme which have just been propounded by Mr. Lowe, and examine the value and importance of these.

1.—What the Revised Code will actually *do,* is to reduce considerably the grants at present contributed by the State towards the support of schools for the poor. This is what it will certainly and indisputably do. It may do other things besides, but about its doing these other things there is much dispute; about its effecting a reduction of existing grants there is no dispute. The reduction may be more or less great; Sir James Shuttleworth, the best of authorities on such a matter, estimates it at two-fifths, or £175,000 a year, of the money now annually paid; Archdeacon Sinclair, representing the National Society, estimates it at forty per cent (the same thing). Even Mr. Lowe admits that there will be a loss, although he declares such an estimate of it as the above to be exaggerated. It is possible that this estimate may not be exactly correct; but that the reduction will be considerable, no one who has any real acquaintance with the subject denies. It is probably safe to reckon it at nearly two-fifths of the present annual grant.

The heads of a public department are not, in general, the persons most forward in proposing to contract the operations of their own department, and to reduce its expenditure. Of any such want of self-denying disinterestedness the heads of our Education Department cannot be accused. They have propounded a scheme which—while it dismays and discourages the supporters of that system of State-aid to public education, which the infinite zeal and adroitness of Sir James Shuttleworth, the infinite moderation and sagacity of Lord Lansdowne, founded in this country with so much difficulty—delights and animates all the bitterest adversaries of that system. It is from these adversaries, almost as much surprised as rejoiced, that the framers of the Revised Code have received the warmest approval. A clergyman, well known in the North Midland Counties for his uncompromising opposition to all State-interference in national education, procured from a Yorkshire meeting, filled with ardent Voluntaries who shared his own opinions, a vote of entire adhesion to the new Code. Mr. Crossley, member for the West Riding, an Independent and a Voluntary, declared at an Education Conference lately held, that 'the new Minute of the Privy Council had given fresh heart and life to the opponents of the system.' Those members of the late Education Commission who, though not refusing to sign their names to the recommendations of their fellow Commissioners, signed them with the reservation that to the principle of State-intervention in this matter they were still opposed, confess that while the action of the majority of their own body was at variance with their wishes, the present action of the Committee of Council is quite in conformity with them. 'It is a step in the right direction,' says Mr. Miall. 'The penny will become a halfpenny, the halfpenny will become a farthing, and the farthing nothing at all.'

We will not stop here to ask how it is that the Education Department should itself have promulgated a Code such as those most hostile to the very existence of that department would have been glad to promulgate had they possessed the power. The secretary who drew up the new Code should have been Mr. Miall; the vice-president who defended it should have been Mr. Baines. But this is a mere question of persons. What we are here concerned to ask, what the general reader will care to know is, on what grounds the reduction to be effected by the new Code is proposed; why its authors have been, as they profess, induced to make it.

2.—These grounds are the following. 'The duty of a State in public education is,' it is said, 'when clearly defined, to obtain the greatest possible quantity of reading, writing, and arithmetic for the greatest number.' These are, so far as the State is concerned, 'the education of the people.' To obtain the greatest possible quantity of these is 'the requirement of a State;' and to attempt to give this greatest possible quantity is 'to attempt to give as much as the State can be expected to give.' To give this is 'the one thing which the elementary schools of the State are bound to do, just as the one thing a brewer is bound to do is to make good beer.' But the State has hitherto given more than this. It has paid for a machinery of instruction extending itself to many other things besides this. It has thus been paying for discipline, for civilization, for religious and moral training, for a superior instruction to clever and forward children—all of them matters quite out of its province to pay for: it has not exclusively kept its grants for the matters exclusively meriting them, the reading, writing, and arithmetic.

In thus acting, the State has of course been extravagant. But not only has it been extravagant, inasmuch as it has been paying for what it had no business to pay for: by attending to this it has relaxed its attention to those elementary matters which alone concerned it. These have suffered in consequence. While inspectors were reporting on the tone and general influence of a school, on the discipline and behaviour of the children, on the geography and history of the first class, the indispensable elements, the reading, writing, and arithmetic, were neglected.

The Education Commission reported 'that the children attend long enough to afford an opportunity of teaching them to read, write, and cipher; but that a large proportion of them, in some districts, do not even learn to read; that they do not write well; and that they learn their arithmetic in such a way as to be of little practical use in after life.' They declared their opinion that, 'even under the present conditions of school age and attendance, it would be possible for at least *three-fifths* of the children on the books of the schools to learn to read and write without conscious difficulty, and to perform such arithmetical operations as occur in the ordinary business of life.' They came to the conclusion that 'the existing system has hitherto educated successfully only one-fourth of its pupils.' Seven-twentieths of the present body of scholars in our State-aided schools ought to read, write, and cipher well, who do not.

At the same time, the Commissioners bore the strongest testimony to the superiority of these schools in discipline, in method, in general instruction, to all elementary schools not aided by the State.

Well then, it was said, here has the State been creating a system which 'suits admirably in all points but one, but that one unfortunately is *the education of the people*.' It was proposed to cure the error by paying solely for the reading, writing, and arithmetic actually taught, and by lowering the standard of instruction. The 'principles involved in the Code which are really worth contending for, are,' it was declared, '*payment by results;* requiring all managers to make their own terms with teachers, and *the lowering the standard of popular education*.'

But we must remark here that another 'principle' also was said to be 'involved' in the new Code, along with these principles of payment by results and lowering the standard of popular education. This other principle is no less than—what do our readers think?—'the *extending more widely the area and benefit* of popular education.' This, they will naturally say, is a most important addition. This 'principle' is undoubtedly, if it be involved in the new Code, one well 'worth contending for.' And it therefore urgently behoves us to be well assured whether it is really involved in the new Code or no; for we may be very sure that the two points on which, in the House of Commons, the framers of the Code will chiefly rely for winning to it the support of the country gentlemen, and indeed of that large body of members with fair intentions but without special acquaintance with the subject, whose votes must decide the fate of the new scheme, will be these—1. That the Code will repress the exorbitant pretensions of schoolmasters, and reduce the over-ambitious instruction of their highest classes; 2. *That it will carry instruction into the 'waste places' of the country*, and, in Dr. Vaughan's words, 'extend the advantages of education, to a certain though limited amount, to a larger number than heretofore.'

Now the plain truth is, that to hold out this expectation that the new Code will extend the advantages of education to the waste places of the country, to places too poor or too neglected to obtain these advantages under the present system, is to hold out an expectation utterly and entirely delusive. Its framers should be challenged to prove *how* the new Code will do this. We hope they will be pressed very closely on this point. The present system, they will keep saying—Mr. Lowe said it the other day—leaves untouched many of the most necessitous places in the country; it helps most those who can best help themselves. True, let them be answered, this is a just reproach to bring against the old system; *only show us how your new system will in this respect do better*. 'Somebody or other must gain,' it is said, 'by a redistribution in which so many are said to lose.' But this is not a case of *redistribution*, but of reduction. Two-fifths of the sum at present contributed by the State to the support of schools for the poor are to be suddenly taken away. Why *must* 'somebody or other,' among the maintainers of such schools, gain by this? On the contrary, Archdeacon Sinclair declares, '*everybody* loses.' And so far are the 'waste places' of the country from gaining, that they will be among the heaviest losers. We assert this deliberately; let the framers of the Revised Code disprove it if they can. Take the very type of a 'waste place:' some remote rural village in Wiltshire or Nottinghamshire, with a school of about forty children; the school of this place would obtain from the Committee of Council under the Revised Code annual assistance to the amount of £10; at the present moment it can obtain from them, without having to fulfil one condition which it would not have to fulfil under the Revised Code, and the attendance of the scholars being reckoned as precisely the same in both cases—it can obtain £30. Let the country gentleman who complains that the present system leaves poor and remote districts untouched, while it lavishes its aid on wealthy centres of population, and who hopes for some amendment in this respect from the new Code, behold the amendment which he will actually obtain!

The principles really involved in the new Code remain, therefore, those stated above—*payment by results*, those results being understood to be good reading, good writing, and good arithmetic, the proper 'requirement of a State' from the schools which it aids; and the lopping off of all payments hitherto made for anything else. In other words, *reduction* and a *prize-scheme*.

The proposal of the Royal Commissioners had been very different. They had proposed two grants; one of them to be paid, as at present, for the general maintenance of the school and its machinery if these were such as to deserve maintaining at all; in other words, 'in consideration of the discipline, efficiency, and general character of the school,'—of all those matters not touched by an individual examination of the scholars in reading, writing, and arithmetic,—duly attested by the inspector; the other, like the new sole grant established by the Revised Code, to be paid in direct reward of proficiency, proved by examination, of individual scholars in the three branches of instruction, supposed to be suffering—'in consideration of the attainment of a certain degree of knowledge in reading, writing, and arithmetic.' Thus the Royal Commissioners proposed two grants: a *maintenance-grant* and a *prize-grant*. But the money for one of these grants they proposed to raise by a rate. An education-rate it is, or is supposed to be, impossible at present to introduce in this country; so one of the two grants proposed by the Commissioners the Privy Council authorities resolved to abandon. They selected for sacrifice that one which from all their own previous practice and traditions they might have been expected to retain, the *maintenance-grant;* a contribution, not in the nature of prizes for the proficiency, in certain subjects, of individual scholars, but in the nature of assistance towards the payment of teachers, towards the general support of the school. They adopted, as henceforth their sole grant, that one which was new and foreign to their traditions and practice, the *prize-grant*. No aid was henceforth to be given towards the maintenance of teachers, the support of the school, in consideration of the school's 'discipline, efficiency, and general character;' but in consideration of each examination successfully passed before the inspector, by scholars fulfilling certain conditions of age and attendance, in reading, writing, and arithmetic, a certain reward was to be paid. This was called payment by results; and the reduction of two-fifths on the total contribution of the State will arise from limiting the State's contribution to a payment for reading, writing, and arithmetic only, and only for proved proficiency in these.

It is sometimes alleged, indeed, that the aid of the State will still, under the Revised Code, be partly given in consideration of the 'discipline, efficiency, and general character' of the school, inasmuch as on the inspector's unfavourable report of these, one-half of the grant which we have called the prize-grant may be stopped. But this allegation is really, when closely looked into, quite illusory; as illusory as the allegation that the new Code will carry instruction into the waste places of the country, now neglected. It amounts to this; that the elementary schools of England, already mulcted by the new Code of two-fifths of the sum which they formerly received for maintaining their discipline, efficiency, and good general character, may be mulcted one and a half-fifth more, if, with their reduced rate of aid, they fail still to maintain these. This is not the old payment for maintaining these matters; it is a new penalty for not maintaining them. The sole objects judged worthy of the grants of the State are the reading, writing, and arithmetic; but of these grants part is forfeited if the objects no longer deemed worthy of State-grants are not provided for all the same. Singular encouragement for these latter! Religion, according to Mr. Lowe's latest revision of his plan, is to be *encouraged* in a similar manner; that is, some more of the grant is to be forfeited if the religious instruction is found to have been neglected. These forfeitures, however, will seldom be pronounced. Inspectors are, after all, human; and where so much aid has been stopped already, an inspector will probably try very hard not to see anything which might force him to stop more.

State-aid to popular education diminished in amount, and administered under the conditions of a prize-scheme for proved proficiency in reading, writing, and arithmetic, on the plea that the State has hitherto been paying for matters with which it has no concern, that 'the greatest quantity of reading, writing, and arithmetic for the greatest number' is 'the requirement of the State,' is, so far as the State is concerned, 'the education of the people;' on the plea that this State-requirement has hitherto been ill satisfied because attention was not exclusively enough given to it, that it will be satisfied better when attention is concentrated upon it and withdrawn from supererogatory matters; —this is in fact, stripped of all official details and plainly expressed, the meaning of the original Revised Code. We have now to examine the merit of these pleas.

3.—We will take the last plea first. It is founded on the declaration of the Royal Commissioners that a very large proportion of the scholars, even in inspected schools, carry very little instruction away with them; that even under the present conditions of school-age and attendance a much greater number of children might 'learn to read and write without conscious difficulty, and to perform such arithmetical operations as occur in the ordinary business of life;' that, in fact, 'so many as seven-twentieths of the children ought to learn as much as this, even under the present conditions, who do not.' Now, is this true? About the fact, that a very large proportion of the scholars, even in inspected schools, carry very little instruction away with them when they leave school, there can be no doubt: the inspectors themselves declare it; the Royal Commissioners are careful to assure us that they assert this on the authority of the inspectors themselves, and not on that of their own Assistant-Commissioners. But what are we to say to the next assertion of the Royal Commissioners, that, this fact being granted, it is, even under the present conditions of school-age and attendance, remediable; that even now seven-twentieths of the scholars ought to learn to read, write, and cipher much better than they do? As to the truth of this second assertion, there is by no means the same agreement. School-teachers deny it, school-managers deny it, Sir James Shuttleworth denies it, the most experienced of the inspectors deny it. They declare the fact of the ignorance in which so many poor children, after passing through our elementary schools, still remain; but they give an explanation of this fact which is not that of the Royal Commissioners. 'We know this,' says Mr. Watkins, '*and we know also the cause.* It is the shortness of school-life. You cannot cram into the space of two or three years the instruction which ought to occupy five or six. Yet this is what is being done now, and must be done so long as the present inexorable demands of labour continue.' The Royal Commissioners, however, will not admit such an explanation as this; they attribute the ignorance complained of to other causes; to the neglect of the lower classes of his school by the master, to his over-ambitious teaching of the higher classes, to his imperfect teaching of the elementary parts of instruction, reading, writing, and arithmetic, to all. They say that reading, writing, and arithmetic might be much better taught than they are now, and to a much greater number. Who is in the right, and where lies the real truth in this matter?

Everything depends here upon a rigid exactitude in the use of terms. And there has been, on the contrary, much laxity. Sir James Shuttleworth and others have shown with triumph, from the reports of the inspectors, that a vastly greater proportion of scholars than that given by the Commissioners, are returned as reading, writing, and ciphering fairly or well. It has been retorted with equal triumph that this only proves how fallacious these reports of the inspectors are; for this proportion, calculated from their reports, is quite inconsistent with the state of imperfect instruction known to exist, and indeed admitted elsewhere by the inspectors themselves. The truth is, the terms *fair* and *good*, when applied to the reading, writing, and arithmetic of our elementary schools, are not always used in precisely the same sense, and do not carry, to the minds of all who hear them used, precisely the same impression.

We wish to avoid all unnecessary detail, so we will illustrate this from the case of reading only. If, when we speak of a scholar reading fairly or well, we merely mean that reading in his accustomed lesson-book, his provincial tone and accent being allowed for, his want of home-culture and refinement being allowed for, some inevitable interruptions in his school attendance being allowed for, he gets through his task fairly or well, then a much larger proportion of scholars in our inspected schools than the one-fourth assigned by the Royal Commissioners, may be said to read fairly or well. And this is what the inspectors mean when they return scholars as reading fairly or well. Such reading as this might honestly be said to meet sufficiently the requirement of the Commissioners that a scholar shall 'read without conscious difficulty.' Holding the Commissioners fast to this expression of theirs, we may safely assert that—whatever may be the value of their assertion that as many of the scholars as three-fifths *may be* taught, even under the present conditions of school age and attendance, to 'read without conscious difficulty'—the assertion that as few of the scholars as one-fourth *are actually* at present taught so to read is completely erroneous.

But the truth is, the Commissioners presently shift their terms a little. In order to read *fairly* or *well*, it is no longer enough to read *without conscious difficulty;* it is necessary to read *in an intelligent manner.*

It is necessary, to use Dr. Vaughan's words, that the scholar shall be able to *read the Bible with intelligence;* it is necessary, to use the words of one of the ablest and most ardent of the Assistant-Commissioners—Mr. Fraser—that he shall be able to *read the newspaper with sufficient ease to be a pleasure to himself and to convey information to listeners.* The Commissioners, in adopting these words, no longer confine themselves to the requirement that the scholar shall *read without conscious difficulty;* they understand by fair or good reading something more than this. They abandon what may be called the scholastic and professional acceptation of these terms; they adopt the acceptation of them current in the world and among the educated classes.

Now if it is understood by the assertion that a child in an elementary school reads fairly or well, that he reads in an intelligent manner, that he can read the Bible with intelligence, that he can read the newspaper sufficiently well to be a pleasure to himself and his hearers, then no doubt the inspectors, in reporting so large a proportion of children in inspected schools as reading fairly or well, have asserted what is most untrue. If this is what is understood by reading fairly or well, the Commissioners, in declaring that not more than one-fourth of the children in inspected schools now read fairly or well, have asserted what is most true. Whether they are equally right in asserting that at least three-fifths of them *ought*, even under present conditions, to learn to read fairly or well in this sense, is quite another question.

But the inspectors have themselves given the clearest proof that they at least do not use the terms *fairly* or *well* in this absolute sense. Mr. Norris, who has been much quoted on this point, expressly tells us that the newspaper-test is one which he has applied only in his good schools, and that even these good schools failed to stand it. 'Where I found a school *much above par in reading*,' he says, 'I tested the *first class* by giving them a newspaper and telling them to read aloud some paragraph; but in not more than 20 out of 169 schools did I find a first class able to read a newspaper at sight.' He, at any rate, does not mean when he says that a poor child goes through his reading-lesson well or fairly, can read without conscious difficulty, that he is an *intelligent* reader, can *read the newspaper so as to give pleasure to himself and others*. He knows very well, as all persons know who are familiar with the poor and their life, and who do not take their standards from the life of the educated classes, that the goodness of a poor child's reading is something relative, that absolute standards are here out of place.

The Commissioners are certainly mistaken if they imagine that three-fifths of the children in our elementary schools can, under the present conditions, be brought to read *fairly* or *well* in the absolute sense, which, by slightly shifting their terms, they have come to attach to these words. What renders impossible the attainment by so many of a power so considerable—a power which is a real lasting acquirement for the whole life—is the utter want of care for books and knowledge in the homes from which the great majority of them come forth, to which the great majority of them return; in a word, the general want of civilization in themselves and in those among whom they pass their lives. It is the advance of them and their class in civilization which will bring them nearer to this power, not the confining them to reading-lessons, not the striking out lessons on geography or history from the course of our elementary schools. Intelligent reading—reading such as to give pleasure to the reader himself and to his hearers—is a very considerable acquirement; it is not very common even among the children of the rich and educated class. When children in this class possess it, they owe it not to the assiduity with which they have been taught reading and nothing but reading, but partly to natural aptitude, far more to the civilizing and refining influences, the current of older and educated people's ideas and knowledge, in the midst of which they have been brought up. It may safely be said that the religious teaching and the general information given in schools for the poor supply—most imperfectly indeed, but still in some sort or other supply—a kind of substitute for this current, the loss of which would do harm to those mechanical parts of instruction on which it is now proposed to lay exclusive stress. Some remarks in the *Guardian* newspaper bring this out very well. 'Reading,' it is there said, 'is not a merely mechanical art; good reading requires many of the qualities of good oratory; nor will the most elaborate drill enable dulness and ignorance to wear the appearance of intelligent skill. The *general intellectual cultivation* which in late years we have all been promoting in schools is the best preparation for such reading as will please and interest reader and hearer alike.' And the Commissioners themselves quote the case of a school at Greenwich, in which backward readers, kept to reading-lessons only, were found to make less progress even in reading than others equally backward whose lessons were of a more varied cast. The most experienced inspectors, too, declare that the schools in which the general instruction is best are precisely the schools in which the elementary instruction is best also.

The Commissioners, therefore, probably overestimated both the actual neglect of elementary instruction in schools for the poor, and the possible improvement in it which the creating a prize-grant exclusively for proficiency in this instruction might bring about. But after all, the Commissioners proposed still to keep what we have called the *maintenance-grant*—the grant by which aid is given to a school not as a mere machine for teaching reading, writing, and arithmetic, but as a living whole with complex functions, religious, moral, and intellectual. So far as a school by its full and efficient discharge of all these functions acts beneficially on the elementary instruction, the Commissioners helped it still so to act; for they proposed still to assist the school in the full and efficient discharge of all of them. But the same cannot be said of the framers of the Revised Code, who withdraw the subsidy altogether, and leave only a system of prizes for three particular subjects. Yet an advocate of this Code—the Assistant-Commissioner whom we have already quoted, Mr. Fraser—has published a pamphlet, of which the whole scope is this—that the new Code really tends to promote the acquirement of general information in schools, certainly will not tend to discourage it, because (as we have already shown) good reading is impossible without general information and intelligence. Was there ever such reasoning heard of? If for the very object you have in view, good reading, cultivation in other subjects is necessary, why cut off all grants for these subjects in the hope of thereby getting better reading? How are you thus brought one step nearer to the end you have in view? How are you not rather pushed several steps farther back from it? The schools even with these auxiliary subjects encouraged by your grants have failed to produce reading good enough to satisfy you, and you hope, by discouraging these, to make them produce better. Thus it turns out that by persisting to teach just what you rebuke them for teaching, the schools are to produce the result which you desire! And when, in spite of your rebuke, in spite of the withdrawal of your grants, they have persisted in giving some general cultivation, as that without which good reading is impossible, you turn round and assure them that after all the best friends of this general cultivation are yourselves!

This plea, then, for the change introduced by the Revised Code—that elementary instruction has suffered from the undue attention given to higher instruction, that it will be amended by concentrating upon it the exclusive encouragement of the State—cannot stand. We pass to the other plea, that the State has hitherto been paying for matters with which it has no concern; that the requirement of the State from the schools which it aids is the greatest possible quantity of reading, writing, and arithmetic for the greatest number, and this alone.

Mr. Cumin, perhaps the cleverest of the Assistant-Commissioners, declares that the parents of our poor scholars care solely for good elementary instruction for their children, that they care nothing about the higher instruction generally superadded to this, that the higher instruction is due to the ambitiousness of the teacher or to the requirements of the Privy Council Office. A little more experience would have convinced Mr. Cumin that this is often by no means so. A little more experience would have shown him teachers and managers struggling with difficulty against the demand for ornamental accomplishments for their children by parents who imagine that these tend to make ladies and gentlemen of them; it would have shown him teachers excusing themselves for teaching geography in their lower classes by the plea that if they did not teach something of this kind the parents would remove their children to private schools which professed to teach more subjects; it would have shown him the scholars of the highest class themselves putting a pressure upon the master to teach them mathematics or French or even Latin. He would have found that one of the most successful baits by which private schools, more expensive and less efficient, draw scholars away from public schools, is the lure of a more ambitious programme. There is a great deal of folly in all this; but the source of it lies in something natural and respectable—the strong desire of the lower classes to raise themselves. The faults of the teachers themselves, so visible, so pardonable, and so little pardoned, proceed from this desire. It is by no means clear to us that this effort of the humbler classes towards a higher stage of civilization deserves no assistance from the State. It certainly requires direction, and the only way of obtaining the right to give it direction is to give it some assistance. The present, however, is an unpropitious time for dwelling on this topic. That tide of reactionary sentiment against everything supposed to be in the least akin to democracy which, in presence of the spectacle offered by America, is now sweeping over Europe, it is useless at this moment to try to stem. *Now is your hour and the power of darkness.* Democracy, by its faults and extravagances, has almost deserved even so undiscriminating a reaction. But while forbearing at this inauspicious time to press the claims of the higher instruction of the lower classes upon

State-encouragement,* let the friends of these claims steadily refuse to ignore them. When a writer in *Blackwood's Magazine* contemptuously tells the parish schoolmaster that 'if he thinks that the men whom the State wants for "cutting and polishing" the little boys and girls of the labouring classes are those who claim a social equality with surgeons and lawyers, he very much mistakes the feeling of the country,' let us remind him that Coleridge, certainly no levelling Radical, desired 'a schoolmaster in every parish who in due time, and under condition of a faithful performance of his arduous duties, *should succeed to the pastorate*, so that both he and the pastor should be labourers in different compartments of the same field, *with such difference of rank as might be suggested in the names pastor and sub-pastor, or as now exists between rector and curate.*' Let us repeat the wise admonition of M. de Rémusat to the upper classes, uttered only the other day: 'Attaquez avec courage tous les problèmes de l'avenir de la société où le sort vous a placés, *en pénétrant avec intelligence et avec sympathie dans les sentiments qui l'animent et dans les pensées qui la guident, en formant avec elle ces liens de solidarité morale sans lesquels tous les avantages de l'éducation ou de la fortune excitent l'envie et ne donnent pas l'influence.*'

But, whatever may be the case as to the higher instruction, it is surely beyond a doubt that the 'discipline, efficiency, and general character' of its elementary schools are 'requirements of a State,' as well as the successful teaching of reading, writing, and arithmetic. Yet for these, to which the Royal Commissioners expressly devoted a grant from the State, the Revised Code gives nothing. Two-fifths of the money which now goes to maintain these, it takes away, on the plea that even with this reduction good reading, writing, and arithmetic may be sufficiently encouraged; and that, when these have been sufficiently encouraged, the State has nothing more to do. Limit the State's duty, in the schools of the nation, to offering a capitation grant for every good reader, writer, and cipherer? You might as well

* 'The poor man's child,' says the excellent President of the Wesleyan Education Committee, Mr. Scott, in his letter to Lord Granville, '*deserves a better education than this new regulation will give.*'

limit the State's duty, in the prisons of the nation, to the offering a capitation grant for every reformed criminal! But in prisons, it will be said, the State has another interest besides the reformation of the criminal—the protection of society. We answer: And so, too, in schools the State has another interest besides the encouragement of reading, writing, and arithmetic—*the protection of society*. It has an interest in them so far as they keep children out of the streets, so far as they teach them—the dull as well as the clever—an orderly, decent, and human behaviour; so far as they civilize the neighbourhood where they are placed. It owes to its schools for the poor something more than *prizes*, it owes them *help for maintenance*. It owes them that very *subsidy* which Mr. Lowe is so indignant at now giving, and so impatient to withdraw. Whether this help is bestowed in the form of a contribution towards the payment of the teachers, or in that of a contribution towards the general expenses of the school, matters little. But for every school-machinery which is thrown out of gear, for every glimmer of civilization which is quenched, for every poor scholar who is no longer humanized, owing to a reduction, on the plea that reading, writing, and arithmetic are all the State ought to pay for in our present State-expenditure for elementary schools, the State will be directly responsible. It will be as responsible as it would be for the harm to society of any deterioration which should be brought about in our prison-system by a reduction, on the plea that reformed criminals are all the State ought to pay for in the present expenditure for prisons.

Lord Stanley said the other day at Leeds that he should be satisfied 'if three-fourths of all those who attend day-schools could be sent out into the world knowing thoroughly how to read, write, and cipher; having acquired, in addition, those habits of order, discipline, and neatness, which a well-managed school gives, and having been taught the elementary truths of religion.' Well, the State, if the Revised Code is adopted, will do something towards giving Lord Stanley satisfaction. It will give prizes for the production of good reading, writing, and ciphering. But for the formation of 'those habits of order, discipline, and neatness, which a well-managed school gives,' it will give nothing. For the inculcation of the elementary truths of religion, it will give nothing. But these, say the advocates of the Revised Code, it is the clergyman's duty to see cared for. True, it is his duty; but what a course for the State, to put a clergyman's duty at variance with his interests! Instead of strengthening his hands, it creates a temptation for him to stimulate in his parish school the secular rather than the religious instruction, and then tells him that it is his duty to overcome this temptation! Why this is as if a highwayman, who puts his pistol to your head and demands your money or your life, were to tell you at the same time that you would be a very cowardly fellow if you did not resist him. 'I should like nothing better,' you might answer, 'than to show a proper spirit, and to do my duty as a man; but I should like also not to have my brains blown out for doing it.'

But even supposing that, alarmed at discovering what grave evils will follow the withdrawal of a large amount of the aid now given to elementary schools, the framers of the Revised Code were to consent to increase their Capitation Grant, so that the amount of this aid should still remain the same, the Revised Code would yet remain open to the most serious objections. The partisans of the Code at first laid great stress on its economy. But it was soon evident that they must not base its excellence on its economy alone; for a Minute abolishing all grants whatever to education would have been more economical still, and therefore more excellent. Of late, therefore, they have changed their ground a little, and all the stress is now laid on the Code's *efficiency*. The concessions just announced somewhat diminish the reduction at first threatened. 'Lord Granville and Mr. Lowe do not,' we are now told, 'propose to diminish the grant, or to exclude one child from a share in it. But it will henceforth be *no work, no pay*.' 'I cannot promise,' says Mr. Lowe, 'that the new scheme will be economical; but if it is not economical, it will be *efficient*.' 'I am not aware,' says Dr. Vaughan, 'that a positive diminution of expenditure is a prominent object of the changes proposed.' But 'who shall complain,' he asks, 'if henceforth the State should say, "What I give, I choose to give as the reward of success; of success in teaching the rudiments?" ' The State, we have said, owes to its elementary schools more than 'prizes for success in teaching the rudiments;' it is a social and political blunder to confine its duty towards such schools to the duty of offering these. If, however, under the name of 'prizes for success in teaching the rudiments,' it gives as much as it formerly gave under the name of 'grants in consideration of the discipline, efficiency, and general character' of schools, the bad consequences of this social and political blunder are no doubt lessened. They are not by any means removed; for it is idle to say that when the State proclaims 'success in teaching the rudiments' to be the sole object of its rewards, other matters, really of vital importance to the State—the humanizing of that multitude of children whose home-training is defective, who are very rude, ignorant, or dull, very unlikely to obtain prizes, and whom, therefore, under the operation of such a Prize-scheme as that proposed, '*it will not pay to teach*;' *—it is idle to say that this, that the forming those 'habits of order, discipline, and neatness,' the inculcating those 'elementary truths of religion,' which Lord Stanley wishes to be formed and inculcated, will not be made in some degree secondary, will not, therefore, to some extent suffer. But even if this were not so, even should the social and political blunder entirely disappear, a great administrative blunder would remain. The State would be forced to appropriate to the *supervision* of public education much too large a proportion of its whole grant for public education; a great deal of money would have to be spent in maintaining inspectors, which would be better spent in maintaining schools. This is the inconvenience of losing sight of the State's proper business. The State's proper business in popular education, is to help in the creation and maintenance of the schools necessary; to cause fit local bodies to be appointed with the function of watching over these schools; and, finally, itself to exercise over these bodies and their performance of their functions, a general supervision. When it goes far beyond this, when it makes its aid a system of prizes requiring the most minute and detailed examinations; when it tries to test the ac-

* The words of the Memorial read by a deputation from the Educational Societies to Lord Granville.

quirements of every individual child to whose instruction it contributes, it goes beyond its province; it invests itself with municipal, not imperial, functions, it creates an administrative expenditure which is excessive. It is as if (to revert to our old comparison of prisons) the State, proposing to support prisons by a capitation grant on reformed criminals, had to ascertain for what criminals the grant was due. The staff of officers to conduct this minute inquisition would absorb funds which might have provided prison-discipline enough to reform scores of criminals. Even at present the cost of inspection forms a very large item in the expenditure of the Committee of Council. Under the operation of the Prize-scheme proposed by the new Code, this cost would be doubled. 'The first piece of statesmanship we have had on this subject' would be guilty of this grave administrative blunder! The last remaining friends of 'voluntary energy and spontaneity' would create a mass of State-mechanism only to be paralleled in China! Examination, we are told, is now the rule of our public service. Yes; but where, except in China, is examination the rule not only for every public servant, but for all those to whom the public servant's action extends? Yet this is the rule which Mr. Lowe institutes, by examining—not his own inspectors before appointment—but every child in the schools which these inspectors visit. This is as if the State undertook, not only to send the exciseman before the Civil Service Commissioners, but to send before them also all the people who drink beer!

Such are the merits of the Revised Code. It will not do what it proposes to do; it will not 'extend the advantages of education to a larger number than heretofore,' and it will not remove 'the unsatisfactory state of elementary instruction in inspected schools.' It will not make the distribution of the Parliamentary grant for education 'more general and more effective.' And, even were it to do what it proposes, the means by which it proposes to do this would still be objectionable; namely, the confining the State's part in popular education to the offering 'prizes for success in teaching the rudiments,' and the compelling the State to institute, in order to test this success, an immense system of individual examination.

Concocted in the recesses of the Privy Council Office, with no advice asked from those practically conversant with schools, no notice given to those who largely support schools, this new scheme of the Council Office authorities—by which they abruptly revolutionize the system which they were appointed to administer, stab in the back the ward committed to their guardianship—has taken alike their friends and enemies by surprise. Their own inspectors, education-societies, school-managers, are astounded. Their enemies, while enjoying their triumph, can hardly believe that they have obtained it so easily. They cannot refrain from scornfully complimenting the Committee of Council on the facility with which it has yielded. 'We learnt with *equal surprise and satisfaction*,' say the Edinburgh Reviewers, 'the prompt and radical remedy which the Lords of the Education Committee were already prepared (as it now appears) to apply to the evils and shortcomings we had endeavoured to point out. The justification of our strictures is therefore complete, since the heads of the department are so conscious of these defects that they have since promulgated a Minute which rescinds the whole of their former code of regulations, and substitutes an entirely new system for that of 1846. All that we take to be proved at present is, that *the old system is irrevocably condemned by the very persons who have administered it*.' And the reviewers applaud the new plan proposed, because it will give 'greater liberty of action to managers, more self-reliance to teachers;' not caring to add that in their opinion it is a great pity managers should not be made yet more free, and teachers yet more self-reliant, by the abolition of all State-aid to them whatever.

But they accept the Revised Code as an instalment, as the 'commencement of the end' of a system of State-aid to national education, that palpable 'defiance of the laws of supply and demand.' The enemies of such a system are relieved to discover that their own maxims are now predominant in the Council Office; that the authorities there are indeed still encumbered with 'this system of which Sir James Shuttleworth was the author,' but that they are convinced that 'it is time to halt,' to 'arrest the growth for the future of this vested interest,' which, by making State-payments to schoolmasters, he created. They find Mr. Lingen, the Secretary, himself deprecating any further extension of the system; apprehending that it must become unmanageable, enlarging on its administrative difficulties. Sir James Shuttleworth, who knows the details of this business at least as well as Mr. Lingen, makes very short work of these administrative difficulties. A more honourable and indefatigable public servant than Mr. Lingen does not exist; but the most indefatigable man sees difficulties in a course for which he has no love. Mr. Lingen's difficulties show the presence, in the heart of the Education Department, of this want of love for the very course which such a department is created to follow.

The present heads of this department would certainly never have instituted it. They cannot well abolish it outright, but they reduce its action as much as possible. They share in their hearts the feelings of those who think the existence of such a department opposed to English habits, and undesirable. Indeed, this existence is opposed to so great a body of English habits and English prejudices, that one wonders how it ever found means to establish itself. It found them, almost entirely, in the zeal and perseverance of one man, Sir James Shuttleworth. He has been taunted with not possessing the graces of style, the skill of the literary artist; but he possesses that which is perhaps almost as useful as these, and which those who taunt him do not always exhibit—a thorough knowledge of this subject of popular education. And how comes he to know it so well? Alas! there is no royal road to knowledge in these matters; he knows it in the only way by which this subject ever can be well known—he knows it because he loves it. Statesmen—and among them Lord Lansdowne deserves to be named the first—who perhaps did not share his zeal, were yet wise and open-minded enough to see the benefits which might be wrought by it. So, in the face of immense prejudice, of angry outcry, of vehement opposition, the Education Department was established. The good which it did, reconciled to it gradually even that body, which by its nature shares most strongly the popular prejudices on this matter, which had been warmest in its opposition, loudest in its outcry—the clergy. Because they have thus outgrown a vain prejudice, the clergy are now reproached with inconsistency, with being debauched by Government grants, with 'relying too little upon personal exertion,' with 'importunately petitioning for public alms.' The old cry, so hollow, yet to the heedless so plausible, is again raised: 'It is time that our schools should be thrown back upon that mode of maintenance which is the most independent.' Independent for whom? For those for whose sake these schools exist—the poor and their children? Is a poor man more independent by receiving help from his squire or his rector towards his child's education, than by receiving it from the State? Are his reasonable wishes as to the kind of that education more likely to be respected by his local, or by his imperial benefactor? To state a commonplace like this fully, is to refute it. Experience, the best of teachers, has convinced the clergy of the hollowness of this and other like commonplaces which once deluded them. Their schools have been dearer to them than their prejudices. As they saw the change gradually worked in the country by the Education Grant—as they began to perceive the benefits for the present and future of a steady current of communication opened, for help, sympathy, and guidance, between the Government of this country and the schools of the lower classes—their prejudices were dispersed or forgotten, and the system which it is now proposed to 'simplify' until it becomes, in Mr. Miall's words, 'nothing at all,' grew precious to them. Their attachment will probably even now save it from destruction. Their experience has been a truer guide to the clergy than has their enlightenment to organs of public opinion, such as the *Guardian* or the *Spectator*, most friendly to the improvement and gradual elevation of the lower classes, but so sensitive to the faults of the present system that they are disposed to welcome the Revised Code for attacking it. To such friends of the lower classes we may well say: *You know not what you do*. It is because there is something *vital* in the connexion established between the State and the lower classes by the old system, that this system—with all its complication, all its expensiveness, all its mistakes, with all the false taste of many of its schoolmasters and students, all their pretentiousness, all their sciolism, all their nonsense—was yet precious; it is because the Revised Code, by destroying—under the specious pleas of simplifying, of giving greater liberty of action to managers—this vital connexion, takes the heart out of the old system, that it is so condemnable.

For it withdraws from popular education, so far as it can, all serious guidance, all initiatory direction by the State; it makes the action of the State upon this as mechanical, as little dynamical, as possible. It turns the inspectors into a set of registering clerks, with a mass of minute details to tabulate, such a mass as must, in Sir James Shuttleworth's words, 'necessarily withdraw their attention from the religious and general instruction, and from the moral features of the school.' In fact the inspector will just hastily glance round the school, and then he must fall to work at the 'log-books.' And this to ascertain the precise state of each individual scholar's reading, writing, and arithmetic. As if there might not be in a school most grave matters needing inspection and correction; as if the whole school might not be going wrong, at the same time that a number of individual scholars might carry off prizes for reading, writing, and arithmetic! It is as if the generals of an army,—for the inspectors have been the veritable generals of the educational army,—were to have their duties limited to inspecting the men's cartouch-boxes. The organization of the army is faulty:—inspect the cartouch-boxes! The camp is ill-drained, the men are ill-hutted, there is danger of fever and sickness. Never mind; inspect the cartouch-boxes! But the whole discipline is out of order, and needs instant reformation:—no matter; inspect the cartouch-boxes! But the army is beginning a general movement, and that movement is a false one; it is moving to the left when it should be moving to the right: it is going to a disaster! That is not your business; inspect, inspect the cartouch-boxes!

'But what was to be done?' cry Mr. Lowe and his friends. 'It was impossible for us,' says Mr. Lowe, 'to remain quiet under the actual imputations cast upon the system.' 'Not being able to avail itself of the suggestion of a county rate, nor yet, *in the face of a recent exposure, to ask Parliament for a large increase of the grant,* all the Committee of Council could do,' say Mr. Lowe's friends, 'was to do as it has done, to *economize;* and it is in its economies that the Minute differs from the report of the Royal Commissioners.' Not quite so; it differs from it, radically, in the principle on which it makes its grants, in that it makes its grants for reading, writing, and arithmetic only, while the Royal Commissioners proposed to make theirs partly for these, but partly also for the 'discipline, efficiency, and general character' of the school. But the Committee of Council was not reduced to one of the three alternatives, of either proposing a county rate, or else asking Parliament, *in the face of a recent exposure*, for a large increase of the grant; or else, those two courses being impossible, economizing. It might surely have made itself quite certain, whether an *exposure* had actually befallen its system, and to what this *exposure* amounted. It might have made some inquiry on this matter of its own officers, whose credit was greatly concerned. It made none. If it had satisfied itself, as we are persuaded it might have satisfied itself, that the Royal Commissioners had not clearly seen the real truth of this matter of the elementary instruction; that *well* and *ill*, in this matter, are relative terms; that of the children in our inspected schools much more than the Commissioners' one-fourth read well, considering their condition and opportunities—very much less than the Commissioners' three-fifths could be brought, with their present condition and opportunities, to read well absolutely;—if it had explained this, if it had declared, as it might have declared with perfect truth, that it had itself emphatically insisted on the importance of the elementary instruction; that it had struggled for its advancement, that it was prepared to struggle for it still;—such an explanation, we are convinced, would have been willingly accepted. The Committee might have proved its sincerity by very simple administrative changes. It had already directed its inspectors to pay special attention to the elementary instruction, but it had retained (and still retains) its crowded programme of subjects for examination. By striking out the great majority of these, by reducing the subjects entered on the official programme from twenty-three to five—religious knowledge, reading, writing, arithmetic, and *general information*—and by directing the inspector to refuse to examine in the last if he be dissatisfied with the results of his examination in the four others; by permitting him to recommend *partial* stoppage of grants when thus dissatisfied (at present he can recommend entire stoppage only)—the Committee of Council, at the same time that it would have somewhat diminished its consumption of stationery (no light merit), would, we feel certain, have done far more to promote elementary instruction than the Revised Code will ever effect.

But we must not forget that we write for the general reader, and that we have promised him to avoid official details as much as possible. We will not trouble him with the very simple expedients by which, as Sir James Shuttleworth shows, the minor administrative knots which fill Mr. Lingen with such dismay—the multiplication of Post-office orders and of petty separate payments in the same school—might have been untied without the sword of the Revised Code. Nor will we discuss even more important changes which it was time to bring about, but which, like the consolidation of small payments just mentioned, might have been brought about without a revolution. The details of the Privy Council Office system have grown up gradually; some of them must have been the result of accident; all of them are fit matter for revision. It can hardly have been by the deliberate judgment of men of sagacity that that meritorious work, *Morell's Analysis of Sentences*, was made the intellectual food of girls of sixteen. It can hardly have been by the deliberate judgment of men of taste that another meritorious work, *Warren's Extracts from Blackstone's Commentaries*, was selected, for the astonishment of Quintilians yet unborn, to be the authorized textbook for readers, the chosen field in which the student of elocution should exhibit his powers. It must have been by an accident that those two odious words, *male* and *female* (for *man* and *woman*, *boy* and *girl*), established themselves so firmly in the vocabulary of a department charged with the propagation of humane letters and refinement, from whence they are invading the common language of the whole country, carrying into the relations of social human life the terminology of the Zoological Gardens. The Revised Code contains, we see, regulations for changing certain matters in the training of pupil-teachers and students. It must have been by an accident that these were omitted. But we will not discuss these things here. We will not discuss the organization of inspection; inspection with its sixty inspectors, all performing the independent functions and receiving something like the salary of inspectors-general, but not chosen (they are far too numerous) with the care with which inspectors-general should be chosen; not possessing (they are far too numerous) that access to their chief by which inspectors-general enlighten him as to what is really going on outside the walls of the central office;—inspection which the Revised Code reorganizes not at all, but proposes to make, by introducing a plan of immense examinations, more vast, more expensive, and more unwieldy. We will only say in passing, that we are convinced the right course to follow is not to increase the number of Privy Council Office inspectors, but rather to reduce it; that the State—instead of attempting itself to carry out a vast system of minute local examinations by means of its own inspectors in chief, highly paid and sent from a distance—should avail itself for such purposes of a local and cheaper machinery, supervising the operations of this by their own inspectors greatly reduced in number. This is what is done in Holland with signal success, and we are sure it might be done here. Our denominational system affords, indeed, peculiar facilities for it. We feel certain that in the case of National schools (which form the vast majority of those aided by the Committee of Council), the ordinary inspection of these would be perfectly well performed by the diocesan inspectors—appointed as at present, but receiving a small allowance from the Committee of Council for their travelling expenses—acting under the supervision of the Committee of Council's inspector in chief, and removeable from the Committee of Council's service (but from that only) by the Lord President. The diocesan inspectors are in general men of precisely the same age, standing, and experience as the majority of the young clerical inspectors. They could hardly be asked to act under the supervision of these; but under the supervision of an inspector in chief much their superior in standing and experience they would willingly act. These inspectors in chief would have large districts, would be few in number (ten or fifteen would probably suffice for all

England), might therefore be selected with great care and discrimination, and would be, like the provincial inspectors in Holland, the only salaried inspectors of the State. As in Holland, they would yearly re-inspect a certain number of the schools inspected by their local inspectors, and would maintain among these uniformity of practice and standard. At the same time, they would form a body of men not too numerous to have concert among themselves, and to communicate with the central office. Similar means might be found to provide for the inspection of British, Wesleyan, or Roman Catholic schools, which lie chiefly in or about the large towns. The inspectors at present are at once very expensive, and a mob. Under the Revised Code they will be still more expensive, and still more a mob.

Finally, we will not even discuss the much vexed question of the teachers' augmentation grants, by its handling of which the Revised Code has raised such a storm. We will not attack this handling. We will even say that the teachers have not, in our opinion, either a vested interest or a legal claim. They have only what is called, in common life, *a very hard case*. We think a payment in consideration of a teacher's place in an examination for honours a bad form of help for the State's help towards school-maintenance to take. We do not think it the State's business itself to hold examinations for honours, any more than we think it its business itself to examine all the little readers in the country. We should be sorry to see less mental life and activity among the young schoolmasters, but we should be glad if this could find its vent and look for its honours (as it is beginning to look for them) in the examinations of bodies such as the London University and its affiliated institutions, rather than in the examinations of a Government Department. The examinations of the Committee of Council should address themselves to ascertain a teacher's *competence* only; there we agree with the framers of the Revised Code. But we think they might have managed to establish this principle for their future operations, without wholly disregarding the hopes, the legitimate confidence, engendered by their own past operations; without throwing twenty thousand persons into despair. So, again, with the aid to training colleges. We do not blame the framers of the Revised Code for wishing to set some limits to this. The State has aided the creation of too many of these institutions, often in the wrong places, and at needless expense. Limitation was necessary. But we could wish some better means had been originally devised for accomplishing this limitation, by processes which the training colleges might have accepted, and which would not have abruptly deranged all their operations; by processes which their inventors might not have been, after all, forced to abandon.

These are matters, however, in which the Council Office authorities might perfectly well have proposed any needful changes, although it behoved them to plan such changes prudently. Every one admits that the old system, *in its details*, was, as Mr. Lowe called it, 'a tentative, provisional, and preliminary one.' But recognising that the mind of the country was not yet ripe for the final settlement of this question of popular education, not able to adopt the county rate of the Royal Commissioners, but explaining what had been the real success of the system they administered, explaining what there was erroneous in the complaints against it, proposing certain salutary administrative changes, the Council Office authorities might, we are convinced, with the cheerful acquiescence of the country, have asked Parliament, not 'for a large increase of their grant,' but for a continuation of their former grant, for the means of carrying on their old system for the present; thus saving intact for the future the vital principle of that system,—the principle, that the State owes to schools for the poor support 'in consideration of their discipline, efficiency, and general character,' and a supervision which addresses itself, above all, to these. *Their strength was to sit still.*

Instead of this, they have accepted with alacrity the first summons of their adversaries, and are cheerfully preparing to abandon all their positions. If these are ever to be reoccupied they will all have to be fought for over again. Instead of reserving this question for the future, they settle it now; by proposing a change which abandons the essential part of their old system, severs all vital connexion between the State and popular education, substitutes for the idea of a *debt* and a *duty* on the

State's part towards this, the idea of a *free gift*, a gratuitous boon of *prizes;* for a supervision of the whole movement of popular education,—its method, its spirit, and its tendency,—a mechanical examination of certain scholars in three branches of instruction. For to this must State-inspection inevitably dwindle, when to these the grants of the State are confined. Where the State's treasure is bestowed, there will its heart be also.

But Lord Granville and Mr. Lowe have just announced certain concessions. Some of these are slight, others are more important. They none of them remove the worst faults of the Code, although two of them partially correct its greatest absurdities. The framers of the Code have actually discovered that they 'pushed their principle too far when they proposed to examine infants under six years of age!' They have positively found out that to discourage the retention in school of all children over eleven years of age is not a good way of promoting popular education! From such quickness of apprehension what might not be expected? But then throughout the whole speech of the real author of this Code—Mr. Lowe—shines clearly forth the spirit which still animates him, and which makes even his concessions valueless. That spirit is a spirit of hostility to the system which he administers, and to its fundamental principles. It is in vain that he declares—to conjure the alarm which he has excited—that 'he has no wish to disturb any of the fundamental principles of the present system.' With his next breath he avows that 'his only plan is to sweep away the existing system.' Reproached with inconsistency, he explains that he only means to sweep away the *annual grants* of the present system. That is, he means to sweep away just what is essential in the present system—its *maintenance-grants*, its recognition of the State's duty to aid schools for the poor 'in consideration of their discipline, efficiency, and general character.' And this he calls 'not disturbing any fundamental principle of the present system!' We suppose he must imagine that the 'fundamental principle of the present system' is its vice-president, and that so long as that functionary subsists, the system is whole. So, again, he consents to spare the training colleges a little longer, but he consents to this unwillingly and with menaces. So, too, forced to give up his examination of infants—forced to mar in this particular the beautiful simplicity of his scheme, forced to admit into it, in some small measure, the accursed thing, the maintenance-grant, the *subsidy*—he relieves his mind by lamenting over the decay of that voluntary spirit which once regarded all State-grants with such jealousy, by intimating that, 'were he at liberty to choose abstractedly what he thought best for the education of the country,' he would have no such grants at all. He has the air of apologizing to the Voluntaries for not being able to give them perfect satisfaction. We are convinced they will receive his apologies most indulgently. His momentary bowing in the house of Rimmon will be forgiven him. It is so evident that his heart is in the right place! It is so manifest that his desires are in the heaven of Voluntaryism with Mr. Baines, even though his practice be condemned to grope a little longer in the earthly gloom of State-connexion!

But of his enmity to the present system, Mr. Lowe gave a yet more striking proof than these apologies. It is understood that the inspectors are, as a body, favourable to that system, and averse to the Revised Code: their reports are quoted in contradiction of the assumptions on which the Code is based. Mr. Lowe determined to punish them. The habits of English public life, the high tone of English public men, in general prescribe to a Minister the most punctilious consideration for those who serve under him. He spares and screens these, though it be to his own hindrance. His generosity in this respect is one of Lord Palmerston's most popular qualities; rather than resist its impulse, he has incurred on more than one occasion serious embarrassment. From no such embarrassment will Mr. Lowe suffer. With the unscrupulousness of passion—growing desperate as the dangers of his 'little subject' thickened round him—he, in his late speech, flung to the winds every restraint of official delicacy. In his Code he had sacrificed the principles of his department; in his speech he sacrificed its persons. The best part of that performance was an elaborate attack upon his own inspectors. Of this Lord Granville is incapable. But Lord Granville is not the real leader in this struggle.

What will be the issue of the discussion now impending? We

have good hopes. The disposition hitherto shown by the House of Commons has been excellent; the attachment of the country at large to a system from which vast practical benefit has been derived is strong. But we are not confident. The friends of the Revised Code are numerous, resolute, and powerful. There is Mr. Lowe, a political economist of such force, that had he been by when the Lord of the harvest was besought 'to send labourers into his harvest,' he would certainly have remarked of that petition that it was 'a defiance of the laws of supply and demand,' and that the labourers should be left to come of themselves. There is the *Times*, which naturally upholds Mr. Lowe. There is the *Daily News*, unable on this subject to shake off what it has shaken off on so many others, a superstitious reverence for old watchwords of those extreme Dissenters, who for the last ten years have seemed bent on proving how little the future of the country is to owe to their intelligence. There are the friends of economy at any price, always ready to check the hundreds of the national expenditure, while they let the millions go. There are the selfish vulgar of the upper classes, saying in their hearts that this educational philanthropy is all rubbish, and that the less a poor man learns except his handicraft the better. There are the clever and fastidious, too far off from its working to see the substantial benefits which a system, at all national, of popular education confers on the lower classes, but offended by its superficial faults. All these will be gratified by the triumph of the Revised Code, and they are many. And there will be only one sufferer;—*the education of the people.*

The "Principle of Examination"

TO THE EDITOR OF THE DAILY NEWS

Sir,—You are, I believe, opposed to State interference with religion or education. But, when the State does interfere with these matters, you have no wish, I am sure, that it should regulate them unwisely rather than wisely. I think, therefore, that your candour will permit me to point out how the partisans of the Revised Code are attempting, by a false use of the admitted value of the principle of examination, to recommend a measure which, as I believe, regulates popular education unwisely.

The principle of individual examination is, it is said, an excellent thing. There is no such test as the examination test. Lord Overstone got on slowly under a teacher who did not apply it to him, and fast under the late Bishop of London who did. Where there is any shrinking, on a school's part, from this test, there must be something unsound in that school; a school's soundness is proved by its being willing to submit to it.

And why should not the State, it is asked, carry out in practice here this principle of individual examination? It carries it out already in Ireland.

The value of the principle of examination, for certain purposes, no one denies. No doubt it is a good thing for the scholar to be examined. No doubt Lord Overstone got on better the more Bishop Blomfield examined him. But the question is—Is it a good thing to make the scholar's success in his examination the sole measure of the payment of those who educate him? If Lord Overstone's father had proposed to Bishop Blomfield to make his son's performance in an examination at the end of the year the basis for fixing what he should pay for that year's schooling, and proposed this before the Bishop could know the admirable talents which Lord Overstone, under his care, was to develop, would the excellent tutor have "willingly submitted"? If he did not submit, ought he to have submitted? Would his "shrinking" from this test have implied that there was "something unsound" even in that tuition which has made Lord Overstone what we see him? Would the Bishop have deserved all the depreciatory sarcasm of Mr. Lowe, all the exquisite amenities of the *Times*, for shrinking from it?

For this is all that the managers of schools are doing. These ravenous sharks, these importunate beggars, these interested filchers of public money, these bad citizens who have subscribed nine millions of their own money to educate the people, are doing no more than this. "Examine our scholars as much as you will," they say; "the more of them the better; all of them if you can. Whether the State should undertake such a task is not a question for us to settle; it is a question of administration and public expense; it is a question for Government and the House of Commons. But the more our scholars are examined, the better for them, and the better we shall be pleased. Only—since we educate a great number of children, of the most various circumstances, the most various attainments—do not make in any school, infant school or juvenile school either, each scholar's success in reaching, under examination, a certain standard, the sole basis of your payments to us. If you do, you will seriously embarrass us. The circumstances of our scholars, the backwardness of their civilisation, must for some time prevent their reaching that standard in numbers sufficient [to protect us] from heavy loss. You are premature by at least twenty years in fixing that standard."

But in Ireland the State examines every child. Let us see what the State really does in Ireland. It is an official regulation that the Inspector shall examine every child. So much the better for the school. But if the children fail to reach a certain standard, does the Irish school lose its grants? It does not.

This, then, is not the "principle of examination" of the Revised Code. This is examination used as a stimulus, not as a machine for measuring payment.

In Dublin, in a school filled with the children of poor weavers of the Liberty, every child, we will say, is examined by the

Inspector. Great numbers of them fail to come up to the standard of the Revised Code. Yet progress is being made with them, much good is being done to them, they are far better where they are than in the streets. Accordingly, their school receives its grant notwithstanding the examination failure.

In London, in a school filled with the children (not infants) of poor weavers of Spitalfields, every child will under the Revised Code be examined by the Inspector. Great numbers of them will fail: so backward are they, so long neglected, so physically feeble. Yet most of the good they get, they get from that school. But now the "principle of examination" is to become a reality. There is to be no "shrinking." It is to be "no work no pay." The grant will sink to nothing, and the school managers will be left to enjoy perfect "liberty of action."

The opponents of the Revised Code value the "principle of examination" as much as Lord Overstone. It is this false use of it which they deprecate.—I am, &c.,

A LOVER OF LIGHT.

The Code Out of Danger

The too-famous Code is safe at last. The third revision of it has been accepted by the House of Commons. The concessions offered by the Government were really considerable; and members had no desire to immerse themselves, without absolute necessity, after Easter as well as before Easter, in the mysteries of capitation-grants, pupil-teachership, and grouping by age. The fight was warm, but it is over; and Mr. Lowe has swum to shore with two principles in his mouth. The Opposition having forced him to abandon a great deal else, are content to see him land with these two principles, shake himself, and set about putting them in operation. They are careful to tell him, however, that they let him try them as an experiment, and on his own responsibility; and that of the success of his operations with them they are by no means sanguine.

But meanwhile Mr. Lowe has, at least, these two principles safe, and, like a prudent general, he puts the best face he can on his situation. Henceforth he is enabled "to know no one financially but the manager of a school." Henceforth he is empowered "to have some individual examination of the scholars." These, he declares, are advantages of "immense importance." As the House is kind enough to allow him to enjoy these, "he is quite willing to give up everything else." Mr. Lowe is thankful for small mercies. His devout aspiration to "know no one financially but the manager of a school" was really a very innocent longing, to which nobody wished to oppose the slightest obstacle, and which he might have gratified without raising any commotion. His desire "to have some individual examination of the scholars" is equally unexceptionable. But his desire, in its original and unmodified state, was a great deal more than this.

He himself, in his second speech on Monday night, told us what it was. It was, not only "to have some individual examination of the scholars," but "*to make the payments depend on that examination, and on nothing else.*" The fruition of this, his true original desire, has been denied him. He himself confesses it with a sigh: "payment by results exists no longer in the present code." His adversaries never objected to individual examination; they objected to making individual examination the sole means of payments. To this objection they have compelled Mr. Lowe to yield. All their success is here.

To have succeeded here is much. A principle far more real and important than either of Mr. Lowe's two principles has been saved. In direct contradiction to Mr. Lowe it has been successfully maintained, that to give rewards for proved good reading, writing, and arithmetic is *not* the whole duty of the State towards popular education. Mr. Lowe wished to limit the State's part in popular education to crowning with rewards the summit of the edifice, when the edifice had been reared to its summit. If, for want of means on the builders' part, it failed to reach that summit, he was for leaving it to stand incomplete, or to fall to ruin. According to him, until certain results were achieved, the State's duty did not commence. Thus popular education might have disappeared altogether before the State would have become bound to lend it its aid. Such a negation of the State's responsibility the House of Commons refused to sanction. They affirmed the State's obligation to assist in building up popular education, as well as to crown it when it was built. They declared the State bound to help in providing means for popular education, as well as to reward results. They forced Mr. Lowe to institute, in addition to his proposed grant for the latter only, a grant for the former also. Payment by results, therefore, as really desired by Mr. Lowe, exists no longer in the present Code.

On establishing it, in a mutilated form, in that Code, Mr. Lowe has expended all his strength. Two-thirds of the State's grant are to depend upon individual examination. Mr. Lowe has been able to carry his principle of payment by results thus far. The energy and resolution which have been required for this would probably have sufficed to found a solid national system of popular education. The old system had nearly served its time. It had for its basis, indeed, two invaluable principles, without which no good system of popular education is possible; the recognition of the State's duty to aid in providing for its people the means of instruction; the recognition of the State's right to demand from those to whom it entrusts the task of giving that instruction, the guarantee of the certificate. Both these principles Mr. Lowe renounces; and his renunciation of them delivered him logically helpless to Mr. Walter, who urged with truth that just so far as you adopt, in paying your schools, Mr. Lowe's test of results, the certificate test becomes a superfluity. The arguments by which Mr. Lowe tried to invalidate this proposition were so transparently worthless that even the *Times* refuses to endorse them. But the two principles, in spite of their renunciation by Mr. Lowe and the logical difficulty into which this renunciation brought him, are in themselves true; to have had them for its basis is the grand merit of the old system. All the superstructure, however, raised upon this basis, needed remodelling. Here was a great opportunity to produce a statesman-like and enduring work, and all Mr. Lowe has accomplished is to produce a scheme which Lord Granville, indeed, apparently hopes will be a "permanent settlement," but which the majority of those who sanction it sanction with distrust, and which Mr. Lowe himself declares it would be absurd to regard as final. And why has Mr. Lowe been driven to rest contented with this lame and impotent conclusion? Simply because he was so blindly zealous for one principle—his principle of payment by results,—that he could care for nothing else. And this principle itself is profoundly false. Of the hundreds who repeat, like parrots, the cry of "payment by results," not one in fifty has considered what it really means. It means, in the present case, that the right way to make a bad scholar better is to cripple the school which teaches him. The scholar is imperfect, and to remedy this, you diminish the school's means of perfecting him. It is as if you sought to remedy the under-feeding of inmates of a union workhouse by reducing the dietary; or the insubordination of inmates of a prison by letting the walls tumble down. You will pay, or refuse payment, you cry, according to examination. Yes; but the proper object for reward or penalty, in respect of examination, is the *examinee*. Is it on him that your reward or your penalty will alight? No. Is it on his teacher? Undoubtedly, where a great number of scholars do ill, there must, in general, be fault in the teacher; in this case, to dismiss the teacher would probably be a better plan than to diminish his means of subsistence; still, to punish him in either way is not unjust. Well, does your penalty fall on the teacher? No. On whom then does it fall? On the school. It is as we said at first: a lame man walks ill, and to make him walk better, you break his crutches.

This is payment by results, as Mr. Lowe has devised it. If stringently carried out, it would produce serious embarrassment; even carried out as it probably will be, it will produce considerable irritation. But in the long run it will be found, we imagine, more and more difficult to carry it out stringently. The inspector, who sees a school with his eyes, will always feel differently towards it from the clerk who sees it only in the Council Office register. He will always have a reluctance to disable it. Gradually the inevitable "fair" of this too indulgent official will do its work. Examination-grants will be paid by wholesale. The State will again be granting money for the education of little ploughboys quite unable to read aloud Mr. Lowe's speeches in the papers "in a manner to give pleasure to themselves and the hearers." For a time the young impostors will go on without detection. But one day a penetrating philosopher like Dr. Hodgson will drop from the clouds among them. He will hear them sing a stave of "Rule Britannia;" he will set them to answer "a few questions on digestion." From the manner in which they perform these tasks, his powerful intelligence will instinctively discern that they are ignorant of reading, writing, and arithmetic. A Royal Commission will trumpet this discovery to the world. The tempest will again arise. The House of Commons will be tormented anew with a subject which it does not understand, and which it will not master. All the familiar figures will reappear. The amiable Mr. Walpole will lament, at unnecessary length, his own too great moderation. The excellent Mr. Henley will be incredibly dull. The well-meaning Mr. Adderley will denounce, in the thinnest of Houses, a curse against centralization. Out of the House, Archdeacon Allen will address, from "Prees, Salop," a letter to every newspaper. Canon Girdlestone, and other *nolumus episcopari* clergymen, will extol the wisdom of the existing Government. The *Times* will thunder, the *Telegraph* whistle, the *Star* scream. All the foundations of the educational deep will once more be broken up. When that second deluge approaches, may we have for the Noah to build us our ark a wiser carpenter than Mr. Lowe!

Ordnance Maps

The notice which newspapers attract to a subject is vivid, but it is transient. To-day's topic is not yesterday's, and will not be to-morrow's; Folly has to be shot flying, and is soon out of the reach of danger. No one talks now of the Salisbury scandals; no one gives an ill-natured thought to that wise old Canon, who, no doubt, as he looks at his son-in-law in his stall, and opens his newspaper without finding his own name in it, thanks God that he held his tongue, and waited for the sure deliverance of time. A fortnight hence nobody will ask the etymology of *reindeer;* and Colonel Burnaby, now (they say) ill from the annoyance which his attainments in philology have brought upon him, will be going about as usual with his *Johnson* in his carpet-bag, well and cheerful as if nothing had happened.

Before a similar oblivion quite covers the Ordnance Surveyors and Sir Henry James—household words as the *Times* made them a few weeks ago,—we want to recall attention to them for one moment. It is just possible, though not, we fear, very probable, that they may be now setting themselves in silence to amend the errors with which they have been reproached. In that case it would be a pity they should not know that in what they have hitherto heard about their errors they have by no means heard the worst of themselves.

The Ordnance Surveyors have been reproached with letting the nomenclature of their maps become obsolete; the names of places are left (it is said) just as they stood forty or fifty years ago; new railways, new roads, new churches, new groups of houses are not marked in. And this in the maps of a country which changes so fast as England! There is much truth in this charge; but it is not the charge which a real lover of maps would be disposed to press most warmly. The imperfect nomenclature of the older Ordnance maps is no doubt a grievance, but the worn out condition of their plates is a far worse one. The writing of an old map is inaccurate, but its shading is a great deal more than inaccurate. The dark shading is all blurred, and the fine shading is all gone.

By its shading a good map becomes, to the lover of maps, almost a picture; it shows him all the relief and configuration of a county. He can trace, in those finely graduated lines, mountain and valley, slope and plain, open ground and woodland, in all their endless variety. It is by the completeness and beauty of their shading that modern maps distinguish themselves from ancient most advantageously. But the Ordnance sheet of Oxford or Cheltenham which one buys at the present day is, in its shading, little superior to the county map of a hundred years ago. It cannot be denied that the Ordnance Surveyors have done a good deal to amend the obsolete nomenclature of their maps. To amend their effaced shading they have done nothing. They have, indeed, in some of the most worn of their sheets, attempted a little detestable patching here and there; but the remedy is worse than the disease. A lover of maps would in general be only too happy if he could obtain the unworn sheet of thirty years ago, with all its imperfections of writing, in exchange for the indistinct catalogue of names which he now buys under the title of an Ordnance sheet. Names he can put in or correct for himself, but he cannot restore shading. He is therefore not very grateful to the Ordnance Surveyors for doing the former for him, so long as they neglect to do the latter. They give him, indeed, in the sheets already mentioned of Oxford and Cheltenham, the Great Western and the London and North Western Railways; but where, he sorrowfully asks, is the Cumnor hill country on the right bank of the Thames, as the original map gave it? Where is Bredon Hill, with all its beautiful staging from the plain to its summit? As they were in the Roman maps of Britain—absent.

As is usual in England, the defects of the Ordnance Survey are at once attributed to its being a Government work, and it is proposed to cure them by leaving the map of England to be made by private enterprise. A more absurd proposition it would be hard to conceive. What English private enterprise produces in the way of map-making one has only to walk down the Strand to see. The truth is, map-making is by no means an English speciality; the taste of our general public for maps, as for cooking, is not yet cultivated enough to demand a very superior article; it is satisfied with less than what in several other countries is demanded. Not only are the Government maps in England inferior to the maps made in Germany or Switzerland, but our private enterprise-maps are inferior to them in still greater degree. Nothing was more noticeable for any map-lover who went and came between London and Paris during the Italian war of 1859, than the difference between the maps of the seat of war exposed for sale in the shops of the two capitals. No doubt the best and most expensive foreign map of North Italy might be bought in London as well as in Paris; but the maps manufactured in London to meet the common home demand were daubs which in Paris would have been unsaleable. Mr. Stanford is a most intelligent and enterprising map-seller—much the best, probably, now that Mr. Arrowsmith has become somnolent, to be found in London; but his shop is not yet that of Andriveau or of Artaria. A sheet of the English Ordnance Survey can be obtained at Andriveau's; but a sheet of the map of France by the *état-major* could not a year or two ago be obtained in London without sending to Paris expressly for it; and we greatly doubt whether it is obtainable here at this moment.

Neither on the Continent nor in England, however, would the ordinary public demand ensure a supply of maps of first-rate excellence. As a mere matter of trade, a Swiss publisher would not think it worth his while to go to the expense of preparing such maps as the Dufour map of Switzerland, or a Viennese tradesman such maps as we have just seen in the Austrian department of the International Exhibition. A tradesman's business is simply to make money, and he can make it with less risk by publishing inferior maps to these. But a government is not a tradesman; and the governments of civilized European countries have very properly thought it their business to get first-rate maps made of the countries under their rule, whether the making should prove a good trade speculation or no. To perform this duty, governments have at their disposal in the scientific branches of their armies an instrument superior to any which private enterprise can employ. The English government could not well shirk the duty of providing a map of England; but, in discharging this duty, it has been hampered as only an English government is hampered, and it has shown an irresolution such as only an English executive can display. The history of our Ordnance Survey and of the Select Committees which have kindly undertaken to be its nursing fathers, is the satire of administration under a Parliamentary Government. But it was a folly of the late Mr. Joseph Hume (and with all his usefulness he had many) which made the deterioration of the English Ordnance map a necessity. He procured the reduction of its price to 2s. for a full sheet, and to 6d. for a quarter sheet. Even the general public were willing to get good maps when they were to be given away at this rate; and the demand which followed wore out the plates. Modern science has supplied the Ordnance Surveyors with means by which, for their new sheets, the wear and tear of incessant engraving can be avoided. It will be long before electrotyped maps equal for beauty and clearness the best engraved ones; still, the preservation of the new plates has been rendered possible. But, meanwhile, the old plates are spoilt.

The whole matter lies in a nutshell. It is the duty of a Government to provide a good map of its country, and to keep that map in good order; but it is not its duty to provide cheap maps for the million. If, however, it chooses to assume this latter duty, it cannot thereby get rid of the former. If the English government thinks itself bound to sell its map of Oxfordshire at sixpence a sheet, it is bound to renew the plates as fast as the great demand caused by this low price wears them out. If this cannot be done by reason of the expense, that proves that the price of the Ordnance maps is at present fixed too low. For a Government's first and indispensable duty in the way of map-making is (we cannot repeat it too often), to provide a *good* map of its country, not to provide a *cheap* one. The cheapness or dearness is a secondary consideration for it; the first consideration is excellence. When an excellent map has been once secured, then let private enterprise bring this out on a reduced scale, and let Mr. Stanford sell the performances of private enterprise as cheap as he will. To compete in the sale of cheap maps with Mr. Stanford, is no part of a Government's business.

To this day the Ordnance Surveyors seem unable to comprehend this. Sir Henry James, reproached with the imperfection of his maps, talks to us about new means of multiplying impressions of them. Let him clearly understand what is expected of him. It is expected that he shall have a first-rate map of England on the one-inch scale (which is very nearly the scale adopted in other European countries), producible at the demand of an English or foreign purchaser; and that, if he is precluded by his present conditions of price from having this, he should, instead of writing letters to the *Times* about photo-zincography, address an urgent representation to his official superior, the War Minister, and get those conditions altered. His map of Cumberland (if it is ever going to appear) will even then, probably, be inferior to the Dufour map of Lucerne just published; but at any rate he will no longer be compelled to offer to a foreigner, who asks for our Government map of Kent or Devonshire, a production discreditable to the English nation and Government, and hardly superior to the old French map of Cassini.

Mr. Walter and Schoolmasters' Certificates

"Curses," says an Eastern proverb, which Southey has taken for the motto to one of his poems, "curses are like young chickens, they always come home to roost." For *curses* read *claptraps*, and the proverb applies admirably to the situation in which Mr. Lowe at this moment finds himself. "Claptraps are like young chickens, they always come home to roost."

Even the general public by this time knows pretty well what a certificate of merit is. It is a document, issued by a department of State, attesting that the holder has passed a satisfactory examination in the subjects of elementary instruction. In every country of Europe the elementary schoolmaster has to provide himself with such a document. It appears that Mr. Walter, the member for Berkshire, has at Bearwood a valued schoolmaster without this appendage. His own favourite fox being thus without a tail, Mr. Walter has been led to entertain doubts as to the utility of tails in general. Gradually the whole question of tails has been explored by him, and he has arrived at an absolute conviction of their inutility. Henceforth he is an infidel as to tails. Like all great infidels, he is not satisfied till he can dethrone the idol which he condemns; he cries out with Voltaire,—"*écrasons l'infâme!*" His own schoolmaster, devoid of a tail, suffers under an unjust slight so long as tails are prized. The schoolmasters of the neighbourhood, who wear these bushy honours thick upon them, flap them provokingly on the ground when Mr. Walter or his schoolmaster pass by. "Let us have done with this nonsense," cries Mr. Walter. "Results are everything: tails without works are nothing. Instead of asking whether a schoolmaster has a certificate, let us ask what results he produces in the reading, writing, and arithmetic of his scholars. Let the State pay simply for these results, and ask no questions as to the person of those who have produced them. Let us have free trade in education. *Sursum corda.* Down with tails!"

It is easy to make a triumphant defence of tails, and to show Mr. Walter's proposal to be an absurdity of the first magnitude. He proposes an administrative impossibility. The State cannot possibly accomplish this minute inquisition into results; it cannot possibly scrutinize every single item of the work done for it. If it attempts this, one of two things must happen: either the scrutiny must be made with inadequate means, and then it will be a mere farce; or it must be made with adequate means, and then it will prove so ruinously expensive that it cannot be continued six months. What the State can really do is, in the first place, by examining the future functionary, to ascertain that he is in a certain degree competent for his function; and in the second place, by examining from time to time samples of his work, to ascertain that he actually fulfils his function properly. This is the universal practice of all rational administration. Mr. Walter says:—"Instead of examining the functionary beforehand, and samples of his work afterwards, examine all his work when he is in discharge of his function." The State may reply: —"Why do you thus rob me of a security which I can take, and substitute for it a security which I cannot take? When you engage a doctor for your union, you take a man with a diploma, you keep your eye on his work, and you dismiss him if he does it badly; you do not forego the security of the diploma, examine every single case of illness treated by your practitioner, and pay or dismiss him according to the success of that treatment. You ask me:—'Why should the intending practitioner give me the security of his certificate?' Rather let me ask you:—'Why should he not?' "

But Mr. Walter is fortunate. He addresses his proposal to a department of State which is precluded from giving him this plain answer. He has to deal with a Minister who has himself used all Mr. Walter's clap-traps, and who now finds them turned against himself. *Let us have free trade in education*, is a cry of which Mr. Lowe is the original proprietor. Last year he and the *Times* thought they could not let us hear it too often. Last year

Mr. Lowe was never weary of disparaging all securities except this one security of results; he could not sufficiently scout the notion of paying for "means," instead of solely paying for "results;" he had no words strong enough to express his scorn for the hollowness of the old system of the Privy Council Office. He rated tails very cheap then. If he defends them now, it is not because he believes in them a bit more than Mr. Walter does, but because Mr. Walter's crusade against them threatens him with a personal embarrassment. Mr. Walter's motion threatens Mr. Lowe's measure of last year with a practical, immediate *reductio ad absurdum.* That measure,—extolled only by enemies of all State aid to education, by clergymen in search of a bishopric, or by officials to whom all the works of their superiors are very good; condemned most by those who had studied popular education most, and happily described by the best Review of the best educated country in Europe, Switzerland, as "*une soi-disant réforme, inintelligente et mal combinée,*"—that measure rested with its whole weight upon a principle on which Mr. Walter's motion, also, wholly rests; the principle that the State's business in popular education is to ascertain whether or no each child in a school can read, write, and cypher, and to pay accordingly. The absurdity of this principle is proved, as we have already said, the moment it is attempted to give full practical effect to it. Mr. Lowe hoped to avoid this test; he had to deal with but a small portion of the elementary schools of England, and these he hoped to be able, or to pretend to be able, to pay by results. Mr. Walter presents him with an addition of 15,000 schools, and Mr. Lowe begins to perceive what "payment by results" really means administratively. Payment by results would, he told us, ensure one of two blessings—economy or efficiency. It is to be hoped its blessing of efficiency may be great; for assuredly, if Mr. Walter's motion passes, its blessing of economy will be small.

Mr. Norris, a painstaking Inspector, and laudably studious of the goodwill of his superiors, has in this difficulty come to Mr. Lowe's assistance. Mr. Norris begins action by general reflections on the utility of the certificate; by a eulogy on tails in the abstract. What he says is true, but, in the contest between

Mr. Walter and Mr. Lowe, not to the point. Mr. Walter's strength lies in Mr. Lowe's inability to use these topics; in Mr. Lowe's own well-remembered cries for free trade in education and payment by results. Mr. Norris then changes his tactics a little. "Let us distinguish," he says: "there are tails and tails. There is the old corrupt tail, and there is the pure and reformed branch which Mr. Lowe has instituted. There is the money-bearing certificate and the barren certificate. The moment the State ceases to pay money to the holder of a certificate, all the blemishes of the certificate-test disappear, all its beauties come out in full bloom." "Fine words," replies the inexorable Mr. Walter; "but free trade in education? but payment by results? So long as you insist on the certificate, money-bearing or barren, you have neither." Mr. Norris then quits the thorny regions of intellectual dispute. He soars into the empyrean of the moral sphere. "Profane man," he cries from above to Mr. Walter, "you know not what you are attacking. There exists in the certificate a mysterious virtue. Like the precious glass in the Middle Ages, which indicated the approach of poison, the certificate—that wonderful, that almost divine instrument—has the power of indicating the approach of intemperance. I have come in contact with uncertificated schoolmasters, of whose general sobriety I could not but feel grave doubts. The hue of Bacchus was on their nose and the odour of juniper upon their lips. I have presented to them the certificate-test and they have shivered into a thousand pieces. Drunkenness is the English vice; and an engine which thus detects drunkenness must be preserved at any sacrifice of logic." Having said this, Mr. Norris passes into the heavens out of our sight.

Meanwhile, Mr. Walter's motion will soon be in the House of Commons. The Goddess of Unreason counts many votaries in that august assembly; and how any matter, which is not a matter of party, but only a matter of good government and good sense, may be there decided, it is impossible to foretell. Mr. Norris's attempt to defend the certificate-test on transcendental grounds is vain. The sun shines both on the evil and on the good, and the certificate rewards both the purple-nosed and the pale-nosed. To defend the certificate-test upon the true grounds is for Mr. Lowe impossible. But it is to be hoped that the House of Commons will save Mr. Lowe from the due results of his own impolicy. It is to be hoped they will say, "You have given us a measure of which Mr. Walter's proposed measure is certainly the legitimate consequence. But then your own measure is said to have none of the signs of life about it; weighty authorities were and are against it; we permitted its introduction only on trial and on your responsibility; the whole question of education will probably soon have to be re-opened by us. Let us leave things for the present as they are. Let us destroy no more of the old system, until we are sure that we have not destroyed too much of it already. Let us have no more of payment by results, until we are sure that what we have of it will give us satisfaction. Let us at any rate reject Mr. Walter's proposal as premature." This is the course which the best friends of education must wait to see the House of Commons take. They will have real ground for uneasiness should the House take a different course, and insist on embarrassing Mr. Lowe by carrying out Mr. Lowe's own doctrines. Even amidst that uneasiness, however, it will be impossible to repress a smile at seeing the engineer hoist by his own petard. *Tu l'as voulu, Georges Dandin, tu l'as voulu!*

A French Eton
or
Middle-Class Education and the State

Forgetting those things which are behind, and reaching forth unto those things which are before.

ST. PAUL

A lively and acute writer, whom English society, indebted to his vigilance for the exposure of a thousand delinquents, salutes with admiration as its Grand Detective, some time ago called public attention to the state of the "College of the Blessed Mary" at Eton. In that famous seat of learning, he said, a vast sum of money was expended on education, and a beggarly account of empty brains was the result. Rich endowments were wasted; parents were giving large sums to have their children taught, and were getting a most inadequate return for their outlay. Science, among those venerable towers in the vale of the Thames, still adored her Henry's holy shade; but she did very little else. These topics, handled with infinite skill and vivacity, produced a strong effect. Public attention, for a moment, fixed itself upon the state of secondary instruction in England. The great class, which is interested in the improvement of this, imagined that the moment was come for making the first step towards that improvement. The comparatively small class, whose children are educated in the existing public schools, thought that some inquiry into the state of these institutions might do good. A Royal Commission was appointed to report upon the endowments, studies, and management of the nine principal public schools of this country—Eton, Winchester, Westminster, Charterhouse, St. Paul's, Merchant Taylors', Harrow, Rugby, and Shrewsbury.

Eton was really the accused, although eight co-respondents were thus summoned to appear with Eton; and in Eton the investigation now completed will probably produce most reform. The reform of an institution which trains so many of the rulers of this country is, no doubt, a matter of considerable importance. That importance is certainly lessened if it is true, as the *Times* tells us, that the real ruler of our country is "The People," although this potentate does not absolutely transact his own business, but delegates that function to the class which Eton educates. But even those who believe that Mirabeau, when he said, *He who administers, governs,* was a great deal nearer the truth than the *Times,* and to whom, therefore, changes at Eton seem indeed matter of great importance, will hardly be disposed to make those changes very sweeping. If Eton does not teach her pupils profound wisdom, we have Oxenstiern's word for it that the world is governed by very little wisdom. Eton, at any rate, teaches her aristocratic pupils virtues which are among the best virtues of an aristocracy—freedom from affectation, manliness, a high spirit, simplicity. It is to be hoped that she teaches something of these virtues to her other pupils also, who, not of the aristocratic class themselves, enjoy at Eton the benefit of contact with aristocracy. For these other pupils, perhaps, a little more learning as well, a somewhat stronger dose of ideas, might be desirable. Above all, it might be desirable to wean them from the easy habits and profuse notions of expense which Eton generates—habits and notions graceful enough in the lilies of the social field, but inconvenient for its future toilers and spinners. To convey to Eton the knowledge that the wine of Champagne does not water the whole earth, and that there are incomes which fall below 5,000*l.* a year, would be an act of kindness towards a large class of British parents, full of proper pride, but not opulent. Let us hope that the courageous social reformer who has taken Eton in hand may, at least, reap this reward from his labours. Let us hope he may succeed in somewhat reducing the standard of expense at Eton, and let us pronounce over his offspring the prayer of Ajax:—"O boys, may you be cheaper-educated than "your father, but in other respects like him; may you have the "same loving care for the improvement of the British officer, "the same terrible eye upon bullies and jobbers, the same "charming gaiety in your frolics with the 'Old Dog Tray;'— "but may all these gifts be developed at a lesser price!"

But I hope that large class which wants the improvement of

secondary instruction in this country—secondary instruction, the great first stage of a liberal education, coming between elementary instruction, the instruction in the mother tongue and in the simplest and indispensable branches of knowledge on the one hand, and superior instruction, the instruction given by universities, the second and finishing stage of a liberal education, on the other—will not imagine that the appointment of a Royal Commission to report on nine existing schools can seriously help it to that which it wants. I hope it will steadily say to the limited class whom the reform of these nine schools (if they need reform) truly concerns—*Tua res agitur*. These nine schools are by their constitution such that they profess to reach but select portions of the multitudes that are claiming secondary instruction; and, whatever they might profess, being nine, they *can* only reach select portions. The exhibition which the Royal Commissioners have given us of these schools is indeed very interesting; I hope it will prove very useful. But, for the champions of the true cause of secondary instruction, for those interested in the thorough improvement of this most important concern, the centre of interest is not there. Before the English mind, always prone to throw itself upon details, has by the interesting Report of the Public School Commissioners been led completely to throw itself upon what, after all, in this great concern of secondary instruction, is only a detail, I wish to show, with all the clearness and insistance I can, where the centre of interest really lies.

[I]

To see secondary instruction treated as a matter of national concern, to see any serious attempt to make it both commensurate with the numbers needing it and of good quality, we must cross the Channel. The Royal Commissioners have thought themselves precluded, by the limits of their instructions, from making a thorough inquiry into the system of secondary instruction on the Continent. I regret that they did not trust to the vast importance of the subject for procuring their pardon even if they somewhat extended their scope, and made their survey of foreign secondary instruction exact. This they could have done only by investing qualified persons with the commission to seek, in their name, access to the foreign schools. These institutions must be seen at work, and seen by experienced eyes, for their operation to be properly understood and described. But to see them at work the aid of the public authorities abroad is requisite; and foreign governments, most prompt in giving this aid to accredited emissaries, are by no means disposed to extend it to the chance inquirer.

In 1859 I visited France, authorised by the Royal Commissioners who were then inquiring into the state of popular education in England, to seek, in their name, information respecting the French primary schools. I shall never cease to be grateful for the cordial help afforded to me by the functionaries of the French Government for seeing thoroughly the objects which I came to study. The higher functionaries charged with the supervision of primary instruction have the supervision of secondary instruction also; and their kindness enabled me occasionally to see something of the secondary schools—institutions which strongly attracted my interest, but which the Royal Commissioners had not authorised me to study, and which the French Minister of Public Instruction had not directed his functionaries to show me. I thus saw the Lyceum, or public secondary school, of Toulouse—a good specimen of its class. To make clear to the English reader what this class of institutions is, with a view of enabling him to see, afterwards, what is the problem respecting secondary instruction which we in this country really have to solve, I will describe the Toulouse Lyceum.

Toulouse, the chief city of the great plain of Languedoc, and a place of great antiquity, dignity, and importance, has one of the principal lyceums to be found out of Paris. But the chief town of every French department has its lyceum, and the considerable towns of every department have their communal colleges, as the chief town has its lyceum. These establishments of secondary instruction are attached to academies, local centres of the Department of Public Instruction at Paris, of which there are sixteen in France. The head of an academy is called its "rector," and his chief ministers are called "academy-inspectors." The superintendence of all public instruction (under the general control of the Minister of Public Instruction at Paris) was given by M. Guizot's education-law to the academies; that of primary instruction has been, in great measure, taken away from them and given to the prefects; that of secondary or superior instruction still remains to them. Toulouse is the seat of an academy of the first class, with a jurisdiction extending over eight departments; its rector, when I was there in 1859, was an ex-judge of the Paris Court of Cassation, M. Rocher, a man of about sixty, of great intelligence, courtesy, and knowledge of the world. Ill-health had compelled him to resign his judgeship, and the Minister of Public Instruction, his personal friend, had given him the rectorate of Toulouse, the second in France in point of rank, as a kind of dignified retreat. The position of rector in France much resembles that of one of our heads of houses at Oxford or Cambridge. M. Rocher placed me under the guidance of his academy-inspector, M. Peyrot; and M. Peyrot, after introducing me to the primary inspectors of Toulouse, and enabling me to make arrangements with them for visiting the primary schools of the city and neighbourhood, kindly took me over the lyceum, which is under his immediate supervision.

A French lyceum is an institution founded and maintained by the State, with aid from the department and commune. The communal colleges are founded and maintained by the commune, with aid from the State. The Lyceum of Toulouse is held in large and somewhat gloomy buildings, in the midst of the city; old ecclesiastical buildings have in a number of towns been converted by the Government into public-school premises. We were received by the *proviseur*, M. Seignette. The provisor is the chief functionary—the head master—of a French lyceum; he does not, however, himself teach, but manages the business concerns of the school, administers its finances, and is responsible for its general conduct and discipline; his place is one of the prizes of French secondary instruction, and the provisor, having himself served a long apprenticeship as a teacher, has all the knowledge requisite for superintending his professors. He, like the professors, has gone through the excellent normal school out of which the functionaries of secondary instruction are taken, and has fulfilled stringent conditions of training and examination. Three chaplains—Roman Catholic priests—have the charge of the religious instruction of the lyceum; a Protestant minister, however, is specially appointed to give this instruction to pupils whose parents are of the reformed faith, and these pupils attend, on Sundays, their own Protestant places of worship. The lyceum has from three to four hundred scholars; it receives both boarders and day-scholars. In every lyceum which receives boarders there are a certain number of *bourses*, or public scholarships, which relieve their holders from all cost for their education. The school has three great divisions, each with its separate schoolrooms and playground. The playgrounds are large courts, planted with trees. Attached to the institution, but in a separate building, is a school for little boys from six to twelve years of age, called the *Petit Collège;* here there is a garden as well as a playground, and the whole school-life is easier and softer than in the lyceum, and adapted to the tender years of the scholars. In the *Petit Collège*, too, there are both boarders and day-scholars.

The schoolrooms of the lyceum were much like our schoolrooms here; large bare rooms, looking as if they had seen much service, with their desks browned and battered, and inscribed with the various carvings of many generations of schoolboys. The cleanliness, order, and neatness of the passages, dormitories, and sick-rooms were exemplary. The dormitories are vast rooms, with a teacher's bed at each end; a light is kept burning in them all the night through. In no English school have I seen any arrangements for the sick to compare with those of the Toulouse Lyceum. The service of the *infirmary*, as it is called, is performed by Sisters of Charity. The aspect and manners of these nurses, the freshness and airiness of the rooms, the whiteness and fragrance of the great stores of linen which one saw ranged in them, made one almost envy the invalids who were being tended in such a place of repose.

In the playground the boys—dressed, all of them, in the well-known uniform of the French schoolboy—were running, shouting, and playing, with the animation of their age; but it is not by its playgrounds and means of recreation that a French lyceum, as compared with the half-dozen great English public schools, shines. The boys are taken out to walk, as the boys at Winchester used to be taken out to *hills;* but at the end of the French schoolboy's walk there are no *hills* on which he is turned loose. He learns and practises gymnastics more than our schoolboys do; and the court in which he takes his recreation is somewhat more spacious and agreeable than we English are apt to imagine a *court* to be; but it is a poor place indeed —poor in itself and poor in its resources—compared with the *playing-fields* of Eton, or the *meads* of Winchester, or the *close* of Rugby.

Of course I was very desirous to see the boys in their schoolrooms, and to hear some of the lessons; but M. Peyrot and M. Seignette, with all the good-will in the world, were not able to grant to an unofficial visitor permission to do this. It is something to know what the programme of studies in a French lyceum is, though it would be far more interesting to know how that programme is practically carried out. But the programme itself is worth examining: it is the same for every lyceum in France. It is fixed by the Council of Public Instruction in Paris, a body in which the State, the Church, the French Academy, and the scholastic profession, are all represented, and of which the Minister of Public Instruction is president. The programme thus fixed is promulgated by the Minister's authority, and every lyceum is bound to follow it. I have before me that promulgated by M. Guizot in 1833; the variations from it, up to the present day, are but slight. In the sixth, or lowest class, the boys have to learn French, Latin, and Greek Grammar, and their reading is Cornelius Nepos and Phædrus, and, along with the fables of Phædrus, those of La Fontaine. For the next, or fifth class, the reading is Ovid in Latin, Lucian's Dialogues and Isocrates in Greek, and *Télémaque* in French. For the fourth, besides the authors read in the classes below, Virgil in Latin and Xenophon in Greek, and, in French, Voltaire's *Charles XII*. For the third, Sallust and Cicero are added in Latin, Homer and Plutarch's *Moralia* in Greek; in French, Voltaire's *Siècle de Louis XIV.*, Massillon's *Petit Carême*, Boileau, and extracts from Buffon. For the second class (our fifth form), Horace, Livy, and Tacitus, in Latin; in Greek, Sophocles and Euripides, Plato and Demosthenes; in French, Bossuet's *Histoire Universelle*, and Montesquieu's *Grandeur et Décadence des Romains*. The highest class (our sixth form) is divided into two, a rhetoric and a philosophy class; this division—which is important, and which is daily becoming, with the authorities of French Public Instruction, an object of greater importance—is meant to correspond to the direction, literary or scientific, which the studies of the now adult scholar are to take. In place of the Pindar, Thucydides, Lucan, and Molière, of the rhetoric class, the philosophy class has chemistry, physics, and the higher mathematics. Some instruction in natural science finds a place in the school-course of every class; in the lower classes, instruction in the elements of human physiology, zoology, botany, and geology; in the second class (fifth form), instruction in the elements of chemistry. To this instruction in natural science two or three hours a week are allotted. About the same time is allotted to arithmetic, to special instruction in history and geography, and to modern languages; these last, however, are said to be in general as imperfectly learnt in the French public schools as they are in our own. Two hours a week are devoted to the correction of composition. Finally, the New Testament, in Latin or Greek, forms a part of the daily reading of each class.

On this programme I will make two remarks, suggested by comparing it with that of any of our own public schools. It has the scientific instruction and the study of the mother-tongue which our school-course is without, and is often blamed for being without. I believe that the scientific instruction actually acquired by French schoolboys in the lower classes is very little, but still a boy with a taste for science finds in this instruction an element which keeps his taste alive; in the special class at the head of the school it is more considerable, but not, it is alleged, sufficient for the wants of this special class, and plans for making it more thorough and systematic are being canvassed. In the study of the mother-tongue the French school-boy has a more real advantage over ours; he does certainly learn something of the French language and literature, and of the English our schoolboy learns nothing. French grammar, however, is a better instrument of instruction for boys than English grammar, and the French literature possesses prose works, perhaps even poetical works, more fitted to be used as classics for schoolboys than any which English literature possesses. I need not say that the fitness of works for this purpose depends on other considerations than those of the genius alone, and of the creative force, which they exhibit.

The regular school-lessons of a lyceum occupy about twenty-two hours in the week, but among these regular school-lessons the lessons in modern languages are not counted. The lessons in modern languages are given out of school-hours; out of school-hours, too, all the boarders work with the masters at preparing their lessons; each boarder has thus what we call a private tutor, but the French schoolboy does not, like ours, pay extra for his private tutor: the general charge for board and instruction covers this special tuition.

Now I come to the important matter of school-fees. These are all regulated by authority; the scale of charges in every lyceum and communal college must be seen and sanctioned by the academy-inspector in order to have legality. A day-scholar in the Toulouse Lyceum pays, in the lowest of the three great divisions of the school, 110f. (4*l.* 8*s.* 4*d.*) a year; in the second division he pays 135f. (5*l.* 8*s.* 4*d.*); in the third and highest division, 180f. (7*l.* 4*s.* 2*d.*) If he wishes to share in the special tuition of the boarders, he pays from 2*l.* to 4*l.* a year extra. Next, for the boarders. A boarder pays, for his whole board and instruction, in the lowest division, 800f. (32*l.*) a year; in the second division, 850f. (34*l.*); in the highest division, 900f. (36*l.*) In the scientific class the charge is 2*l.* extra. The payments are made quarterly, and always in advance. Every boarder brings with him an outfit (*trousseau*) valued at 500f. (20*l.*): the sum paid for his board and instruction covers, besides, all expense for keeping good this outfit, and all charges for washing, medical attendance, books, and writing materials. The meals, though plain, are good, and they are set out with a propriety and a regard for appearances which, when I was a boy, graced no school-dinners that I ever saw; just as, I must say, even in the normal schools for elementary teachers, the dinner-table in France contrasted strongly, by its clean cloth, arranged napkins, glass, and general neatness of service, with the stained cloth, napkinless knives and forks, jacks and mugs, hacked joints of meat, and stumps of loaves, which I have seen on the dinner-table of normal schools in England. With us it is always the individual that is filled, and the public that is sent empty away.

Such may be the cheapness of public school education, when that education is treated as a matter of public economy, to be administered upon a great scale, with rigid system and exact superintendence, in the interest of the pupil and not in the interest of the school-keeper.* But many people, it will be said, have no relish for such cast-iron schooling. Well, then, let us look at a French school not of the State-pattern—a school without the guarantees of State-management, but, also, without the uniformity and constraint which this management introduces.

A day or two after I had seen the Toulouse Lyceum, I started for Sorèze. Sorèze is a village in the department of the Tarn, a department bordering upon that in which Toulouse stands; it contains one of the most successful private schools in France, and of this school, in 1859, the celebrated Father Lacordaire was director. I left Toulouse by railway in the middle of the day; in two hours I was at Castelnaudary, an old Visigoth place, on a hill rising out of the great plain of Languedoc, with immense views towards the Pyrenees on one

* *L'administration des lycées est complètement étrangère à toute idée de spéculation et de profit,* says the Toulouse prospectus which lies before me; "A lyceum is managed not in the least as a matter of speculation or profit;" and this is not a mere advertising puff, for the public is the real proprietor of the lyceums, which it has founded for the education of its youth, and for that object only; the directors of the lyceum are simple servants of the public, employed by the public at fixed salaries.

side and the Cevennes on the other. After rambling about the town for an hour, I started for Sorèze in a vehicle exactly like an English coach; I was outside with the driver, and the other places, inside and outside, were occupied by old pupils of the Sorèze school, who were going there for the annual *fête*, the *Speeches*, to take place the next day. They were, most of them, young men from the universities of Toulouse and Montpellier; two or three were settled in Paris, but, happening to be just then at their homes, at Béziers or Narbonne, they had come over like the rest: they seemed a good set, all of them, and their attachment to their old school and master was more according to one's notions of English school-life than French. We had to cross the *Montagne Noire*, an outlier of the Cevennes; the elevation was not great, but the air, even on the 18th of May in Languedoc, was sharp, the vast distance looked grey and chill, and the whole landscape was severe, lonely, and desolate. Sorèze is in the plain on the other side of the *Montagne Noire*, at the foot of gorges running up into the Cevennes; at the head of these gorges are the basins from which the *Canal du Midi*—the great canal uniting the Mediterranean with the Atlantic—is fed. It was seven o'clock when we drove up the street, shaded with large trees, of Sorèze; my fellow-travellers showed me the way to the school, as I was obliged to get away early the next morning, and wanted, therefore, to make my visit that evening. The school occupies the place of an old abbey, founded in 757 by Pepin the Little; for several hundred years the abbey had been in the possession of the Dominicans, when, in Louis the Sixteenth's reign, a school was attached to it. In this school the king took great interest, and himself designed the dress for the scholars. The establishment was saved at the Revolution by the tact of the Dominican who was then at its head; he resumed the lay dress, and returned, in all outward appearance, to the secular life, and his school was allowed to subsist. Under the Restoration it was one of the most famous and most aristocratic schools in France, but it had much declined when Lacordaire, in 1854, took charge of it. I waited in the monastic-looking court (much of the old abbey remains as part of the present building) while my card, with a letter which the Papal Nuncio at Paris, to whom I had been introduced through Sir George Bowyer's kindness, had obtained for me from the Superior of the Dominicans, was taken up to Lacordaire; he sent down word directly that he would see me; I was shown across the court, up an old stone staircase, into a vast corridor; a door in this corridor was thrown open, and in a large bare room, with no carpet or furniture of any kind, except a small table, one or two chairs, a small book-case, a crucifix, and some religious pictures on the walls, Lacordaire, in the dress of his order, white-robed, hooded, and sandalled, sat before me.

The first public appearance of this remarkable man was in the cause of education. The Charter of 1830 had promised liberty of instruction; liberty, that is, for persons outside the official hierarchy of public instruction to open schools. This promise M. Guizot's celebrated school law of 1833 finally performed; but, in the meantime, the authorities of public instruction refused to give effect to it. Lacordaire and M. de Montalembert opened in Paris, on the 7th of May, 1831, an independent free school, of which they themselves were the teachers; it was closed in a day or two by the police, and its youthful conductors were tried before the Court of Peers and fined. This was Lacordaire's first public appearance; twenty-two years later his last sermon in Paris was preached in the same cause; it was a sermon on behalf of the schools of the Christian Brethren. During that space of twenty-two years he had run a conspicuous career, but on another field than that of education; he had become the most renowned preacher in Europe, and he had re-established in France, by his energy, conviction, and patience, the religious orders banished thence since the Revolution. Through this career I cannot now attempt to follow him; with the heart of friendship and the eloquence of genius, M. de Montalembert has recently written its history; but I must point out two characteristics which distinguished him in it, and which created in him the force by which, as an educator, he worked, the force by which he most impressed and commanded the young. One of these was his passion for firm order, for solid government. He called our age an age "which does not know how to obey—*qui ne sait guère* "*obéir*." It is easy to see that this is not so absolutely a matter of reproach as Lacordaire made it; in an epoch of transition society may and must say to its governors, "Govern me ac- "cording to my spirit, if I am to obey you." One cannot doubt that Lacordaire erred in making absolute devotion to the Church (*malheur à qui trouble l'Église!*) the watch-word of a gifted man in our century; one cannot doubt that he erred in affirming that "the greatest service to be rendered to "Christianity in our day was to do something for the revival "of the mediæval religious orders." Still, he seized a great truth when he proclaimed the intrinsic weakness and danger of a state of anarchy; above all, when he applied this truth in the moral sphere he was incontrovertible, fruitful for his nation, especially fruitful for the young. He dealt vigorously with himself, and he told others that the first thing for them was to do the same; he placed character above everything else. "One may have spirit, learning, even genius," he said, "and "not *character;* for want of character our age is the age of "miscarriages. Let us form Christians in our schools, but, first "of all, let us form Christians in our own hearts; the one great "thing is *to have a life of one's own.*"

Allied to this characteristic was his other—his passion, in an age which seems to think that progress can be achieved only by our herding together and making a noise, for the antique discipline of retirement and silence. His plan of life for himself, when he first took orders, was to go and be a village curé in a remote province in France. M. de Quélen, the Archbishop of Paris, kept him in the capital as chaplain to the Convent of the Visitation; he had not then commenced the *conférences* which made his reputation; he lived perfectly isolated and obscure, and he was never so happy. "It is with delight," he wrote at this time, "that I find my solitude deepening "round me; 'one can do nothing without solitude,' is my grand "maxim. A man is formed from within, and not from with- "out. To withdraw and be with oneself and with God, is "the greatest strength there can be in the world." It is impossible not to feel the serenity and sincerity of these words.

Twice he refused to edit the *Univers;* he refused a chair in the University of Louvain. In 1836, when his fame filled France, he disappeared for five years, and these years he passed in silence and seclusion at Rome. He came back in 1841 a Dominican monk; again, at Notre Dame, that eloquence, that ineffable *accent,* led his countrymen and foreigners captive; he achieved his cherished purpose of re-establishing in France the religious orders. Then once more he disappeared, and after a short station at Toulouse consigned himself, for the rest of his life, to the labour and obscurity of Sorèze. "One of the great "consolations of my present life," he writes from Sorèze, "is, "that I have now God and the young for my sole companions." The young, with their fresh spirit, as they instinctively feel the presence of a great character, so, too, irresistibly receive an influence from souls which live habitually with God.

Lacordaire received me with great kindness. He was above the middle height, with an excellent countenance; great dignity in his look and bearing, but nothing ascetic; his manners animated, and every gesture and movement showing the orator. He asked me to dine with him the next day, and to see the school festival, the *fête des anciens élèves;* but I could not stop. Then he ordered lights, for it was growing dark, and insisted on showing me all over the place that evening. While we were waiting for lights he asked me much about Oxford; I had already heard from his old pupils that Oxford was a favourite topic with him, and that he held it up to them as a model of everything that was venerable. Lights came, and we went over the establishment; the school then contained nearly three hundred pupils—a great rise since Lacordaire first came in 1854, but not so many as the school has had in old days. It is said that Lacordaire at one time resorted so frequently to expulsion as rather to alarm people.

Sorèze, under his management, chiefly created interest by the sort of competition which it maintained with the lyceums, or State schools. A private school, in France, cannot be opened without giving notice to the public authorities; the consent of these authorities is withheld if the premises of the proposed school are improper, or if its director fails to produce a certificate of probation and a certificate of competency—that is, if he has not served for five years in a secondary school, and passed the authorised public examination for secondary teachers. Finally, the school is always subject to State-inspection, to ascertain that the pupils are properly lodged and fed, and that the teaching contains nothing contrary to public morality and to the laws; and the school may be closed by the public authorities on an inspector's report, duly verified. Still, for an establishment like the Sorèze school, the actual State-interference comes to very little; the Minister has the power of dispensing with the certificate of probation, and holy orders are accepted in the place of the certificate of competency (the examination in the seminary being more difficult than the examination for this latter). In France the State (Machiavel as we English think it), in naming certain matters as the objects of its supervision in private schools, means what it says, and does not go beyond these matters; and, for these matters, the name of a man like Lacordaire serves as a guarantee, and is readily accepted as such.

All the boys at Sorèze are boarders, and a boarder's expenses here exceed by about 8*l.* or 10*l.* a year his expenses at a lyceum. The programme of studies differs little from that of the lyceums, but the military system of these State schools Lacordaire repudiated. Instead of the vast common dormitories of the lyceums, every boy had his little cell to himself; that was, after all, as it seemed to me, the great difference. But immense stress was laid, too, upon physical education, which the lyceums are said too much to neglect. Lacordaire showed me with great satisfaction the stable, with more than twenty horses, and assured me that all the boys were taught to ride. There was the *salle d'escrime*, where they fenced, the armoury full of guns and swords, the shooting gallery, and so on. All this is in our eyes a little fantastic, and does not replace the want of cricket and football in a good field, and of freedom to roam over the country out of school-hours; in France, however, it is a good deal; and then twice a week all the boys used to turn out with Lacordaire upon the mountains, to their great enjoyment as the Sorèze people said, the Father himself being more vigorous than any of them. And the old abbey school has a small park adjoining it, with the mountains rising close behind, and it has beautiful trees in its courts, and by no means the dismal barrack-look of a lyceum. Lacordaire had a staff of more than fifty teachers and helpers, about half of these being members of his own religious order—Dominicans; all co-operated in some way or other in conducting the school. Lacordaire used never to give school-lessons himself, but scarcely a Sunday passed without his preaching in the chapel. The highest and most distinguished boys formed a body called *the Institute,* with no governing powers like those of our sixth form, but with a sort of common-room to themselves, and with the privilege of having their meals with Lacordaire and his staff. I was shown, too, a *Salle d'Illustres,* or Hall of Worthies, into which the boys are introduced on high days and holidays; we should think this fanciful, but I found it impressive. The hall is decorated with busts of the chief of the former scholars, some of them very distinguished. Among these busts was that of Henri de Larochejaquelein (who was brought up here at Sorèze), with his noble, speaking countenance, his Vendean hat, and the heart and cross on his breast. There was, besides, a theatre for public recitations. We ended with the chapel, in which we found all the school assembled; a Dominican was reading to them from the pulpit an edifying life of a scapegrace converted to seriousness by a bad accident, much better worth listening to than most sermons. When it was over, Lacordaire whispered to me to ask if I would stay for the prayers or go at once. I stayed; they were very short and simple; and I saw the boys disperse afterwards. The gaiety of the little ones and their evident fondness for the *Père* was a pretty sight. As we went out of chapel, one of them, a little fellow of ten or eleven, ran from behind us, snatched, with a laughing face, Lacordaire's hand, and kissed it; Lacordaire smiled, and patted his head. When I read the other day in M. de Montalembert's book how Lacordaire had said, shortly before his death, "I have always tried to serve

"God, the Church, and our Lord Jesus Christ; besides these, I "have loved—oh, dearly loved!—children and young people," I thought of this incident.

Lacordaire knew absolutely nothing of our great English schools, their character, or recent history; but then no Frenchman, except a very few at Paris who know more than anybody in the world, knows anything about anything. However, I have seen few people more impressive; he was not a great modern thinker, but a great Christian orator of the fourth century, born in the nineteenth; playing his part in the nineteenth century not so successfully as he would have played it in the fourth, but still nobly. I would have given much to stay longer with him, as he kindly pressed me; I was tempted, too, by hearing that it was likely he would make a speech the next day. Never did any man so give one the sense of his being a natural orator, perfect in ease and simplicity; they told me that on Sunday, when he preached, he hardly ever went up into the pulpit, but spoke to them from his place "*sans façon*." But I had an engagement to keep at Carcassonne at a certain hour, and I was obliged to go. At nine I took leave of Lacordaire and returned to the village inn, clean, because it is frequented by the relations of pupils. There I supped with my fellow-travellers, the old scholars; charming companions they proved themselves. Late we sat, much *vin de Cahors* we drank, and great friends we became. Before we parted, one of them, the Béziers youth studying at Paris, with the amiability of his race assured me (God forgive him!) that he was well acquainted with my poems. By five the next morning I had started to return to Castelnaudary. Recrossing the *Montagne Noire* in the early morning was very cold work, but the view was inconceivably grand. I caught the train at Castelnaudary, and was at Carcassonne by eleven; there I saw a school, and I saw the old *city* of Carcassonne. I am not going to describe either the one or the other, but I cannot forbear saying, Let everybody see the *cité de Carcassonne*. It is, indeed, as the antiquarians call it, the Middle Age Herculaneum. When you first get sight of the old city, which is behind the modern town—when you have got clear of the modern town, and come out upon the bridge over the Aude, and see the walled *cité* upon its hill before you—you rub your eyes and think that you are looking at a vignette in *Ivanhoe*.

Thus I have enabled, as far as I could, the English reader to see what a French lyceum is like, and what a French private school, competing with a lyceum, is like. I have given him, as far as I could, the facts; now for the application of these facts. What is the problem respecting secondary instruction which we in this country have to solve? What light do these facts throw upon that problem?

[II]

For the serious thinker, for the real student of the question of secondary instruction, the problem respecting secondary instruction which we in England have to solve is this:—Why cannot we have throughout England—as the French have throughout France, as the Germans have throughout Germany, as the Swiss have throughout Switzerland, as the Dutch have throughout Holland—schools where the children of our middle and professional classes may obtain, at the rate of from 20*l.* to 50*l.* a year, if they are boarders, at the rate of from 5*l.* to 15*l.* a year if they are day-scholars, an education of as good quality, with as good guarantees, social character, and advantages for a future career in the world, as the education which French children of the corresponding class can obtain from institutions like that of Toulouse or Sorèze?

There is the really important question. It is vain to meet it by propositions which may, very likely, be true, but which are quite irrelevant. "Your French Etons," I am told, "are no "Etons at all; there is nothing like an Eton in France." I know that. Very likely France is to be pitied for having no Etons, but I want to call attention to the substitute, to the compensation. The English public school produces the finest boys in the world; the Toulouse Lyceum boy, the Sorèze College boy, is not to be compared with them. Well, let me grant all that too. But then there are only some five or six schools in England to produce this specimen-boy; and they cannot produce him cheap. Rugby and Winchester produce him at about 120*l.* a year; Eton and Harrow (and the Eton school-boy is perhaps justly taken as the most perfect type of this highly-extolled class) cannot produce him for much less than 200*l.* a year. *Tantæ molis erat Romanam condere gentem*—such a business is it to produce an article so superior. But for the common wear and tear of middling life, and at rates tolerable for middling people, what do we produce? What do we produce at 30*l.* a year? What is the character of the schools which undertake for us this humbler, but far more widely-interesting production? Are they as good as the Toulouse Lyceum and the Sorèze College? That is the question.

Suppose that the recommendations of the Public School Commissioners bring about in the great public schools all the reforms which a judicious reformer could desire;—suppose that they produce the best possible application of endowments, the best possible mode of election to masterships; that they lead to a wise revision of the books and subjects of study, to a reinforcing of the mathematics and of the modern languages, where these are found weak; to a perfecting, finally, of all boarding arrangements and discipline: nothing will yet have been done towards providing for the great want—the want of a secondary instruction at once reasonably cheap and reasonably good. Suppose that the recommendations of the Commissioners accomplish something even in this direction—suppose that the cost of educating a boy at Rugby is reduced to about 100*l.* a year, and the cost of educating a boy at Eton to about 150*l.* a year—no one acquainted with the subject will think it practicable, or even, under present circumstances, desirable, to effect in the cost of education in these two schools a greater reduction than this. And what will this reduction amount to? A boon—in some cases a very considerable boon—to those who now frequent these schools. But what will it do for the great class now in want of proper secondary instruction? Nothing: for in the first place these schools are but two, and are full, or at least sufficiently full, already; in the second place, if they were able to hold all the boys in England, the class I speak of would still be excluded from them—excluded by a cost of 100*l.* or 150*l.* just as much as by a cost of 120*l.* or 200*l.* A certain number of the professional class, with incomes quite inadequate to such a charge, will, for the sake of the future establishment of their children, make a brave effort, and send them to Eton or Rugby at a cost of 150*l.* or 100*l.* a year. But they send them there already, even at the existing higher rate. The great mass of middling people, with middling incomes, not having for their children's future establishment in life plans which make a public school training indispensable, will not make this effort, will not pay for their children's schooling a price quite disproportionate to their means. They demand a lower school-charge—a school-charge like that of Toulouse or Sorèze.

And they find it. They have only to open the *Times*. There they read advertisement upon advertisement, offering them, "conscientiously offering" them, in almost any part of England which suits their convenience, "Education, 20*l.* per "annum, no extras. Diet unlimited, and of the best description. "The education comprises Greek, Latin, and German, French "by a resident native, mathematics, algebra, mapping, globes, "and all the essentials of a first-rate commercial education." Physical, moral, mental, and spiritual—all the wants of their children will be sedulously cared for. They are invited to an "Educational Home," where "discipline is based upon moral in-"fluence and emulation, and every effort is made to combine "home-comforts with school-training. Terms inclusive and "moderate." If they have a child with an awkward temper, and needing special management, even for this particular child the wonderful operation of the laws of supply and demand, in this great commercial country, will be found to have made perfect provision. "Unmanageable boys or youths (up to twenty "years) are made perfectly tractable and gentlemanly in one "year by a clergyman near town, whose peculiarly persuasive "high moral and religious training at once elevates," &c. And all this, as I have said, is provided by the simple, natural operation of the laws of supply and demand, without, as the *Times* beautifully says, "the fetters of endowment and the inter-"ference of the executive." Happy country! happy middle classes! Well may the *Times* congratulate them with such fervency; well may it produce dithyrambs, while the newspapers of less-favoured countries produce only leading articles; well may it declare that the fabled life of the Happy Islands is already beginning amongst us.

But I have no heart for satire, though the occasion invites it. No one, who knows anything of the subject, will venture to affirm that these "educational homes" give, or can give, that which they "conscientiously offer." No one, who knows anything of the subject, will seriously affirm that they give, or can give, an education comparable to that given by the Toulouse and Sorèze schools. And why? Because they want the securities which, to make them produce even half of what they offer, are indispensable—the securities of supervision and publicity. By this time we know pretty well that to trust to the principle of supply and demand to do for us all that we want in providing education is to lean upon a broken reed. We trusted to it to give us fit elementary schools till its impotence became conspicuous; we have thrown it aside, and called upon State-aid, with the securities accompanying this, to give us elementary schools more like what they should be; we have thus founded in elementary education a system still, indeed, far from perfect, but living and fruitful—a system which will probably survive the most strenuous efforts for its destruction. In secondary education the impotence of this principle of supply and demand is as signal as in elementary education. The mass of mankind know good butter from bad, and tainted meat from fresh, and the principle of supply and demand may, perhaps, be relied on to give us sound meat and butter. But the mass of mankind do not so well know what distinguishes good teaching and training from bad; they do not here know what they ought to demand, and, therefore, the demand cannot be relied on to give us the right supply. Even if they knew what they ought to demand, they have no sufficient means of testing whether or no this is really supplied to them. Securities, therefore, are needed. The great public schools of England offer securities by their very publicity; by their wealth, importance, and connexions, which attract general attention to them; by their old reputation, which they cannot forfeit without disgrace and danger. The appointment of the Public School Commission is a proof, that to these moral securities for the efficiency of the great public schools may be added the material security of occasional competent supervision. I will grant that the great schools of the Continent do not offer the same moral securities to the public as Eton or Harrow. They offer them in a certain measure, but certainly not in so large measure: they have not by any means so much importance, by any means so much reputation. Therefore they offer, in far larger measure, the other security—the security of competent supervision. With them this supervision is not occasional and extraordinary, but periodic and regular; it is not explorative only; it is also, to a considerable extent, authoritative.

It will be said that between the "educational home" and Eton there is a long series of schools, with many gradations; and that in this series are to be found schools far less expensive than Eton, yet offering moral securities as Eton offers them, and as the "educational home" does not. Cheltenham, Bradfield, Marlborough, are instances which will occur to every one. It is true that these schools offer securities; it is true that the mere presence, at the head of a school, of a distinguished master like Mr. Bradley is, perhaps, the best moral security which can be offered. But, in the first place, these schools are thinly scattered over the country; we have no provision for planting such schools where they are most wanted, or for insuring a due supply of them. Cheltenham, Bradfield, and Marlborough are no more a due provision for the Northumberland boy than the Bordeaux Lyceum is a due provision for the little Alsatian. In the second place, Are these schools cheap? Even if they were cheap once, does not their very excellence, in a country where schools at once good and cheap are rare, tend to deprive them of their cheapness? Marlborough was, I believe—perhaps it still is—the cheapest of them; Marlborough is probably just now the best-taught school in England; and Marlborough, therefore, has raised its school-charge. Marlborough was quite right in so doing, for Marlborough is an individual institution, bound to guard its own interests and to profit by its own successes, and not bound to provide for the general educational wants of the country. But what makes the school-charge of the Toulouse Lyceum remain moderate, however eminent may be the merits of the Toulouse masters, or the successes of the Toulouse pupils? It is that the Toulouse Lyceum is a public institution, administered in view of the general educational wants of France, and not of its own individual preponderance. And what makes (or made, alas!) the school-charge of the Sorèze College remain moderate, even with a most distinguished and attractive director, like Lacordaire, at its head? It was the organisation of a complete system of secondary schools throughout France, the abundant supply of institutions, with at once respectable guarantees and reasonable charges, fixing a general mean of school-cost which even the most successful private school cannot venture much to exceed.

After all, it is the "educational home," and not Bradfield or Marlborough, which supplies us with the nearest approach to that rate of charges which secondary instruction, if it is ever to be organised on a great scale, and to reach those who are in need of it, must inevitably adopt. People talk of the greater cheapness of foreign countries, and of the dearness of this; everything costs more here, they say, than it does abroad; good education, like everything else. I do not wish to dispute, I am willing to make some allowance for this plea; one must be careful not to make too much, however, or we shall find ourselves to the end of the chapter with a secondary instruction failing just where our present secondary instruction fails—a secondary instruction which, out of the multitude needing it, a few, and only a few, make sacrifices to get; the many, who do not like sacrifices, go without it. If we fix a school-charge varying from 25*l.* to 50*l.* a year, I am sure we have fixed the outside rate which the great body of those needing secondary instruction will ever pay. Sir John Coleridge analyses this body into "the clergy of moderate or con-"tracted incomes" (and that means the immense majority of the clergy), "officers of the army and navy, medical men, "solicitors, and gentry of large families and small means." Many more elements might be enumerated. Why are the manufacturers left out? The very rich, among these, are to be counted by ones, the middling sort by hundreds. And when Sir John Coleridge separates "tenant-farmers, small landholders, "and retail tradesmen," into a class by themselves, and proposes to appropriate a separate class of schools for them, he carries the process of distinction and demarcation further than I can think quite desirable. But taking the constituent parts of the class requiring a liberal education as he assigns them, it seems to me certain that a sum ranging from 25*l.* to 50*l.* a year is as much as those whom he enumerates can in general be expected to pay for a son's education, and as much as they need be called upon to pay for a sound and valuable education, if secondary instruction were organised as it might be. It must be remembered, however, that a reduced rate of charge for boarders, at a good boarding-school, is not by any means the only benefit to the class of parents in question—perhaps not even the principal benefit—which the organisation of secondary instruction brings with it. It brings with it, also, by establishing its schools in proper numbers, and all over the country, facilities for bringing up many boys as day-scholars who are now brought up as boarders. At present many people send their sons to a boarding-school when they would much rather keep them at home, because they have no suitable school within reach. Opinions differ as to whether it is best for a boy to live at home or to go away to school, but there can be no doubt which of the two modes of bringing him up is the cheapest for his parents; and those (and they are many) who think that the continuation of home-life along with his schooling is far best for the boy himself, would enjoy a double benefit in having suitable schools made accessible to them.

But I must not forget that an institution, or rather a group of institutions, exists, offering to the middle classes, at a charge scarcely higher than that of the 20*l.* "educational home," an education affording considerable guarantees for its sound character. I mean the College of St. Nicholas, Lancing, and its affiliated schools. This institution certainly demands a word of notice here, and no word of mine, regarding Mr. Woodard and his labours, shall be wanting in unfeigned interest and respect for them. Still, I must confess that, as I read Mr. Woodard's programme, and as I listened to an excellent sermon from the Dean of Chichester in recommendation of it, that programme and that sermon seemed to me irresistibly to lead towards conclusions which they did not reach, and the conclusions which they did reach were far from satisfying. Mr. Woodard says with great truth: "It may be asked, Why cannot the shop-"keeper-class educate their own children without charity? It "may be answered, Scarcely any class in the country does edu-"cate its own children without some aid. Witness the enormous "endowments of our Universities and public schools, where the "sons of our well-to-do people resort. Witness our national "schools supported by State grants, and by parochial and na-"tional subscriptions. On the other hand, the lower middle class" (Mr. Woodard might quite properly have said the middle class in general), "politically a very important one, is dependent to "a great extent for its education on private desultory enterprise. "This class, in this land of education, gets *nothing* out of the "millions given annually for this purpose to every class except "themselves." In his sermon Dr. Hook spoke, in his cordial, manly way, much to the same effect.

This was the grievance; what was the remedy? That this great class should be rescued from the tender mercies of private desultory enterprise? That, in this land of education, it should henceforth get something out of the millions given annually for this purpose to every class except itself? That in an age when "enormous endowments,"—the form which public aid took in earlier ages, and taking which form public aid founded in those ages the Universities and the public schools for the benefit, along with the upper class, of this very middle class which is now, by the irresistible course of events, in great measure excluded from them—that in an age, I say, when these great endowments, this mediæval form of public aid, have ceased, public aid should be brought to these classes in that simpler and more manageable form which in modern societies it assumes—the form of public grants, with the guarantees of supervision and responsibility? The Universities receive public grants; for—not to speak of the payment of certain professors * by the State—that the State regards the endowments of the Universities as in reality public grants, it proves by assuming to itself the right of interfering in the disposal of them; the elementary schools receive public grants. Why, then, should not our secondary schools receive public grants? But this question Mr. Woodard (I do not blame him for it, he had a special function to perform) never touches. He falls back on an Englishman's favourite panacea—a subscription. He has built a school at Lancing, and a school at Shoreham, and he proposes to build a bigger school than either at Balcombe. He asks for a certain number of subscribers to give him contributions for a certain number of years, at certain rates, which he has calculated. I cannot see how, in this way, he will be delivering English secondary instruction from the hands of "private desultory "enterprise." What English secondary instruction wants is these two things: sufficiency of provision of fit schools, sufficiency of securities for their fitness. Mr. Woodard proposes to establish one great school in Sussex, where he has got two already. What sort of a provision is this for that need which is, on his own showing, so urgent? He hopes, indeed, that "if the public "will assist in raising this one school, it will lead to a general "extension of middle class education all over England." But in what number of years? How long are we to wait first? And then we have to consider the second great point—that of *securities*. Suppose Mr. Woodard's hopes to be fulfilled—suppose the establishment of the Balcombe school to have led to the establishment of like schools all over England—what securities shall we have for the fitness of these schools? Sussex is not a very large and populous county, but, even if we limit ourselves to the ratio adopted for Sussex, of three of these schools to a county, that gives us 120 of them for England proper only,

* These professors are now nominally paid by the University; but the University pays them in consideration of the remission to her, by the State, of certain duties of greater amount than the salaries which the State used to pay to these professors. They are still, therefore, in fact, paid by the State.

without taking in Wales. I have said that the eminence of the master may be in itself a sound security for the worth of a school; but, when I look at the number of these schools wanted, when I look at the probable position and emoluments of their teachers, I cannot think it reasonable to expect that all of them, or anything like all, will be provided with masters of an eminence to make all further guarantees unnecessary. But, perhaps, they will all be affiliated to the present institution at Lancing, and, in some degree, under its supervision? Well, then, that gives us, as the main regulative power of English secondary instruction, as our principal security for it, the Provost and Fellows of St. Nicholas College, Lancing. I have the greatest, the most sincere respect for Mr. Woodard and his coadjutors—I should be quite ready to accept Mr. Woodard's name as sufficient security for any school which he himself conducts—but I should hesitate, I confess, before accepting Mr. Woodard and his colleagues, or any similar body of private persons, as my final security for the right management of a great national concern, as the last court of appeal to which the interests of English secondary instruction were to be carried. Their constitution is too close, their composition too little national. Even if this or that individual were content to take them as his security, the bulk of the public would not. We saw this the other day, when imputations were thrown out against Lancing, and our proposed security had to find security for itself. It had no difficulty in so doing; Mr. Woodard has, it cannot be repeated too often, governed Lancing admirably; all I mean is—and Mr. Woodard himself would probably be the first to agree with me—that, to command public confidence for a great national system of schools, one needs a security larger, ampler, more national, than any which, by the very nature of things, Mr. Woodard and his friends can quite supply.

But another and a very plausible security has been provided for secondary instruction by the zeal and energy of Mr. Acland and Dr. Temple; I mean, the Oxford and Cambridge Middle Class Examinations. The good intentions and the activity of the promoters of these examinations cannot be acknowledged too gratefully; good has certainly been accomplished by them: yet it is undeniable that this security also is, in its present condition, quite insufficient. I write, not for the professed and practised educationist, but for the general reader; above all, for the reader of that class which is most concerned in the question which I am raising, and which I am most solicitous to carry with me—the middle class. Therefore, I shall use the plainest and most unprofessional language I can, in attempting to show what the promoters of these University examinations try to do, what they have accomplished, wherein they have failed. They try to make *security* do for us all that we want in the improvement of our secondary education. They accept the "educational "homes" at present scattered all over the country; they do not aim at replacing them by other and better institutions; they do not visit or criticise them; but they invite them to send select pupils to certain local centres, and when the pupils are there, they examine them, class them, and give prizes to the best of them. Undoubtedly this action of the Universities has given a certain amount of stimulus to these schools, and has done them a certain amount of good. But any one can see how far this action falls, and must fall, short of what is required. Any one can see that the examination of a few select scholars from a school, not at the school itself, not preceded or followed by an inspection of the school itself, affords no solid security for the good condition of their school. Any one can see that it is for the interest of an unscrupulous master to give all his care to his few cleverest pupils, who will serve him as an advertisement, while he neglects the common bulk of his pupils, whose backwardness there will be nobody to expose. I will not, however, insist too strongly on this last mischief, because I really believe that, serious as is its danger, it has not so much prevailed as to counterbalance the benefit which the mere stimulus of these examinations has given. All I say is, that this stimulus is an insufficient security. Plans are now broached for reinforcing University examination by University inspection. There we get a far more solid security. And I agree with Sir John Coleridge, that a body fitter than the Universities to exercise this inspection could not be found. It is indispensable that it should be exercised in the name, and on the responsibility, of a great public body; therefore the Society of Arts, which deserves thanks for its readiness to help in improving secondary instruction, is hardly, perhaps, from its want of weight, authority, and importance, qualified to exercise it: but whether it is exercised by the State, or by great and august corporations like Oxford and Cambridge, the value of the security is equally good; and learned corporations, like the Universities, have a certain natural fitness for discharging what is, in many respects, a learned function. It is only as to the power of the Universities to organise, equip, and keep working an efficient system of inspection for secondary schools that I am in doubt; organisation and regularity are as indispensable to this guarantee as weight and authority. Can the Universities organise and pay a body of inspectors to travel all over England, to visit, at least once in every year, the four or five hundred endowed schools of this country, and its unnumbered "educational homes;" can they supply a machinery for regulating the action of these gentlemen, giving effect to the information received from them, printing their reports, circulating them through the country? The French University could; but the French University was a department of State. If the English Universities cannot, the security of their inspection will be precarious; if they can, there can be no better.

No better *security*. But English secondary instruction wants, I said, two things: sufficient provision of good schools, sufficient security for these schools continuing good. Granting that the Universities may give us the second, I do not see how they are to give us the first. It is not enough merely to provide a staff of inspectors and examiners, and still to leave the children of our middle class scattered about through the numberless obscure endowed schools and "educational homes" of this country, some of them good,* many of them middling, most of them

* A friendly critic, in the *Museum*, complains that my censure of private schools is too sweeping, that I set them all down, all without exception, as utterly bad;—he will allow me to point to these words as my answer. No doubt there are some masters of cheap private schools who are doing honest and excellent work; but no one suffers more than such men themselves do from a state of things in which, from the bad-

bad; but none of them great institutions, none of them invested with much consideration or dignity. What is wanted for the English middle class is *respected* schools, as well as *inspected* ones. I will explain what I mean.

The education of each class in society has, or ought to have, its ideal, determined by the wants of that class, and by its destination. Society may be imagined so uniform that one education shall be suitable for all its members; we have not a society of that kind, nor has any European country. We have to regard the condition of classes, in dealing with education; but it is right to take into account not their immediate condition only, but their wants, their destination—above all, their evident pressing wants, their evident proximate destination. Looking at English society at this moment, one may say that the ideal for the education of each of its classes to follow, the aim which the education of each should particularly endeavour to reach, is different. Mr. Hawtrey, whose admirable and fruitful labours at St. Mark's School entitle him to be heard with great respect, lays it down as an absolute proposition that the *family is the type of the school.* I do not think that is true for the schools of all classes alike. I feel sure my father, whose authority Mr. Hawtrey claims for this maxim, would not have laid it down in this absolute way. For the wants of the highest class—of the class which frequents Eton, for instance—not *school a family*, but rather *school a little world*, is the right ideal. I cannot concede to Mr. Hawtrey that, for the young gentlemen who go to Eton, our grand aim and aspiration should be, in his own words, "to make their boyhood a joyous one, by gentle usage and "friendly confidence on the part of the master." Let him believe me, the great want for the children of luxury is not this sedulous tenderness, this smoothing of the rose-leaf for them; I am sure that, in fact, it is not by the predominance of the family and parental relation in its school-life that Eton is

ness of the majority of these schools, a discredit is cast over them all, bad and good alike; no one would gain more by obtaining a public, trustworthy discrimination of bad from good, an authentic recognition of merit. The teachers of these schools would then have, in their profession, a career; at present they have none.

strongest: and it is well that this is so. It seems to me that, for the class frequenting Eton, the grand aim of education should be to give them those good things which their birth and rearing are least likely to give them: to give them (besides mere book-learning) the notion of a sort of republican fellowship, the practice of a plain life in common, the habit of self-help. To the middle class, the grand aim of education should be to give largeness of soul and personal dignity; to the lower class, feeling, gentleness, humanity. Here, at last, Mr. Hawtrey's ideal of the *family* as the type for the school, comes in its due place; for the children of poverty it is right, it is needful to set oneself first to "make their boyhood a joyous one, by gentle usage and "friendly confidence on the part of the master;" for them the great danger is not insolence from over-cherishing, but insensibility from over-neglect. Mr. Hawtrey's labours at St. Mark's have been excellent and fruitful, just because he has here applied his maxim where it was the right maxim to apply. Yet even in this sphere Mr. Hawtrey's maxim must not be used too absolutely or too long. Human dignity needs almost as much care as human sensibility. First, undoubtedly, you must make men feeling; but the moment you have done that, you must lose no time in making them magnanimous. Mr. Hawtrey will forgive me for saying that perhaps his danger lies in pressing the spring of gentleness, of confidence, of child-like docility, of "kindly feeling of the dependent towards the patron who is "furthering his well-being" a little too hard. The energy and manliness, which he values as much as any one, run perhaps some little risk of etiolating. At least, I think I can see some indications of this danger in the reports—pleasing as in most respects they are—of his boys' career in the world after they have left school. He does so much for them at St. Mark's, that he brings them to the point at which the ideal of education changes, and the prime want for their culture becomes identical with the prime want for the culture of the middle classes. Their fibre has been suppled long enough; now it wants fortifying.

To do Eton justice, she does not follow Mr. Hawtrey's ideal; she does not supple the fibre of her pupils too much; and, to do the parents of these pupils justice, they have in general a wholesome sense of what their sons do really most want, and are not by any means anxious that school should over-foster them. But I am afraid our middle classes have not quite to the same degree this just perception of the true wants of their offspring. They wish them to be comfortable at school, to be sufficiently instructed there, and not to cost much. Hence the eager promise of "home comforts" with school teaching, all on "terms inclusive and moderate," from the conscientious proprietor of the educational home. To be sure, they do not get what they wish. So long as human nature remains what it is, they never will get it, until they take some better security for it than a prospectus. But suppose they get the security of inspection exercised by the Universities, or by any other trustworthy authority. Some good such an inspection would undoubtedly accomplish; certain glaring specimens of charlatanism it might probably expose, certain gross cases of mishandling and neglect it might put a stop to. It might do a good deal for the school teaching, and something for the home comforts. It can never make these last what the prospectuses promise, what the parents who believe the prospectuses hope for, what they might even really have for their money; for only secondary instruction organised on a great and regular scale can give this at such cheap cost, and so to organise secondary instruction the inspection we are supposing has no power. But even if it had the power, if secondary instruction were organised on a great and regular scale, if it were a national concern, it would not be by ensuring to the offspring of the middle classes a more solid teaching at school, and a larger share of home comforts than they at present enjoy there (though certainly it would do this), that such a secondary instruction would confer upon them the greatest boon. Its greatest boon to the offspring of these classes would be its giving them great, honourable, public institutions for their nurture—institutions conveying to the spirit, at the time of life when the spirit is most penetrable, the salutary influences of greatness, honour, and nationality—influences which expand the soul, liberalise the mind, dignify the character.

Such institutions are the great public schools of England and the great Universities; with these influences, and some others to which I just now pointed, they have formed the upper class of this country—a class with many faults, with many shortcomings, but imbued, on the whole, and mainly through these influences, with a high, magnanimous, governing spirit, which has long enabled them to rule, not ignobly, this great country, and which will still enable them to rule it until they are equalled or surpassed. These institutions had their origin in endowments; and the age of endowments is gone. Beautiful and venerable as are many of the aspects under which it presents itself, this form of public establishment of education, with its limitations, its preferences, its ecclesiastical character, its inflexibility, its inevitable want of foresight, proved, as time rolled on, to be subject to many inconveniences, to many abuses. On the Continent of Europe a clean sweep has in general been made of this old form of establishment, and new institutions have arisen upon its ruins. In England we have kept our great school and college foundations, introducing into their system what correctives and palliatives were absolutely necessary. Long may we so keep them! but no such palliatives or correctives will ever make the public establishment of education which sufficed for earlier ages suffice for this, nor persuade the stream of endowment, long since failing and scanty, to flow again for our present needs as it flowed in the middle ages. For public establishments modern societies have to betake themselves to the State; that is, to *themselves in their collective and corporate character*. On the Continent, society has thus betaken itself to the State for the establishment of education. The result has been the formation of institutions like the Lyceum of Toulouse; institutions capable of great improvement, by no means to be extolled absolutely, by no means to be imitated just as they are; but institutions formed by modern society, with modern modes of operation, to meet modern wants; and in some important respects, at any rate, meeting those wants. These institutions give to a whole new class—to the middle class taken at its very widest—not merely an education for whose teaching and boarding there is valid security, but something—not so much I admit, but something—of the same enlarging, liberalising sense, the sense of belonging to a great and honourable public institution, which

Eton and our three or four great public schools give to our upper class only, and to a small fragment broken off from the top of our middle class. That is where England is weak, and France, Holland, and Germany are strong. Education is and must be a matter of public establishment. Other countries have replaced the defective public establishment made by the middle ages for their education with a new one, which provides for the actual condition of things. We in England keep our old public establishment for education. That is very well; but then we must not forget to supplement it where it falls short. We must not neglect to provide for the actual condition of things.

I have no pet scheme to press, no crotchet to gratify, no fanatical zeal for giving this or that particular shape to the public establishment of our secondary instruction. All I say is, that it is most urgent to give to the establishment of it a wider, a truly public character, and that only the State can give this. If the matter is but once fairly taken in hand, and by competent agency, I am satisfied. In this country we do not move fast; we do not organise great wholes all in a day. But if the State only granted for secondary instruction the sum which it originally granted for primary—20,000*l.* a year—and employed this sum in founding scholarships for secondary schools, with the stipulation that all the schools which sent pupils to compete for these scholarships should admit inspection, a beginning would have been made; a beginning which I truly believe would, at the end of ten years' time, be found to have raised the character of secondary instruction all through England. If more than this can be attempted at first, Sir John Coleridge, in his two excellent letters on this subject to the *Guardian*, perfectly indicates the right course to take: indeed, one could wish nothing better than to commit the settlement of this matter to men of such prudence, moderation, intelligence, and public character as Sir John Coleridge. The four or five hundred endowed schools, whose collective operations now give so little result, should be turned to better account; amalgamation should be used, the most useful of these institutions strengthened, the most useless suppressed, the whole body of them be treated as one whole, destined harmoniously to co-operate towards one end. What should be had in view is to constitute, in every county, at least one great centre of secondary instruction, with low charges, with the security of inspection, and with a public character. These institutions should bear some such title as that of *Royal Schools*, and should derive their support, mainly, of course, from school-fees, but partly, also, from endowments—their own, or those appropriated to them—and partly from scholarships supplied by public grants. Wherever it is possible, wherever, that is, their scale of charges is not too high, or their situation not too unsuitable, existing schools of good repute should be adopted as the *Royal Schools*. Schools such as Mr. Woodard's, such as King Edward's School at Birmingham, such as the Collegiate School at Liverpool, at once occur to one as suitable for this adoption; it would confer upon them, besides its other advantages, a public character which they are now without. Probably the very best medicine which could be devised for the defects of Eton, Harrow, and the other schools which the Royal Commissioners have been scrutinising, would be the juxtaposition, and, to a certain extent, the competition, of establishments of this kind. No wise man will desire to see root-and-branch work made with schools like Eton or Harrow, or to see them diverted from the function which they at present discharge, and, on the whole, usefully. Great subversive changes would here be out of place; it is an addition of new that our secondary instruction wants, not a demolition of old, or, at least, not of this old. But to this old I cannot doubt that the apparition and operation of this desirable new would give a very fruitful stimulus; as this new, on its part, would certainly be very much influenced and benefited by the old.

The repartition of the charge of this new secondary instruction, the mode of its assessment, the constitution of the bodies for regulating the new system, the proportion and character of functions to be assigned to local and to central authority respectively, these are matters of detail and arrangement which it is foreign to my business here to discuss, and, I hope, quite foreign to my disposition to haggle and wrangle about. They are to be settled upon a due consideration of circumstances, after an attentive scrutiny of our existing means of operation, and a discriminating review of the practice of other countries. In general, if it is agreed to give a public and coherent organisation to secondary instruction, few will dispute that its particular direction, in different localities, is best committed to local bodies, properly constituted, with a power of supervision by an impartial central authority, and of resort to this authority in the last instance. Of local bodies, bad or good, administering education, we have already plenty of specimens in this country; it would be difficult for the wit of man to devise a better governing body for its purpose than the trustees of Rugby School, or a worse governing body than the trustees of Bedford School. To reject the bad in the examples offering themselves, to use the good, and to use it with just regard to the present purpose, is the thing needful. Undoubtedly these are important matters; but undoubtedly, also, it is not difficult to settle them properly; not difficult, I mean, for ordinary good sense, and ordinary good temper. The intelligence, fairness, and moderation which, in practical matters, our countrymen know so well how to exercise, make one feel quite easy in leaving these common-sense arrangements to them.

I am more anxious about the danger of having the whole question misconceived, of having false issues raised upon it. One of these false issues I have already noticed. People say: "After all, your Toulouse Lyceum is not so good as Eton." But the Toulouse Lyceum is for the middle class, Eton for the upper class. I will allow that the upper class, amongst us, is very well taken care of, in the way of schools, already. But is the middle class? The Lyceum loses, perhaps, if compared with Eton; but does it not gain if compared with the "Classical and Commercial "Academy?" And it is with this that the comparison is to be instituted. Again, the French Lyceum is reproached with its barrack life, its want of country air and exercise, its dismalness, its rigidity, its excessive supervision. But these defects do not come to secondary instruction from its connexion with the State; they are not necessary results of that connexion; they come to French secondary instruction from the common French and continental habitudes in the training of children and school-boys—habitudes that do not enough regard physical well-being and play. They may be remedied in France, and men's attention is now strongly drawn to them there; there has even been a talk of moving the Lyceums into the country, though this would have its inconveniences. But, at any rate, these defects need not attend the public establishment of secondary instruction in England, and assuredly, with our notions of training, they would not attend them. Again, it is said that France is a despotically-governed country, and that its Lyceums are a part of its despotism. But Switzerland is not a despotically-governed country, and it has its Lyceums just as much as France. Again, it is said that in France the Lyceums are the only schools allowed to exist, that this is monopoly and tyranny, and that the Lyceums themselves suffer by the want of competition. There is some exaggeration in this complaint, as the existence of Sorèze, and other places like Sorèze, testifies; still the restraints put upon private enterprise in founding schools in France, are, no doubt, mischievously strict; the refusal of the requisite authorisation for opening a private school is often vexatious; the Lyceums would really be benefited by the proximity of other, and sometimes rival, schools. But who supposes that any check would ever be put, in England, upon private enterprise in founding schools? Who supposes that the authorisation demanded in France for opening a private school would ever be demanded in England, that it would ever be possible to demand it, that it would ever be desirable? Who supposes that all the benefits of a public establishment of instruction are not to be obtained without it? It is for what it does itself that this establishment is so desirable, not for what it prevents others from doing. Its letting others alone does not prevent it from itself having a most useful work to do, and a work which can be done by no one else. The most zealous friends of free instruction upon the Continent feel this. One of the ablest of them, M. Dollfus, lately published in the *Revue Germanique* some most interesting remarks on the defects of the French school system, as at present regulated. He demands freedom for private persons to open schools without any authorisation at all. But does he contest the right of the State to have its own schools, to make a public establishment of instruction? So far from it, he treats this as a right beyond all contestation, as a clear duty. He treats as certain, too, the right of the State to inspect all private schools once opened, though he denies the right, and the good policy, of its putting the present obstacles in the way of opening them.

But there is a catchword which, I know, will be used against me. England is the country of cries and catchwords; a country where public life is so much carried on by means of parties must be. That English public life should be carried on as it is, I believe to be an excellent thing; but it is certain that all modes of life have their special inconveniences, and every sensible man, however much he may hold a particular way of life to be the best, and may be bent on adhering to it, will yet always be sedulous to guard himself against its inconveniences. One of these is, certainly, in English public life, the prevalence of cries and catchwords, which are very apt to receive an application, or to be used with an absoluteness, which do not belong to them; and then they tend to narrow our spirit and to hurt our practice. It is good to make a catchword of this sort come down from its stronghold of commonplace, to force it to move about before us in the open country, and to show us its real strength. Such a catchword as this: *The State had better leave things alone*. One constantly hears that as an absolute maxim; now, as an absolute maxim, it has really no force at all. The absolute maxims are those which carry to man's spirit their own demonstration with them; such propositions as, *Duty is the law of human life*, *Man is morally free*, and so on. The proposition, *The State had better leave things alone*, carries no such demonstration with it; it has, therefore, no absolute force; it merely conveys a notion which certain people have generalised from certain facts which have come under their observation, and which, by a natural vice of the human mind, they are then prone to apply absolutely. Some things the State had better leave alone, others it had better not. Is this particular thing one of these, or one of those?—that, as to any particular thing, is the right question. Now, I say, that education is one of those things which the State ought not to leave alone, which it ought to establish. It is said that in education given, wholly or in part, by the State, there is something eleemosynary, pauperising, degrading; that the self-respect and manly energy of those receiving it are likely to become impaired, as I have said that the manly energy of those who are too much made to feel their dependence upon a parental benefactor, is apt to become impaired. Well, now, is this so? Is a citizen's relation to the State that of a dependent to a parental benefactor? By no means; it is that of a member in a partnership to the whole firm. The citizens of a State, the members of a society, are really a partnership; "a partnership," as Burke nobly says, "in all science, "in all art, in every virtue, in all perfection." Towards this great final design of their connexion, they apply the aids which co-operative association can give them. This applied to education will, undoubtedly, give the middling person a better schooling than his own individual unaided resources could give him; but he is not thereby humiliated, he is not degraded; he is wisely and usefully turning his associated condition to the best account. Considering his end and destination, he is bound so to turn it; certainly he has a right so to turn it. Certainly he has a right—to quote Burke again—"to a fair portion of all which "society, *with all its combinations of skill and force*, can do in "his favour." Men in civil society have the right—to quote Burke yet once more (one cannot quote him too often)—as "to the acquisitions of their parents and to the fruits of their "own industry," so also "*to the improvement of their offspring*, "*to instruction in life*, and to consolation in death."

How vain, then, and how meaningless, to tell a man who, for the instruction of his offspring, receives aid from the State, that he is humiliated! Humiliated by receiving help for himself as an individual from himself in his corporate and associated capacity! help to which his own money, as a tax-payer, contributes, and for which, as a result of the joint energy and intelligence of the whole community in employing its powers, he himself deserves some of the praise! He is no more humiliated than one is humiliated by being on the foundation of the Charterhouse or of Winchester, or by holding a scholarship or a fellowship at Oxford or Cambridge. Nay (if there be any humiliation here), not so much. For the amount of benefaction, the amount of obligation, the amount, therefore, I suppose, of humiliation, diminishes as the public character of the aid becomes more undeniable. He is no more humiliated than when he crosses London Bridge, or walks down the King's Road, or visits the British Museum. But it is one of the extraordinary inconsistencies of some English people in this matter, that they keep all their cry of humiliation and degradation for help which the State offers. A man is not pauperised, is not degraded, is not oppressively obliged, by taking aid for his son's schooling from Mr. Woodard's subscribers, or from the next squire, or from the next rector, or from the next ironmonger, or from the next druggist; he is only pauperised when he takes it from the State, when he helps to give it himself!

This matter of State-intervention in the establishment of public instruction is so beset with misrepresentation and misconception, that I must, before concluding, go into it a little more fully. I want the middle classes (it is for them, above all, I write), the middle classes so deeply concerned in this matter, so numerous, so right-intentioned, so powerful, to look at the thing with impartial regard to its simple reason and to its present policy.

[III]

The State mars everything which it touches, say some. It attempts to do things for private people, and private people could do them a great deal better for themselves. "The State," says the *Times*, "can hardly aid education without cramping and "warping its growth, and mischievously interfering with the "laws of its natural development." "Why should persons in "Downing Street," asks Dr. Temple, "be at all better qualified "than the rest of the world for regulating these matters?" Happily, however, this agency, at once so mischievous and so blundering, is in our country little used. "In this country," says the *Times* again, "people cannot complain of the State, because "the State never promised them anything, *but, on the contrary*, "*always told them it could do them no good*. The result is, none "are fed with false hopes." So it is, and so it will be to the end. "This is something more than a system with us; *it is usage, it* "*is a necessity*. We shall go on for ages doing as we have done."

Whether this really is so or not, it seems as if it *ought* not to be so. "Government," says Burke (to go back to Burke again), "is a contrivance of human wisdom to provide for human "wants. Men have a right that these wants should be provided "for by this wisdom." We are a free people, we have made our own Government. Our own wisdom has planned our contrivance for providing for our own wants. And what sort of a contrivance has our wisdom made? According to the *Times*, a contrivance of which the highest merit is, that it candidly avows its own impotency. It does not provide for our wants, but then it "always told us" it could not provide for them. It does not fulfil its function, but then it "never fed us with false "hopes" that it would. It is perfectly useless, but perfectly candid. And it will always remain what it is now; it will always be a contrivance which contrives nothing: this with us "is "usage, it is a necessity." Good heavens! what a subject for self-congratulation! What bitterer satire on us and our institutions could our worst enemy invent?

Dr. Temple may well ask, "Why should persons in Downing "Street be at all better qualified than the rest of the world for "regulating such matters as education?" Why should not a sporting rector in Norfolk, or a fanatical cobbler in Northamptonshire, be just as good a judge of what is wise, equitable, and expedient in public education, as an Education Minister? Why, indeed? The Education Minister is a part of our contrivance for providing for our wants, and we have seen what that contrivance is worth. It might have been expected, perhaps, that in contriving a provision for a special want, we should have sought for some one with a special skill. But we know that our contrivance will do no good, so we may as well let Nimrod manage as Numa.

From whence can have arisen, in this country, such contemptuous disparagement of the efficiency and utility of State-action? Whence such studied depreciation of an agency which to Burke, or, indeed, to any reflecting man, appears an agency of the greatest possible power and value? For several reasons. In the first place, the government of this country is, and long has been, in the hands of the aristocratic class. Where the aristocracy is a small oligarchy, able to find employment for all its members in the administration of the State, it is not the enemy, but the friend of State-action; for State-action is then but its own action under another name, and it is itself directly aggrandised by all that aggrandises the State. But where, as in this country, the aristocracy is a very large class, by no means conterminous with the executive, but overlapping it and spreading far beyond it, it is the natural enemy rather than the friend of State-action; for only a small part of its members can directly administer the State, and it is not for the interest of the remainder to give to this small part an excessive preponderance. Nay, this small part will not be apt to seek it; for its interest in its order is permanent, while its interest in State-function is transitory, and it obeys an instinct which attaches it by preference to its order. The more an aristocracy has of that profound political sense by which the English aristocracy is so much distinguished, the more its members obey this instinct; and, by doing so, they signally display their best virtues, moderation, prudence, sagacity; they prevent fruitful occasions of envy, dissension, and strife; they do much to insure the permanence of their order, its harmonious action, and continued predominance. A tradition unfavourable to much State-action in home concerns (foreign are another thing) is thus insensibly established in the Government itself. This tradition, this essentially aristocratic sentiment, gains even those members of the Government who are not of the aristocratic class. In the beginning they are overpowered by it; in the end they share it. When the shepherd Daphnis first arrives in heaven, he naturally bows to the august traditions of his new sphere—*candidus insuetum miratur limen Olympi*. By the time the novelty of his situation has worn off, he has come to think just as the immortals do; he is now by conviction the foe of State-interference; the worthy Daphnis is all for letting things alone—*amat bonus otia Daphnis*.

Far from trying to encroach upon individual liberty, far from seeking to get everything into its own hands, such a Government has a natural and instinctive tendency to limit its own functions. It turns away from offers of increased responsibility or activity; it deprecates them. To propose increased responsibility and activity to an aristocratic Government is the worst possible way of paying one's court to it. The *Times* is its genuine mouthpiece, when it says that the business of Government, in domestic concerns, is negative—to prevent disorder, jobbery, and extravagance; that it need "have no notion of se-"curing the future, not even of regulating the present;" that it may and ought to "leave the course of events to regulate itself, "and trust the future to the security of the unknown laws of "human nature and the unseen influences of higher powers." This is the true aristocratic theory of civil government: to have recourse as little as possible to State-action, to the collective action of the community; to leave as much as possible to the individual, to local government. And why? Because the members of an artistocratic class are preponderating individuals, with the local government in their hands. No wonder that they do not wish to see the State overshadowing them and ordering them about. Since the feudal epoch, the palmy time of local government, the State has overlaid individual action quite enough. Mr. Adderley remembers with a sigh that "Houses of "Correction were once voluntary institutions." Go a little further back, and the court of justice was a voluntary institution; the gallows was a voluntary institution; voluntary, I mean, in Mr. Adderley's sense of the word voluntary—not depending on the State, but on the local government, on the lord of the soil, on the preponderating individual. The State has overlaid the feudal gallows, it has overlaid the feudal court of justice, it has overlaid the feudal House of Correction, and finally, says Mr. Adderley, "it has overlaid our school-system." What will it do next?

In the aristocratic class, whose members mainly compose and whose sentiment powerfully pervades the executive of this country, jealousy of State-action is, I repeat, an intelligible, a profoundly natural feeling. That, amid the temptations of office, they have remained true to it is a proof of their practical sense, their sure tact, their moderation—the qualities which go to make that *governing spirit* for which the English aristocracy is so remarkable. And perhaps this governing spirit of theirs is destined still to stand them in good stead through all the new and changing development of modern society. Perhaps it will give them the tact to discern the critical moment at which it becomes of urgent national importance that an agency, not in itself very agreeable to them, should be used more freely than heretofore. They have had the virtue to prefer the general interest of their order to personal temptations of aggrandising themselves through this agency; perhaps they will be capable of the still higher virtue of admitting, in the general interest of their country, this agency, in spite of the natural prejudices and the seeming immediate interest of their own order. Already there are indications that this is not impossible. No thoughtful observer can have read Lord Derby's remarks last session on the regulation of our railway system, can have followed the course of a man like Sir John Pakington on the Education question, can have watched the disposition of the country gentlemen on a measure like Mr. Gladstone's Government Annuities Bill, without recognising that political instinct, that governing spirit, which often, in the aristocratic class of this country, is wiser both than the unelastic pedantry of theorising Liberalism, and than their own prejudices.

The working classes have no antipathy to State-action. Against this, or against anything else, indeed, presented to them in close connexion with some proceeding which they dislike, it is, no doubt, quite possible to get them to raise a cry; but to the thing itself they have no objection. Quite the contrary. They often greatly embarrass their Liberal friends and patrons from other classes, one of whose favourite catchwords is *no State-interference*, by their resolute refusal to adopt this Shibboleth, to embrace this article of their patrons' creed. They will join with them in their Liberalism, not in their crotchets. Left to themselves, they are led, as by their plain interest, so, too, by their natural disposition, to welcome the action of the State in their behalf.

It is the middle class that has been this action's great enemy. And originally it had good reason to be its enemy. In the youth and early manhood of the English middle class, the action of the State was at the service of an ecclesiastical party. This party used the power of the State to secure their own predominance, and to enforce conformity to their own tenets. The stronghold of Nonconformity then, as now, was in the middle class; in its struggle to repel the conformity forced upon it, the middle class underwent great suffering and injustice; and it has never forgotten them. It has never forgotten that the hand which smote it—the hand which did the bidding of its High Church and prelatical enemies—was the hand of the State. It has confronted the State with hostile jealousy ever since. The State tried to do it violence, so it does not love the State; the State failed to subdue it, so it does not respect the State. It regards it with something of aversion and something of contempt. It professes the desire to limit its functions as much as possible, to restrict its action to matters where it is indispensably necessary, to make of it a mere tax-collector and policeman—the hewer of wood and drawer of water to the community.

There is another cause also which indisposes the English middle class to increased action on the part of the State. M. Amédée Thierry, in his "History of the Gauls," observes, in contrasting the Gaulish and Germanic races, that the first is characterised by the instinct of intelligence and mobility, and by the preponderant action of individuals; the second, by the instinct of discipline and order, and by the preponderant action of bodies of men. This general law of M. Thierry's has to submit to many limitations, but there is a solid basis of truth in it. Applying the law to a people mainly of German blood like ourselves, we shall best perceive its truth by regarding the middle class of the nation. Multitudes, all the world over, have a good deal in common; aristocracies, all the world over, have a good deal in common. The peculiar national form and habit exist in the masses at the bottom of society in a loose, rudimentary, potential state; in the few at the top of society, in a state modified and reduced by various culture. The man of the multitude has not yet solidified into the typical Englishman; the man of the aristocracy has been etherealised out of him. The typical Englishman is to be looked for in the middle class. And there we shall find him, with a complexion not ill-suiting M. Thierry's law; with a spirit not very open to new ideas, and not easily ravished by them; not, therefore, a great enthusiast for universal progress, but with a strong love of discipline and order, —that is, of keeping things settled, and much as they are; and with a disposition, instead of lending himself to the onward-looking statesman and legislator, to act with bodies of men of his own kind, whose aims and efforts reach no further than his own. Poverty and hope make man the friend of ideals, therefore the multitude has a turn for ideals; culture and genius make man the friend of ideals, therefore the gifted or highly-trained few have a turn for ideals. The middle class has the whet neither of poverty nor of culture; it is not ill-off in the things of the body, and it is not highly trained in the things of the mind; therefore it has little turn for ideals: it is self-satisfied. This is a chord in the nature of the English middle class which seldom fails, when struck, to give an answer, and which some people are never weary of striking. All the variations which are played on the endless theme of *local self-government* rely on this chord. Hardly any local government is, in truth, in this country, exercised by the middle class; almost the whole of it is exercised by the aristocratic class. Every locality in France—that country which our middle class is taught so much to compassionate—has a genuine municipal government, in which the middle class has its due share; and by this municipal government all matters of local concern (schools among the number) are regulated; not a country parish in England has any effective government of this kind at all. But what is meant by the habit of local self-government, on which our middle class is so incessantly felicitated, is its habit of voluntary combination, in bodies of its own arranging, for purposes of its own choosing—purposes to be carried out within the limits fixed for a private association by its own powers. When the middle class is solemnly warned against State-interference, lest it should destroy "the habit of self-reliance and love of local self-government," it is this habit, and the love of it, that are meant. When we are told that "nothing can be more dangerous than these "constant attempts on the part of the Government to take from "the people the management of its own concerns," this is the sort of management of our own concerns that is meant; not the management of them by a regular local government, but the management of them by chance private associations. It is our habit of acting through these associations which, says Mr. Roebuck, saves us from being "a set of helpless imbeciles, totally "incapable of attending to our own interests." It is in the event of this habit being at all altered that, according to the same authority, "the greatness of this country is gone." * And the middle class, to whom that habit is familiar and very dear, will never be insensible to language of this sort.

Finally, the English middle class has a strong practical sense and habit of affairs, and it sees that things managed by the Government are often managed ill. It sees them treated sometimes remissly, sometimes vexatiously; now with a paralysing want of fruitful energy, now with an over-busy fussiness, with rigidity, with formality, without due consideration of special circumstances. Here, too, it finds a motive disinclining it to trust State-action, and leading it to give a willing ear to those who declaim against it.

Now, every one of these motives of distrust is respectable. Every one of them has, or once had, a solid ground. Every one of them points to some virtue in those actuated by it, which is not to be suppressed, but to find true conditions for its exercise. The English middle class was quite right in repelling State-action, when the State suffered itself to be made an engine of the High Church party to persecute Nonconformists. It gave an excellent lesson to the State in so doing. It rendered a valuable service to liberty of thought and to all human freedom. If State-action now threatened to lend itself to one religious party against another, the middle class would be quite right in again thwarting and confining it. But can it be said that the State

* Mr. Roebuck, in his recent excellent speech at Sheffield, has shown that in popular education, at any rate, he does not mean these maxims to apply without restriction. But perhaps it is a little incautious for a public man ever to throw out, without guarding himself, maxims of this kind; for, on the one hand, in this country such maxims are sure never to be lost sight of; on the other, but too many people are sure always to be prone to use them amiss, and to push their application much further than it ought to go.

now shows the slightest disposition to take such a course? Is such a course the course towards which the modern spirit carries the State? Does not the State show, more and more, the resolution to hold the balance perfectly fair between religious parties? The middle class has it in its own power, more than any other class, to confirm the State in this resolution. This class has the power to make it thoroughly sure—in organising, for instance, any new system of public instruction—that the State shall treat all religious persuasions with exactly equal fairness. If, instead of holding aloof, it will now but give its aid to make State-action equitable, it can make it so.

Again, as to the "habits of self-reliance and the love of local "self-government." People talk of Government *interference*, Government *control*, as if State-action were necessarily something imposed upon them from without; something despotic and self-originated; something which took no account of their will, and left no freedom to their activity. Can any one really suppose that, in a country like this, State-action—in education, for instance—can ever be that, unless we choose to make it so? We can give it what form we will. We can make it our agent, not our master. In modern societies the agency of the State, in certain matters, is so indispensable, that it will manage, with or without our common consent, to come into operation somehow; but when it has introduced itself without the common consent—when a great body, like the middle class, will have nothing to say to it—then its course is indeed likely enough to be not straightforward, its operation not satisfactory. But, by all of us consenting to it, we remove any danger of this kind. By really agreeing to deal in our collective and corporate character with education, we can form ourselves into the best and most efficient of voluntary societies for managing it. We can make State-action upon it a genuine local government of it, the faithful but potent expression of our own activity. We can make the central Government that mere court of disinterested review and correction, which every sensible man would always be glad to have for his own activity. We shall have all our self-reliance and individual action still (in this country we shall always have plenty of them, and the parts will always be more likely to tyrannise over the whole than the whole over the parts), but we shall have had the good sense to turn them to account by a powerful, but still voluntary, organization. Our beneficence will be "beneficence acting *by rule*" (that is Burke's definition of law, as instituted by a free society), and all the more effective for that reason. Must this make us "a set "of helpless imbeciles, totally incapable of attending to our own "interests?" Is this "a grievous blow aimed at the independence "of the English character?" Is "English self-reliance and inde- "pendence" to be perfectly satisfied with what it produces already without this organisation? In middle-class education it produces, without it, the educational home and the classical and commercial academy. Are we to be proud of that? Are we to be satisfied with that? Is "the greatness of this country" to be seen in that? But it will be said that, awakening to a sense of the badness of our middle-class education, we are beginning to improve it. Undoubtedly we are; and the most certain sign of that awakening, of those beginnings of improvement, is the disposition to resort to a public agency, to "beneficence work- "ing *by rule*," to help us on faster with it. When we really begin to care about a matter of this kind, we cannot help turning to the most efficient agency at our disposal. Clap-trap and commonplace lose their power over us; we begin to see that, if State-action has often its inconveniences, our self-reliance and independence are best shown in so arranging our State-action as to guard against those inconveniences, not in foregoing State-action for fear of them. So it was in elementary education. Mr. Baines says that this was already beginning to improve, when Government interfered with it. Why, it was because we were all beginning to take a real interest in it, beginning to improve it, that we turned to Government—to ourselves in our corporate character—to get it improved faster. So long as we did not care much about it, we let it go its own way, and kept singing Mr. Roebuck's fine old English stave about "self-reliance." We kept crying just as he cries now: "nobody has the same interest "to do well for a man as he himself has." That was all very pleasant so long as we cared not a rush whether the people were educated or no. The moment we began to concern ourselves about this, we asked ourselves what our song was worth. We asked ourselves how the bringing up of our labourers and artisans—they "doing for themselves," and "nobody having the "same interest to do well for a man as he himself has"—was being done. We found it was being done detestably. Then we asked ourselves whether casual, precarious, voluntary beneficence, or "beneficence acting by rule," was the better agency for doing it better. We asked ourselves if we could not employ our public resources on this concern, if we could not make our beneficence act upon it by rule, without losing our "habits of "self-reliance," without "aiming a grievous blow at the inde-"pendence of the English character." We found that we could; we began to do it; and we left Mr. Baines to sing in the wilderness.

Finally, as to the objection that our State-action—our "be-"neficence working by rule"—often bungles and does its work badly. No wonder it does. The imperious necessities of modern society force it, more or less, even in this country, into play; but it is exercised by a class to whose cherished instincts it is opposed—the aristocratic class; and it is watched by a class to whose cherished prejudices it is opposed—the middle class. It is hesitatingly exercised and jealously watched. It therefore works without courage, cordiality, or belief in itself. Under its present conditions it must work so, and, working so, it must often bungle. But it need not work so; and the moment the middle class abandons its attitude of jealous aversion, the moment they frankly put their hand to it, the moment they adopt it as an instrument to do them service, it will work so no longer. Then it will not bungle; then, if it is applied, say, to education, it will not be fussy, baffling, and barren; it will bring to bear on this concern the energy and strong practical sense of the middle class itself.

But the middle class must make it do this. They must not expect others to do the business for them. It is they whose interest is concerned in its being done, and they must do it for themselves. Why should the upper class—the aristocratic class—do it for them? What motive—except the distant and not very peremptory one of their general political sense, their instinct for taking the course which, for the whole country's sake, ought to be taken—have the aristocratic class to impel them to go counter to all their natural maxims, nay, and to all their seeming interest? They do not want new schools for their children. The great public schools of the country are theirs already. Their numbers are not such as to overflow these few really public schools; their fortunes are such as to make the expensiveness of these schools a matter of indifference to them. The Royal Commissioners, whose report has just appeared, do not, indeed, give a very brilliant picture of the book-learning of these schools. But it is not the book-learning (easy to be improved if there is a will to improve it) that this class make their first care; they make their first care the tone, temper, and habits generated in these schools. So long as they generate a public spirit, a free spirit, a high spirit, a governing spirit, they are not ill-satisfied. Their children are fitted to succeed them in the government of the country. Why should they concern themselves to change this state of things? Why should they create competitors for their own children? Why should they labour to endow another class with those great instruments of power—a public spirit, a free spirit, a high spirit, a governing spirit? Why should they do violence to that distaste for State-action, which, in an aristocratic class, is natural and instinctive, for the benefit of the middle class?

No; the middle class must do this work for themselves. From them must come the demand for the satisfaction of a want that is theirs. They must leave off being frightened at shadows. They may keep (I hope they always will keep) the maxim that self-reliance and independence are the most invaluable of blessings, that the great end of society is the perfecting of the individual, the fullest, freest, and worthiest development of the individual's activity. But that the individual may be perfected, that his activity may be worthy, he must often learn to quit old habits, to adopt new, to go out for himself, to transform himself. It was said, and truly said, of one of the most unwearied and successful strivers after human perfection that have ever lived—Wilhelm von Humboldt—that it was a joy to him to feel himself modified by the operation of a foreign influence. And this may well be a joy to a man whose centre of character and whose moral force are once securely established. Through this he makes growth in perfection. Through this he enlarges his being and fills up gaps in it; he unlearns old prejudices and learns new excellences; he makes advance towards inward light and freedom. Societies may use this means of perfection as well as individuals, and it is a characteristic (perhaps the best characteristic) of our age, that they are using it more and more. Let us look at our neighbour, France. What strikes a thoughtful observer most in modern France, is the great, wide breach which is being made in the old French mind; the strong flow with which a foreign thought is pouring in and mixing with it. There is an extraordinary increase in the number of German and English books read there, books the most unlike possible to the native literary growth of France. There is a growing disposition there to pull to pieces old stock French commonplaces, and to put a bridle upon old stock French habitudes. France will not, and should not, like some English liberals, run a-muck against State-action altogether; but she shows a tendency to control her excessive State-action, to reduce it within just limits where it has overpassed them, to make a larger part for free local activity and for individuals. She will not, and should not, like Sir Archibald Alison, cry down her great Revolution as the work of Satan; but she shows more and more the power to discern the real faults of that Revolution, the real part of delusion, impotence, and transitoriness in the work of '89 or of '91, and to profit by that discernment.

Our middle class has secured for itself that centre of character and that moral force which are, I have said, the indispensable basis upon which perfection is to be founded. To securing them, its vigour in resisting the State, when the State tried to tyrannise over it, has contributed not a little. In this sense, it may be said to have made way towards perfection by repelling the State's hand. Now it has to enlarge and to adorn its spirit. I cannot seriously argue with those who deny that the independence and free action of the middle class is now, in this country, immutably secure; I cannot treat the notion of the State now overriding it and doing violence to it, as anything but a vain chimera. Well, then, if the State can (as it can) be of service to the middle class in the work of enlarging its mind and adorning its spirit, it will now make way towards perfection by taking the State's hand. State-action is not in itself unfavourable to the individual's perfection, to his attaining his fullest development. So far from it, it is in ancient Greece, where State-action was omnipresent, that we see the individual at his very highest pitch of free and fair activity. This is because, in Greece, the individual was strong enough to fashion the State into an instrument of his own perfection, to make it serve, with a thousand times his own power, towards his own ends. He was not enslaved by it, he did not annihilate it, but he used it. Where, in modern nations, the State has maimed and crushed individual activity, it has been by operating as an alien, exterior power in the community, a power not originated by the community to serve the common weal, but entrenched among them as a conqueror with a weal of its own to serve. Just because the vigour and sturdiness of the people of this country have prevented, and will always prevent, the State from being anything of this kind, I believe we, more than any modern people, have the power of renewing, in our national life, the example of Greece. I believe that we, and our American kinsmen, are specially fit to apply State-action with advantage, because we are specially sure to apply it voluntarily.

Two things must, I think, strike any one who attentively regards the English middle class at this moment. One is the intellectual ferment which is taking place, or rather, which is beginning to take place, amongst them. It is only in its commencement as yet; but it shows itself at a number of points, and bids fair to become a great power. The importance of a change, placing in the great middle class the centre of the intellectual life of this country, can hardly be over-estimated. I have been reproved for saying that the culture and intellectual life of our highest class seem to me to have somewhat flagged since the last century. That is my opinion, indeed, and all that I see and hear strengthens rather than shakes it. The culture of this class is not what it used to be. Their value for high culture, their belief in its importance, is not what it used to be. One may see it in the public schools, one may see it in the universities. Whence come the deadness, the want of intellectual life, the poverty of acquirement after years of schooling, which the Commissioners, in their remarkable and interesting report, show us so prevalent in our most distinguished public schools? What gives to play and amusement, both there and at the universities, their present overweening importance, so that home critics cry out: "The real studies of Oxford are its games," and foreign critics cry out: "At Oxford the student is still the mere school-"boy"? The most experienced and acute of Oxford heads of houses told me himself, that when he spoke to an undergraduate the other day about trying for some distinguished scholarship, the answer he got was: "Oh, the men from the great "schools don't care for those things now; the men who care "about them are the men from Marlborough, Cheltenham, and "the second-rate schools." Whence, I say, does this slackness, this sleep of the mind, come, except from a torpor of intellectual life, a dearth of ideas, an indifference to fine culture or disbelief in its necessity, spreading through the bulk of our highest class, and influencing its rising generation? People talk as if the culture of this class had only changed; the Greek and Roman classics, they say, are no longer in vogue as they were in Lord Chesterfield's time. Well, if this class had only gone from one source of high culture to another; if only, instead of reading Homer and Cicero, it now read Goethe and Montesquieu;—but it does not; it reads the *Times* and the *Agricultural Journal*. And it devotes itself to practical life. And it amuses itself. It is not its rising generation only which loves play; never in all its history has our whole highest class shown such zeal for enjoying life, for amusing itself. It would be absurd to make this a matter of reproach against it. The triumphs of material progress multiply the means of material enjoyment; they attract all classes, more and more, to taste of this enjoyment; on the highest class, which possesses in the amplest measure these means, they must needs exercise this attraction very powerfully. But every thoughtful observer can perceive that the ardour for amusement and enjoyment, often educative and quickening to a toil-numbed working class or a strait-laced middle class, whose great want is expansion, tends to become enervative and weakening to an aristocratic class—a class which must rule by superiority of all kinds, superiority not to be won without contention of spirit and a certain severity. I think, therefore, both that the culture of our highest class has declined, and that this declension, though natural and venial, impairs its power.

Yet in this vigorous country everything has a wonderful ability for self-restoration, and he would be a bold prophet who should deny that the culture of our highest class may recover itself. But however this may be, there is no doubt that a liberal culture, a fulness of intellectual life, in the middle class, is a far more important matter, a far more efficacious stimulant to national progress, than the same powers in an aristocratic class. Whatever may be its culture, an aristocratic class will always have at bottom, like the young man in Scripture with great possessions, an inaptitude for ideas; but, besides this, high culture or ardent intelligence, pervading a large body of the community, acquire a breadth of basis, a sum of force, an energy of central heat for radiating further, which they can never possess when they pervade a small upper class only. It is when such a broad basis is obtained, that individual genius gets its proper nutriment, and is animated to put forth its best powers; this is the secret of rich and beautiful epochs in national life; the epoch of Pericles in Greece, the epoch of Michael Angelo in Italy, the epoch of Shakspeare in England. Our actual middle class has not yet, certainly, the fine culture, or the living intelligence, which quickened great bodies of men at these epochs; but it has the forerunner, the preparer, the indispensable initiator; it is traversed by a strong intellectual ferment. It is the middle class which has real mental ardour, real curiosity; it is the middle class which is the great reader; that immense literature of the day which we see surging up all round us,—literature the absolute value of which it is almost impossible to rate too humbly, literature hardly a word of which will reach, or deserves to reach, the future,—it is the middle class which calls it forth, and its evocation is at least a sign of a widespread mental movement in that class. Will this movement go on and become fruitful: will it conduct the middle class to a high and commanding pitch of culture and intelligence? That depends on the sensibility which the middle class has for *perfection;* that depends on its power to *transform itself*.

And it is not yet manifest how far it possesses this power. For—and here I pass to the second of those two things which particularly, I have said, strike any one who observes the English middle class just now—in its public action this class has hitherto shown only the power and disposition to *affirm itself*, not at all the power and disposition to *transform itself*. That, indeed, is one of the deep-seated instincts of human nature, but of vulgar human nature—of human nature not high-souled and aspiring after perfection—to esteem itself for what it is, to try to establish itself just as it is, to try even to impose itself with its stock of habitudes, pettinesses, narrownesses, shortcomings of every kind, on the rest of the world as a conquering power. But nothing has really a right to be satisfied with itself, to be and remain itself, except that which has reached perfection; and nothing has the right to impose itself on the rest of the world as a conquering force, except that which is of higher perfection than the rest of the world. And such is the fundamental constitution of human affairs, that the measure of right proves also, in the end, the measure of power. Before the English middle class can have the right or the power to assert itself absolutely, it must have greatly perfected itself. It has been jokingly said of this class, that all which the best of it cared for was summed up in this alliterative phrase—*Business and Bethels:* and that all which the rest of it cared for was the *Business* without the *Bethels*. No such jocose and slighting words can convey any true sense of what the religion of the English middle class has really been to it; what a source of vitality, energy, and persistent vigour. "They who wait on the "Lord," says Isaiah, in words not less true than they are noble, "*shall renew their strength;*" and the English middle class owes to its religion not only comfort in the past, but also a vast latent force of unworn life and strength for future progress. But the Puritanism of the English middle class, which has been so great an element of strength to them, has by no means brought them to perfection; nay, by the rigid mould in which it has cast their spirit, it has kept them back from perfection. The most that can be said of it is, that it has supplied a stable basis on which to build perfection; it has given them character, though it has not given them culture. But it is in making endless additions to itself, in the endless expansion of its powers, in endless growth in wisdom and beauty, that the spirit of the human race finds its ideal; to reach this ideal, culture is an indispensable aid, and that is the true value of culture. The life of aristocracies, with its large and free use of the world, its conversance with great affairs, its exemption from sordid cares, its liberation from the humdrum provincial round, its external splendour and refinement, is a kind of outward shadow of this ideal, a prophecy of it; and there lies the secret of the charm of aristocracies, and of their power over men's minds. In a country like England, the middle class, with its industry and its Puritanism, and nothing more, will never be able to make way beyond a certain point, will never be able to divide power with the aristocratic class, much less to win for itself a preponderance of power. While it only tries to affirm its actual self, to impose its actual self, it has no charm for men's minds, and can achieve no great triumphs. And this is all it attempts at present. The Conservative reaction, of which we hear so much just now, is in great part merely a general indisposition to let the middle-class spirit, working by its old methods, and having only its old self to give us, establish itself at all points and become master of the situation. Particularly on Church questions is this true. In this sphere of religion, where feeling and beauty are so all-important, we shrink from giving to the middle-class spirit, limited as we see it, with its sectarianism, its under-culture, its intolerance, its bitterness, its unloveliness, too much its own way. Before we give it quite its own way, we insist on its making itself into something larger, newer, more fruitful. This is what the recent Church-Rate divisions really mean, and the lovers of perfection, therefore, may accept them without displeasure. They are the voice of the nation crying to the *untransformed* middle class (if it will receive it) with a voice of thunder: "The future is not yours!"

And let me say, in passing, that the indifference, so irritating to some persons, with which European opinion has received the break-up of the old American Union has at bottom a like ground. I put the question of slavery on one side; so far as the resolution of that question depends on the issue of the conflict between the North and the South, every one may wish this party or that to prevail. But Mr. Bright and Mr. Cobden extol the old American Republic as something interesting and admirable in itself, and are displeased with those who are not afflicted at its disaster, and not jealous for its restoration. Mr. Bright is an orator of genius; Mr. Cobden is a man of splendid understanding. But why do they refuse to perceive, that, apart from all class-jealousy of aristocracies towards a democratic republic, there existed in the most impartial and thoughtful minds a profound dissatisfaction with the spirit and tendencies of the old American Union, a strong aversion to their unchecked triumph, a sincere wish for the disciplining and correcting of them? And what were the old United States but a colossal expression of the English middle-class spirit, somewhat more accessible to ideas there than here, because of the democratic air it breathed, much more arrogant and overweening there than here, because of the absence of all check and counterpoise to it—but there, as here, full of rawness, hardness, and imperfection; there, as here, greatly needing to be liberalised, enlarged, and ennobled, before it could with advantage be suffered to assert itself absolutely? All the energy and success in the world could not have made the United States admirable so long as their spirit had this imperfection. Even if they had overrun the whole earth, their old national style would have still been detestable, and Mr. Beecher would have still been a heated barbarian. But they could not thus triumph, they could not make their rule thus universal, so long as their spirit was thus imperfect. They had not power enough over the minds of men. Now they are transforming their spirit in the furnace of civil war; with what success we shall in due time see. But the lovers of perfection in America itself ought to rejoice —some of them, no doubt, do rejoice—that the national spirit should be compelled, even at any cost of suffering, to transform itself, to become something higher, ampler, more gracious. To be glad that it should be compelled thus to transform itself, that it should not be permitted to triumph untransformed, is no insult, no unkindness; it is a homage to perfection. It is a religious devotion to that providential order which forbids the final supremacy of imperfect things. God keeps tossing back to the human race its failures, and commanding it to try again.

In the Crusade of Peter the Hermit, where the hosts that marched were not filled after the usual composition of armies, but contained along with the fighters whole families of people —old men, women, and children, swept by the universal torrent of enthusiasm towards the Holy Land—the marches, as might have been expected, were tedious and painful. Long before Asia was reached, long before even Europe was half traversed, the little children in that travelling multitude began to fancy, with a natural impatience, that their journey must surely be drawing to an end; and every evening, as they came in sight of some town which was the destination of that day's march, they cried out eagerly to those who were with them, "*Is this Jerusalem?*" No, poor children, not this town, nor the next, nor yet the next, is Jerusalem; Jerusalem is far off, and it needs time, and strength, and much endurance to reach it. Seas and mountains, labour and peril, hunger and thirst, disease and death, are between Jerusalem and you.

So, when one marks the ferment and stir of life in the middle class at this moment, and sees this class impelled to take possession of the world, and to assert itself and its own actual spirit absolutely, one is disposed to exclaim to it, "*Jerusalem is not* "*yet.* Your present spirit is not Jerusalem, is not the goal you "have to reach, the place you may be satisfied in." And when one says this, they sometimes fancy that one has the same object as others who say the same to them; that one means that they are to yield themselves to be moulded by some existing force, their rival; that one wishes Nonconformity to take the law from actual Anglicanism, and the middle class from the present governing class; that one thinks Anglicanism Jerusalem, and the English aristocratic class Jerusalem.

I do not mean, or wish, or think this, though many, no doubt, do. It is not easy for a reflecting man, who has studied its origin, to feel any vehement enthusiasm for Anglicanism; Henry the Eighth and his parliaments have taken care of that. One may esteem it as a beneficent social and civilising agent. One may have an affection for it from life-long associations, and for the sake of much that is venerable and interesting which it has inherited from antiquity. One may cherish gratitude to it—and here, I think, Mr. Goldwin Smith, who fights against it the battle of the Nonconformists with so much force and so much ability, is a little ungrateful—for the shelter and basis for culture which this, like other great nationally established forms of religion, affords; those who are born in them can get forward on their road, instead of always eyeing the ground on which they stand and disputing about it. But actual Anglicanism is certainly not Jerusalem, and I should be sorry to think it the end which Nonconformity and the middle class are to reach. The actual governing class, again, the English aristocratic class (in the widest sense of the word *aristocratic*)—I cannot wish that the rest of the nation, the new and growing part of the nation, should be transformed in spirit exactly according to the image of that class. The merits and services of that class no one rates higher than I do; no one appreciates higher than I do the value of the relative standard of elevation, refinement and grandeur, which they have exhibited; no one would more strenuously oppose the relinquishing of this for any lower standard. But I cannot hide from myself that while modern societies increasingly tend to find their best life in a free and heightened spiritual and intellectual activity, to this tendency aristocracies offer at least a strong passive resistance, by their eternal prejudices, their incurable dearth of ideas. In modern, rich, and industrial societies, they tend to misplace the ideal for the classes below them; the immaterial chivalrous ideal of high descent and honour is, by the very nature of the case, of force only for aristocracies themselves; the immaterial modern ideal of spiritual and intellectual perfection through culture, they have not to communicate. What they can and do communicate is the material ideal of splendour of wealth, and weight of property. And this ideal is the ideal truly operative upon our middle classes at this moment. To be as rich as they can, that they may reach the splendour of wealth and weight of property, and, with time, the importance, of the actual heads of society, is their ambition. I do not blame them, or the class from which they get their ideal; all I say is, that the good ideal for humanity, the true Jerusalem, is an ideal more spiritual than splendid wealth and boundless property, an ideal in which more can participate. The beloved friends of humanity have been those who made it feel its ideal to be in the things of the mind and spirit, to be in an internal condition separable from wealth and accessible to all—men like St. Francis, the ardent bridegroom of poverty; men like the great personages of antiquity, almost all of them, as Lacordaire was so fond of saying, poor. Therefore, that the middle class should simply take its ideal from the aristocratic class, I do not wish. That the aristocratic class should be able absolutely to assert itself and its own spirit, is not my desire. No, no; they are not Jerusalem.

The truth is, the English spirit has to accomplish an immense evolution; nor, as that spirit at this moment presents itself in any class or description amongst us, can one be perfectly satisfied with it, can one wish it to prevail just as it is.

But in a transformed middle class, in a middle class raised to a higher and more genial culture, we may find, not perhaps Jerusalem, but, I am sure, a notable stage towards it. In that great class, strong by its numbers, its energy, its industry, strong by its freedom from frivolity, not by any law of nature prone to immobility of mind, actually at this moment agitated by a spreading ferment of mind, in that class, liberalised by an ampler culture, admitted to a wider sphere of thought, living by larger ideas, with its provincialism dissipated, its intolerance cured, its pettinesses purged away,—what a power there will be, what an element of new life for England! Then let the middle class rule, then let it affirm its own spirit, when it has thus perfected itself.

And I cannot see any means so direct and powerful for developing this great and beneficent power as the public establishment of schools for the middle class. By public establishment they may be made cheap and accessible to all. By public establishment they may give securities for the culture offered in them being really good and sound, and the best that our time knows. By public establishment they may communicate to those reared in them the sense of being brought in contact with their country, with the national life, with the life of the world; and they will expand and dignify their spirits by communicating this sense to them. I can see no other mode of institution which will offer the same advantages in the same degree.

I cannot think that the middle class will be much longer insensible to its own evident interests. I cannot think that, for the pleasure of being complimented on their self-reliance by Lord Fortescue and the *Times*, they will much longer forego a course leading them to their own true dignity instead of away from it. I know that with men who have reached or passed the middle of life, the language and habits of years form a network round the spirit through which it cannot easily break; and among the elder leaders of the middle class there are men whom I would give much to persuade—men of weight and character, like Mr. Baines, men of character and culture too, like Mr. Miall—whom I must not, I fear, hope to persuade. But among the younger leaders of this class—even of that part of it where resistance is most to be apprehended, among the younger Dissenting ministers, for instance—there exists, I do believe, a disposition not fixedly averse to the public establishment of education for the middle classes—a willingness, at any rate, to consider a project of this kind on its merits. Amongst them particularly is the ferment and expansion of mind, of which I have spoken, perceptible; their sense of the value of culture, and their culture itself, increases every day. Well, the old bugbear which scares us all away from the great confessed means of best promoting this culture—the religious difficulty, as it is called—is potent only so long as these gentlemen please. It rests solely with themselves to procure the public establishment of secondary instruction upon a perfectly equitable basis as regards religious differences. If its establishment is suffered to fix itself in private hands, those hands will be the clergy's. It is to the honour of the clergy—of their activity, of their corporate spirit, of their sense of a pressing want—that this should be so. But in that case the dominant force in settling the teaching in these schools will be clerical. Their organisation will be ecclesiastical. Mr. Woodard tells us so himself; and indeed he (very naturally) makes a merit of it. This is not what the Dissenters want, neither is it what the movement of the modern spirit tends to. But when instruction has once been powerfully organised in this manner, it is very difficult for the State afterwards to interfere for the purpose of giving effect to the requirements of the modern spirit. It is met by vested interests—by legitimate vested interests—not to be conciliated without great delay and difficulty. It is not easy for the State to impose a conscience clause on primary schools, when the establishment of those schools has been for the most part made by the clergy. It is not easy to procure the full benefits of the national universities to Nonconformists, when Anglicanism has got a vested interest in the colleges. Neither will it be easy hereafter, in secondary instruction, to settle the religious difficulty equitably, if the establishment of that instruction shall have been effected by private bodies in which clerical influence predominates.

I hope the middle class will not much longer delay to take a step on which its future value and dignity and influence so much depend. By taking this step they will indirectly confer a great boon upon the lower class also. This obscure embryo, only just beginning to move, travailing in labour and darkness, so much left out of account when we celebrate the glories of our Atlantis, now and then, by so mournful a glimpse, showing itself to us in Lambeth, or Spitalfields, or Dorsetshire; this immense working class, now so without a practicable passage to all the joy and beauty of life, for whom in an aristocratic class, which is unattainable by them, there is no possible ideal, for whom in a middle class, narrow, ungenial, and unattractive, there is no adequate ideal, will have, in a cultured, liberalised, ennobled, transformed middle class, a point towards which it may hopefully work, a goal towards which it may with joy direct its aspirations.

Children of the future, whose day has not yet dawned, you, when that day arrives, will hardly believe what obstructions were long suffered to prevent its coming! You who, with all your faults, have neither the aridity of aristocracies, nor the narrow-mindedness of middle classes, you, whose power of simple enthusiasm is your great gift, will not comprehend how progress towards man's best perfection—the adorning and ennobling of his spirit—should have been reluctantly undertaken; how it should have been for years and years retarded by barren commonplaces, by worn-out clap-traps. You will wonder at the labour of its friends in proving the self-proving; you will know nothing of the doubts, the fears, the prejudices they had to dispel; nothing of the outcry they had to encounter; of the fierce protestations of life from policies which were dead and did not know it, and the shrill querulous upbraiding from publicists in their dotage. But you, in your turn, with difficulties of your own, will then be mounting some new step in the arduous ladder whereby man climbs towards his perfection; towards that unattainable but irresistible lode-star, gazed after with earnest longing, and invoked with bitter tears; the longing of thousands of hearts, the tears of many generations.

Critical and Explanatory Notes

The principal studies of Arnold's writings on education are by F. G. Walcott, "Matthew Arnold and the Growth of Democratic Education in England," a University of Michigan doctoral dissertation of 1945 that is regrettably unpublished, and W. F. Connell, *The Educational Thought and Influence of Matthew Arnold* (London: Routledge and Kegan Paul, 1950). A comprehensive history of all the problems under discussion is J. W. Adamson's *English Education, 1789–1902* (Cambridge: at the University Press, 1930).

Three books have been used so often that they are referred to in these notes only by short titles: *The Letters of Matthew Arnold to Arthur Hugh Clough*, ed. H. F. Lowry (London: Oxford University Press, 1932); *Matthew Arnold's Books: Toward a Publishing Diary*, ed. William E. Buckler (Geneva: E. Droz, 1958); and *The Note-Books of Matthew Arnold*, ed. H. F. Lowry, Karl Young, and W. H. Dunn (London: Oxford University Press, 1952). G. W. E. Russell's collection of *Letters of Matthew Arnold, 1848–1888* is available in so many editions that page references are little help; nearly all the letters quoted here without other reference may be found by their date in his collection. A very few passages are from unpublished manuscripts.

In the identification of French and Dutch names, the editor has depended heavily upon Pierre Larousse's *Grand dictionnaire universel du XIXe. siècle*, the *Nieuw Nederlandsch Biografisch Woordenboek*, the *Winkler Prins Encyclopaedie*, and *The Oxford Companion to French Literature.*

[THE POPULAR EDUCATION OF FRANCE]

On June 30, 1858, a Royal Commission was appointed under the chairmanship of the Duke of Newcastle "to consider and report what Measures, if any, are required for the Extension of sound and cheap elementary Instruction to all Classes of the People." The Commission resolved to appoint ten assistant commissioners to investigate various aspects of popular education in England, and two more to go to the Continent on similar missions. On January 25, 1859,* Fitzjames Stephen, secretary to the Education Commission, wrote to Arnold privately to inquire whether he would accept one of the latter posts. "The salary would be £50 a month, 15/- a day allowance & expenses of locomotion." The Committee of Council had already given its consent. Arnold called on Stephen two days later. At first his mission was to include France and the French-speaking countries, Belgium, Switzerland, and Piedmont. "I cannot tell you how much I like the errand, and above all, to have the French district," Arnold wrote to his sister Frances. Mark Pattison was appointed to visit the German-speaking countries. After some alterations in the plan, Arnold reported upon France, the French cantons of Switzerland, and Holland, and Pattison reported upon Germany alone.

Arnold left London on the evening of March 15 and reached Paris the next morning. His family followed on the nineteenth and remained with him for nearly six weeks, while he obtained for himself the necessary introductions and authorizations for his investigation and laid the basis of his study by conferring with the men who knew the French educational system best: he talked personally to Guizot, Villemain, Magin, Cousin, the Duc de Broglie, and Eugène Rendu, all of them authors of works he used in his report.

On April 30 he went to Brittany for eight days: Nantes (April 30), Quimper (May 3–5), Auray, with an excursion to Carnac (May 6), and Rennes (May 7). He was in Paris on the eighth and ninth, then took the night train on the tenth to Bordeaux. On the thirteenth he made the expedition to Blanquefort that he describes at some length in his report. Next morning he went to Toulouse. From there on May 18 he went to Sorèze, and next day to Carcassonne. On May 22 he wrote from Nîmes that he had visited Arles that day and would see Avignon the next.

A fortnight later he was in Holland, his wife again with him but not the children. Most of the week of June 5 they spent at The Hague; on the eleventh they went to Amsterdam. The next day, Sunday, he visited Zaandam, and on Monday made a day's

* Russell misdates the letter in which Arnold tells his sister of this offer.

excursion to Haarlem to visit the teacher training school. On June 15 they left Amsterdam for Utrecht; next day they journeyed through Rotterdam and Antwerp to Brussels, and on the seventeenth were again in Paris.

From there the itinerary was: June 23–24, Nancy; June 25–27, Strasbourg; June 28, Basel; June 29–30, Bern; and July 1, Geneva. On July 3 they went to Vevey, on the fifth to Martigny, and from there made a pleasure excursion to Chamonix. On July 9 they returned to Geneva for five days, then went to Lausanne for four (fourteenth to seventeenth). When he learned that the schools were to be closed for the long vacation, he canceled his proposed visit to Fribourg and Neuchâtel and journeyed through Geneva to Lyon on the eighteenth. They took the night train to Paris on the twentieth and reached the capital the next morning. There Arnold left his wife for two or three days while he visited the departments of the Center. The first two weeks in August he was with his family at Dover, returned to Paris for eleven days on the fourteenth, and ended his travels on August 26 in London. During these last days he worked on his report with Magin and Villemain; of the former he remarked, "I like him more and more, and shall make, I think, with his help, a very interesting report." The letters home from this four-months' tour are given with unusual fullness in Russell's edition; there can be little doubt that the intimate knowledge he gained of France and the personal acquaintance with her statesmen and literary men were of the first importance to the development of his career as a writer.

The writing of the report did not begin for several months. Late in December he was tempted to return to Paris—partly for the gaiety of the society, but "my great inducement in going back would be to see and talk to Cousin, who has himself had a Report to make much like that on which I am engaged. I should also, now that I know and have read so much about popular education in France, much like to see Guizot again, and to ask him some questions. However, I don't much think I shall go. The most important and difficult part of my Report is pretty well formed in my head now, and going back to Paris might give me a new start in some direction or other which would unsettle me, and give me all to do again." He was busily at work on it during January 1860; on the twentieth he reported to his mother that he had been all week at the British Museum, assembling his materials. "I have not even yet composed more than a sentence or two here and there of the Report as it will actually appear, though I have covered a good many sheets with notes and extracts." The last of the French portion of the report was sent to the printer on March 20. By that time Switzerland was done and Holland lacked only a table for its appendix; these sections followed eight days later.

It is not certain when he made the decision to print the report separately on his own account; presumably it was before October 29, when he indicated to his mother that he planned to prepare an introduction to his foreign report. On December 17 he told her that the commissioners had given him leave, and leave also to make some additions; he had already arranged with Longmans to publish at his own risk, and expected the book to appear in February 1861. It needed, he thought, "a good deal of re-touching . . . in order to be sufficiently de-officialized for general reading," but a glance at the Textual Notes will show how little seemed really to suffice. He restored one long passage (pp. 158:37–164:24) that had appeared in the initial "Strictly Confidential" printing but had been dropped from the officially published report, presumably at the request of his superiors: it is a passage that makes clear his view of the American culture and contains also the germ of his later essay on "The Literary Influence of Academies." The only other assistant commissioner to publish his report separately was Arnold's friend Cumin, who also made use of Longmans. *The Popular Education of France* was published about May 4, 1861, only a few weeks after its appearance as part of the Newcastle Commission's report; the price was 10*s.* 6*d.* The end papers were (somewhat ironically) devoted to advertising the complete works of Lord Macaulay.

The Introduction gave Arnold the most trouble. On February 13 he complained of "introduction-writing"; a month later, it still went slowly as he struggled against a bad cold, rheumatism, and headache: "It needs so much tact as to how much and how little to say that I am never satisfied with it." Only on March 28 could he report that he had finished a draft of it and had corrected nearly all the proof sheets of the rest of the book. "My health improves as I get out of the wood. I am not yet quite sure how the introduction will do—but I shall manage to lick it into some shape." In many ways the Introduction is the keystone of his thinking about politics and education; his republication of it as an independent essay in 1879 under the title "Democracy" suggests his own sense of its importance. (In the autumn of 1864 he had been tempted to include it in the first collection of *Essays in Criticism:* "It is one of the things I have taken most pains with, and it will come in very well."—Buckler, *Matthew Arnold's Books,* p. 68.) Though his opinion of the failure of American culture was by no means new, it received striking confirmation and emphasis in his eyes from the Secession: "I see Bright goes on envying the Americans," he wrote to his mother on January 20, 1860, "but I cannot but think that the state of things with respect to their *national character,* which, after all, is the base of the only real grandeur or prosperity, becomes graver and graver. It seems as if few stocks could be trusted to grow up properly without having a priesthood and an aristocracy to act as their schoolmasters at some time or other of their national existence." The events of 1860, when he was meditating his Introduction, did little to alter his judgment.

Reviewers might disagree with Arnold's doctrines, but they had reason to be grateful to an assistant commissioner who composed a government report with all the care of an artist. Its style was remarkably different from his polemic articles and his literary essays—far less allusive, perfectly straightforward, and remarkably clear. It is the only one of his books to be documented fully in footnotes; one can see the wide range of his investigation and the care with which he worked. He himself was content with it and professed an indifference to its sale: "The great thing is to produce nothing of which, if it comes into broad light, you will be ashamed; and then whether it *does* come into broad light or no need not much trouble you." One calculation was overlooked in this light-hearted assertion: in October 1862, he was staggered by a bill of more than £80 from Longmans, the extent to which the sale of the book had failed to meet its cost. This sum was greater than all the income he had yet received from more than thirteen years of publication. The stock of copies still on hand, with those of *Merope,* was transferred from Longmans to Macmillan in 1883.

Motto: Burke, "Thoughts on the Cause of the Present Discontents," *Works* (London, 1852), III, 147 (nearly two-thirds through the essay).

4:1–6. Eighth paragraph of the same essay.

6:37–38. Mirabeau, *Correspondance* [*avec*] *de La Marck,* II, 75.

7:17–19. See Spinoza, *Ethics,* Part III, Propositions 6–7: "Unaquaeque res, quantum in se est, in suo esse perseverare conatur. Conatus, quo unaquaeque res in suo esse perseverare conatur, nihil est praeter ipsius rei actualem essentiam."

9:17–23. Ed. of 1836, I, 40–41 (two-thirds through Chapter I) and I, 87 (conclusion of Chapter III).

12:13–15. Sir James Parke, judge of the court of exchequer from 1834 to 1855, was raised to a life peerage by letters patent dated January 16, 1856, but the Lords, after long debate, determined that the crown had lost by disuse the power of creating peers for life and declined to let him take his seat. Parke was then given a hereditary peerage.

14:34–38. For Wood's anecdote, see Arnold, *Prose Works*, ed. Super, I, 108. Chesterfield's letters are those to his son, February 22 and May 27, 1748 (O.S.), and November 1750 (to await his son's arrival in Paris). All insist upon the necessity of knowing Greek and Latin if one is to live at ease in the best society.

15:2. Vergil *Aeneid* v. 231.

17:6. The *Constitutionnel*, founded in 1815 during the Hundred Days, was Bonapartist in sympathies; in 1851 it studiously prepared public opinion to accept the *coup d'état* that made Louis Napoleon Emperor.

17:8. The *Morning Star* was founded as a penny newspaper by the Radicals of the Manchester school on March 17, 1856; Cobden contributed to its capital and Bright's brother-in-law was its first editor. After October 13, 1869, it was absorbed by the *Daily News*.

17:13–14. Samuel Butler, *Hudibras*, I, i, 215–16.

20:28–29. The Act of Uniformity, the Five-mile Act, the Conventicle Act, and the Corporation Act were measures passed by the first Restoration Parliament in 166:–65 to provide for the suppression of the Nonconformist sects.

21:7. See Philippians 4:12.

21:9–10. See Matthew 9:12.

22:14. The term "Classical and Commercial Academy" covered the multitude of private schools set up primarily for middle-class patrons, in rivalry with the endowed "public" schools and "free" grammar schools.

26:37–38. See note to 294:25.

29:25–26. Matthew 5:48; Philippians 3:13. The conclusion of the latter verse became the motto at the head of *A French Eton.*

30:6. Henry Wellesley, first Earl Cowley, a career diplomat, was British ambassador in Paris from 1852 to 1867.

30:9. Gustave Rouland, a lawyer and a whole-hearted adherent of the *coup d'état* of December 2, 1851, became minister of Public

Instruction on August 13, 1856, and held that post until June 24, 1863.

30:23. Alfred Magin [-Marrens] was inspector general of primary instruction from 1854 to 1862, author of textbooks in geography and history, and translator of Terence. See p. 34:36.

31:4. Granville George Leveson-Gower, second Earl Granville, as lord president of the Privy Council was the superior of the vice-president of the Committee of Council on Education; before the creation of the vice-presidency in 1857 the lord president himself presided over the committee and he remained its spokesman in the House of Lords.

31:5. François Guizot (1787–1874), distinguished both as historian and statesman, was minister of Public Instruction from October 11, 1832, to April 15, 1837 (except for a few months in 1836). He was Louis Philippe's chief minister from 1841 until the Revolution of 1848; thereafter he did not hold political office.

31:9. Jean-Jacques Rapet was author of textbooks in French grammar, of a *Manual of Legislation and Administration of Primary Instruction* (1860) and of a *Course of Study of Primary Schools.* About *The Popular Education of France,* Rapet wrote to the author when he read his copy: "Si, après avoir passé quelque temps en Angleterre pour étudier l'organisation de son système d'éducation, je venais à publier le résultat de mes études, je m'estimerais trop heureux que mon travail eût la même valeur que le vôtre, et *surtout qu'il reproduisît les faits avec la même exactitude.*" "That is the sort of testimony I like," Arnold remarked as he underlined the last words.—*Letters to Clough,* ed. Lowry, p. 156. In the spring of 1862 Rapet made an official visit to England and Arnold was able to repay his assistance in kind. Arnold commemorated him in an article entitled "A French Worthy" in the *Pall Mall Gazette* for November 8, 1882.

31:22–23. See p. 182:37–38.

31:37. The monitorial (or mutual) system, established in England by Andrew Bell and Joseph Lancaster at the turn of the century, had been known in France, at least in principle, fully as early. It involved the use of a single schoolmaster in the school; he taught the monitors, and the monitors taught the other pupils. The vogue of this method gave impetus to the attempts in both countries to establish popular instruction on a national scale. The simultaneous system, practiced by the Brethren of the Christian Schools in

France, was the teaching of large groups together, in classes sometimes larger than a hundred. The Brethren steadfastly resisted official pressure to adopt the monitorial system. See p. 114:10–18.

32:23. Joseph Kay was younger brother of Sir James Kay-Shuttleworth, "founder of English popular education."

34:20–30. Magin, III, 184–85.

35:10–23. Vallet de Viriville, pp. 72, 199–200. A prebend is "any portion of the cathedral revenues set aside for the support of the clergy attached to it."—*Catholic Encyclopedia.*

36:2–4. The Declaration of the Clergy of France, drawn up by Bossuet, approved by the bishops, and made law by royal decree on March 23, 1682, established for France the independence of the temporal power and traditional rights of the Gallican church against encroachment by the Holy See. The Concordat of 1801 between Napoleon and the Pope established the principle that religion in France should be subject to whatever police regulation should be necessary for the public peace. In giving the Concordat the force of law on April 8, 1802, the government put forth a set of provisions regulating both Protestant and Catholic religion in France: these provisions were the *articles organiques,* and were long opposed by the Holy See as claiming for the State too much power over church administration.

36:7–10. Vallet de Viriville, p. 91.

36:10–17. A. Rendu, *Essai sur l'instruction publique* (Paris, 1819), I, 305; II, 371.

36:20–21. *Ibid.*, I, 290.

36:22–30; 37:6. Domat, Rousseaud de Lacombe, and Bonald are quoted by Rendu, I, 288, 289; III, 338–40.

37:30. St. Patroclus, a recluse, built Colombiers monastery, in Berry, France, for his disciples. He died in 577. "Deux simples pâtres, saint Patrocle, natif du Berri, et un autre du nom de Léobin, s'instruisirent aux lettres chrétiennes et devinrent, à leur tour, la lumière de leur époque."—Vallet de Viriville, p. 71.

38:9–29. Vallet de Viriville, pp. 270–71. The act of 1696 ordered "that a school be established, and a schoolmaster appointed in every parish [of Scotland]; and it further ordered that the landlords should be obliged to build a school-house, and a dwelling-house for the use of the master; and that they should pay him a salary, exclusive of the fees of his scholars; which should not fall short of £5. 11*s.* 1*d.* a year, nor exceed £11. 2*s.* 2*d.*"—H. Barnard, *National Education in Europe* (2d edition; Hartford, Conn., 1854), p. 652.

39:6–21. A. Rendu, *Essai,* I, 275–76.

39:21–33. Vallet de Viriville, p. 271n.

39:34–41:9. *Ibid.*, pp. 243–45.

41:10–42:3. A. Rendu, *Essai,* I, 15–30, 46.

42:9–17. *Ibid.*, I, 57, 47–48n.

42:23–30. *Ibid.*, I, 130–31, 133.

42:33–38. *Ibid.*, I, 33.

43:3. Pierre-Paul Royer-Collard (1763–1845) was distinguished by his integrity throughout all the vicissitudes of French politics during his lifetime. A moderate royalist under Napoleon, he nevertheless was made professor of the history of philosophy at the Sorbonne in 1811. He was an influential adviser of Louis XVIII at his restoration and author of the law reorganizing the French universities and making their professors no longer dependent on the crown for their posts. He was first president of the new commission that governed the University (see p. 62:31–32), but not, strictly speaking, education minister. His remark on the brethren will be found in A. Rendu, *Essai,* II, 590.

43:38–39. Eugène Rendu, *De l'Instruction primaire à Londres dans ses rapports avec l'état social* (2d edition; Paris, 1853) and *De l'Éducation populaire dans l'Allemagne du Nord et de ses rapports avec les doctrines philosophiques et religieuses* (Paris, 1855).

43:20–44:11. Vallet de Viriville, pp. 271–73.

44:18. Abel-François Villemain (1790–1870), professor at the Sorbonne, academician, historian, and critic, was minister of Public Instruction for some four years under Louis Philippe. His list of instructional establishments at the time of the Revolution (No. 25) is reprinted in Vallet de Viriville, p. 276.

45:13–16. See Vallet de Viriville, p. 272; A. Rendu, *Essai,* II, 338.

46:1–48:7. Vallet de Viriville, pp. 279–80, 282, 284; A. Rendu, *Essai,* I, 248, 263–64; II, 339–40, 342.

46:26. Charles-Maurice de Talleyrand-Périgord (1754–1838) was the most brilliant French diplomat of his day; his tremendous abilities won him high posts in every administration and his shrewd self-interest kept him on the successful side of every revolution.

47:7. Antoine-Nicolas de Condorcet (1743–94), philosopher and mathematician, was for a time president of the Legislative Assembly and was member of the committee of the Convention charged with preparing a new constitution.

47:25. Antoine-François Fourcroy (1755–1809), chemist and colleague of Lavoisier, as councillor of state under Napoleon reorganized public instruction in the provinces.

48:11–49:15. A. Rendu, *Essai*, II, 342–46. The *décadi* was the day of rest, the final day of the Republican ten-day week.

49:23–50:26. *Ibid.*, I, 251; II, 347–50, 354.

49:29–30. See Matthew 24:15.

51:1–31. Vallet de Viriville, pp. 284–85, and a summary of the law Arnold printed in his appendix.

51:4. Pierre-Claude-François Daunou (1761–1840), priest and historian, after the fall of Robespierre was a leader in legislative, scientific, and educational reform.

51:32. Arnold described his meeting with Guizot in a letter to his wife on April 28, 1859.

54:10–20. A. Rendu, *Essai*, II, 359–61.

54:29–55:8. *Ibid.*, II, 365–66.

55:15–56:2. Vallet de Viriville, pp. 297–99, 301–2. The decree of March 17, 1808, is printed in Lewis Goldsmith, ed., *Recueil de décrets, ordonnances, traités de paix, manifestes, proclamations, discours, &c. &c. de Napoléon Bonaparte. . . . Extraits du Moniteur* (London, 1813), III, 276–94.

56:7–29. A. Rendu, *Essai*, I, 235–36, 220–21.

56:30–36; 57:1–5. Vallet de Viriville, pp. 304–8.

57:23–25. Article 107.

57:28–30. Article 38.

58:1–6. Article 109.

58:21. Louis de Fontanes (1757–1821) continued the tradition of the didactic poets of the eighteenth century with a verse *Essay on Astronomy*, a poem *On Nature and Man*, and a translation of Pope's *Essay on Man.*

58:25–59:19. A. Rendu, *Essai*, II, 402, 413–16.

59:34. Charles Jourdain (1817–86) devoted his life to education and to writing on the relation of philosophy to religion. His father, Amable-Louis-Marie (1788–1818), was an orientalist.

60:6–17. Jourdain, *Budget*, pp. 180, 176. Adrien, Comte Lezay de Marnésia, was named prefect of Rhin-et-Moselle in 1806 and of Bas-Rhin in 1811. He died in 1814. Lazare-Nicolas-Marguerite Carnot (1753–1823), the "organizer of victory" for the armies of early republican France and one of the five directors of 1795, was Napoleon's minister of the interior during the Hundred Days.

61:1–8. Jourdain, *Budget*, p. 176.

61:26–27. The Declaration of Breda on April 4, 1660, set forth the policy to which Charles II pledged himself on his return to England; in effect it left to Parliament the task of untangling the difficulties that had been caused by the Rebellion.

62:3–15. Vallet de Viriville, p. 305 (but without the passages Arnold puts in quotation marks).

62:22–25. "France Before the Revolution," tr. J. S. Mill, in A. de Tocqueville, *Memoir, Letters, and Remains* (London, 1861), I, 241–53 (reprinted from *Westminster Review*, April 1836).

62:33–39. F. de La Mennais, "Sur les attaques dirigées contre les Frères des Écoles chrétiennes," *Le Conservateur*, I, 297, 299, 300–301 (November 1818); quoted by A. Rendu, *Essai*, III, 317, 322–23, 327.

63:3–28. A. Rendu, *Essai*, III, 303–5, 312–14, 295–97.

63:29. Denis Frayssinous (1765–1841), titular bishop of Hermopolis, was grand master of the University from 1822 and minister of Ecclesiastical Affairs and Public Instruction from 1824 to 1828; he retained the portfolio of Ecclesiastical Affairs until the revolution of 1830.

64:8. Antoine-François-Henri Lefebvre de Vatimesnil (1789–1860), an arch-conservative lawyer and secretary-general of the Ministry of Justice, became minister of Public Instruction and grand master of the University in 1828. He proved vigorous and enlightened, but his term of office was only a little more than one year.

64:15. Martial-Côme-Annibal, Comte de Guernon-Ranville (1787–1866), royalist magistrate, was minister of Public Instruction and grand master of the University from November 1829 to the July revolution of 1830. The July Ordinances, signed by the ministers of Charles X on July 25, 1830, suppressed the newspapers and dissolved the liberal Chamber of Deputies in a final attempt to assert the power of the throne; instead, they precipitated the revolution. Guernon-Ranville was imprisoned for six years thereafter.

64:29–31. See note to p. 69:13–17.

65:17–20. "Tout-à-coup parut l'ordonnance du 8 avril 1824. Elle donna plein pouvoir aux évêques: . . . mais, à l'exception d'un petit nombre de diocèses, cet absolu pouvoir du clergé sur l'instruction primaire n'eut pas des résultats heureux. L'Université vit naître de tous côtés, sans pouvoir y porter remède, le désordre et la confusion; les instituteurs clandestins et indignes, trop peu surveillés ou faiblement réprimés, se multiplièrent. . . . Chose remarquable! l'ordonnance de 1824 semblait avoir pour object principal la réforme et la prospérité des écoles catholiques, et elle leur a été généralement fatale; tandis que les écoles protestantes, qui étaient restées sous l'empire des ordonnances de 1816 et de 1820, n'ont pas cessé de prospérer."—*Bulletin universitaire*, II, 173–74 (November 1830).

65:34. Achille-Charles, Duc de Broglie (1785–1870), held several portfolios under the July monarchy, including that of minister of Public Instruction and grand master of the University from August 11 to November 8, 1830.

66:32–35. Paul Lorain was in charge of the inspection of schools in the Department of Indre-et-Loire in 1833 and became Academy rector of Lyon. The inspection of 1833 was a comprehensive survey of French schools by 490 inspectors; their reports, summarized by Lorain, were to form the basis for the work of improvement provided by the law of June 28.

Chapter VII: Arnold's principal authority is E. Kilian, *Manuel législatif et administratif de l'instruction primaire* (Paris, 1838–39), which contains the law of 1833, official decrees that augment it, and a full commentary. Arnold reprints the law of 1833 in an appendix not given in this edition.

68:28–69:5. Guizot's *Exposé des motifs* is printed in Kilian, pp. 1–18, and his covering letter to the schoolmasters on pp. 19–26. The passages Arnold quotes or summarizes are on pp. 4–5.

69:13–17. *Le Moniteur universel*, LXXXVIII, 1433–36 (May 22, 1833), reporting the session of the House of Peers the preceding day at which Victor Cousin presented the new elementary education bill on behalf of the government: "Le principe de liberté, s'il était admis comme principe unique, serait un obstacle invincible à l'universalité de l'instruction. Remarquez que les communes pauvres n'attirent guère l'instituteur privé; de sorte que ce seraient précisément ceux qui ont le plus besoin de l'instruction primaire qui en seraient presque infailliblement privés."—p. 1434, col. 2.

69:33–35. Kilian, *Manuel*, p. 2.

71:35–36. See p. 77.

73:14–21. Jourdain, *Budget*, p. 184. Jean-Denis-Marie Cochin (1789–1841), lawyer and philanthropist, was noted for his strenuous efforts to relieve poverty and spread instruction. The XIIth arrondissemont is in the eastern part of the city; it now includes the Gare de Lyon.

74:36–38. The words Arnold quotes appear on p. 282.

75:8. Narcisse-Achille, Comte de Salvandy (1795–1856), was minister of Public Instruction and grand master of the University from 1845 to the end of Louis Philippe's reign.

76:3. Lazare-Hippolyte Carnot (1801–88), second son of the director, was a vigorous minister of Public Instruction in the Provisional Government from February 24 to July 5, 1848.

76:29. Louis-Adolphe Thiers (1797–1877), author of the long *History of the Consulate and the Empire*, was a politician whose greatest success was still in the future—the leadership of the republican government after the fall of Napoleon III.

77:35–37. Arnold's table, showing the number of accused, convicted, and acquitted persons from 1826 to 1850, reveals a decline in the last decade, despite an increasing population.

83:20–29. *Bulletin universitaire*, III, 234, 295. The "many interesting instructions written by M. Guizot" to which Arnold alludes may be found in this official *Bulletin*.

83:32–84:3. *Ibid.*, IV, 390.

86:17–31. *Ibid.*, III, 234, 100, 236–37.

92:27. Arnold's tables deal with the cost of state elementary education in France. His Table I is Jourdain's Table VI (pp. 300–301), with a footnote based on Jourdain's Tables VII–VIII (pp. 302–3); his Table II is Jourdain's Table XXVIII (p. 322); his Table III is Jourdain's XXIX (p. 323); and his Table IV is Jourdain's XXXI (p. 325).

102:2. Horace *Odes* I.xii.47–48.

102:25–26. E. Rendu, *De l'Instruction primaire à Londres* (2d edition; Paris, 1853), p. 92.

106:19. A "British school" was one supervised and supported by the British and Foreign School Society, a nondenominational society founded in 1814 by dissenters and radicals.

111:12–13. I.e., to the doctrines of the Roman Catholic Church as defined by the Council of Trent, 1545–63.

114:6–9. "Les maîtres conviendront avec le Frère directeur de ceux qui pourraient être changés, et qu'il ne sera pas à propos de changer cette fois, ou parce qu'ils sont encore fort jeunes, *ou parce qu'il en faut laisser quelques-uns dans chaque leçon ou dans chaque ordre de leçon, qui sachent assez bien lire pour animer les autres et pour leur servir de modèles, pour les former à bien s'exprimer et à bien prononcer distinctement les lettres, les syllabes, ou les mots, et à bien faire les pauses.*"—Rendu quotes the 1812 edition of the *Conduite des écoles chrétiennes*.

114:10. See note to p. 31:37.

114:30–115:1. A minute of the Committee of Council on Education (of which Kay-Shuttleworth was secretary) on December 21, 1846, established the pupil-teacher system as a means of recruiting a professional body of teachers: "Boys and girls of at least thirteen years of age and of good moral character were to be indentured for five years as apprentices to head teachers, provided that these boys and girls showed capacity to teach and passed a very elementary examination. . . . Grants would be made from Government direct to the instructors of these 'pupil teachers.' . . . On completion of the apprenticeship, pupil teachers were to be admissible to a competitive examination, the successful candidates, or 'Queen's Scholars,' being awarded exhibitions of £20–30, to be held for three years or less at a normal school."—J. W. Adamson, *English Education, 1789–1902*, p. 144.

118:16–20. See Guizot, *Mémoires*, III, 79–80.

120:5–6. Guizot (*Mémoires*, III, 80–83) pays high tribute to Jean-Marie de Lamennais (1775–1861), founder of the Congregation of Christian Teaching, and his brother, the writer Félicité de Lamennais (1782–1854), whom Arnold also describes in his essay on Maurice de Guérin.

121:17. The "National schools" were those of the National Society for Promoting the Education of the Poor in the Principles of the Established Church throughout England and Wales.

122:21. In *England and the Italian Question* (1859); see Arnold, *Prose Works*, ed. Super, I, 90.

123:5. The Gironde is a maritime department of southwestern France, notable for its excellent wine. The principal city, Bordeaux, is the seat of the academy.

123:27–28. The French under Junot were defeated by the English under Wellesley (Wellington) at Vimeiro in Portugal on August 21, 1808. By the Convention of Cintra, signed nine days later, the French army, with their arms and artillery, evacuated Portugal and were returned to France.

125:22. The Irish Board of National Education prepared and published a series of reading books, maps, and textbooks that were very popular in England, though in the opinion of the Newcastle Commission they left much to be desired. The *Third Book of Lessons* contains twenty-two reading lessons devoted to natural history—"The Wolf," "The Fox," "The Lion," "The Deer," "Swallows," "Spiders," "Bees," "The Salmon," "The Cod," etc.

126:8–10. Arnold repeated his complaint against the English reading books in his inspectoral report of January 1861: "The candour with which school inspectors in France avowed to me their dissatisfaction with the school-books in use there, led me to reflect on the great imperfection exhibited by our school-books also. I found in the French schools good manuals for teaching special subjects—a good manual for teaching arithmetic, a good manual for teaching grammar, a good manual for teaching geography; what was wanting there, as it is wanting with us, was a good *reading-book*, or course of reading-books. It is not enough remembered in how many cases his reading-book forms the whole literature, except his Bible, of the child attending a primary school. If then, instead of literature, his reading-book, as is too often the case, presents him with a jejune encyclopaedia of positive information, the result is, that he has, except his Bible, no literature, no *humanizing* instruction at all. If, again, his reading-book, as is also too often the case, presents him with bad literature instead of good—with the writing of second or third-rate authors, feeble, incorrect, and colourless—he has not, as the rich have, the corrective of an abundance of good literature to counteract the bad effect of trivial and ill-written school-books; the second or third-rate literature of his school-book remains for him his sole, or, at least, his principal literary standard. Dry scientific disquisitions, and literary compositions of an inferior order, are indeed the worst possible instruments for teaching children to read well. But besides the fault of not fulfilling this, their essential function, the ill-compiled reading-books I speak of have, I say, for the poor scholar, the graver fault of actually doing what they can to spoil his taste, when they are nearly his only means for forming it. I have seen school-books belonging to the cheapest, and therefore most popular series in use in our primary schools, in which far more than half of the poetical extracts were the composition either of the anonymous compilers themselves, or of American writers of the second and third order; and these books were to be some poor child's Anthology of a literature so varied and so powerful as the English! To this defectiveness of our reading-books I attribute much of that grave and discouraging deficiency in anything like literary taste and feeling, which even well-instructed pupil-teachers of four or five years' training, which even the ablest students in our training schools, still continue almost invariably to exhibit; a deficiency, to remedy which, the progressive development of our school system, and the very considerable increase of information among the people, appear to avail little or nothing. I believe that nothing would so much contribute to remedy it as the diffusion in our elementary schools of reading-books of which the contents were really well selected and interesting. Such lessons would be far better adapted than a treatise on the atmosphere, the steam-engine, or the pump, to attain the proper end of a reading-book, that of teaching scholars to read well; they would also afford the best chance of inspiring quick scholars with a real love for reading and literature in the only way in which such a love is ever really inspired, by animating and moving them; and if they succeeded in doing this, they would have this further advantage, that the literature for which they inspired a taste would be a good, a sound, and a truly refining literature; not a literature such as that of most of the few attractive pieces in our current reading-books, a literature over which no cultivated person would dream of wasting his time."—House of Commons, *Sessional Papers*, 1861, XLIX, 158–60.

126:38–39. In his report of January 1861, D. Middleton, inspector for Church of Scotland schools, who had been conducting a campaign for better reading-books, wrote: "The school reading-books now publishing are greatly superior to most of their predecessors, simpler and clearer in style, more interesting and less pedantic. This is true, both of the prose and verse, now offered for school-reading."—*Ibid.*, p. 240. Both Nelson's School Series and Longmans' Graduated Series of Reading-Lesson Books were just now making their appearance.

127:26. The Cantal and the Creuse are two mountainous departments in the Auvergne, in Central France, in the academy district of Clermont; they are without large towns, without industry, and in the nineteenth century were rapidly losing population through emigration.

133:2. The Borough Road Training School (in South London) of the British and Foreign School Society was one of those that came under Arnold's inspection.

133:7–8. The Home and Colonial Infant School Society was organized in 1836 to train schoolmistresses somewhat on Pestalozzian principles.

133:25. Horace *Epistles* I.xi.27.

136:9–25. The program of studies in the English training schools was much criticized. Nassau W. Senior, a member of the Newcastle Commission, published in his *Suggestions on Popular Education* (London, 1861) samples of the pedantic examination questions set for students in these institutions (pp. 323–33).

137:21. Hippolyte-Nicolas-Honoré Fortoul (1811–56), a warm adherent of the politics of Louis Napoleon, was rewarded with the portfolio of Public Instruction on the morrow of the *coup d'état* of December 2, 1851, and held it until his death.

144:28–29. See note to p. 121:17.

154:7–9. Sir John Pakington's Education (No. 2) Bill, proposing to establish a rate (or local tax) for education on the ground that the voluntary system had broken down, had its first reading on March 16, 1855, was printed, and was debated again on May 2 and June 11, but was withdrawn before its second reading. Its language is typical of the legislative style: "The said Committee of Council on Education shall, in such Manner as they may deem most convenient, and they are hereby empowered to transfer to the Account of the School Committee of any Borough, Union, or Parish *the Moiety* or equal Share or Proportion of any Grant made by such school Committee as the Committee of Council may have approved: Provided always . . ." &c. (Bill No. 59, Session 1854–55; House of Commons, *Sessional Papers*, 1854–55, II, 245–68.) Pakington in 1858 moved the resolution by which the Newcastle Commission was set up, in the service of which Arnold wrote the present study.

155:3–4. "C'est la grandeur de notre pays (je ne veux pas dire c'était) que le succès purement matériel et actuel n'y suffit pas, et que les esprits ont besoin d'être satisfaits en même temps que les intérêts."

156:28. Sir Robert Peel, in 1846.

160:13–14. On September 29, 1859, Arnold wrote to Clough: "So long as *segnities* is, as Spinoza says, with *superbia* the great bane of man, it will need the stimulant of literary work or something equally rousing, to overcome this, and to educe out of a man what virtue there is in him."—*Letters to Clough*, ed. Lowry, p. 151. He used the same allusion at the beginning of his essay on "The Literary Influence of Academies."

160:17–18. The Delphic oracle said this of Socrates; see Plato *Apology* 21.

160:20–21. Pope, *Essay on Criticism*, II, 15; Pope's word is "learning."

162:1. "In him the savage virtue of the Race, / Revenge, and all ferocious thoughts were dead."—Wordsworth, "Song at the Feast of Brougham Castle," lines 165–66. Arnold remembered the phrase imperfectly and the context not at all.

162:7. Jules Michelet (1798–1874) devoted his life to writing a *History of France*, the most famous example of vivid, romantic, declamatory, picturesque narrative history. He held the chair of history at the Collège de France from 1838 to 1851, when his refusal to swear allegiance to the Second Empire forced him into retirement. Arnold was introduced to Michelet in Paris in 1847 by Philarète Chasles; upon his arrival on the educational mission of 1859 he wrote to inquire (April 10) if he might call on Michelet, "et de vous demander quelques renseignements sur la condition actuelle de vos populations urbaines et rurales dont on m'a recommandé, dans le but de ma mission, de m'informer avec soin, et sur laquelle personne autant que vous, Monsieur, ne serait en état de me donner des informations utiles."—J.-M. Carré, *Michelet et son temps* (Paris, 1926), p. 181.

162:17–18. An allusion to the "Nil admirari" of Horace *Epistles* I.vi.1.

162:27. The family of Montmorency, one of the most ancient and distinguished of France, was proclaimed by Henry IV the first family after the royal house. It included a number of grand constables of France. The Birons became a ducal family under Henry IV, when one of them was marshal of France. The same ruler made the Rohans a ducal family; they too were among the most ancient noble families of France.

162:35. The Institut de France, a learned society, includes five *académies*, the senior of which is the Académie française.

166:23–24. The British minister at Bern was Captain Edward Alfred John Harris, R.N.; the British Consul at Geneva was Armand Pictet.

167:22–23. Neuchâtel, a county from the twelfth century and a sovereign principality after the Treaty of Westphalia (1648), was nominally ruled by the king of Prussia from the time of Frederick I early in the eighteenth century. The principality became the only nonrepublican member of the Swiss Confederation in 1815. In 1848 a peaceful revolution established a republican form of government which the Prussian king, as hereditary prince, refused to recognize. A royalist conspiracy in 1856 led to negotiations by which in the following year the king of Prussia renounced his claims to sovereignty.

167:34. In 1843 the seven Roman Catholic cantons formed a "Sonderbund," or separate league, upon the question of the suppression of monasteries and the expulsion of the Jesuits. Four years later the Diet voted that the Sonderbund was contrary to the Federal Pact of 1815. The seven cantons withdrew from the Diet, which enforced its position by arms; the War of the Sonderbund lasted from November 10 to 29 and ended with the surrender of the rebellious cantons. In 1848 the Confederation adopted a new constitution.

176:26–27. Jean-Baptiste Girard (1765–1850), a Franciscan, acquired a European reputation as director of the primary schools of Fribourg from 1804 to 1823. He aroused the opposition of the Jesuits and the hierarchy by introducing the mutual system into the schools; the system was declared to be "immoral and irreligious" and Girard was relieved of his post.

179:1–3. The philosopher Victor Cousin (1792–1867), minister of Public Instruction in 1840, brought out studies of public instruction in Prussia and other German states (1833) and in Holland (1837).

179:6–8. The famous zoologist and paleontologist Georges Cuvier (1769–1832) and the humanist educator François-Joseph-Michel Noël (1755–1841) reported to the Imperial University on public education in the Dutch provinces in execution of an imperial decree of December 13, 1810.

181:3–4. Jan Nieuwenhuyzen (1724–1806). In a century and a quarter his society had established 324 popular libraries, 140 savings banks, and 50 nursery schools.

181:12. *Moore's Almanack* was a paper-bound, thirty-two page annual that contained, along with its calendar, predictions of the weather, astrological forecasts for important people and nations, moral advice, recipes for making ginger beer and removing corns, and indeed the usual paraphernalia of works of this kind. It was published, in Arnold's day, by T. Goode, of Clerkenwell, who also published "several Comic quarto books and Broad Sheets."

181:26. Johannes Henricus van der Palm (1763–1840), theologian and man of letters, was a university professor who as agent of National Education (1799–1806) devoted himself principally to elementary education and spelling reform.

181:30. Rutger Jan Schimmelpenninck (1761–1825) was a Dutch statesman and diplomat, onetime ambassador to London.

181:32. Adriaan van den Ende (1768–1846) was van der Palm's

adviser from 1800 and the principal author of the law of April 3, 1806, that bore the latter's name.

187:27. Pieter Johannes Prinsen (1777–1854) became head of the school of the Society for the Public Good in Haarlem in 1801, and became director of the first Dutch National training college for teachers when it was established in that city in 1816. He held the post until his death. His reputation as an educator was international.

190:21–32. Arnold is following Laveleye's summary of Cousin (*Débats sur l'enseignement*, p. 6); the quotations are Laveleye's words, not Cousin's.

192:19–22. Schools in Ireland received direct support from the government through the National Board. An account of the resistance to religious teaching in them is given by William Fraser, *Our Educational Enterprises*, pp. 9–28.

193:23. Émile de Laveleye (1822–92) first won a reputation as a brilliant contributor to French literary journals, then devoted himself almost entirely to the study of political and economic matters.

193:34–35. Guillaume Groen van Prinsterer (1801–76) was a prominent member of the upper chamber of the Dutch legislature from 1849 to 1866, except for his five-year retirement (1857–62) in protest of the new education law.

196:9. Michael Hendrik Godefroi (1813–82) was a member of the Dutch legislature for more than a quarter of a century and was the first Jew to hold a ministerial portfolio (Justice, from 1860 to 1862).

198:36. Justinus Jacobus Leonard van der Brugghen (1804–63), minister of Justice from 1856 to 1858, was a firm advocate of the mixed state school in the debate over the law of 1857.

199:22. For the theology of the Dutch University of Groningen, see p. 194:19–25. The University of Tübingen, in Württemberg, gave its name to the rationalist school of "higher criticism" of the Bible led by F. C. Baur and best known in England through D. F. Strauss's *Leben Jesu*. Utrecht was the seat of a Roman Catholic archbishop and the principal center of the Jansenist Church of Holland as well. Geneva is the home of Calvinism.

204:1. Francis, ninth Lord Napier, was minister to Holland in 1859–60; the secretary of the Legation was William Robert Ward.

204:3. Hendrik Vollenhoven (1816–89) was referendary for Education, Art, and Science from 1848 to 1875, for Education alone until his retirement in 1881.

204:5. Jacob George Hieronymous van Tets van Goudriaan (1812–85) was minister of Internal Affairs from 1858 to 1860, and later Finance minister.

204:10. Jacob de Witte van Citters (1817–76) was school inspector in South Holland from 1855 to 1865, a man of high reputation for his work in the improvement of education.

210:37–38. Third paragraph from the end of the essay.

Notes to Canceled Passages

384:16–19. Burke, "Thoughts on the Cause of the Present Discontents," *Works* (London, 1852), III, 133 (one-third through the essay).

385:15. Terence *Phormio* 454.

[THE TWICE-REVISED CODE]

The history of state aid to schools and the sense of state responsibility for the education of the people in England was one of halting steps, bitter opposition, and sad disagreements even among those who believed that education was indeed the duty of the state. Actually, the start was made in Ireland only fourteen years after the Union (that is, in 1814); the establishment there of the Board of Commissioners of National Education seventeen years later gave Ireland an administrative authority over education two years before the first appropriation was made in England, and was therefore responsible (among other things) for the development of the series of elementary school reading books that, to Arnold's distress, provided the chief intellectual and aesthetic stimulus for the children of the poor in English schools.

On August 17, 1833, the House of Commons voted £20,000 for the building of schoolhouses in England and Wales, and £10,000 for the same purpose in Scotland; the grant was afterward made annual. There was no provision for setting up a government education authority; the money was dispensed by the Treasury directly to the two principal societies engaged in the education of the poor, the National Society of the Established Church and the undenominational British and Foreign School Society. From the outset the state was conceived to have an interest in aiding the education only of the poor, and even here the interest was considered to be limited to assisting voluntary efforts. Those who could be regarded as able to pay for the education of their own children were expected to do so.

By an Order in Council of April 10, 1839, the superintendence of parliamentary grants in aid of education was given to a committee of the Privy Council named for the purpose, with the lord president of the Council (at that time, fortunately, the Marquis of Lansdowne) as its chairman. Its nonparliamentary secretary for ten years was Sir James Kay-Shuttleworth, a vigorous proponent of state support for education. Grants were no longer made through the two school societies, and one of the committee's first acts in administering its funds was to insist that all schools aided by state money submit to inspection by the agents of the Council and comply with the standards it might set up. The Committee of Council, it will be seen, had not been established by Parliament and worked not within a framework of parliamentary legislation but by rules of its own framing, embodied in various Minutes, the most important of which was that of December 21, 1846, that provided an elaborate system of state encouragement and control in the training, certification, and payment of teachers. The Committee of Council was dependent on Parliament only for grants of money, and the only way in which Parliament could call its activities into question was during the debate on the annual appropriation. This rose from £30,000 in 1839 to £813,441 in 1861; in addition to its original purpose of aiding the building of schools and its newer use in the training of teachers, it was by a Minute of April 1853 applied also to a capitation grant—a sum given to the schools in proportion to the number of pupils in attendance, provided certain other conditions were fulfilled.

Every education bill proposed in Parliament failed of enactment, but an Order in Council of February 25, 1856, established an Education Department under the Committee of Council on Education, and Parliament provided for a vice-president of the Committee of Council who should be a member of the House of Commons (since the lord president was customarily a peer). Both president and vice-president would, of course, resign with their governments whenever the political balance shifted to the other party. The first vice-president was W. F. Cowper (later Cowper-Temple) in 1857–58; C. B. Adderley held the post during the Conservative administration of 1858–59, and Robert Lowe, a Liberal, from 1859 to

1864. Meantime, after a year's illness, Kay-Shuttleworth resigned in 1849 and was succeeded as secretary by Ralph R. W. Lingen. On April 15, 1851, Arnold became one of Her Majesty's inspectors.

The Newcastle Commission, appointed before Lowe took office, reported on March 18, 1861. On July 29 Lowe laid on the table of the House of Commons at the very close of its session a new Minute, entirely revising the distribution of government grants for education; essentially it reduced all aid to a single grant to the schools in proportion to the number of pupils who, having attended a certain minimum number of days, should pass satisfactorily examinations in reading, writing, and arithmetic given by the state's inspectors. The aim of the Revised Code was in part, though not quite frankly, to reduce government expenditure (still very high in consequence of the Crimean War), in part to secure administrative efficiency, in part to bring education into accord with Lowe's avowed principles of free trade, of supply and demand. The catchword of "payment by results" was persuasive to many, but not at all to the managers of the schools and their teachers, whose unanimous and vigorous protest made itself heard during the ensuing summer and autumn when Parliament was not in session. The Revised Code entirely reversed the direction of state aid to education which had been given by Kay-Shuttleworth.

Arnold on October 30, 1861, told his mother that he had "settled with Froude to give an article on the new Code in the next [December] Fraser (but I do not wish this mentioned)." A week later he complained that he had been unable to write the article because Shuttleworth was bringing out an 80-page pamphlet, of which he must take cognizance. This proved so effective (though "the matter is hardly enough treated in its first principles for my taste") and so many other pamphlets on the subject were advertised that by mid-November, busied also with the composition of his "Last Words on Translating Homer," he determined to defer his article another month. "My object is rather to sum up the controversy, to give the general result of the whole matter, and to have the last word." By the first of the year he had put off the article for yet another month: "It is a ticklish thing to do as I must blame the office, and it is sure to be soon guessed who the article is by." As the deadline for the February number approached he had still done nothing with his article; then Froude suggested that he defer it to the March number.

The delay, as it turned out, was much to his advantage. On February 13, 1862, Lowe and Granville introduced the Revised Code in their respective Houses, Lowe with an especially long speech in its defense that was undiplomatically hard on the school managers and teachers for claiming a selfish "vested interest" and upon the Education Department's inspectors for misrepresenting the state of education. He announced, however, certain alterations he was willing to make in the new Minute (hence Arnold's title of *Twice-Revised*). By February 19 Arnold had completed reading proofs of his article and "retouching and adding as was necessary" to take Lowe's speech into account. "It will be very long, but I think not dull," he told his mother. "As to the article making a *sensation*, that I by no means expect. I never expect anything of mine to have exactly the popular quality necessary for making a sensation, and perhaps I hardly wish it. But I daresay it will be read by some influential people in connexion with the debate which will soon come on." "I think you will find [it] lively," he told her again a week later, "and presenting the subject in its *essence*, free from those details with which it is generally encumbered, and which make 'outsiders' so afraid of it." "I am surprised myself," he said in reply to one of her comments, "at the length of many of the sentences in my article, but I find that for every new thing I write there comes a style which I find natural for that particular thing, and this tendency I never resist." Froude paid Arnold £13.17.6 for the (anonymous) article.

One measure of his success was the request of Shuttleworth and his Anti-Code Committee for permission to reprint the article as a pamphlet for distribution to members of Parliament. Arnold conceived it might give the Conservative leaders, Lord Derby and Disraeli, just the briefs they needed to speak from. He found the parliamentary opponents of the Code taking "the very ground I could wish them to take, namely, that the State has an interest in the primary school as a *civilising agent*, even prior to its interest in it as an *instructing agent*. . . . If we can get this clearly established in this discussion a great point will have been gained for the future dealings of the State with education, and I shall hope to see State-control reach in time our middle and upper schools." By March 19 he learned that twenty copies of the pamphlet reprint had been delivered to his home in Chester Square.

Despite his reassurances to his mother, he seems to have been somewhat worried over the possibility of reprisal by his superiors. "I don't think, however, they can eject me, though they can, and perhaps will, make my place uncomfortable," he told his wife. "If thrown on the world I daresay we should be on our legs again before very long. Any way, I think I have owed as much as this to a cause in which I have now a deep interest, and always shall have, even if I cease to serve it officially." Only two years earlier, on the eve of his departure to study the schools of France, he had told his sister, Mrs. W. E. Forster, "You know that I have no special interest in the subject of public education, but a mission like this appeals even to the general interest which every educated man cannot help feeling in such a subject." Now he and his brother-in-law were fully committed, each at some risk to his career. The single reprisal, however, if it could be called such, was the refusal to publish part of his inspectoral report of January 1862, ostensibly because it was drawn from his French experience, of which his report had already been printed at public expense, but actually, as he presumed, because of its opposition to the Revised Code that was then under debate.—House of Commons, *Sessional Papers*, 1864, IX, 66–67.

212:1–5. At the meeting of the Canterbury Diocesan Education Society at Maidstone on October 3, 1861, the archbishop of Canterbury (John Bird Sumner) is reported to have said that "he trusted that the feeling of the country was such that nothing that was really useful [in the present system of national grants to education] would be suffered to be changed. What had transpired during the last few weeks showed that there was a great desire to mitigate what might appear severe in the Minute [the Revised Code], and to argue the question on principles of common sense." —*Times*, October 4, 1861, p. 10, col. 4.

212:15. James Kay Shuttleworth, *Letter to Earl Granville, K.G., on the Revised Code of Regulations Contained in the Minute of the Committee of Council on Education Dated July 29th, 1861* (London, 1861).

212:25–29. "Schools which have had hitherto a Master with a low certificate or with none, and no Pupil-Teacher, will be no sufferers by the withdrawal [under the Revised Code] of payments from these sources, while in many cases the attendance of their Scholars is steadier than in larger places, . . . [so] that in some rural Schools the new Minute will at once add a considerable sum to their present limited resources."—Charles John Vaughan, *The Revised Code of the Committee of Council on Education Dispassionately Considered* (Cambridge and London, 1861), p. 32.

213:7, 12–14. The Revised Code was on the calendar for debate on March 25. The modifications Arnold discusses at the end of his article were announced to Parliament by Lord Granville and by Lowe on February 13, 1862; in the same speech Lowe admitted that there might be a loss to the schools under the new code, but insisted that it was possible for the schools to avoid loss by doing their job well.

213:21–23. "The 'Revised Code' . . . cuts off about two-fifths of the annual grants of elementary schools. . . . It requires [their managers] in one year to raise £175,000, in addition to their present resources, or to cut down to the extent, in which they fail to do this, the machinery of their schools."—Shuttleworth, p. 3.

213:24. John Sinclair (1797–1875), archdeacon of Middlesex, was secretary of the National Society from 1839.

213:31. The actual result, as reported by a modern historian, was that "the grant which stood in 1861 at £813,441 had fallen by more than £176,000 in 1865."—J. W. Adamson, *English Education, 1789–1902*, p. 231 (corrected).

214:2. Henry, third Marquis of Lansdowne (1780–1863), was a most respected senior statesman among the Whigs. From the first he was a warm advocate of state assistance for education, accompanied by the right of inspection, and as lord president of the Privy Council (1830–41, 1846–52) he presided over the Committee of Council on Education. Arnold was his private secretary from 1847 to 1851 and owed to him the appointment as inspector of schools.

214:10. The "voluntary system" was opposed altogether to state intervention in education, either through subsidy or through control. Since sheer individualism was obviously inadequate, the voluntaries supported the great education societies like the British and the National.

214:11. Francis Crossley, of a very wealthy carpet-manufacturing family, was a Liberal M.P. from 1852 until his death in 1872. He was created a baronet in 1863.

214:15–19. The Report of the Education Commission, dated March 18, 1861, was signed by the Duke of Newcastle, Sir John Taylor Coleridge, W. C. Lake, William Rogers, Goldwin Smith, Nassau W. Senior, and Edward Miall. The *Times* commented on Saturday, March 30, p. 8, c. 3: "Some members of the Commission, probably including Mr. Miall, retain the belief that Government assistance is both superfluous and prejudicial; but the dissentients, after reserving their own opinion, concur in the recommendations of their colleagues, on the assumption that Parliament will not for the present be disposed to rely exclusively on voluntary measures of education." According to the *D.N.B.*, Goldwin Smith was the other voluntary.

214:23. Edward Miall (1809–81), an aggressive nonconformist politician, opposed state education and urged separation of church and state. He was editor of the *Nonconformist*, a weekly publication dedicated to "The Dissidence of Dissent and the Protestantism of the Protestant Religion." He represented the dissenters on the Newcastle Commission.

214:32. Edward Baines (1800–1890), at eighteen editor of the *Leeds Mercury*, represented that borough in the House of Commons from 1859 to 1874. A Congregationalist, he took a strong part in all matters that interested the dissenters and was a leading voluntary in education.

214:37–215:6. "Mr. [Gathorne] Hardy . . . impressed on the meeting the necessity of attending to lesser instruction, instead of that more glittering and specious instruction which was commonly given. . . . By giving [a child] the lower education, they were giving as much as the State could be expected to give—the means of making himself a useful member of society in that state to which it had pleased God to call him. . . . The duty of the State clearly defined . . . is, to obtain, in exchange for the money which is expended in the annual grant for Education, the instruction of poor children in reading, writing, and arithmetic,—and that not of a few selected specimens, but of all the children who regularly attend the school. . . . How about the main object of the [present] system [of grants to schools]—the greatest quantity of reading, writing, and arithmetic for the greatest number? The system suits admirably in all points but one; but that one, unfortunately, is the education of the people. . . . The State should make its payments dependent on its requirements; and . . . those requirements are reading, writing, and arithmetic. . . . The Archbishop of Canterbury expressed, with characteristic mildness, an opinion that the present system was overdone by carrying education to an unnecessary extent. . . . These observations . . . are another tribute to the general principle for which we contend—that of lowering the standard of education and diffusing elementary instruction wider."—*Times,* October 5, 1861, p. 8, cols. 4–5.

215:26–216:6. "[The children] do attend long enough to afford an opportunity of teaching them to read, write, and cypher. A large proportion of them, however, in some districts do not learn even to read; at least, their power of reading is so slight, so little connected with any intelligent perception of its importance, and so much a matter of mere mechanical routine, as to be of little value to them in after-life, and to be frequently forgotten as soon as the school is left. The children do not generally obtain the mastery over elementary subjects which the school ought to give. They neither read well nor write well. They work sums, but they learn their arithmetic in such a way as to be of little practical use in common life. Their religious instruction is unintelligent, and to a great extent confined to exercises of merely verbal memory." "The present conditions of school attendance are such that three-fifths of the children resorting to elementary schools attend sufficiently to be able with proper instruction to learn to read and write with tolerable ease, and to cipher well enough for the purposes of their condition in life, besides being grounded in the principles of religion." "It appears that even in the best schools, only about one-fourth of the boys attain the highest class, and are considered by the Inspectors to be 'successfully educated.' . . . We have strong testimony to the marked superiority of inspected over uninspected schools, and to the stimulus which inspection supplies."—*Report of the Commissioners Appointed to Inquire into the State of Popular Education in England* (London, 1861), I, 154, 225, 273.

216:7–15. See note to p. 214:37.

216:35–37. Vaughan, *Revised Code*, p. 9. The words are not his, but those of a clergyman in his deanery.

217:7–8. To the House of Commons on February 13, 1862; reported in the *Times* next day, p. 5, col. 6, bottom.

217:18–19. "So far from helping the hitherto unaided rural schools, the Revised Code will financially ruin many whose existence is dependent upon the amount of Parliamentary aid they now receive."—Archdeacon Sinclair in a memorial to Lord Granville, December 10, 1861; reported in the *Times* next day, p. 10, col. 4. See note to p. 230:13.

218:4–18. *Report of the Education Commission*, I, 544–45. What Arnold refers to as the "prize-grant" was to be paid out of the county (or borough) rate after the pupils were examined by the county (or borough) examiners; the "maintenance-grant" was to be paid out of the general taxation of the country, on recommendation of the Privy Council's inspectors.

220:34–221:1. The Reverend Frederick Watkins was inspector of the Church of England schools in Yorkshire; he made this statement in his report for 1860. Arnold quotes Watkins' words not directly but as abridged by Lord Stanley in his address at Leeds, reported in the *Times*, October 23, 1861, p. 8 (see p. 228: 28).

221:12–16. Shuttleworth, *Letter to Granville*, pp. 6–9n, quoting the inspectors' reports for 1860–61.

222:13–14. "[The Revised Code] would give energy to our determination that, whatever else our scholars may or may not be, at least they shall be qualified to read the Bible, to write necessary letters, and to keep their household accounts." "If there be one thing which we ought, even on religious grounds, to desire and to insist upon, it is, intelligent and intelligible reading. Without this, the Bible itself must remain practically a sealed book."—Vaughan, *Revised Code*, pp. 27, 45.

222:16–18. "It is quite possible to teach a child . . . by the time that he is 10 years old, . . . [to] read a common narrative—the paragraph in the newspaper that he cares to read—with sufficient ease to be a pleasure to himself and to convey information to listeners."—James Fraser, in *Report of the Education Commission*, II, 46.

223:5. The Reverend J. P. Norris was inspector of Church of England schools in Chester, Shropshire, and Staffordshire.

224:20–24. *Report of the Education Commission*, I, 262.

225:7–12. "There is no danger under this system of tests, more than under any other, of education, or even of instruction, sinking into mere mechanical routine. The power of reading well presupposes, indeed demands, a considerable amount of mental culture and refinement."—James Fraser, *The Revised Code, . . . Its Principles, Tendencies, and Details* (London, 1861), pp. 9–10. Fraser later became bishop of Manchester.

225:38–226:5. Patrick Cumin (1823–90) matriculated at Balliol College, Oxford, a year later than Arnold. He was appointed assistant commissioner under the Newcastle Commission, to report upon the state of popular education in the maritime districts of Bristol and Plymouth. Arnold seems somewhat to misrepresent Cumin's report, as did the article in *Blackwood's* to which he refers lower in the paragraph (XCI, 84–85, 92): Cumin in fact says very much what Arnold says (*Report of the Education Commission*, III, 26–27).

226:34–35. "This is your hour, and the power of darkness."—Luke 22:53.

227:2–7. "The Poor and their Public Schools: the New Minute," *Blackwood's Edinburgh Magazine*, XCI, 98 (January 1862).

227:8–14. "On the Constitution of the Church and State," Chapter vi; *Works*, ed. W. G. T. Shedd (New York, 1853), VI, 58.

227:36–38. The Reverend John Scott was principal of the Wesleyan Training College, Horseferry Road, Westminster, one of those regularly inspected by Arnold. Arnold alludes to the pamphlet *Letter of the Wesleyan Committee of Education to the Right Honourable Earl Granville, K.G., on the Revised Educational Code* (1861). "Scott, the head of the Wesleyans, is enchanted with [my] article, and has taken a number of copies of the reprint for circulation," Arnold told his mother on March 19.

228:13–14. The new appropriation, according to Lowe, would encourage the schools "to raise the quality of [their] education—it is a spur to improvement—it is not a mere subsidy, but a motive of action."—*Times*, February 14, 1862, p. 6, col. 6.

228:28–34. Lord Stanley spoke as president of the Leeds Mechanics' Institution and Literary Society at its annual *soirée*, October 21, 1861; his talk was reported in the *Times*, October 23, p. 8, col. 6. Stanley was the son of the Conservative leader, the Earl of Derby, and was himself a politician of importance.

229:29–32. Leading article, *Times*, February 14, 1862, p. 8, col. 5.

229:32–34. Lowe's speech to the House of Commons, February 13, 1862; reported in the *Times* next day, p. 6, col. 6.

229:34–230:1. Vaughan, *Revised Code*, pp. 17, 22.

230:13–17. On December 10, 1861, "a deputation of managers, directors, and teachers of schools receiving the Government grant throughout various parts of the country" waited upon Granville and Lowe to present a memorial urging the withdrawal of the new minute (the "Revised Code"). Their memorial, presented on behalf of the delegation by Archdeacon Sinclair, asserted (among other things) that the new code "tends to exclude from school dull and irregular scholars, and those whose home training is most defective (the very class of children for whose benefit the Parliamentary grant should be made most available), for such scholars it will not pay to teach."—*Times*, December 11, 1861, p. 10, col. 4.

231:13–14. Leading article, *Times*, February 14, 1862, p. 8, col. 5.

232:12–29. "Note on Minute of the Committee of Council on Education of the 29th July," *Edinburgh Review* (American edition), CXIV, 300–301 (October 1861). The first article of the July number had been devoted to the report of the Newcastle Commission and such kindred books as Arnold's *Popular Education of France*.

233:2–4. R. R. W. Lingen (1819–1905), Kay-Shuttleworth's successor to the post of secretary of the Committee of Council on Education, testified before the Newcastle Commission on November 30, 1859, that it would not be possible to extend the current system of government grants without considerable changes, because the multiplicity of payments already made the internal complication of the department far greater than that of other departments. "The only way in which you could extend the system would be by simplifying the payments; and simplification really means either not appropriating the money or not following out the appropriation so strictly as you do now. For those reasons I think that the present system . . . is not capable of extension to the whole country."—*Report of the Education Commission*, VI, 76. Lingen, whose post made him the administrative head of the department in which Arnold worked, held that position for twenty years—longer than any other secretary to the Committee on Education. He had been a fellow of Balliol while Arnold was an undergraduate there. Arnold was on amiable terms with him socially, though he regarded him as a bureaucrat in the office.

234:28–32. The *Spectator* was from the first convinced that popular elementary education, of which it was a warm advocate, was best ensured by the principle of payment by results; the new revisions announced by Lowe on February 13 removed the *Spectator*'s reservations, and it flatly declared that "the new code was a necessary and courageous reform."—"The New Minute on Education," XXXIV, 1030–31 (September 21, 1861), and "The Revised Code," XXXV, 206–7 (February 22, 1862).

234:33. "Forgive them, for they know not what they do."—Luke 23:34.

235:10–12. Shuttleworth, *Letter to Granville*, p. 38.

235:32–34. "Lord Granville and myself felt that we could not sit still in the face of that Report without showing the House and the country that we had done all in our power to remedy this state of things. . . . It would be impossible for us to remain quiet under the imputations cast upon the system now administered." —Lowe in the House of Commons, February 13, 1862; *Times*, February 14, p. 6, col. 2, and p. 7, col. 2.

235:34–236:2. Leading article, *Times*, October 5, 1861, p. 8, col. 5.

237:10–15. Shuttleworth, *Letter to Granville*, pp. 64–66. In his speech in the House of Commons on February 13 Lowe complained of these administrative details that afflicted his department.

237:23. J. D. Morell, *The Analysis of Sentences Explained and Systematized. With an Exposition of the Fundamental Laws of Syntax. . . . Revised, and Furnished with Illustrative Exercises* (9th edition; London, 1858). This popular handbook of syntax was first published in 1852; its author was one of Arnold's fellow inspectors. In his inspectoral report for 1861 (dated January 1862), Arnold explained his view more fully: "I am inclined to think that for the ordinary pupil-teacher the text books of grammar which he uses are much too elaborate. These aim at showing the *rationale* of grammar and of the terms and laws of grammar; but this is a stage of doctrine for which the pupil is, in this case, seldom ripe; he has memory to master the rules of grammar, but seldom understanding to master its metaphysics. . . . He will hardly analyse an intricate passage correctly according to the metaphysical principles of Dr. Morell's *Analysis*. But he may be brought, if his teaching takes in somewhat less and keeps him to this more steadily, to parse a sentence a good deal better than he does now. And the true aim of a boy's mental education,—to give him the power of doing a thing right,—will in this way best be followed. The best intelligence of the *rationale* of grammar is that which gradually comes of itself, after such a discipline, in minds with a special aptitude for this science. Such minds are few; but the minds with some aptitude or other for which the discipline of learning to do a thing right will be most beneficial, are numerous. And to the young, grammar gives this discipline best when it limits itself most."—House of Commons, *Sessional Papers*, 1862, XLII, 134–35.

237:25–26. *Select Extracts from Blackstone's Commentaries, Carefully Adapted to the Use of Schools and Young Persons*, ed. Samuel Warren (London, 1837). The book is equipped with notes, glossary, and questions for study.

238:20–22. For the system of school inspection in Holland, see pp. 182–83, 202.

239:16. The augmentation grant was a supplement provided by the government to increase the salaries of schoolmasters who had qualified by examination for certain classes of certificates; its abolition under the Revised Code was much attacked as a failure to fulfill a quasi-contractual obligation, since schoolmasters had entered the profession in the expectation of receiving this increase in due course. The figure of "twenty thousand persons" is drawn from the memorial presented to Lord Granville (see note to p. 230:13), and somewhat speciously includes "Lecturers in Training Colleges, schoolmasters and schoolmistresses, and pupil-teachers," with whom, it was asserted, the Revised Code "cancels positive engagements."

240:14–15. Lowe to the Commons, February 13, 1862; *Times*, February 14, p. 5, col. 6.

240:29–30. "For the Egyptians shall help in vain, and to no purpose: therefore have I cried concerning this, Their strength is to sit still."—Isaiah 30:7.

241:6–7. "For where your treasure is, there will your heart be also."—Matthew 6:21; Luke 12:34. Arnold's sister Frances was apparently somewhat distressed by his use of scriptural quotations; he replied (in a letter to his mother): "At a time when religion penetrated society much more than it does now and in the seventeenth century they were very common, and, if they are used seriously, I see no objection to them. Burke used them, even in his time. The Bible is the only book well enough known to quote as the Greeks quoted Homer, sure that the quotation would go home to every reader, and it is quite astonishing how a Bible sentence clinches and sums up an argument. 'Where the State's treasure is bestowed,' etc., for example, saved me at least half a column of disquisition. The Methodists do not mind it the least; they like it, and this is much in its favour."

241:12–242:8. Arnold quotes from Lowe's address to the House of Commons on February 13, 1862, as reported in the *Times* the next day (pp. 5–7). There was laughter in the House when Lowe admitted that "we carried our principle too far when we proposed to examine infants under 6 years of age." The Revised Code originally provided that no grant might be made to a night school for a student who was under thirteen, but that a grant might be made to a day school for only one year after the student became eleven; the new modification lowered the former age to twelve in order to bring the two together.

242:11–12. "In this thing the Lord pardon thy servant [Naaman], that when my master goeth into the house of Rimmon to worship there, and he leaneth on my hand, and I bow myself in the house of Rimmon: when I bow down myself in the house of Rimmon, the Lord pardon thy servant in this thing."—II Kings 5:18.

242:30–36. Arnold had some misgivings, practical as well as ethical, in attacking in print his two superior officers; but, as he told his mother, "Lowe's attack on the inspectors quite relieved me from all scruples in dealing with him, and I think my comments on his proceedings will be found vivacious."

243:7–8. "Therefore said [Jesus] unto them, The harvest truly is great, but the labourers are few: pray ye therefore the Lord of the harvest, that he would send forth labourers into his harvest."—Luke 10:2. Lowe, in defending the abandonment of augmentation grants, insisted that "there is nothing more certain in economical science than that wages do not depend on Government bounties, but on the great law of demand and supply."—*Times*, February 14, 1862, p. 7, col. 1.

243:11. "The *Times* was one of the few newspapers which approved the Code; but in this connexion that journal meant Robert Lowe himself, then one of its leader-writers."—Adamson, *English Education*, pp. 226–27. Arnold assured his mother that Lowe dared not show any resentment of his article, "as he does precisely the same thing himself in the *Times*. Whenever he has a grudge at the Ministry of which he is a subordinate member he attacks it *there*. So I feel quite safe, and in hopes of having done something to ward off the heaviest blow dealt at civilisation and social improvement in my time."

243:12. The *Daily News* remained firm for the principle of payment based on the result of examinations in reading, writing, and arithmetic: it reasserted its stand in leading articles on March 22 and 25.

[THE "PRINCIPLE OF EXAMINATION"]

The full debate on the Revised Code was forced by resolutions for its modification introduced by Spencer Walpole. On the day on which these were to come before the House, March 25, 1862, there appeared in the *Daily News* a letter signed "A Lover of Light" that answered effectively those critics of the educational system who thought it perfectly reasonable to insist that pupils should demonstrate their achievements by examination before any grant were made to their teachers and schools. The negotiations between Arnold and the editor of the *Daily News* ("who is for the Code and behaved very well in printing my . . . letter") were managed by Patrick Cumin. That evening's parliamentary debate led to significant modifications of the Code, due chiefly, in Arnold's opinion, to his brother-in-law William Forster—"his earnestness, his thorough knowledge of the subject, and the courage which his reputation for honesty gave to other Liberals to follow him in opposing the Code." "I find William thinks my letter in answer to Lord Overstone one of the most telling and useful strokes in the whole contest," Arnold wrote to his wife.

In the House of Lords on March 20, 1862, Lord Overstone rose to express "his fervent hope that the people of England would perceive the value of the principle of examination as a test of the efficiency of a school. His own early history had proved to him the importance of this principle. In the public school which he had attended an imperfect system of examination prevailed; but he passed thence under the hands of the late Bishop of London, to whom he owed a deep debt of gratitude for having first taught him the full value of examinations, and the necessity of continuing them in every form as the only means of rendering a man's reading really efficient. The people of this country might rest assured that where a school submitted willingly to the test of examination the system of instruction followed there was a sound one; and, on the other hand, they might with certainty come to an opposite conclusion whenever they found an unwillingness or an inability to undergo such a test."—*Times*, March 21, p. 7, col. 3. The briefer summary of the speech on the middle page (8, col. 4) uses this language: "Lord Overstone defended the system of examinations, and insisted that when there was any shrinking from that test there was something unsound in the school which refused to submit to it. Having severely reflected on much of the opposition with which the Revised Code had been met, he trusted that in spite of that opposition the people of this country would insist on paying only for results." In the next column a leading article praised Lord Overstone's "singularly judicial and business-like remarks," which "really settle the question."

Samuel Jones Loyd, created Baron Overstone in 1860, as head of the London and Westminster Bank was one of the richest men in England and one of the most influential in forming the government's monetary and banking policies. He was educated first at Eton, then for a year under Charles James Blomfield, rector of

St. Botolph, Bishopsgate, and later (1828–56) bishop of London. Lord Overstone's wife was the sister of Ichabod Charles Wright, the translator of Dante and Homer and a contemporary of Overstone's at Eton.

[THE CODE OUT OF DANGER]

When Lowe was considering what compromise he might offer on the Revised Code in response to Walpole's resolutions, Arnold had high hopes that the government would be defeated on the issue, or at least that Lowe would resign. Neither event occurred, though Lowe's unpopularity was now so great that his resignation was forced two years later on the question of his suppression of certain of his inspectors' reports. The compromises he offered were so great as to be humiliating in the light of his earlier speeches, but the new Code retained as a partial basis for the distribution of grants the examination of the pupils in reading, writing, and arithmetic by the Education Department's inspectors. "Payment by results" remained in the picture of English education until after Arnold's death. And therefore, despite some triumph for his principles, he had (as he told his mother) "one more shot at the Code yet." Cumin was editor of the new weekly *London Review;* to him Arnold sent his satiric remarks on the compromise, published anonymously on May 10, 1862, as "The Code out of Danger"; he received three guineas in payment.

247:11–14. In the parliamentary debate on May 5, Spencer Walpole, Conservative M.P. for the University of Cambridge, said that he apprehended difficulties would still be found to exist in the working of the much-modified Revised Code. "I cannot accept it as a final settlement, until I see that it really meets the requirements of the country upon this question."—*Times*, May 6, 1862, p. 8, col. 5.

247:15–22. "This measure [the new Code] cannot be regarded, without the greatest arrogance and presumption on my part, as a final one; but there are [two] principles from which I am not disposed to go back. One is, that we should do away with all appropriated grants, and know no one financially but the manager of a school. The other is, that we should have, under such modifications as the House of Commons may be pleased to allow, some individual examination of the scholars. Those two principles I could not relinquish, for of their immense importance I was well aware; but as the House was kind enough to allow me to retain them, I was quite willing to give up anything else."—Lowe in the House of Commons, May 5, 1862; *Times*, May 6, p. 9, col. 3.

248:1–7. "We proposed . . . another kind of security—that which was called payment by results, on a strict examination of children grouped according to age, the payments depending on that examination, and on nothing else. . . . Payment by results exists no longer in the present code."—*Ibid.*, p. 10, col. 2 (Lowe in reply to Walter's motion).

249:10–15. John Walter, Liberal M.P. for Berkshire and proprietor of the *Times*, intruded into the debate on the Code a resolution "That to require the employment of certificated masters by managers of schools, as an indispensable condition of their participation in the Parliamentary grant, is inexpedient and inconsistent with the principle of payment for results which forms the basis of the Revised Code." Lowe opposed the resolution, and it lost by a bare seven votes. "Nothing but the general wish to stop all discussion on this and, indeed, on most subjects, for the present year, could have prevented the House from adopting Mr. Walter's resolution," said the *Times* next day (May 6, p. 11, col. 2). "All the answer attempted last night was, that, appropriate as the alteration might have been under the Revised Code, supposing that to remain in its original integrity, it could not find place in the system when the grant no longer depends on examination alone. This can mean nothing, except that it is desirable to stop further discussion. The injustice remains, and next Session it will find a voice as potent as that which has arrested the revision of the Code and drowned even the voice of a Royal Commission." Since Lowe was a writer of leading articles for the *Times*, his difference with its proprietor contained the seeds of embarrassment. See pp. 257–61.

249:26–27. *Othello*, II, i, 162.

250:24–25. See p. 222:17–18.

250:26–27. Under the Newcastle Commission, W. B. Hodgson was an assistant commissioner appointed to inquire into the state of elementary education in London.

250:36. Spencer Walpole, whose resolutions forced the government to modify its Education Code so drastically, opened the debate of May 5 with a long speech to explain why, despite misgivings, he would accept the modifications and, by withdrawing his resolutions, not force the matter to a vote.

250:37. Joseph W. Henley, Conservative M.P. for Oxfordshire, spoke long and discursively after Walpole sat down; his principal point (but only one of many) seemed to be that the Council's concern for education must not be entirely secular.

250:38. Charles B. Adderley, Conservative M.P. for North Staffordshire and vice-president of the Committee of Council on Education when the Newcastle Commission was set up, remarked: "If there were any one single object of interest to the country that ought not to be centralized or in the hands of the Government, and which ought to be remitted to local hands and placed under local management, it was the system of education."—*Times,* May 6, 1862, p. 9, col. 2.

251:2. John Allen, vicar of Prees, near Shrewsbury, and archdeacon of Salop, had been an inspector of schools. His letter in the *Times* of April 2, 1862, p. 9, col. 6, advocated even more rigorous application of "payment by results" than the Revised Code set out to require.

251:3. Edward Girdlestone, vicar of Wapley and canon of Bristol, published a letter in the *Times* of February 21, 1862, p. 7, col. 6, hailing "the masterly speeches of Lord Granville and Mr. Lowe" and rejoicing that "a few months more, probably, . . . will suffice to convert many of the fiercest opponents of the Revised Code into its warmest supporters." It is often supposed that when a clergyman is offered a bishopric, he must reply humbly with the formula "Nolo episcopari"—"I do not wish to be a bishop" (when of course he does). Arnold's expression is therefore the equivalent of his "clergymen in search of a bishopric," p. 259:12.

[ORDNANCE MAPS]

Like his father, Arnold was a great walker; when he traveled the assize circuit as marshal to his father-in-law, Justice Wightman, he never tired of sight-seeing. Writing on July 20, 1862, to ask if his sister Frances could find one of their father's maps at Fox How, he remarked, "The ordnance map is the greatest possible pleasure to me, even in a dull country—I have it now for all the places we go to on circuit, except Ipswich." When, therefore, the subject of the Ordnance Survey maps came up for discussion in the *Times,* Arnold volunteered to write upon it for his friend Cumin's *London Review.* He finished his article at the Athenaeum Club on the afternoon of November 26, too late (as it turned out) for the last number in November: "It is the one thing I cannot manage, to be ready to the exact day named." Accordingly, it was published (anonymously) on December 6. Arnold was paid six guineas for this and an article on Spinoza's *Tractatus* (which appears in vol. III of the present edition).

252:3. "Eye Nature's walks, shoot Folly as it flies, | And catch the Manners living as they rise."—Pope, *Essay on Man*, I, 13–14.

252:10–13. During the Exeter race meeting in the autumn of 1862, Lt.-Col. Edwyn S. Burnaby of the Grenadier Guards wagered a fellow officer £5 even money that "raindeer" was spelled with an "a," and supported his opinion with his view of the etymology of the word. Next day, when the discussion was resumed, the fellow officer wagered £1 to £100 with another man that the word was spelled with an "a." Col. Burnaby, who said he was a very bad speller and always carried Johnson's *Dictionary* about with him to assist him in writing letters, then referred to that authority and found it allowed only the "a" spelling. The sportsman who stood to lose £100 first denied that Johnson had been fixed as the authority, then charged that there had been collusion against him. The matter was taken up by the stewards of the Jockey Club in connection with a charge that Burnaby had deliberately arranged to have one of his horses lose a race, and was the subject of indignant leading articles in the *Times* of November 6, 1862, p. 6, November 7, p. 8, and November 13, p. 8.

252:14–16. Sir Henry James (1803–77) was director-general of the Ordnance Survey from 1854 to 1875. His principal achievement was devising a new photographic process for the reproduction of the maps, called photozincography. The debate over the current state of the maps was touched off by a letter signed "Surveyor" in the *Times* for September 17, 1862, p. 6, col. 5, objecting that the Ordnance Survey maps had hardly been altered since they were engraved, some as early as 1809: "And yet we see large sums annually voted for the Ordnance Survey, sums that in the hands of civil engineers or private surveyors would have sufficed to give to the public most accurate and correct maps." The *Times* supplied a leading article on September 22, p. 6, col. 4, critical of the Ordnance Survey; Sir Henry James's letter on the same day (p. 7, col. 3) asserted that things were not so bad as they seemed; Edward Stanford, of 6 Charing Cross, who had supplied "Surveyor" with his maps, offered in a letter on the twenty-third (p. 10, col. 6) to undertake the publication of up-to-date maps if only the government would not compete against him. Another leading article and further correspondence followed. Sir Henry James's letters on photozincography (October 9, p. 11, and November 4, p. 10) make no reference to this debate.

253:28–31. By 1861 ninety sheets had been published (out of a proposed 110) of the English maps on the scale of one inch to the mile. On the Oxford map (#13) the railways were inserted in 1848; on the Cheltenham map (#44), in 1842.

253:31–32. On January 22, 1862, two months after Clough's death, Arnold wrote to his widow about some of Clough's lines: "I shall take them with me to Oxford, where I shall go alone after Easter;—and there, among the Cumnor hills where we have so often rambled, I shall be able to think him over as I could wish." The Cumnor Hills became the setting for "Thyrsis."

254:20. The family of Arrowsmith produced a very distinguished collection of large maps and charts, as well as school texts in geography, from 1790. The last of them, John Arrowsmith (1790–1873), nephew of the founder, retired from the active publication of maps at his establishment in Soho Square in 1861.—*D.N.B.*

254:21. J. Andriveau-Goujon was a Parisian bookseller and publisher of atlases.

254:22. Artaria & Cie. was a Viennese firm that published and sold maps, music, and engravings, and acted also as distributor of the official state maps of Austria.

254:32–33. The International Exhibition in South Kensington was opened on May 1, 1862.

255:12. Joseph Hume (1777–1855), from Montrose, was a leading radical in Parliament, "indefatigable in exposing every kind of extravagance and abuse," who "spoke longer and oftener and probably worse than any other private member" and "served on more committees of the House of Commons than any other member." —*D.N.B.*

256:19. The maps of Switzerland published from 1842 to 1864 under the direction of General G. H. Dufour were magnificently shaded to show the relief and beautifully engraved. That for Lucerne, no. 8, was published in 1861. The scale was one centimeter to a thousand meters (somewhat less than an inch to the mile).

256:23. The maps of France by César and Jacques Cassini de Thury appeared in 1744–93.

[MR. WALTER AND THE SCHOOLMASTERS' CERTIFICATES]

After the failure of his resolution of May 5, 1862, John Walter continued his campaign for abandoning the requirement of certificated teachers as an indispensable condition of state aid to schools. In the early spring of 1863 he announced that he was introducing his resolution again; he did so on May 5, exactly a year after the former debate, and once again it was defeated. In Arnold's *Note-Books* (ed. Lowry, p. 570) for April 1863 is the entry: "Compose the articles on Walter's Motion." This was corrected to "one article," and then, when the task was completed, canceled. The article appeared anonymously in the *London Review* for April 11, 1863; Arnold was paid two guineas for it.

257:1–3. The motto of Southey's *Curse of Kehama.*

257:12–14. Bearwood, near Reading, was Walter's home, writing from which he told J. P. Norris on November 20, 1862: "My own schoolmaster was trained at Battersea, where he passed an excellent examination 15 years ago. He has been teaching ever since with remarkable success, and stands deservedly high in his profession; but it would be a downright insult to ask him to go up for a third and fourth class certificate, and equally unreasonable to expect him, at the age of 33, to compete for a higher one."—*Times*, December 30, 1862, p. 4, col. 3. The correspondence between Walter and Norris (one of the inspectors of schools) on this subject took up three and a half columns of the *Times* and was also published by Walter as a pamphlet.

257:14–15. Arnold alludes to the Aesopic fable of "The Fox That Had Lost His Tail."

257:20–21. "Écrasez l'infâme" was used as a kind of watchword in many of Voltaire's letters, directed against "la basse et infâme superstition qui déshonore tant d'États."

257:26–27. "Tails without works" parodies "faith without works," one of the doctrinal cruxes between Protestantism and Roman Catholicism.

258:3. "Let us lift up our hearts," from the Preface to the Canon of the Mass.

258:24. The "union" is one of the districts (unions of several parishes) set up as the administrative units of the Poor Law of 1834.

258:34. Lowe as vice-president of the Committee of Council on Education was the minister responsible to the House of Commons for the working of that department. He was also a writer of leading articles for the *Times,* of which Walter was proprietor.

259:27–28. "We have it proved as an undoubted fact that so far from these unassisted districts which receive no aid from the State doing nothing for themselves, there are no less than 15,000 schools now existing which do not receive one farthing of the public money, and I contend that there should be some attempt on the part of the Government to distribute this money more fairly and impartially."—Walter in the House of Commons, May 5, 1862; *Times,* May 6, p. 9, col. 6.

260:16–28. Arnold is having his fun with Norris' replies to Walter in the *Times* of December 30, 1862: "I often went to a new school, found a teacher newly appointed by a careless clergyman. . . . I examine his school, find signs of clever teaching and the order unexceptionable. But the man has the look of a dram-drinker, and I notice a certain unmistakeable shrinking under his reproof, which tells a tale of blows when no one is present. I am persuaded myself that the man is morally unfit for his post. . . . But what am I to do? The day's inspection has furnished me with no *producible* proofs of unfitness. . . . In 1853 . . . inspectors were allowed to require the attendance at the annual collective examination of all uncertificated teachers whose schools applied for annual grants. . . . *In a few years teachers of doubtful character, such as I have alluded to above, disappeared from our annual grant schools.* No mere adventurer would face that certificate examination, occupying a whole week, and requiring a twelvemonth's preparation. A man must be in earnest to do that. . . .

"At all events, now that we have done so much to reform [our pupil-teacher and certificate system through the Revised Code], and to place our teachers upon a more wholesome footing—give our plans a fair trial. . . . I quite concur . . . that in respect of practical usefulness as teachers, there is no great superiority in those who hold a high degree over those who hold a low degree of certificate. . . . Under the Revised Code all are to be classed at first in a fourth degree, and are to rise to the higher degrees according to their practical usefulness."—P. 4, cols. 4, 6.

260:18–19. Venetian glass was said to shiver at the approach of poison.—N. M. Penzer, ed., *The Ocean of Story* (London, 1924),

I, 110n. Hence Elizabeth Barrett wrote ("Sonnets from the Portuguese," IX): "Nor breathe my poison on thy Venice-glass."

261:21–22. "Vous l'avez voulu, vous l'avez voulu, George Dandin, vous l'avez voulu, cela vous sied fort bien, et vous voilà ajusté comme il faut; vous avez justement ce que vous méritez."—Molière, *George Dandin, ou Le Mari confondu,* end of Act I.

[A FRENCH ETON]

At the beginning of his visit to France for the Newcastle Commission Arnold was careful to secure from the Papal Nuncio a letter of introduction to Lacordaire: "I pick up a good deal that is very interesting and instructive, and the French ecclesiastics, I must say, are not the least interesting objects among those which I see," he told his mother on May 8, 1859. Soon after he completed his official report on the elementary education of France, a writer using the pseudonym of "Paterfamilias" touched off a pamphlet and journalistic debate by sharply pointing out in a *Cornhill* article of May 1860 that education at the large, wealthy public schools (and at Eton in particular) was woefully poor, owing in great part to the irresponsibility of the masters and governors. He gained support almost at once in a pamphlet by another Old Etonian, Sir John Taylor Coleridge, father of Arnold's close friend John Duke Coleridge. Arnold had never thought it possible to separate the problem of elementary education from that of higher education, nor that of educating the poor from the problem of educating the more prosperous middle class. Doubtless only the immediate demands of the debate on the Revised Code caused him to defer entering the discussion on secondary education as long as he did, but the activities of the Clarendon Commission (appointed July 18, 1861, to inquire into all aspects of the nine most distinguished public schools) and the partial victory over the Revised Code led him to throw what light he could upon the whole question of secondary education on the basis of his French experience. When, therefore, he planned to write an article a month to earn money for a trip to Rome, as he told his mother on November 27, 1862, "A French Eton" was already planned for the March issue of *Macmillan's Magazine;* though it took advantage in its title of the current investigation of the public schools, it really was not at all concerned with the aristocratic education they offered, but with secondary education of another class altogether. March passed; in April he promised it to Macmillan for his June number. On May 15 he reported that he had done reading for the article but had not been able to screw himself up to begin writing it. All through July he drove himself to work on it; the positive deadline of the twentieth slipped by and it still was not done. At last, on August 1, when he was traveling on circuit with his father-in-law, he completed one article, but now it seemed that he would need a second, "to appear in October or November." Part I was published in *Macmillan's* in September 1863 (and reprinted in Boston by *Littell's Living Age* on October 10). In the middle of November, with not a word yet written of his Oxford lecture on Joubert for the twenty-eighth of that month, he imagined he could write his second part early in December: "I am anxious about [it], as the prejudices are strong, and I want to prevail against them; this cannot be done without prodigies of persuasion," he told his mother. By December 2 his second part was another month away: he promised Macmillan he could have it for the February number; "then I am going to retire into a hermitage."—Buckler, *Matthew Arnold's Books*, p. 105. The half of this promise he kept, writing the article at the Athenaeum Club from eleven to three daily in the middle of January. "I am really labouring hard to *persuade*," he told his sister on the eve of its appearance, "and have kept myself from all which might wound, provoke, or frighten, with a solicitude which I think you will hardly fail to perceive, and which will perhaps amuse you; but to school oneself to this forbearance is an excellent discipline, if one does it for the right objects." "In the long-run one makes enemies by having one's brilliancy and ability praised; one can only get oneself really accepted by men by making oneself forgotten in the people and doctrines one recommends," he wrote to his mother. "In doing the second part of my 'French Eton' . . . I have felt how necessary it was to keep down many and many sharp and telling things that rise to one's lips, and which one would gladly utter if one's object was to show one's own abilities." And when Macmillan praised the article, Arnold told him he was "quite sure the whole future of the middle classes depends upon their giving a public establishment to their education and so getting their minds more opened and their characters more dignified. There is a ferment among them just now which seems to me to give one a chance; but what it will all lead to, we shall see in time."—Buckler, *Matthew Arnold's Books*, p. 105.

But Arnold had not yet had all his say; he told Macmillan he would have a concluding part in the hands of the printer by February 18. This rashness he quickly repented; he promised it then for April, but the difficulties of inspection under the new code were too great, and try as he would, he could not bring it into shape until the deadline for the May number. Meantime, other papers were noticing his articles: the *Spectator* wrote vigorously in support of him on February 13, and Miall's *Nonconformist* on February 10, following its editor's usual line, warned that Arnold had no notion of the depth of the feeling against State interference. "But I have," he told his mother, "—of the depth of the feeling among the *Dissenting ministers*, who have hitherto greatly swayed the middle class. But I shall come to this in my next article. I mean, as I told Fan [his unmarried sister] in the autumn, to deliver the middle class out of the hands of their Dissenting ministers. The mere difficulty of the task is itself rather an additional incentive to undertake it." The agony of labor was rewarded with some self-satisfaction: "I have written, to my own mind, nothing better."

And so on May 6 he proposed that Macmillan bring out the three articles in pamphlet form, "that they may be more handy for use in the discussions about Middle Class Education which are certainly about to set in." Only ten days later he returned the corrected proofs, and Macmillan hoped to have it out—"a pleasant and attractive booklet"—within another week or so.—Buckler, pp. 107–8. It was advertised in the *Athenaeum* of June 4 at a price of 2*s.* 6*d.* in cloth. For the magazine articles Arnold was paid ten guineas, twelve guineas, and fourteen pounds, but the booklet met the same fate as his French report: more than three years later he was speaking of dividing the losses on it with the publisher.—Buckler, p. 109.

Yet it was in his eyes one of his most important works to date; and we, who can foresee the lecture on "Culture and Its Enemies" three years later, are bound to agree, just as we are certain to regard his description of Lacordaire at Sorèze as one of his most fascinatingly lively bits of writing. (Arnold sent a copy of the book to Emerson in Concord, in the expectation that the account of Lacordaire and the general reflections on the English middle class would interest him.) Other influential journals took up the cause, and recommended his book as their text. Grant Duff, M.P. for Elgin, in his annual report to his constituency on October 27, urged his audience to read it. Arnold, indeed, was eager that it should not escape the eyes of its possible friends in Parliament:

copies of the articles were sent to Sir John Pakington (whose motion had set up the Newcastle Commission) and Richard Cobden, and the booklet to Gladstone. Pakington's acknowledgment contained high praise of Arnold's French report. Cobden a little disappointed him by writing (Arnold reported) that "his main interest was in the condition of the lower class. But I am convinced that nothing can be done effectively to raise this class except through the agency of a transformed middle class; for, till the middle class is transformed, the aristocratic class, which will do nothing effectively, will rule."—Arnold to his mother, February 2 and 11, 1864; Arnold's letters to Cobden are published by W. H. G. Armytage, "Matthew Arnold and Richard Cobden in 1864," *Review of English Studies*, XXV, 249–54 (July 1949). Recalling the debates on the Revised Code, and especially Lingen's passion for simplifying administration, Arnold speculated with amusement on the "*malaise* of the Council Office, as they see me gradually bringing to their fold fresh sheep whom they by no means want"; he sent the pamphlet to the economizing Gladstone "rather as Member for the University than as Chancellor of the Exchequer." When, therefore, Lord Granville, still president of the Council, and Lowe, now out of office, publicly dissented from his thesis in speeches at the distribution of certificates to successful candidates in the Oxford Local Examinations, Arnold was not surprised; he merely regarded the remarks as publicity for his book. "I cannot conceive anything more graphic and more picturesque," said Granville, "than his description of certain classes of schools in France, but though, no doubt, there is much in what he says that is worthy of reflection, I own that I entirely dissent from his conclusion that it is desirable for the State here to take upon itself the establishment of large schools all over the country, and, in fact, educate the whole of the middle classes in this country."—*Times*, November 17, 1864, p. 12, cols. 3–4; Lowe's speech at Nottingham is reported in the *Times* of October 29, p. 5, with the allusion to Arnold in col. 4. By that time the government had already announced its intention to appoint a commission that would inquire into the education given in schools not within the scope of the Newcastle Commission and the Clarendon Commission, and thereby acknowledged the possibility, at least, that the whole educational problem in England was one.

Arnold's remark to Gladstone forecast the direction in which he himself was to be drawn: "In a now twelve years' acquaintance with British schools all over the country and with their promoters, I have perhaps had more than common opportunities for studying the English middle class—and particularly one of its strongest and most characteristic parts,—the Protestant Dissenters; this, and the reflexions such a study irresistibly awakened, is my excuse for touching a subject which is certainly social and political rather than literary."—W. H. G. Armytage, "Matthew Arnold and W. E. Gladstone," *University of Toronto Quarterly*, XVIII, 220 (April 1949).

Motto: Philippians 3:13.

262:1–5. Perhaps Sir John Taylor Coleridge, in *Public School Education: a Lecture Delivered at the Athenaeum, Tiverton* (London, 1860). Coleridge, nephew of the poet, was a scholar at Corpus Christi College, Oxford, with Thomas Arnold, his lifelong friend; Coleridge's son, John Duke Coleridge, was at Balliol with Matthew Arnold, and theirs too was a lifelong friendship. Some of the most eloquent passages of Coleridge's lecture are a tribute to Dr. Arnold's regime at Rugby.

262:10–11. Thomas Gray, "Ode on a Distant Prospect of Eton College," lines 3–4.

263:5–6. Mirabeau, *Correspondance* [*avec*] *de La Marck*, II, 75; see p. 6:37–38.

263:10–11. "Behold, my son, with how little wisdom the world is governed."—Axel, Count Oxenstierna, Swedish chancellor, in a letter to his son, 1648.

263:22–23. "Consider the lilies of the field, how they grow; they toil not, neither do they spin."—Matthew 6:28.

263:32. "O my boy, mayst thou be happier than thy father, but like him in all else."—Sophocles *Ajax* 550–51.

264:11. Plautus *Rudens* 1148.

265:35–266:7. See p. 80.

267:33. The Sisters of Charity were a nursing order founded by St. Vincent de Paul in 1633.

268:35–36. A didactic romance by Fénelon (1699).

273:2–3. Sir George Bowyer (1811–83), lawyer and a member of Parliament from 1852 to 1868, was converted to Roman Catholicism in 1850 and was one of England's leading Catholic laymen.

273:13. The Charter of 1830, drawn up by the Chamber of Deputies, was accepted by Louis Philippe as the basis of his rule, and was the constitution of France until he was forced to abdicate by the revolution of 1848.

273:18–19. Charles-Forbes-René, comte de Montalembert (1810–70) was an eloquent speaker and writer on behalf of a liberal Catholicism, especially with regard to education and the limits of Church participation in secular affairs. Arnold met him at one of Gladstone's breakfasts late in May 1858.

273:18–26. Arnold draws for his account of Lacordaire's career upon Montalembert, *Le Père Lacordaire* (Paris, 1862). The story of their attempt to found a free school is on pp. 35–37; of Lacordaire's final appearance in Paris on p. 234.

273:38–274:2. *Ibid.*, p. 107.

274:7–11. *Ibid.*, pp. 66, 106.

274:18–22. *Ibid.*, pp. 245, 239, 268.

274:26–31. *Ibid.*, pp. 86–88, 98.

274:32–37. *Ibid.*, pp. 92, 168; see *Note-Books,* ed. Lowry, pp. 16, 18.

275:1–5. *Ibid.*, pp. 91, 102–3.

275:8–12. *Ibid.*, pp. 240–41, 261.

277:20. Henri du Vergier, comte de La Rochejaquelein (1772–94), a cadet at the military school at Sorèze when the French Revolution broke out, became the generalissimo of the Vendéen insurrection against the revolutionary government in 1793. He was a bold and skillful leader in a futile cause, in which he lost his life.

277:36–278:2. Montalembert, *Lacordaire,* pp. 263–64.

280:5. Vergil *Aeneid* I.33.

281:17–21, 31–34. "Education, £20 per annum, no extras, at Wimberley-House, Fulham, Middlesex, conducted by Mr. T. Cooper and able masters. Diet unlimited and of the best description. The education comprises Greek, Latin, and German, French by a resident native, mathematics, algebra, mapping, globes, and all the essentials of a first-rate commercial education. The house and grounds are extensive. Inspection of domestic arrangements is earnestly invited. Highest references given."

"Unmanageable boys or youths (up to 20 years) made perfectly tractable and gentlemanly in one year, by a clergyman near town, of 30 years' experience, whose peculiarly persuasive, high moral and religious training at once elevates children of peculiar tempers and dispositions (because not understood) to the level of others. A most liberal education, including modern languages, successful preparation for every examination and vocation in life, and every gentlemanly comfort, on moderate terms. Address Alpha, No. 27, Watling-street, E.C."—*Times,* Thursday, April 16, 1863, p. 16, c. 1 (and frequently repeated).

282:19–21. The annual grant administered by the Committee of Council on Education; the first grant was made in 1833, and in 1839 the "accompanying security" required all schools that received aid to submit to inspection.

283:20–21. Cheltenham College was founded in 1841, Marlborough College in 1843, and Bradfield College (near Reading) in 1850.

283:24. George Granville Bradley (1821–1903), a contemporary of Arnold's at Rugby and later a master there, was headmaster of Marlborough from 1858 to 1870; thereafter he became master of University College, Oxford, and dean of Westminster. His daughter, Margaret L. Woods, has recorded some of her reminiscences of Arnold in *Essays and Studies*, XV, 7–19 (1929).

283:37–38. Marlborough raised its charges in 1860 to £52 10*s.* per annum for sons of clergymen, £70 for sons of laymen. Bradley wrote to Macmillan when he read this statement to say that his fees had been raised not because of the success of the school but because the former terms were insufficient to meet expenses. "But he says in his letter he agrees with every word I have written, which from the master of such a school, is a great thing," Arnold told his mother. See also Buckler, *Matthew Arnold's Books*, pp. 106–7.

284:35–285:1, 4–7. See note to p. 295:28.

285:37–38. Nathaniel Woodard (1811–91) established a society in 1848 to promote the education of the lower middle classes. His scheme was ambitious and he proved skillful in raising vast sums for the construction of schools, but at the time Arnold wrote only three Woodard schools were in existence, at Hurstpierpont, Lancing, and (temporarily) Shoreham, all in Sussex. It was now proposed to build permanent quarters for the last; the cornerstone for the school at Ardingly (Sussex) was laid on July 12, 1864. Woodard actually did have a scheme for training and certifying his own teachers. Woodard, Robert Lowe, and Arnold all received honorary degrees of D.C.L. at the same Encaenia at Oxford in June 1870.

286:5. Walter Farquhar Hook (1798–1875), dean of Chichester from 1859, was one of the most vigorous proponents of a national system of elementary education.

288:23–26. At the beginning of 1862 allegations were made that the Woodard schools enforced Romish practices. The charges alarmed the friends of the schools so much as to lead Woodard to submit to an examination by his visitor, the bishop of Chichester, in consequence of which he was entirely cleared at the end of 1863.

288:34–36. Thomas Dyke Acland and Frederick Temple (then

an inspector of schools) in 1857 set up experimentally a voluntary uniform examination for students in the middle class schools of Cornwall, Devon, and Somerset, in order to give some standard of attainment as well as some measure of the effectiveness of the schools. They then quickly persuaded the universities of Oxford and Cambridge to undertake the task throughout England; from 1858 the two universities examined schoolboys at two levels, those under fifteen (or sixteen for Cambridge) and those under eighteen, examinations were held simultaneously at the universities and at other places, and success in the higher level was rewarded at Oxford by the title of associate in arts. The examinations became known also as the Oxford and Cambridge Local Examinations.

289:35–37. See note to p. 295:28.

290:1. The Society of Arts, chartered in 1847 under the presidency of the Prince Consort, was successor to the Society for the Encouragement of Arts, Commerce, and Manufactures, founded nearly a century earlier. The Great Exhibition of 1851 and the International Exhibition of 1862 were fathered by it. In 1856 it began to give certificates based on examinations in science, mathematics, history, and other subjects to members of the "artisan class" who belonged to the mechanics' educational institutions that made up the Society's Union of Institutions.

290:33–35. "Mr. Arnold must know as well as we do, that he cannot be better aware of the faults of the bad private schools, or more heartily incensed against them, than are the friends and conductors of good private schools. Yet by the uncompromising swing of his besom of destruction he has swept away, and deprived himself of, the sympathy and the co-operation of many good men and true, who think as justly and feel as strongly as he does on the disgraceful quackery of the 'educational homes' on the one hand, and on the deplorable gullibility of their dupes on the other." —"Middle Class Public Schools," *The Museum: and English Journal of Education,* n.s. I, 15 (April 2, 1864).

291:17. Stephen Hawtrey, a mathematical assistant at Eton and incumbent of a parish in Windsor, about 1847 founded St. Mark's School in an abandoned washerwoman's cottage in Windsor as a means of educating the choirboys of his parish. His several pamphlets on the school reflect the tone Arnold ascribes to him, but I do not find the passages to which Arnold specifically refers. It was Hawtrey's opinion that the small school, like Eton, should stand *in loco parentis* to its boys.

294:24–25. "Arnold uses [this] phrase some sixteen times in his essays. Although Burke uses both the words *collective* and *corporate* in describing the State, he nowhere uses the exact phrase that Arnold credits him with here. The closest statement comes in the *Appeal* [*from the New to the Old Whigs, Works* (Boston, 1880)], IV, 169–70, and in the *Reflections* [*on the Revolution in France, ibid.*], III, 359, 361."—R. C. Tobias, *Matthew Arnold and Edmund Burke* (Ann Arbor: University Microfilms, 1958), p. 173n.

295:21. Made in 1833, for England and Wales. An additional £10,000 was appropriated for assisting the construction of schools in Scotland.

295:28–30. *Guardian*, November 18 and 25, 1863.

297:10–12. Bedford School was refounded about he time Rugby was founded, in the mid-sixteenth century, through a charitable trust set up in perpetuity by Sir William Harper and endowed (like Rugby) with land in Middlesex. The Corporation almost up to the time of Arnold's writing appropriated the income from the trust to purposes other than the school, which by 1855 was in a thoroughly unsatisfactory state, trustees quarrelling with masters and refusing to erect the necessary new buildings because their whole interest was in the Commercial School. The completion of new buildings in 1861 led in five years to a doubling of the number of boys at the school.—F. A. M. Webster, *Our Great Public Schools* (London, 1937), pp. 21–25.

298:32–299:4. Charles Dollfus, "Le Lycée et la liberté d'enseignement," *Revue germanique et française*, XXVI, 385–404 (August 1, 1863).

300:9–10. "Reflections on the Revolution in France," *Works* (London, 1852), IV, 230 (not quite halfway through the essay).

300:19–25. *Ibid.*, IV, 198 (one-fifth through the essay).

301:26–28. "I hope that the House of Commons will support the new Code, because it is the first step towards decentralizing our elementary education. I do not undervalue the good done by the Minutes of 1846. They have set before the country models of good schools, and have taught us a most valuable lesson. This is precisely what a Government can occasionally do for a people. But a time comes when the lesson ought to cease. Either it has been learnt, or the people have shown that they cannot learn it. In the former case Government interference is needless; in the latter useless; in both cases wrong. People who work in offices in Downing-street are not in the long run wiser or better than people who live in the country. We have learnt the lesson. Now that we have learnt it, leave us to ourselves to work it out. See as closely and as carefully as you like that we are doing our work, but do not interfere more than you positively must with our mode of doing it."—F. Temple, "The Revised Code," *Times*, March 25, 1862, p. 5. Arnold intended to reply to this letter publicly (in the *Daily News*) when it first appeared, but the government's modification of the code in the face of criticism made a reply unnecessary. "Temple's letter is really a string of thumping assertions with a bit of claptrap at the end. To most of the assertions the answer is simply—'not true,'" Arnold told his mother.

302:3–6. "Reflections," IV, 199.

302:31–32. Nimrod was "the mighty hunter before the Lord" of Genesis 10:9; Numa was the legendary second king of Rome, to whose wisdom and piety the Romans attributed many of their religious institutions and laws.

303:30–31, 34. Vergil *Eclogues* V. 56, 61.

304:20–30. In the House of Commons on March 27, 1862; *Times*, March 28, p. 7, col. 1.

305:12–14. Thirty bills providing for the introduction of various railway companies into metropolitan London were presented to the 1863 session of Parliament. Lord Derby, in opposing one of these, which would have authorized the Great Eastern Railway to construct a terminus on Finsbury Circus, remarked that the Circus "was the great resort of the poorer classes on fine days, . . . the only place where, within a moderate distance, the people could obtain healthy exercise and a free circulation of air. . . . He thought that their Lordships would be astonished if it were proposed to take Grosvenor Square, or Berkeley Square, or St. James's Square for a railway station, and to take every house for that purpose. Yet those squares were infinitely of less importance than Finsbury Circus to the densely crowded population of the City of London." He urged the defeat of the particular bill, with a view to ascertaining a general solution to the problem, "not in the interests of the companies, but of the public."—*Hansard's Parliamentary Debates*, 3rd ser., CLXIX, cols. 623–27 (House of Lords, February 23, 1863).

305:15. Sir John Pakington, heir of a Worcestershire estate that had been in his family since the reign of Henry VIII, was an important conservative politician who, though he disliked "the democratic spirit which had recently been making such strides," introduced unsuccessful education bills in 1855 and 1857 which were far in advance of the views of his own party and of the liberals.—*D.N.B.* He became something of a watchdog over the Minutes of the Committee of Council on Education when Lowe attempted to use these as the instrument of reducing state support for education (as in 1864, when he proposed to reduce government support to a school by the amount of its income from endowment). On December 28, 1863, in a speech at Kidderminster, Sir John recommended *The Popular Education of France* as a book which "ought to be read by all who took an interest in the subject, and wished to know what was our own condition as compared with other civilized nations."—*Times*, December 30, 1863, p. 4, col. 5.

305:17–18. Gladstone's Government Annuities Bill of 1864, aimed at allowing the working man to purchase small annuities and life insurance from the government instead of leaving him at the mercy of hundreds of unsound Friendly societies and Assurance societies, was conceived as supplementing his Post Office Savings Banks, established in 1861. It was a proposal which would not benefit the class of men who sat in Parliament and which would never become a vital issue in an election, so that its passage by the Commons on June 20 was regarded as the measure of Gladstone's greatness as a leader.—John Morley, *Life of William Ewart Gladstone* (New York: The Macmillan Company, 1932), II, 52–53.

306:16–17. "Let them live; but let them be hewers of wood and drawers of water unto all the congregation."—Joshua 9:21.

306:19–25. Amédée Thierry, *Histoire des Gaulois* (7th ed.; Paris, 1866), I, 4.

307:35–308:8. J. A. Roebuck, in the debate on the Government Annuities Bill on March 7, 1864, took the dogmatic liberal position founded on Mill's essay *On Liberty:* "It was laid down as a rule by all political writers that whatever concerned the individual himself should be left to him to do, that the Government which endeavoured to interfere in such matters almost always failed, and that, in fact, a paternal Government was a great nuisance. . . . There was nobody who had the same interest to do well for a man as he himself had; in other words, self-interest prompted every man to do all he could for himself, making him more industrious, more sagacious, and a better instrument for the furtherance of his own business than any other person could possibly be. . . . Nothing could be more dangerous than these constant attempts on the part of the Government to take from the people the management of their own concerns. The effect of them, if successful, would be to make the people a set of helpless imbeciles, totally incapable of attending to their own interests; and then, he would ask, what would become of the greatness of this country?"—*Times*, March 8, 1864, p. 7, col. 2. Baines spoke on the same side as Roebuck in this debate.

308:32–34. On Wednesday evening, May 18, 1864, Roebuck spoke at the annual conference of the Yorkshire Union of Mechanics Institutions at Sheffield, and with Baines on the platform behind him, remarked: "The class of political economists drove their opinions a good deal further than I think their principles justified them. . . . I believe my honourable friend behind me objects to the state interfering in the education of the people. I do not. Many years [ago] . . . I advocated a system of national education. . . . I am quite certain that every year that passes over our heads will confirm the people and the Parliament of England in the opinion that the education of the people is among its first, its greatest, and most important duties."—*Times*, May 20, 1864, p. 11, col. 1.

310:4. "Reflections," IV, 198.

310:35–36. See note to p. 307:35.

312:35–38. "Humboldt a subi les influences les plus diverses, celles des hommes aussi bien que celles des événements. Bien loin de se prémunir contre ces influences, . . . il s'applaudissait de se sentir modifié par une action étrangère, et suivait sans résistance la direction nouvelle où elle le poussait momentanément."—P. Challemel-Lacour, "Guillaume de Humboldt. II. Les Études," *Revue germanique et française*, XXVIII, 348 (February 1864).

313:23. Sir Archibald Alison, archconservative Scottish judge, published a ten-volume *History of Europe During the French Revolution* and an eight-volume *History of Europe from the Fall of Napoleon in 1815 to the Accession of Louis Napoleon in 1852*, intended "to show the corruption of human nature and the divine superintendence of human affairs; or, as Disraeli said, . . . to prove that Providence was on the side of the tories."—*D.N.B.*

313:26–27. See pp. 46–50.

314:32–35. See p. 14:32–38. The *Athenaeum* focused its review of *The Popular Education of France* (July 6, 1861, pp. 15–16) upon the Introduction and devoted more than a column to Arnold's view of the aristocracy in the eighteenth century: "This period of mohocks and patrician ruffianism Mr. Arnold selects as an era remarkable for the refinement, dignity, and high culture of our aristocracy,—the humour of the assertion being heightened by [the evidence adduced in his] foot-note. . . . We lay aside Mr. Arnold's essay with no increase of respect for his practical ability."

315:10–11. Probably Edward Hawkins, provost of Oriel from 1828 to 1882, and head of the college, therefore, while Arnold was fellow there as well as during Arnold's tenure of the Poetry professorship. A correspondent from Eton refuted Arnold's general statement by listing the academic honors won by Etonians at Oxford and Cambridge in 1862 and 1863.—*Macmillan's Magazine*, X, 175–76 (June 1864).

316:15–16. Matthew 19:16–22.

317:31–33. Isaiah 40:31.

318:33. The Church Rate was a tax levied by the vestry for the repair of the parish church. Since it was enforceable upon the nonconformists of the parish as well as the members of the Established Church, it was vigorously opposed by the Liberals, who made almost annual attempts in Parliament to repeal the compulsory rating power of the vestries. Though the divisions were sometimes very close and the bill passed the House of Commons in 1858, 1860, and 1867, the Lords did not concur until 1868.

318:36. "I heard a voice from heaven, . . . as the voice of a great thunder."—Revelation 14:2.

319:29–30. Henry Ward Beecher lectured to huge audiences in England in the autumn of 1863; his impassioned censure of English behavior toward the Federal Government, especially in the *Trent* affair, called forth vigorous criticism such as the *Saturday Review*'s remarks on "irresponsible spouters," on "the feminine reasoning and effeminate passion of political preachers."—XVI, 566 (October 31, 1863). For what Arnold called "the celebrated misprint about Beecher's colouring," see Textual Notes.

320:7–18. J. F. Michaud, *History of the Crusades*, translated by W. Robson (London, 1852), I, 59–60 (end of Book I).

323:10–11. A pamphlet by Hugh, Earl Fortescue, *Public Schools for the Middle Classes* (London, 1864) is summarized and contrasted with Arnold's *A French Eton* in the *Saturday Review*, XVIII, 389–90 (September 24, 1864). In the opinion of the reviewer, Lord Fortescue very much exaggerates the spirit of independence on the part of the middle class in matters of education: "He leaves Mr. Lowe far behind in the tilt which he rides against bureaucracy. [In his view,] not only is political economy violated, but the manliness of the English character is undermined by the acceptance of public money for educational purposes." The pamphlet appeared late in February 1864.

Textual Notes

[THE POPULAR EDUCATION OF FRANCE]

60.* *Strictly confidential.* | Education Commission. | Report | of | Matthew Arnold, Esq., | Foreign Assistant Commissioner. | London: | Printed by George E. Eyre and William Spottiswoode, | Printers to the Queen's Most Excellent Majesty. | For Her Majesty's Stationery Office. | 1860.

61r. Education Commission. | Reports | of the | Assistant Commissioners | Appointed to Inquire into | the State of Popular Education | in Continental Europe | and on | Educational Charities in England | and Wales. | 1861. | Vol. IV. | Presented to both Houses of Parliament by Command of Her Majesty. | London: | Printed by George E. Eyre and William Spottiswoode, | Printers to the Queen's Most Excellent Majesty. | For Her Majesty's Stationery Office. | 1861.

Matthew Arnold, Esq., M.A., "Report on the Systems of Popular Education in use in France, Holland, and the French Cantons of Switzerland," pp. 13–160.

61p. The | Popular Education of France | with Notices of That of | Holland and Switzerland | By | Matthew Arnold, M.A. | Foreign Assistant-Commissioner to the Commissioners Appointed to Inquire into | the State of Popular Education in England: | Professor of Poetry in the University of Oxford: | One of Her Majesty's Inspectors of Schools. | London | Longman, Green, Longman, and Roberts | 1861 | *The right of translation is reserved*

This is the earliest edition with the "Introduction."

79. Mixed Essays | By | Matthew Arnold | London | Smith, Elder, & Co., 15 Waterloo Place | 1879 | [*All rights reserved*]

Also issued with the imprint: New York | Macmillan and Co., | 1880.

* For 60 read 1860, etc.

An identical "Second Edition" was published in London in 1880.

"Democracy" [Introduction to *The Popular Education of France*], pp. 1–47.

80. Passages from | the Prose Writings | of | Matthew Arnold | London | Smith, Elder, & Co., 15 Waterloo Place | 1880 | [*All rights reserved*]

Also issued with the imprint: New York | Macmillan and Co., | 1880

83m. Mixed Essays | Irish Essays | and Others | By | Matthew Arnold | New York | Macmillan and Co. | 1883

"Democracy," pp. 1–35.

03. Mixed Essays | By | Matthew Arnold | *Popular Edition* | London: Smith, Elder, & Co. | New York: The Macmillan Company | 1903

From the same setting of type as 79; not collated.

The following passages appear in 80: 5:34–6:30 (pp. 115–17, headed "Good of Aristocracy"); 8:3–10:6 (pp. 121–24, headed "Democratic Equality"); 11:24–12:26 (pp. 117–19, headed "Weak Side of Aristocracy"); 19:3–12 (pp. 160–61, headed "State Action"); 24:30–25:23 (pp. 101–3, headed "Athenian Culture"); 26:29, 26:36–27: 2, 27:5–28:26 (pp. 161–63, headed "What Is the State?"); 160:28–161:11 (pp. 114–15, headed "Priesthoods and Aristocracies").

Introduction: Democracy. *Title* Introduction 61p; Democracy 79, 83m; *the two combined in the present edition only.*

Motto. *only in* 61p

3:1. In the following account of popular education in 61p

3:2–3. Continent, the State and its action are occasionally spoken of in a way which, if quite unexplained, is likely, I know, to offend some of 61p

3:7. that it neither would 61p

3:12. community. According to the long-cherished convictions of a great many, it is for the public interest that Government should be confined, as far as possible, to the bare and indispensable functions of a police officer and a revenue collector. It is to be always the mere delegated hand of the nation, never its originating head. 61p

3:15. has taken deep root 61p, 79

4:7. ¶The wish for a more deliberate and systematically reasoned action on the part of the State in dealing with education in this country, is more than once expressed or implied in the following pages. In this introduction I propose to 61p

4:25. since the Revolution has long 61p

5:5. had the air and style 61p

5:23. they may be Ministers 61p

5:27-28. of grandeur and dignity 61p

5:33. are not precisely fitted 61p

5:34-35. influence a vigorous 80

5:36. I had occasion lately, in 61p

6:7. by habitually dealing 61p

6:12. of its people 61p

6:13. welfare possible for them; 61p

6:37–38. *To quote once more from two men, very unlike, but both of them such perspicacious observers, and such weighty authorities, on any matter of politics—Mirabeau and Burke. *Administrer . . . là.* And Burke says: "Constitute government how you please, infinitely the greater part of it must depend upon the exercise of the powers which are left at large to the prudence and uprightness of ministers of state." 61p

7:3. administers the State, 61p

7:36. all freedom; but 61p

8:5–6. its character contrasted with that of liberty, which can magnanimously 61p

8:22. *no* ¶ 61p

9:10. importance and culture 61p

9:24. which is so impetuously 61p

10:37. to having done so 61p

11:21. delusion: I 61p

11:25. this instinct 61p

11:31. a fine idea, of 80

11:32. nation: but 61p

12:1. aristocracies, to retain them or to replace them 61p

12:21. actually be 61p; would on the whole be 80

13:24. But it is 61p

13:34–35. deference, eminent superiority 61p

14:1. record: if 61p

14:9. decorum: perhaps 61p

14:10. better; I 61p

14:20. but it was 61p

14:24. *no* ¶ 61p

15:8–9. still to be seen 61p

15:11. of their order takes 61p
15:21. constantly attracted and assimilated,) 61p
15:34. the tendency . . . as it really is. 61p
16:7–8. answer:—*Nothing but the influence of the State.* 61p
16:18. notice first: 61p
16:25. in the one, 61p
17:6. But, when the 61p
17:15–16. *not in* 61p
17:24. become weakly prone 61p
18:5. himself. Not only the greatness of nations, but their very unity, depends on this. In fact, unless a nation's action is inspired by an ideal commanding the respect of the many as higher than each ordinary man's own, there is nothing to keep that nation together, nothing to resist the dissolvent action of innumerable and conflicting wills and opinions. *Quot homines, tot sententiæ*, and one man's opinion is as good as another's:—there is no basis for a real unity here. In this regard, what is now passing in the United States of America is full of instruction for us. I hear numberless English lamenting the disruption of the American Union; they esteem it a triumph for the enemies of all freedom, a discouragement for the principles of self-government, as they have been long understood and put in practice in this country as well as in America. I, on the contrary, esteem it a great and timely lesson to the over-individualism of the English character. We in England have had, in our great aristocratical and ecclesiastical institutions, a principle of cohesion and unity which the Americans had not; they gave the tone to the nation, and the nation took it from them; self-government here was quite a different thing from self-government there. Our society 61p
18:6. democratic: who will give the tone 61p
18:7. That is the question. 61p
18:8. *no* ¶ 61p
18:12. national unity and greatness, 61p
18:20. for a noble national spirit, and therefore for unity, which 61p
18:22–24. be ours: the multitude in power, with no ideal to elevate or guide it; the spirit of the nation vulgarised; unity imperilled because there is no institution grand enough to unite round. 61p
19:6. allowing to government 80
19:8. whether it may not 61p
19:18. democracy. Almost 61p

19:27–28. to retain the whole Middle Ages. 61p

20:10–11. The State lent 61p

20:16. activity of the State, 61p

20:17. intervention of Government in 61p

20:35. whenever this was 61p

21:16–17. which are indeed mean and insignificant, if compared 61p

21:24–25. which I am making, I impose on myself the rule carefully to abstain from 61p

21:26–31. them. I do not presume to discuss in what manner the world of facts is to adapt itself to the changed world of ideas which I have been describing. I offer general considerations,—presented, I hope, without offensiveness, as I am sure they have been formed without prejudice—considerations suggested by watching the course of men and classes in this country, to the silent reflection of thinking minds. This an isolated individual, however humble, may fairly attempt; more he cannot attempt properly; perhaps the time has not yet come for more to be attempted at all. But one breach of my own rule I shall here venture to commit, by dwelling for a moment 61p

22:16. Harrow; the 61p

22:17 them; nay, 61p

22:24. them; by 61p

22:26–28. which the knowledge of these classes is not in itself at present able 61p

22:28. supply; by 61p

22:30. not in itself 61p

22:34. closely: economical, 61p

23:4. would be nothing in 61p

23:8–9. value; it 61p

23:11. which they desire. 61p

23:24. them; such 61p

23:26. admires them more 61p

23:27. who admire them 61p

23:33. for the ideas it possesses: of 61p

24:1–2. achieved at least as much; but of one 61p

24:3. thought, it has been 61p

24:6. great and useful. 61p

24:21–22. ensure two things; 61p

24:36. fatal: culture 61p

24:38. dangerous: the 61p

25:12. monuments; in 61p

25:13. or by the 61p
25:21. world so much 61p
25:37. in itself 61p
26:1. dulled: but 61p
26:2. consider that, as we have seen, this high tone of feeling supplies a principle of cohesion by which a nation is kept united; that without this, not only its nobleness is endangered, but its unity. Another consideration is, that the middle classes, remaining 61p
26:3. narrow and somewhat harsh and unattractive 61p
26:8–9. activity: in 61p
26:17–26. middle class has . . . its own . . . it can . . . in its . . . it does not now ensure . . . it ought . . . it has . . . it had not; now it has. . . . let it now show itself . . . let it check . . . let it no 61p
26:25. to prevent the action 61p
26:27. take for granted 61p, 79
26:36–38. purposes. The state is the representative 61p
27:22. each in his own 61p
27:23–24. under . . . opinion, *not in* 61p
28:10. or of an 80
28:14. thing that can be done 80
28:14–15. as nearly as 80
28:18–20. it; it is its own action which it suffers . . . free it . . . its affairs . . . its own power. 61p
28:22. of its deliberative proceedings, may 61p
29:12. A far graver 61p
29:13. change, because a change at variance with maxims far less sound and habits far less salutary,—to reduce 61p
29:22–23. for all nations the one thing needful is . . . their own . . . they themselves may 61p
29:29. is the nearest 61p

Both the tentative form of the Report (60) and the final form (61r) were divided into three principal parts, France, Switzerland, and Holland, each in turn divided into numbered sections as indicated below, and each followed by the appropriate appendices. These appendices were gathered at the end of 61p, and one new appendix, the translation of the Dutch "Law of the 13th August 1857, on Primary Instruction" was added. The "Introduction" was not in 60, 61r. A few passages of 60 that were dropped from 61r were restored to 61p as indicated below; chief among these was 158:37–164:24.

30, Salutation: Sir, 60; My Lord Duke and Gentlemen, London, June 1860. 61r; *no salutation* 61p

30:1–3. Having had the honour to be entrusted by the Royal Commissioners with the charge 60; Having had the honour to be entrusted by you with the charge of reporting on 61r

31:29. far superior 60, 61r

31:36–37. It is not 60, 61r

32:1. that the Royal Commissioners are appointed. 60; that the present Commission has been appointed. 61r

32:13. so alike to . . . so alike to . . . so alike to 60, 61r

32:15. Moreover, the 60, 61r

32:16. historians; that 60, 61r

Section I of 60, 61r became Chapters II–III of 61p

35:1. Church from 60, 61r

35:24. arrogated the right to govern public 60, 61r

36:29. in a realm 60, 61r

37:19–20. But I hope that the Commissioners will allow me, having made this profession of faith, to point 60; But I hope that I may be allowed, having made this profession of faith, to point 61r

38:26. a historical 60, 61r

38:32–37. *not in* 60, 61r

40:9–10. girls, developed this 60, 61r

41:24. have been in the 60, 61r

41:27. now there must 60, 61r

41:36–37. those given, from official returns, at p. [93–94] of this Report. 60, 61r

42:15. as the term; 60, 61r

42:18. their master's 60, 61r

44:16. point are almost entirely wanting. 60, 61r

Section II of 60, 61r became Chapters IV–VI and the first ¶ of Chapter VII in 61p

46:25. escape the most 60, 61r

46:26. of this commission 60, 61r

47:14. the profits should 60, 61r

47:31. 1792 60, 61r, 61p; *corrected by Ed.*

48:32. would admit." 60, 61r

50:27. of teachers, for the 60, 61r

51:36. of this report. 60, 61r

53:5. shed such an 60, 61r

54:2. to our upper 60, 61r

54:11. It merely 60, 61r

54:27–29. leave a blank as serious as the disappearance of the village-school now. 60, 61r

60:18–21. l'instruction primaire . . . l'amélioration de la société; . . . but qu'il 60, 61r, 61p; *corrected from* Moniteur.
62:5. February the 17th, 60, 61r
63:19. left exploded institutions 60, 61r
65:6. The Commissioners have seen 60, 61r
Section III of 60, 61r runs from Chapt. VII, ¶ 2, through Chapt. VIII, ¶ 2 of 61p
72:17–20. In 1847 . . . 2,176,079. *not in* 60, 61r
72:34–35. *not in* 60, 61r
72:35. p. 81. 61p; *corrected by Ed.*
73:19–20. 2,000*l*.; they 60, 61r
74:37. vol. iii. 60, 61r, 61p; *corrected by Ed.*
76:1. no ¶; The Revolution, however, 60, 61r
76:27. 10th, 60, 61r, 61p; *corrected by Ed.*
77:2. governs public institutions in *mispr.* 60.
77:37. of this report. 60, 61r
78:9. which, for the rest, the 60, 61r
78:25. March the 15th, 60, 61r
Section IV of 60, 61r became Chapt. VIII, from ¶ 3 to the end, of 61p
78:27. March the 9th, 60, 61r
82:15. in great numbers 60
82:22. but the Commissioners are not 60; but it must not be supposed that 61r
82:24. constantly exceeded 60
83:27. natural tolerance *mispr.* 60, 61r
83:34. 1838, 60, 61r, 61p; *corrected by Ed.*
83:38. p. 382. 60, 61r, 61p; *corrected by Ed.*
86:37. p. 99. 60, 61r, 61p; *corrected by Ed.*
87:6. in each. The 60, 61r
87:16. to call the Commissioners' attention 60; to call attention 61r
89:20. But the Commissioners must be well aware that already 60; But you must be well aware that already 61r
89:32. is but the 60, 61r
89:36–37. The Commissioners, I am convinced, would excite 60; You would excite, I am convinced, . . . which you little 61r
90:1. of your labours 61r
Section V of 60, 61r became Chapt. IX of 61p
92:1. The Commissioners will 60; You will 61r

92:2. show to them both 60; show to you both 61r
92:27. of this Report. 60, 61r
93:26. number belongs to 60, 61r
93:27. under male teachers. 60, 61r
95:14–15. commissions, and central delegates 60, 61r
96–97. *The tables in 60 differ in details from those in 61r, 61p, and do not balance.*
96:28–29. From fees paid by scholars 60; From families:—By fees paid by scholars 61r
96:30. From payments made by normal 60; By payments made by normal 61r
97:10–11. Leaving a deficiency of 208,680 *f.* 25 *c.*, or, in round numbers, 8,340*l.*, to be carried to the next year. 60
97:19. about 400,000*l.* 60
97:23. 210,400*l.* (nearly 60
97:23–26. departments), for the complement of regular charges which it had undertaken to make good; 64,000*l.* it granted for the additional expenses which have been detailed, and for local inspection it granted a sum, in round numbers, of 32,880*l.* 60
97:25–26. 146,400*l.;* it granted for the additional . . . detailed, 60,400*l.* 61r
98:3. 10,430*l.* 60
98:5–6. 1,710,430*l.;* let us say, in round numbers, one million and 60; 1,710,470*l.;* less than one million and 61r
98:8. 1,750,000*l.;* 60; 1,710,000*l.;* 61r
98:9. contributed about nine seventeenths 60
98:11. two seventeenths and a half; and 60
98:12. benevolence about four seventeenths. 60
98:13. altogether about 1,350,000*l.;* 60
98:14. produced nearly two-thirds of 60
98:16. most strike the Commissioners in 60; most strike you in 61r
98:20–21. expenditure of one million and 60; expenditure of less than one million and 61r
98:32–34. primary instruction. The sum of one million and three-quarters sterling, therefore, is more exact than it appears. 60
99:5. for 1,750,000*l.* 60
99:8–9. two-thirds . . . two-thirds 60
99:10. for 1,350,000*l.*, more than 33,000 schools 60
99:11. millions and a quarter of 60
99:26. The Commissioners will also, 60; You will also, 61r

99:35. 392,000*l.* 60; 396,000*l.* 61r
101:37. 160*l.* a-year. 60, 61r
101:37–38. The . . . 28,887*l.* *not in* 60, 61r
Section VI of 60, 61r became Chapt. X of 61p
105:1. The Commissioners are now 60; You are now 61r
105:2. They will 60, 61r, *the latter erroneously*
105:23. spare the Commissioners 60, 61r
106:6. playground; this 60, 61r
106:36. be a full 60, 61r
107:32–33. of Paris. Parents, 60, 61r
107:35. children; the 60, 61r
109:8–9. mislead the Commissioners if I allowed them 60; mislead you if I allowed you 61r
109:12. mislead them if I let them 60, 61r, *the latter erroneously*
114:35–115:1. popular education, Sir James Shuttleworth. In naming 61r
115:2. implore the Commissioners that they will use their powerful influence to preserve 60; implore you to use your powerful influence to preserve 61r
115:3. unimpaired. Entreat ministerial 61r
115:5. times; entreat Chancellors 61r
115:7. here; entreat the Privy 61r
115:21. of twenty-five, and an 60, 61r
117:14. it is usual 60
117:16. Many of them 60
118:10. state to the Commissioners the conclusion 60, 61r
118:15. almost always have the 60, 61r
118:37. Père 60, 61r, 61p; *corrected by Ed.*
119:13. The Commissioners must 60; You must 61r
119:26–40. *not in* 60, 61r
120:38–41. *not in* 60, 61r
121:4. If the Commissioners must not 60; If you must not 61r
121:5. must they think 60; must you think 61r
121:12. the one than the 60, 61r
121:36–38. *not in* 60, 61r
122:9. important, Sir, to call the Commissioners' attention 60; important to call your attention 61r
122:31–34. *not in* 60, 61r
Section VII of 60, 61r became Chapt. XI of 61p
123:1. carry the Commissioners 60, 61r
123:2. ask them, 60, 61r

124:27. Paris: among 60, 61r
126:27. of them books and 60, 61r
126:36. The Commissioners will 60; You will 61r
126:38–39. *not in* 60, 61r
127:2. and taught by 60, 61r
127:16–17. the Commissioners will 60; you will 61r
127:28. and the Commissioners will, 60; and you will, 61r
127:34. curé; when 60, 61r
129:15. if the Commissioners will 60; if you will 61r
129:21. Warwickshire or Lincolnshire 60, 61r
129:23–130:7. an impression . . . nightfall *not in* 61r
130:36–38, 131:26–39. *not in* 60, 61r
132:12–17, 32–34. *not in* 61r
132:14–15. Yet nothing is despicable, which 60
132:17. nation. The Commissioners may rely upon it, ten thousand Frenchmen of the lower orders could not have been found, who, placed in a remote dependency of their country, while the soil yet trembled under their feet with the last throes of a convulsion which had shaken all the empire, would have preferred a private interest to their country's need, or who, had they preferred it for a moment, would not have been rallied instantly to their standards by an appeal to their patriotism. 60
132:23. conduct the Commissioners to 60; conduct you to 61r
133:27. intended, Sir, to describe to the Commissioners a Protestant 60
133:29. I forbear to trouble them. 60, 61r, *the latter erroneously*
Section VIII of 60, 61r became Chapt. XII of 61p
134:2. describe to the Commissioners what 60
134:11. describe to the Commissioners that 60
135:26–27. truly; and to 60
135:27. give to a 60, 61r
136:6. unduly meagre, 60, 61r
136:38. first year pay 100 francs, 60, 61r
137:29. good certificates of conduct 60, 61r, 61p; *corrected by Ed.*
140:11. wearied the Commissioners by 60; wearied you by 61r
140:17. remind the Commissioners, that 60, 61r
Section IX of 60, 61r became Chapt. XIII and the first ¶ of Chapt. XIV in 61p
142:1. Let me now, Sir, briefly sum up 60; Let me now, briefly sum up 61r
142:13. right; when 60, 61r

142:15. give to the Commissioners some important information on it; 60, 61r

142:23. well, no doubt, if 60, 61r

142:27. its deplorable ravages; 60, 61r

147:21. prefect almost invariably acts 60, 61r

150:1. numbers have they yet, 60, 61r

150:2–3. schools, what proportion of the population remains wholly untaught, what 60, 61r

150:4–5. questions, Sir, which, as I have told the Commissioners, cannot 60; questions, which, as I have told you, cannot 61r

150:17. deceiving the Commissioners if I led them to 60; deceiving you if I led you to 61r

150:24–31, 151:21–22. *not in* 60, 61r

151:27–40, 152:28–39. *not in* 60, 61r

Section X of 60, 61r became Chapt. XIV from ¶ 2 to the end, in 61p

153:3. all the Commissioners' indulgence 60; all your indulgence 61r

153:4. exhibit to them this 60

153:20–21. culture, they do actually receive it; 60, 61r

154:5. Let the Commissioners compare, 60, 61r

154:7. of this Report, 60, 61r

155:5. to the Commissioners what 60; to you what 61r

155:9. all. There 60, 61r

155:21. functions towards the 60, 61r

155:25. the position of 60, 61r

157:38. question. The State, in trying to found a system of public schools, is met by the objection that conscience is violated if a man has to contribute, as a public taxpayer, to the support of schools in which a religion which he disapproves may be taught. Will it treat this sort of objection as what it is; as a phantom having really no ground in reason at all; as really not even a proposition cognizable by the reason, but, at best, the fancy of a conscience tormented into morbid irritability? Will it encourage 60

158:7. The Commissioners will be 60; You will be 61r

158:9. ¶Now I say that, in France, about such an objection as this, the State would not hesitate one moment; it would boldly (to use a French expression) pass over its body. It will be rejoined, 60, 61r

158:10. can crush unreason or 60, 61r

158:26. France, if not warmly hostile to him, yet coldly 60, 61r

158:30. unreason. ¶Our constitutional sympathies must not here mislead us. There is a rational theory of despotism, and on that theory the present Government of France takes its stand. I fully and heartily believe that the indirect and ulterior effect of despotism upon a people's reason and intelligence is baneful. But reason can entertain the theory of despotism as it can entertain the theory of republicanism or constitutionalism; it is not an eternal prescript of reason which pronounces in favour of the one or the other, it is a long experience of the balance of advantages. Till that balance is patent to all the world, reason is not violated by maintaining one theory against the others. The example of Plato is there to show, if any example were needed, that the highest intelligence may go along with the greatest dislike to popular power. The French State upholds at present the despotic theory, on the ground that this theory is accepted by the sentiment of France; but it treats the pretensions of the opposing theories as powers to which it must give way to-morrow if the sentiment of France espoused them,—for they are *rational*. But, when a priest 60

158:37–164:24. *not in* 61r

159:4. But, Sir, there 60

159:7–9. but which the Commissioners, who give a wider scope to their inquiries, will certainly 60

160:6–7. has certainly not 60

160:8–9. comparatively high education, without correctives, the 60

161:3. to them. But 80

161:5. lofty and grand 80

161:7. was lofty, little 80

161:37–38. *not in* 60

162:2–3. is ineradicably operant 60

162:16. as the truest and most eloquent 60

163:1. of intellect, science, and letters, 60

163:6. I confess, Sir, that 60

164:22. Well, then, Sir, to 60

164:25. ¶I say, then, in conclusion, that at the present moment the French government offers to its people a national system of education, which, though very 61r

164:29. higher. I say, that this system 61r

164:32. In England, meanwhile, what is the system of education offered to our people by its Government? A system not national, 61r

The part headed "Switzerland" has, in 60, 61r, three sections: I, 166:1–172:37; II, 173:1–175:33; III, 175:34–178:13.
166:29. of this Report. 60, 61r
167:10–11. state very briefly to the Commissioners the result, 60; state briefly the result, 61r
170:8–9. as the Commissioners will ask themselves,— 60; as you will ask yourselves,— 61r
170:19. what do the Commissioners suppose?— 60, 61r
170:36. *du* 5 60, 61r; *du* 6 61p
171:23. at work or at home. 60, 61r
172:17. words, Sir, are 60
174:18. of the female students, 60, 61r
174:23. for male students . . . for female students 60, 61r
174:24–25. a male student's . . . a female student's 60, 61r
175:27. are also left to fulfil 60, 61r
176:24–25. When the Commissioners are informed . . . they will not, 60; When you are informed . . . you will not, 61r
177:37–38. which a highly-instructed people lives and works that makes it interesting, 60, 61r
The part headed "Holland" has, in 60, 61r, six sections: I, 179:1–187:10; II, 187:11–196:26; III, 196:27–199:22; IV, 199:23–203:6; V, 204:1–208:4; VI, 208:5–end.
180:9–10. reprinting, the Commissioners have probably never seen; 60, 61r
181:28. education-law 60, 61r; educational law 61p
185:16. examinations of 60, 61r
187:37. p. 33. 60, 61r, 61p; *corrected by Ed.*
188:25. not without justice, 61r
189:1. This being so, what could 60, 61r
194:33. belonged to 60, 61r
198:26. a dogmatic form and 60, 61r
199:29–39. *not in* 60, 61r
200:35–37. *not in* 60, 61r
200:39, *last note.* Art. 35. 60, 61r, 61p; *corrected by Ed.*
201:3. remind the Commissioners 60; remind you 61r
201:28. education obligatory. 60, 61r
205:17. neither the Roman 60, 61r; neither Roman 61p
207:1. Commissioners will perceive that when I assured them that, 60, 61r
207:9–10. and female assistants 60, 61r
207:18. above given. Towards the expense of primary instruction

the Dutch provinces contributed, in 1857, 52,581fl. 17c., about 4,380*l.;* the State contributed 25,490fl. 25c., about 2,120*l.** The rest was defrayed by the communes. 60, 61r

207:37. See *Verslag nopens der Staat der Hooge, Middlebare en Lagere Scholen in het Koningrijk der Nederlanden.* The Hague, 1859; p. 122. See also Tables i. and 60, 61r

207:38. this Report. 60, 61r

208:5. Such, Sir, in 60

208:9. confess to the Commissioners that I 60

208:24 whose flowering period is over. 60

208:36. sober and mechanic spirit 60, 61r

209:24. country of which I have spoken to the Commissioners—in 60; country of which I have spoken—in 61r

209:25–26. and there, indeed, school-legislation may in some respects be injudicious, in some 60, 61r

209:27–28. everywhere I have shown to the Commissioners law, everywhere State-regulation. The Commissioners will judge, whether 60; everywhere I have shown to you law, everywhere State regulation. You will judge, whether 61r

209:31. You will judge, 61r

210:2. of State-control, had 60, 61r

210:4. You will judge, 61r

210:38. London, 1815, vol. vii., p. 416. 60, 61r

211:4. have before mentioned to the Commissioners, supplies 60; have before mentioned, supplies 61r

211, Close. I have the honour to remain | Sir, | Your obedient, humble Servant, | Matthew Arnold. | *To the Secretary to the Royal Commissioners* | *for inquiring into the State of Popular* | *Education in England.* 60; I have . . . remain, | My Lord Duke and Gentlemen, | Your . . . | *To the Royal Commissioners for . . .* 61r; *no close* 61p

[THE TWICE-REVISED CODE]

Fras. Fraser's Magazine LXV, 347–65 (March, 1862). Anonymous.

62. The | Twice-Revised Code. | *Reprinted from 'Fraser's Magazine.'* | London: | Printed by | W. Clowes and Sons, 14, Charing Cross. | 1862.

Anonymous.

212:9. minute, and so *Fras.*
213:25. cent. Even *Fras.*
213:26. such estimates of *Fras.*
213:27. that neither of them may be *Fras.*
213:30–31. reckon it, with Sir James Shuttleworth, at about two-fifths *Fras.*
214:26. here stop *Fras.*
232:23. universally condemned *Fras.*, 62; *corrected from Edinburgh Review.*
237:19. system have *Fras.;* system must have 62

[THE "PRINCIPLE OF EXAMINATION"]

Daily News, March 25, 1862, p. 6, col. 1. Pseudonymous.
245:26. sufficient from heavy loss. *Daily News; corrected for sense.*

[THE CODE OUT OF DANGER]

London Review IV, 429–30 (May 10, 1862). Anonymous.

[ORDNANCE MAPS]

London Review V, 491–92 (December 6, 1862). Anonymous.

[MR. WALTER AND SCHOOLMASTERS' CERTIFICATES]

London Review VI, 374–75 (April 11, 1863). Anonymous.

[A FRENCH ETON]

Macm. *Macmillan's Magazine* VIII, 353–62 (September, 1863); IX, 343–55 (February, 1864); X, 83–96 (May, 1864).
Lit. *Littell's Living Age* LXXIX, 83–90 (October 10, 1863). Part I only, reprinted from *Macm.;* not collated.

64.* A | French Eton; | or, | Middle Class Education | and the State. | By | Matthew Arnold, | *Lately Foreign Assistant Commissioner to the Commissioners appointed to inquire | into the State of Popular Education in England.* | London and Cambridge: | Macmillan and Co. | 1864. | *The right of Translation and Reproduction is reserved.*

65a. Essays in Criticism. | By | Matthew Arnold, | Professor of Poetry in the University of Oxford. | Boston: | Ticknor and Fields. | 1865.

An identical "Second Edition" and "Third Edition," 1866. "A French Eton," pp. 425–506. These American editions have no textual authority and are not collated.

80. Passages from | the Prose Writings | of | Matthew Arnold | London | Smith, Elder, & Co., 15 Waterloo Place | 1880 | [*All rights reserved*]

Also issued with the imprint: New York | Macmillan and Co., | 1880

92. A French Eton | or | Middle-class Education and the State | to which is added | Schools and Universities in France | being part of a volume on 'Schools and Universities | on the Continent' published in 1868 | by | Matthew Arnold | London | Macmillan and Co. | and New York | 1892 | *All rights reserved*

This edition has no textual authority and is not collated.

The following passages appear in 80: 300:5–12 (p. 164, headed "What Is the State?"); 300:26–301:12 (pp. 164–65, headed "State-help Not Degrading"); 316:25–317:3 (p. 153, headed "Ferment"); 320:7–29 (p. 154, headed "Is This Jerusalem?"); 321:15–322:23 (pp. 155–57, headed "The True Jerusalem").

Subtitle, Motto *not in Macm.*

262:26. have thus been *Macm.*

263:1. less if it *Macm.*

263:8. seem really important, *Macm.*

263:18. learning, as well as a *Macm.*

264:15–26. The . . . lies. *not in Macm.*

264:30. I understand that the Royal *Macm.*

264:33. Continent. They will, no doubt, have collected some information upon this subject; for to accomplish perfectly their own duties, even in the narrowest view of them, would be impossible without it. But this information they will have collected either

* For 64 read 1864, etc.

through the English embassies abroad, or by means of private and unofficial inquiry. I regret *Macm.*

265:2. could only have done by *Macm.*

270:17. school-house, too, *mispr. Macm.*

270:32. 800 f. (24*l.*) *erroneously Macm.*

270:33. 850 f. (26*l.*) *erroneously Macm.*

272:8. or three of them were *Macm.*

274:3. for reproach *Macm.*

274:10. in one day *mispr. Macm.*

274:28. of France *Macm.*

275:30–31. in old times *Macm.*

275:33. *no* ¶ *Macm.*

275:35. school of this kind, in *Macm.*

276:20. *no* ¶ *Macm.*

279:10. problem? The answer to these questions I must reserve for a second paper. *Macm.*

279:11. February is beginning; in a day or two Parliament will assemble; the report of the Public School Commissioners will, it is said, be presented almost immediately; and then all the world will have before them Eton, Harrow, Rugby, and the rest of the dissected nine. The probable results of that autopsy I am not going to discuss here. I am sure the exhibition will be very interesting; I hope it will prove very useful. But, for the champions of the true cause of secondary instruction, for those interested in the thorough improvement of this most important concern, the centre of interest is, I repeat it, not there. At this last hour, before the English mind, always prone to throw itself upon details, has completely thrown itself upon what, after all, in this great concern of secondary instruction, is only a detail, I return to the subject, in order to show, with all the clearness and insistance I can, where the centre of interest really lies.

Let me take for granted that the reader has still in his mind the account which I gave of the Toulouse Lyceum and of the Sorèze College; or that, if he has not, he will do me the honour to cast his eye over it. Then I say, for the serious *Macm.*

279:12–13. of secondary instruction, the knot of that question is here:— *Macm.*

283:2–3. The existence of the Royal Commission now sitting is *Macm.*

286:4. programme, as *Macm.*

286:6. to lead to conclusions *Macm.*

286:7. and that the conclusions *Macm.*
287:18. sound schools; *Macm.*
288:22. as my security, *erroneously Macm.*
290:33–38, 291:34–38. *not in Macm.*
292:21. done that, lose no *Macm.*
292:25. the parent who *mispr. Macm.*
292:26. too far. *Macm.*
294:10. establishment, with its *Macm.*
297:30–31. is to be instituted. *Macm.;* is instituted. 64
300:7. of the member *Macm.*
300:18. the right so *Macm.*
300:34. Charterhouse, or at *Macm.*
300:35. or fellowship *Macm.*, 64; or a fellowship 80
301:15–16. must return to it again. I want *Macm.*
304:16. No wonder they *Macm.*
308:9. is very familiar *Macm.*
308:32–39. *not in Macm.*
310:2–3. to the best account *Macm.*
312:23. State-action, in an aristocratic class natural *Macm.*
313:21–22. part to free . . . and to individuals *Macm.*
313:29. indisputable basis *Macm.*
315:38. a short-lived middle class *mispr. Macm.*
316:26. culture, the living *Macm.*
316:27. at creative epochs; 80
317:6. strike him who *Macm.*
317:26. in these two alliterative words— *Macm.*
317:28–29. slighting phrase *Macm.*
318:11. its outward splendour *Macm.*
319:26. could not make *Macm.*
319:30. a painted barbarian. *mispr. Macm.*
320:8. the customary composition *Macm.*
321:16. governing class, the 80
321:28. their secular *Macm.*, 64; their eternal 80
322:6. brilliant wealth *Macm.*, 64; splendid wealth 80
323:10. on this self-reliance *Macm.*
323:11. Fortescue and Mr. Roebuck, they *Macm.*
325:14. will be mounting *Macm.*

Index

A reference to a page of text should be taken to include the notes to that page.

Aargau, 31
Academy, French, 268, 335, 344
accent, 275
Acland, T. D., 288
Adamson, J. W., 327, 340, 352, 360
Adderley, C. B., 250, 304, 348
adequacy, 324
Aesop, 257
age: *see* epoch
Agricultural Journal, 315
agriculture, 48, 90, 137, 152
Aisne, 55
Ajaccio, 155
Ajax, 263
Alais, 150
Albert, Prince Consort, 376
algebra, 281
Alison, Sir Archibald, 313
Allen, John, 251
Alsace, 60, 116, 118, 150, 283
America, 18, 148, 160–61, 208, 226, 314, 319–20, 330–31; Civil War, 161, 319, 331, 381, 385, 387; education, 172, 198; poets, 341
Americanisation, 16, 25, 159, 161, 178
Amsterdam, 181, 184, 190, 328–29
Anaclet, Frère, 118
anarchy, 26, 53, 63, 158, 211, 274
Andriveau-Goujon, J., 254
Antwerp, 187, 329
Archangel, 163
Ardingly, 287, 375
aristocracy, 4–25, 39, 44, 46, 49, 54, 87–89, 153, 160–64, 193, 224, 227, 243, 262–64, 286, 291–94, 297, 303–7, 311–12, 314–16, 318–22, 324–25, 331, 369, 372, 380–81, 385
arithmetic, 41, 48, 51, 57–58, 68, 90, 107, 110–11, 125, 127, 131, 135, 138, 169, 200, 215–21, 224–25, 227–28, 235–36, 241, 248, 250, 257, 259, 269, 341, 349, 353–55, 360, 362
Arles, 328
Armytage, W. H. G., 372–73
Arnold, Frances (sister), 328, 359, 364, 371
Arnold, Frances Lucy (wife), 328–29, 336, 351, 361
Arnold, Mary (mother), 329–31, 349–50, 356, 359–60, 362, 369–72, 375, 378
Arnold, Matthew, "The Code Out of Danger," 362, 397
Continental tour (1859), 30–31, 105, 123, 134, 166, 265–

Arnold, Matthew (*continued*) 66, 271–72, 278–79, 328–29, 344, 351, 369
"Culture and Its Enemies," 371
"Democracy," 330–31, 380
Diaries, ed. W. B. Guthrie, vi
England and the Italian Question, 122, 340
Essays in Criticism, First Series, 331, 398
Essays in Criticism, Second Series, vi
family letters, 327–31, 336, 349–51, 356, 359–62, 364, 369–72, 375, 378
financial losses from books, 331, 371
A French Eton, 332, 369–72, 381, 397–98
"A French Worthy," 333
health, 330
inspectorship, 341–42, 349–52, 356, 358, 371–73
Irish Essays and Others, vi
"Joubert," 370
Letters, ed. G. W. E. Russell, 327–29
Letters to Clough, ed. H. F. Lowry, 327, 333, 343, 366
"Literary Influence of Academies," 330, 343
Matthew Arnold's Books, ed. W. E. Buckler, 327, 331, 370–71
"Maurice de Guérin," 340
Merope, 331
Mixed Essays, vi, 382–83
"Mr. Walter and the Schoolmasters' Certificates," 367, 397
Note-Books, ed. Lowry, Young, and Dunn, 327, 367, 374
On Translating Homer, 5, 332, 349
"Ordnance Maps," 364–65, 397
Passages from the Prose Writings, 383, 398
poems, 278
"The 'Principle of Examination,'" 360–61, 397
Prose Works, ed. R. H. Super, 332, 340
Popular Education of France, 330–31, 333, 357, 371, 379–80, 382–83
Report to the Newcastle Commission, 3, 329–31, 351, 369, 372, 382, 387
style, 331, 350, 370–71
"Thyrsis," 366
"The Twice-Revised Code," 349–50, 396
Unpublished Letters, ed. A. Whitridge, vi
Arnold, Thomas (father), 291, 364, 373
Arrowsmith, John, 254
Artaria & Cie., 254
Asia, 320
Athenaeum, 371, 380
Athenaeum Club, 364
Athens, 25, 56
Atkin, J. R., vi
Atlantic, 272
Atlantis, 324
Aube, 151
Aude, 279
Auray, 328
Austria, 254
Auvergne, 342
Avignon, 328

Bacchus, 260
Baines, Edward, 214, 242, 310–11, 323, 380

Balcombe: *see* Ardingly
Balliol College, Oxford, 355, 357
Baptists, 199
barbarian, barbarism, 7, 47, 162, 210, 319
Barnard, Henry, 32, 334
Barré, Père, 40
Bas-Rhin, 130–31, 336
Basel, 329
Batavian Republic, 181
Battersea Training College, 367
Baur, F. C., 346
Bazas, 119
Bearwood, 257
Bedford School, 297
Beecher, H. W., 319
Belgium, 187, 193, 197, 200–201, 207, 328–29
Bell, Andrew, 333
Benedict XIII, 41–42
Benedictines, 39
Benoît, M., 123–26, 128–30
Berkeley Square, 378
Berkshire, 257, 363
Bern, 329, 344
Berry, 37
Besançon, 131, 151
"best," the, 13
"best self," 19, 28
Béziers, 272, 278
Bible, 186, 192, 196, 198, 222, 269, 341, 346, 355, 359; Apocalypse, 318; Genesis, 251, 302; Isaiah, 240, 317; Joshua, 306; II Kings, 242; Luke, 226, 234, 241, 243; Matthew, 21, 29, 49, 241, 263, 316; Philippians, 21, 29, 262
Birmingham, 296
Biron (family), 162
Black Prince, 123, 129–30
Blackwood's Edinburgh Magazine, 227, 355
Blanquefort, 123, 125–30, 328
Blaye, 119
Blois, 39
Blomfield, C. J., 244–45, 361–62
Boileau-Despréaux, N., 269
Bonald, Louis de, 37
bookkeeping, 169
Bordeaux, 119–20, 123, 125, 130, 134, 136, 283, 328
Borough Road Training College, 133
Bossuet, J.-B., 36, 269
botany, 269
Bourbons, 56
Bowyer, Sir George, 273
Brabant, 207
Bradfield, 283–84
Bradley, G. G., 283, 375
Breda, Declaration of, 61
Bredon Hill, 253
Brethren of Lamennais, 120
Brethren of Marie, 120
Brethren of the Christian Schools, 40–43, 54–55, 58, 62–63, 77, 108, 112–22, 126, 273, 333–34
Bright, John, 319, 331–32
Bristol, 355, 364
British and Foreign School Society, 106–7, 125, 132–33, 143, 192, 198, 232, 239, 347–48, 352, 373
British Museum, 180, 301, 329
Brittany, 72, 120, 328
Broglie, A.-C., duc de, 65, 328
Browning, Elizabeth B., 369
Brugghen, J. J. L. van der, 198
Brussels, 329
Buckler, W. E.: *see* Arnold, M., *Matthew Arnold's Books*
Buffon, G.-L., comte de, 269
Bulletin universitaire, 65, 74, 83, 86
Burke, Edmund, 3–4, 26, 209–10, 300, 302, 310, 359, 377, 384
Burnaby, E. S., 252

"Business and Bethels," 317
Butler, Samuel, *Hudibras*, 17

Cahors, 278
Calais, 55, 163
calligraphy, 116
Calvinism, 34, 346
Cambridge, 89, 266, 290, 300, 362, 376, 381
Canada, 145–46
Canal du Midi, 272
Cantal, 127
Canterbury, Archbishop of, 212, 353
Cape of Good Hope, 181
caprice, 113
Carcassonne, 278–79, 328
Carnac, 328
Carnot, L.-H., 76
Carnot, L.-N.-M., 60, 339
Carré, J.-M., 344
Cassini de Thury, C.-F. & J.-D., 256
Castelnaudary, 271, 278
catchwords, 299
Catholic Encyclopedia, 334
Celts, 163, 306
centralisation, 251
Cévennes, 72, 272
Challemel-Lacour, P., 380
Chamonix, 329
Champagne, 263
Charlemagne, 35–36
Charles II (England), 61
Charles IX (France), 39
Charles X (France), 337
Charterhouse, 262, 300
Chasles, Philarète, 344
Cheltenham, 253, 283, 315, 366
chemistry, 269, 335
Cher, 151
Chester, 355
Chesterfield, Philip, Earl of, 14, 315
Chichester, 286, 375
China, 13, 202, 231
Cicero, 269, 315
Cintra, Convention of, 123
Citters, J. de Witte van, 204
civilisation, civilise, 9, 11, 39, 159, 161–64, 194, 215, 223–24, 226, 228, 245, 254, 321, 350, 360, 379
claptrap, 157–58, 257–58, 310, 325, 378
Clarendon Commission, 262, 264, 280, 283, 296, 312, 315, 369, 372, 399
classics, 25, 54, 68, 86, 188, 315
Clermont, 342
Clough, A. H., 333, 343, 366
Clough, Blanche, 366
Cobden, Richard, 319, 332, 372
Cochin, J.-D.-M., 73
Code Napoléon, 53, 153-54
Cohn, Albert, 107
Coleridge, J. D., Lord, 369, 373
Coleridge, Sir J. T., 284–85, 289, 295, 352, 369, 373
Coleridge, S. T., 227, 373
Collège de France, 344
colonialism, 208, 392
commercial class, 87–88, 281, 286
Common Prayer, Book of, 367
Concord, Mass., 371
Condorcet, A.-N. de, 47
Congregationalism, 353
Connell, W. F., 327
Conservateur, 62
conservatives, 62, 348, 350, 356, 362–64, 378, 380
constitutions, 19, 189, 211, 394
Constitutionnel, 17
Continent, 3, 11–12, 254, 264, 283, 294, 297–98, 328
Conventicle Act, 20
Cooper, T., 374
Cornhill Magazine, 369
Cornwall, 376
Corporation Act, 332

Corpus Christi College, Oxford, 373
Corsica, 155
Côte-d'Or, 54
Coudekerke-Branche, 151
Courbevoie, 134
Cousin, Victor, 31, 64, 67, 69, 93, 179–80, 182, 187–88, 190–92, 328–29
Cowley, Henry, Earl, 30
Cowper-Temple, W. F., 348
Creuse, 127
Crimean War, 349
Crossley, Francis, 214
Crusades, 320
culture, 5, 9–10, 12–15, 17, 23–26, 89, 130, 153, 161–63, 185, 221, 224–25, 292, 306–7, 314–18, 321–24, 330–31, 355, 380
Cumberland, 256
Cumin, Patrick, 225–26, 330, 361, 364
Cumnor Hills, 253, 366
Cuvier, Georges, 179–80, 184, 186–88

Daily News, 243–44, 332, 360–61, 378, 397
Daily Telegraph, 251
Dandin, George, 261
Dante, 362
Daphnis, 303
Daughters of Charity, 55
Daughters of Providence, 55
Daunou, P.-C.-F., 51
Dauzat, M., 123
Davis, A. K., Jr., vi
deliverance, 252, 294
Delphi, 160
democracy, 7–19, 28, 62, 160–63, 177–78, 226, 319, 378, 385
Demosthenes, 269
Derby, Edward, 14th Earl of, 305, 350, 356, 378
despotism, 3, 17–18, 28, 62, 211, 298, 309, 394
Devonshire, 256, 376
Dijon, 151
disinterestedness, 11, 30, 57, 118
Disraeli, Benjamin, 350, 380
Dissent: *see* Protestant
dogma, 43–44, 83–84, 129, 142, 168, 186–87, 190–92, 194–96, 198–99
Dollfus, Charles, 298–99
Domat, Jean, 36
domestic economy, 174
Dominicans, 39, 272–73, 275, 277
Dorsetshire, 324
Doubs, 151
Dover, 329
Dover, Straits of, 163
Downing Street, 301–2, 377
drawing, 90, 116–17
Drenthe, 202
Drôme, 151
Dublin, 245
Duff, M. E. Grant, 371
Dufour, G.-H., 254, 256
Dunkirk, 151
Dunn, W. H.: *see* Arnold, M., *Note-Books*

Edinburgh Review, 232, 356–57
Education Commission: *see* Newcastle Commission
eighteenth century, 11, 14, 314, 336, 380
Elba, 60
electrotyping, 255–56, 365–66
Elgin, 371
Emerson, R. W., 371
Ende, Adriaan van den, 181–82, 187, 191–92
England, English, 52, 333; army, 164, 263, 284, 340; character, 16–18, 29, 63, 148, 156, 161–63, 165, 233, 260, 264, 287, 297, 302, 306, 310–11, 314, 316,

England, English (*continued*) 322, 381, 385, 399; child labour, 125, 150–51, 221; Church, 20, 24, 143–44, 164, 305–6, 308, 318, 320–21, 324, 355, 381, 385; Civil Service Commission, 231; clergy, 100, 121–22, 144, 214, 227, 229, 233–34, 251, 259, 281, 284, 301–2, 306, 323–24, 368, 375; coaches, 272; Commons, House of, 216, 243, 245, 247–48, 250–51, 260–61, 305, 342–43, 347–54, 356–64, 366–68, 377–79, 381; Commonwealth, 61, 337; counties, 110, 145–46, 296, 354; doctors, 258, 284; drunkenness, 260, 368; embassies, legations, consulates, 30–31, 166, 200, 204, 398; Exhibitions of 1851, 1862, 254, 376; free trade, 156; food, 254, 271; government, 3–4, 15, 17, 19, 37, 155–57, 164, 209–10, 242, 245, 247, 251, 253, 255–56, 263, 301–5, 307–10, 312, 364, 366, 368, 372, 377; Government Annuities Bill, 379; Habeas Corpus, 164; history, 163; industry, 110; language, 153–54, 163, 205, 269–70; literature, 270, 313, 316, 341; Lords, House of, 12, 164, 305, 333, 350, 361, 381; newspapers, 164, 281–82; parishes, 34, 98, 121–22, 146, 227, 229, 307, 343, 381; Parliament, 27–28, 153, 212–13, 231, 235–36, 240, 255, 321, 332, 337, 348–50, 352–54, 356, 361, 366, 371–73, 378–81, 399; patriotism, 392; people, 3, 11–13, 16–18, 110, 130, 208, 210, 291, 301, 307, 314, 342, 361, 380; politics, 3–5, 7, 132, 230, 247, 260, 303, 305, 311, 318, 361–62, 373; poor-law unions, 143, 249, 258, 343, 367; population, 32; prelacy, 20, 306; prosperity, 23; railways, 252–53, 305, 366, 378; rates, 218, 235–36, 240, 318, 343, 354, 381; Restoration (1660), 20, 26, 332; Revolution (1688), 3–4; topography, 252, 366

English education, 31; administration, 114, 143, 145, 148, 230, 232–33, 245, 258, 349, 357–58, 372; administrative expense, 99, 103–4, 115, 230–31, 237, 259; attendance, 215, 218, 220–22, 348–49, 351, 353–54; augmentation grants, 115, 212, 239, 260, 358–60; British schools, 106–7, 125, 133, 192, 198, 239, 373; capitation grant, 229, 247, 348; certification of teachers, 100, 103–4, 115, 133, 140–41, 185, 212, 239, 249, 257–60, 348, 351, 358, 363, 367–68; "classical and commercial academies," 22, 281, 297, 310; codes: before 1861, 217, 232, 249, 261, 348, 368, 377; codes: revisions of 1861–62, 212–51, 259, 261, 282, 349–64, 368–69, 371, 378; Committee of Council on Education, 89, 100, 115, 212, 214, 218, 231–32, 235–40, 328, 333, 340, 343, 348, 352, 357, 364, 368, 372, 375, 379; cost, 88, 137, 270, 279–81, 283–85, 293, 296, 312, 322, 375; day schools, 285, 359; denominationalism, 143–44, 238; Department of Science and Art, 104; Education Department, 100, 102, 140, 147, 212–14, 226, 233, 237, 239, 242, 250, 258–59, 348–51, 357, 362; educational homes, 281–85, 289–91, 293, 310, 376; endowments, 262, 280–81, 286, 294–96, 300, 332, 379; examinations, 218, 230–31, 235–39, 241, 244–48, 250, 258–59, 288–89, 354–55, 359–63, 368, 376; grammar schools, 332; infant schools, 128, 241–42, 245–46, 359; infirmaries, 267; inspection and inspectors, 99–100, 102–3, 112–13, 115, 140, 144, 147–48, 212, 215, 218–22, 224, 230–32, 235–39, 241–42, 246, 250, 258–59, 289–90, 293, 295–96, 341–42, 348–50, 354–55, 360, 362, 367–68, 371, 375–76; meals, 271, 281; middle-class, 22–23, 87–89, 263, 279–325, 369–71, 376; National schools, 121–22, 144, 238; needlework schools, 112; night schools, 359; normal schools and colleges, 100, 133–34, 136, 140, 206–7, 239–41, 271, 340–43, 348, 356, 359, 367; parental demands, 226, 281; patrons, 74, 112–13, 234, 292, 301, 373; "payment by results," 216–18, 229–30, 241, 248–50, 257, 259–61, 349, 357, 361–64; playgrounds, 106, 268, 276; primary, 32, 99, 105, 107, 114, 145, 152, 164, 215–16, 219–31, 234, 236–37, 245–46, 249–50, 259, 264, 282, 287, 310, 324, 328, 335, 341–42, 350, 352–54, 357, 363, 369, 375, 377; private, 226, 281–84, 286–88, 290, 293, 297–98, 323, 332, 376; public schools, 22, 53–54, 87–89, 262–64, 267–70, 272, 277–82, 286, 290–93, 295–96, 312, 315, 332, 361, 369, 399; pupil-teachers, 114–15, 134, 186, 204, 237, 247, 340–41, 348, 351, 358–59, 368; religious education, 128, 142–44, 192, 215, 219, 222, 224, 228–30, 235–36, 281, 324, 354–55; religious liberty, 144–45, 158, 323–24; "Royal Schools," 296; rural, 216–17; salaries, 75, 82, 100, 102, 115, 238–39, 287, 328, 358; scholarships, 295–96, 300, 340; school-age, 215, 218, 220, 222, 241, 247, 359; school-books, 125–26, 221, 237, 280, 341–42, 366; school-buildings, 100, 104, 106, 228, 348; school-committees, 133; schoolless children, 109, 216–17, 219, 231; school-managers, 145, 212, 216, 220, 226, 232, 235, 245, 247, 262, 349–50, 352, 356, 362–63; schools, numbers of, 99, 259, 279–80, 283, 287–88, 290, 312; secondary, 22, 87–90, 262, 264–65, 269, 279–80, 282–85, 287–90, 293, 295–98, 323, 350, 369, 399; social effects, 159–65, 335; state grants, 99, 144–45, 213–19, 224–25, 227–45, 248–50, 257–58, 282, 286–87, 295–96, 301, 308–11, 322–23, 340, 347–49, 351–54, 356–63, 367–68, 375, 377, 379, 381; students, abil-

English education (*continued*)
ity of, 107, 110, 134–35, 218–24, 234, 245–46, 249, 342, 356; students, numbers of, 99, 353; subjects of study, 269–70, 280–81; teachers, 100, 102, 115–16, 135–36, 140, 147–48, 212, 216, 220–21, 226–28, 232–34, 239, 250, 260, 280, 288, 292–93, 340, 349–51, 358–59, 367–68; universities, 89, 188, 264, 266, 286–87, 289–90, 293, 314, 324; Vice-Presidency, 101, 241, 302, 333, 348, 364, 368; villages and towns, 125, 136, 216–17; voluntary support, 115, 145, 164, 214, 231–32, 234, 242, 245, 286–87, 301, 309–11, 343, 348, 352–53, 368; Wesleyan schools, 107, 227, 239
epoch, age, 3, 11, 24, 29, 44, 57, 60, 273–74, 294, 313, 316
equality, 5, 8–10, 48
Étienne, Père, 71, 77
Eton, 22, 88, 262–63, 268, 279–81, 283, 291–93, 295–97, 361–62, 369, 376, 381, 399
Euclid, 135
Eure-et-Loir, 151
Euripides, 269
Europe, 7, 10–11, 31, 37, 66, 125, 154, 159–62, 166, 226, 254, 256–57, 259, 273, 291, 294, 319–20, 345
Évreux, 38
executive, 3, 5, 18, 20, 27–28, 71, 281, 303–4
Exeter, 365
expansion, 7–8, 11–13, 316, 318, 323

Falloux, Frédéric, comte de, 76
Fénelon, F. de la Mothe-, *Télémaque*, 268
feudalism, 53, 129, 162, 211, 304
"few," the, 307
Finder, Morris, vi
Finistère, 120
Finsbury Circus, 378
Five-Mile Act, 20
Flanders, 207–8
Fontanes, Louis de, 58–59
Forster, Jane (Arnold), 351
Forster, W. E., 351, 361
Fortescue, Hugh, Earl, 323
Fortoul, H.-N.-H., 78, 135, 137, 155
Fourcroy, A.-F., 47
Fox How, 364
France, French, 30–31, 328; administrative organization, 33, 53, 103–4, 155; army, 11, 102, 123, 151, 164, 336, 340; arrondissements, 33, 71, 73, 79; bishops, 35, 38, 56, 63–64, 72–73, 79, 90, 131, 334, 337; cantons, 33, 44, 79; Center, 329; Chamber of Deputies, 70–71, 74, 79, 337, 373; character, 111, 133, 135–36, 148, 152–53, 158, 161–63, 178, 278, 297, 313; charities, 96, 110–11, 119; Charter of 1830, 273; child labour, 125, 131, 150–51; clergy, 35, 37, 44–46, 49–50, 56, 61, 63–67, 71, 73, 75, 78–81, 84–85, 112, 114, 120–22, 127, 129–30, 136, 138, 140, 144, 146, 157–58, 274, 337, 369; communes, 33–34, 49–51, 54, 58–59, 64, 66, 68–71, 73–74, 78, 80, 82–87, 90, 92, 94–99, 104, 106–8, 119–20, 126–28, 146, 266, 307; Concordat, 34, 36, 53, 143; conscription, 58, 60, 115, 117, 146, 151–52, 162; Constituent Assembly, 46–47; Constitution of 1791, 47; Con-

sulate, 21, 34, 47, 53–54, 58, 211; Convention, 47–49, 51, 53–54, 57, 68; countryside, 123, 125, 128–30, 271–72, 277; *coup d'état* (1851), 332, 343; Courts of Appeal, 56; crime, 42, 77; departments, 33, 51, 54, 58–59, 69–70, 79, 83, 86–87, 94–98, 100, 103, 110, 124–25, 128–29, 137–40, 145, 151, 265–66; Directory, 53, 336; Empire (Napoleon I), 55–60, 63–64, 68, 80, 335–36, 380; Empire (Napoleon III), 78–91, 106, 332, 344, 380; geography, 32; government, 10–11, 16, 35–36, 49, 56–57, 62, 71, 75, 153–55, 157–58, 164, 266, 276, 298, 394; industry, 110–11, 150–51; *Institut*, 51, 162; July monarchy, 64, 67–75, 335, 338–39, 373; language, 48, 68–69, 132, 153–54, 205, 226, 268–70, 281, 333; Legislative Assembly, 47, 57; literature, 268–70, 313; maps, 254, 256; mayors, 33–34, 66, 73–75, 78, 81, 85–86, 108, 121, 126–27, 146; Minister of the Interior, 59, 63, 146–47, 336; newspapers, 132, 164, 337; patriotism, 49, 131, 392; Penal Code, 36; people, 9–11, 17, 22, 32, 45, 110–11, 118, 124, 127, 130–31, 153–55, 208–9, 344; poets, 135, 270; population, 32–33, 48, 50, 143; prefects, 30, 33, 54, 58–59, 61, 64, 71, 73–74, 78–81, 86, 90, 118, 120–21, 126–27, 137–39, 146–47, 266, 336; religions, 34, 63–64, 71–72, 84, 118–19, 143, 199, 267, 273, 275, 334; Restoration, 41, 61–66, 80, 272, 335; Revolution (1789), 3–4, 11, 21, 41–42, 44, 46–52, 54–55, 61, 63, 71, 122, 129, 158, 162, 189, 272–73, 313, 374, 380; Revolution (1830), 64, 337; Revolution (1848), 75–76, 78, 137, 333, 339, 373; savings banks, 103; social conditions, 11, 126–27, 129, 342; States-General, 39, 46; subprefects, 33, 54; taxation, 33, 44, 70, 81, 85, 89, 96–100; Terror, 37; war in Italy, 131–32, 254; wealth, 32; weights and measures, 48, 69

France, education in, academies, 55, 57, 62, 80, 131, 147–48, 265–66; academy-inspectors, 71, 78, 80, 87, 98, 120, 123–24, 137, 146–48, 150, 266, 270, 276; academy-rectors, 30, 55, 57, 59, 61, 64–65, 69, 71, 74, 78, 80, 84, 98, 102, 116, 124, 135, 138–39, 146–47, 266, 338; *adjoints* (*adjointes*), 82, 106–7, 113, 140; administrative expense, 95–98, 103; adult schools, 73, 95–96, 98–99, 113, 150; agriculture, 48, 90, 137, 152; apprentice schools, 96, 98–99; attendance, 125–26, 128, 131, 150–52; bifurcation, 269; boys, 40–41, 43–44, 55, 68, 72, 90, 93–94, 100, 105–7, 112, 117–19, 121, 125–26, 132–33; cantonal committees, 61, 64; cantonal delegates, 79, 81, 95, 103, 121, 146–47; certification of teachers, 49–51, 58–59, 61, 63, 65, 67, 69–70, 73, 77, 79, 86, 90, 95, 103, 106, 112, 116–17, 124, 135, 137–40, 175, 185, 200, 267, 275; col-

France, education in (*cont.*) leges, 21, 44, 47, 64; commission of inquiry (Thiers), 76–77; Commission of Public Instruction, 62–63; communal colleges, 53, 55, 68, 87, 90, 124, 270; communal committees, 71, 73, 78, 84, 86, 146; communal schools, 64–65, 72, 82–83, 100, 107, 112; compulsory attendance, 43, 50–51, 148; congreganist: *see* religious communities; Council of Public Instruction (Imperial, Royal, Superior, etc.), 46, 55, 64, 67, 71, 73, 79–81, 199, 268; denominational, 83–85; departmental council, 54–55, 58, 79, 81, 84, 90, 106, 137–39; descriptions of, 32; district committees, 49, 71, 73–74, 78, 81, 146; domestic, 36; dormitories, 136, 267, 276, 297; endowments, 47, 55–57, 70; "facultative" matters, 68, 90, 94–95, 124, 135, 139, 152; fees and exemption from fees, 44, 49, 51, 54–55, 69–70, 74, 79, 82, 85–87, 89, 94, 96–98, 108, 119, 126–28, 131, 136–37, 150, 270, 276, 284; finances, 51, 59, 64, 70, 72–73, 76, 83, 92, 94–100, 107, 119–20, 339; free, 35, 37, 39, 47, 51, 69, 82, 85, 107, 119, 130–31, 150; girls, 40, 43, 55, 64, 68, 72–73, 90, 93–96, 100, 105, 107–8, 110–12, 117–18, 121, 126–28, 132–33, 152; grammar-schools, 35, 44, 55, 57; Grand-Master of the University, 36, 55, 58–59, 62; history of, 35–91; industrial, 48; infant schools, 73, 95–96, 98, 104, 110, 128; infirmaries, 267, 271; inspection of 1833, 65–66, 72; inspectors-general, 30, 43, 55, 58–59, 73, 97–98, 101, 124, 146, 148; inspectresses, 90, 98; Jewish, 107, 153, 199; jury of instruction, 50–51, 59; law of 3rd Brumaire, year IV, 51, 53, 57; law of 1833, 51, 61, 64, 66–79, 83–86, 145–47, 154, 199, 266, 273, 338; laws of 1850, 1852, 1854, 77–79, 82–86, 90, 108, 126–27, 132, 138–40, 145–46, 153, 159, 266, 333; lay associations, 120; lay education, 51, 157; lay schools, 90, 94–95, 105–8, 110–11, 113, 116–19, 121, 139; libraries, 51; literacy, 38; *lycées*, 22, 53, 55, 57, 87, 265–71, 275–77, 279–84, 294, 297–98, 372; meals, 106, 136, 271, 276–77; medals, 146; mill-schools, 150; Minister of Public Instruction, 30, 43, 56–57, 59, 63–64, 67, 70–71, 74–76, 78–83, 90–92, 98, 101–2, 105, 118, 124, 126–27, 131–32, 135–38, 147–48, 265–66, 268, 276, 335, 338; mixed schools, 82, 93–94, 111, 128; model schools, 60–61, 73; monitors, 107, 113; municipal council, 33, 71, 126; museums, 51; needlework schools, 96, 98–99, 111–12, 127–28, 139; normal schools, 48, 57, 60, 64, 67, 70–74, 78, 80, 86, 95–96, 100, 124, 134–41, 152, 155, 267, 271; "obligatory" matters, 68, 90, 94–95, 124, 135, 139; parochial schools, 43, 112, 121; patrons, 45, 104;

pensions, 70; Petit Collège, 267; playgrounds, 106, 126, 128, 130, 267–68, 276, 297–98; political bias, 48, 57, 76–78, 119, 137; practise schools, 135; priests, 35, 45; primary, 30, 35, 39, 44, 48, 51, 53–55, 57–59, 64, 67, 69, 71–74, 76, 79–80, 83, 87, 92–93, 97–100, 105–33, 135–36, 138, 142, 152, 157, 164, 175, 200, 265–66, 329, 333, 338–39; primary (elementary), 68, 86; primary (superior), 68, 86–87, 90; primary inspectors, 31, 65, 71–74, 80, 84, 94–95, 100–103, 109–10, 112, 114, 117–19, 121, 123–25, 130, 132, 138, 144, 146–48, 266, 341; private (*libre*), 37, 49–50, 56, 59, 69, 79, 87–88, 90, 93–94, 96, 98–99, 112, 120–22, 124, 132, 150, 271, 273, 275–76, 279, 284, 298, 337–38, 372; professors, 267, 335; Protestant, 133–34, 153, 199, 338; provisor, 266–67; religious communities, 37, 39–44, 47, 54–56, 62–65, 71, 73, 77, 80, 90–94, 108, 110–22, 126, 128–29, 132, 134, 139, 272–73, 275, 277; religious education, 35, 37–39, 41, 43, 46, 57, 61, 66, 68–69, 81, 83–85, 106, 111, 116–17, 121–22, 128–29, 138, 142–44, 157, 267, 274, 277; religious liberty, 69, 83–85, 144, 154; Roman Catholic, 143, 199, 338; rural, 37, 43, 59, 74; salaries, 44, 49–51, 54, 70, 74–76, 81, 83, 95, 100–102, 107, 112–13, 124, 126–28, 130, 145, 150–51, 173, 200–201, 271; scholarships, 44, 54, 134, 137–38, 267; school-books, 41, 61, 81, 95–96, 100, 107, 125–26, 130, 271, 333, 341; school-houses, 50–51, 54, 65, 95–96, 104–6, 110–12, 125, 127–30, 145, 148, 205, 266–67, 272–73, 275; schoolless children, 109, 150; schools, numbers of, 47–48, 50, 72, 93–94, 98–99, 125, 152, 284; secondary, 21–22, 44, 53, 55, 58, 80, 87, 97, 265–71, 276, 284, 297; social effects, 150, 153–65; special schools, 48, 140; stagiary schools, 139–40; state support, 21–22, 43, 46, 49–51, 55, 58–61, 64, 67, 69, 72–73, 76, 81, 83, 86–89, 94–98, 122, 125, 128, 131, 149, 155, 164, 200, 209, 266, 271, 295, 297, 313; statistics, 41, 44, 58–59, 64, 67, 72–73, 76, 86–87, 92–104, 109; students, ability of, 107, 110, 134–35, 137; students, numbers of, 44, 72–73, 87, 94, 98–99, 105, 110, 112–13, 115, 120, 125–28, 131–32, 134, 150, 267, 275; Sunday schools, 129; *suppléants*, 82, 106; teachers, 35, 38–39, 43–46, 49–51, 54, 56–59, 61, 64–66, 70–77, 79–83, 85, 93–96, 101–2, 106, 111, 113–17, 119–21, 124, 126–27, 129–30, 132–36, 139–40, 145–47, 150–51, 155, 267, 275–77, 337; technical, 90; uniforms, 268, 272; University, 36, 43, 53, 55–60, 62–65, 67, 78, 80, 88–89, 179, 272, 290, 335, 337; urban, 37, 42; villages and towns, 37, 39, 42–45, 54, 58–59, 66, 74–75, 82, 86, 100, 104, 106–10, 119,

France, education in (*cont.*) 123–32, 136, 336, 338; voluntary support, 73, 87, 96–100, 112, 120, 132
Franciscans, 39, 345
Fraser, James, 222, 225
Fraser, William, 109, 346
Fraser's Magazine, 349, 396
Frayssinous, Denis, 63
Frederick I (Prussia), 344
free trade, 156, 232, 243, 254, 258, 260, 281–82, 349, 360, 365–66
Fribourg, 167, 170, 173–77, 329
Froude, J. A., 349–50

gallicanism, 334
Gard, 150
Gauls, 306
Geerligs, M., 205–6
Geneva, 166–67, 169, 171, 173–75, 199, 329
geography, 48, 90, 106–7, 110, 116, 125, 128, 131, 152, 169, 200, 215, 223, 226, 269, 281, 333, 341, 366
geology, 269
geometry, 135, 152, 200
Gerbaud, Frère, 63
German, Germany, 159, 163, 178, 194, 254, 281, 306, 313; education, 32, 39, 142, 148, 172, 179, 279, 295, 328, 335
Gerson, Jean, 38
Gibraltar, Straits of, 125
Girard, Jean-Baptiste, 176
Girdlestone, Edward, 251
Gironde, 123–24, 127, 134
Gladstone, W. E., 305, 372–74, 379
Glasgow, 109
Godefroi, M. H., 196
Goethe, J. W., 315
Goldsmith, Lewis, *Recueil de décrets, &c.*, 336
Goode, T., 345
government, 3–7, 274
grammar, 107, 125, 131, 138, 169, 200, 237, 264, 268, 333, 341, 358
grand style, 5–6, 321
Granville, Granville George, Earl, 31, 227, 229–30, 241–42, 249, 350, 352, 354, 356, 359, 364, 372
Gray, Thomas, 262
Great Eastern Railway, 378
Great Western Railway, 253
Greece, Greek, 68, 148, 160, 206, 268–69, 281, 314–16, 322, 332, 359
Greenwich, 224
Grenoble, 151
Groen van Prinsterer, Guillaume, 193–94, 196
Groningen, 184, 194, 199, 202
Grosvenor Square, 378
guarantees: *see* securities
Guardian, 224, 234, 284–85, 289, 295
Guernon-Ranville, M.-C.-A., comte de, 64
Guizot, François, 31, 51, 66–69, 71–72, 74, 83–84, 86, 90, 118, 137, 154–55, 266, 268, 273, 328–29
Guthrie, W. B., vi
gymnastics, 50, 90, 268

Haarlem, 182, 184, 187, 205–6, 329
Hague, The, 182, 190, 204–5, 328
Hamilton, Alexander, 18
Happy Islands, 282
Hardy, Gathorne, 353
Harper, Sir William, 377
Harris, E. A. J., 344
Harrow, 22, 88, 140, 262, 280, 283, 296, 399

Haut-Rhin, 131
Haute-Garonne, 152
Haute-Saône, 151
Hawkins, Edward, 315, 381
Hawtrey, Stephen, 291–92
Henley, J. W., 250
Henry IV (France), 36, 344
Henry VI (England), 262
Henry VIII (England), 321, 378
Herculaneum, 278
Hermopolis, 337
history, 90, 107, 125, 131, 152, 169, 200, 215, 223, 269, 333, 376
Hodgson, W. B., 250
Hoijtema, M. van, 197
Holland, 30–31, 328; calendar, 181; conscription, 207; Constitution of 1848, 189, 191, 193, 196; North, 181, 184; people, 195, 202, 208–9; population, 184, 207, 209; public relief, 183–84, 200–201; religious sects, 181, 184, 186, 190–97, 205; South, 207–8, 347
Holland, education in, administration, 183; attendance, 183–84, 189–90, 201–2, 205, 207; certification of teachers, 182, 185, 199–200; communal administration, 183–84, 186, 189, 199–201, 209; compulsory, 201–2; descriptions of, 31–32; fees, 183–84, 188, 200–201, 205; free, 183–84, 188, 205; French schools, 188, 206, 279; grammar-schools, 179; history, 179–203; infant schools, 207; inspection and inspectors, 180, 182–83, 185–87, 197, 199, 201–2, 204, 207, 238–39; intermediate schools, 188, 205–6; Latin schools, 188; law of 1806, 179–90, 192, 194–96, 200–202; law of 1857, 179–80, 189, 195–97, 199–203, 206, 346; legislative debates, 193–96, 198, 207; Minister for the Home Department, 181–82, 185–86, 202, 204; mixed schools, 93, 204–5, 346; normal schools, 181, 186–87, 205–7, 329; poor-schools, 179–80, 183–84, 187, 205–6; primary, 39, 179–81, 183, 186, 188, 200, 202, 205, 207–8; private, 182, 184–87, 189–90, 197, 199–200, 207; public, 182, 184–85, 187, 197, 199, 204, 206–7; pupil-teachers, 114, 186, 201, 204–7; Referendary for Education, 202, 204; religious education, 142, 180–81, 186, 190–97, 202–3, 205; salaries, 82, 183–84, 189, 200–201, 204–5; school-houses, 181, 184, 203, 205–6; school-methods, 185, 187; schools, numbers of, 184, 200, 207; state support, 181, 183, 197, 200, 206, 295; students, numbers of, 184, 189–90, 202, 204–7; Sunday schools, 207; superior, 188; teachers, 181–82, 184–87, 189–92, 195, 199–201, 204–5, 207; universities, 179, 188; villages and towns, 183–85, 187
Holy Land, 320
Home and Colonial Infant School Society, 133
Homer, 5, 14, 269, 315, 359, 362
Hook, W. F., 286
Horace, 162, 269
human nature, 7–8, 12, 68, 199,

human nature (*continued*) 210–11, 228, 230, 292–93, 299, 304, 317–18, 322
Humboldt, Wilhelm von, 312
Hume, Joseph, 255
Hurstpierpont, 375

ideals, ideas, 11–13, 17–19, 21, 23–24, 26, 160–61, 163, 224, 263, 292, 307, 315–16, 318–19, 321–22, 324, 385–86
"Ignorantines": *see* Brethren of the Christian Schools
independence: *see* liberty
India, 392
individualism, 8, 13, 16–18, 21, 25, 113, 304, 306, 309, 311, 313–14, 316–17, 352, 379, 385
Indre-et-Loire, 338
intellect, intellectual, intelligence, 6, 12, 19, 27–28, 48, 57, 70, 74, 136, 153–58, 160–63, 172, 193, 197, 210, 222–25, 227, 243, 250, 260, 297, 302, 306, 314–18, 321, 347, 354, 358, 394
Ipswich, 364
Ireland, 164
Irish Board of National Education, 192, 244–45, 347; reading books, 125, 347
Isocrates, 268
Italy, 254, 316

James, Sir Henry, 252, 256, 365–66
Jansenism, 346
jargon, 237, 330
Jerusalem, 320–22
Jesuits, 39, 66, 176, 345
Jesus, 29, 196, 243
Jews, 34, 107, 143, 160, 186, 190, 194, 196, 199, 205, 346
Jockey Club, 365
Johnson, Samuel, *Dictionary*, 252, 365
Joly, Claude, 38
Jourdain, A.-L.-M., 59
Jourdain, Charles, 59, 72, 87, 101, 336, 338–39
Journal des instituteurs, 131
Junot, A., 340
justice, 304

Kay, Joseph, 32
Kay-Shuttleworth, Sir James, 114–15, 212–14, 220–21, 232–33, 235, 237, 334, 348–50, 357
Kent, 256
Kidderminster, 379
Kilian, Étienne, 87, 199, 338
King's Road, 301

Lacordaire, J.-B.-H., 271–78, 284, 322, 369, 371
La Fontaine, Jean de, 268
Lake, W. C., 352
Lambeth, 324
Lamennais, Félicité de, 120, 337
Lamennais, Jean-Marie de, 120
Lancaster, Joseph, 333
Lancing, 285, 287–88, 375
Landes, 119
Languedoc, 85, 265, 271–72
Lansdowne, Henry, Marquis of, 214, 233, 348
Larochejaquelein, Henri de, 277
Larousse, Pierre, *Grand dictionnaire*, 327
Lasalle, St. Jean-Baptiste de, 40, 42–43, 108, 114, 120
Lateran Councils, 35
Latin, 64, 68, 163, 188, 206, 226, 268–69, 281, 315, 332
Lausanne, 166–67, 171, 174, 329
Laveleye, Émile de, 193, 196–97, 202, 208, 346

Lavoisier, A.-L., 336
Lazarists, 77
Leeds, 228, 353, 355
Legion of Honor, 53, 118, 134, 211
Léobin, 334
Leyden, 188
Lezay de Marnésia, Adrien, comte, 60
liberalism, 26, 62–64, 69, 77, 114, 154–56, 177, 194–95, 305–7, 313, 348, 352, 361, 379, 381
liberty, independence, 3, 5, 7–8, 13, 16–18, 23–24, 29, 48, 50, 63, 69, 121, 145, 156, 177, 189, 199, 210, 246, 303, 307–8, 310–11, 313–14, 381
Libourne, 119
Lierre, 187
Lincolnshire, 129
Lingen, R. R. W., 233, 237, 349, 357, 372
literature, 341–42
Littell's Living Age, 370, 397
Liverpool, 296
Livy, 269
local government and administration, 16, 34, 49–51, 54, 66, 71, 74, 99, 145–47, 156, 165, 183–84, 186, 189, 199, 209, 230, 296–97, 304, 307–9, 313, 354, 364
London, 113, 148, 246, 254, 301, 328–29, 335, 342, 345, 363, 378
London, Bishop of, 244–45, 361–62
London, University of, 89, 239
London and North Western Railway, 253
London and Westminster Bank, 361
London Bridge, 301
London Review, 362, 364, 367, 397
Longman, Green, Longman, and Roberts, 330–31, 342
Lorain, Paul, 65–66
Lorraine, 118
Lot-et-Garonne, 134
Louis XIV, 43, 45
Louis XVI, 272
Louis XVIII, 335
Louis Philippe, 333, 335, 339, 373
Louvain, 275
Lowe, Robert, 213, 217, 228–29, 231, 235, 240–43, 245, 247–51, 257–61, 348–50, 352, 356–60, 362–64, 368, 372, 375, 379, 381
Lowry, H. F.: *see* Arnold, M., *Letters to Clough, Note-Books*
Lucan, 269
Lucerne, 256
Lucian, 268
Lutherans, 34, 184
Lyons, 38, 120, 123, 131, 329, 338

Macmillan, Alexander, 370–71, 375
Macmillan and Co., 331
Macmillan's Magazine, 369–71, 381, 397
Macaulay, Thomas, Lord, 330
Machiavelli, 276
Madison, James, 18
Magin-Marrens, Alfred, 30–31, 34, 92, 102–3, 151, 328–29
Maidstone, 212
"*male* and *female*," 237, 390, 395
Manchester, 109, 123, 332, 355
maps, 252–56, 364–66
Marlborough, 283–84, 315
Marseillaise, 66

Martigny, 329
Mary Virgin, 144
masses: *see* populace
Massillon, J.-B., 269
mathematics, 54, 135, 185, 226, 269, 280–81, 376
maxims, 3, 20, 25, 29, 232, 234, 243, 249, 274, 291–92, 299, 305, 307–8, 310–12
Mediterranean, 272
Médoc, 125
Mennonite, 181
Merchant Taylors' School, 262
Messina, 163
Miall, Edward, 214, 234, 352, 371
Michael Angelo, 316
Michaud, J.-F., 381
Michelet, Jules, 162
middle ages, 19, 45, 154, 260, 274, 278, 286, 294–95
middle class, 19–26, 44, 54, 68, 86–89, 188, 206, 263, 279–82, 284–86, 289–95, 297, 301, 305–25, 332, 369–73, 375, 381
Middleton, D., 342
Midlands, North, 214
military training, 50
Mill, J. S., 337, 379
Mirabeau, Honoré, comte de, 3, 6, 263
modern languages, 68, 188, 204–5, 269–70, 280, 374
modern spirit, modern institutions, 10–11, 24, 29, 37, 39, 57, 143, 154, 158, 160, 188, 253, 255, 274, 294, 305, 309, 311, 313–14, 321, 324
Molière, J.-B., 261, 269
Moniteur, 43, 60, 64, 69, 93, 132, 336
monitorial system, 31, 114, 345
Montagne Noire, 272, 278
Montalembert, C.-F.-R., comte de, 273, 277, 374
Montesquieu, Charles, baron de, 269, 315
Montmartre, Rue du Faubourg, 105
Montmorency (family), 162
Montpellier, 272
Montrose, 366
Moore's Almanack, 181
morality, 6, 10, 23–25, 27, 39, 42, 48–51, 57, 66, 68–70, 77, 83, 111, 119, 122, 132, 137, 142, 155–57, 176, 181, 190, 192, 194–95, 197, 200, 202, 215, 218–19, 224, 227–28, 230, 235–36, 260, 274, 281, 283, 299, 313, 318, 323, 368
Morell, J. D., *Analysis of Sentences*, 237
Morley, John, 379
Morning Star, 17, 251
Moscow, 163
Museum, 290, 376
music, 90, 116, 128, 152, 169, 200, 250
mutual system: *see* monitorial system

Nancy, 30, 107, 134, 148, 329
Nantes, 328
Nantes, Edict of, 43
Napier, Francis, Lord, 204
Napoleon I, 36–37, 41, 47, 53–58, 60, 62, 68, 143, 158, 211, 335–36, 380
Napoleon III, 106, 332, 339, 343, 380
Narbonne, 272
nation: *see* state
national character, 16–18, 24, 29, 155–56, 158–65, 208–10, 314, 316, 319, 331
National Society for Promoting the Education of the Poor, 121–22, 144, 213, 232, 238, 347–48, 352

natural history, 90, 125, 269
Nelson's School Series, 342
Nepos, Cornelius, 268
Neuchâtel, 166, 170, 173–75, 329
Newcastle, Henry, fifth Duke of, 327, 352
Newcastle Commission, 30, 32, 89–90, 214–16, 218, 220–27, 236, 240, 265, 327–28, 330, 340, 343, 349, 352–55, 357, 363–64, 369, 372
newspapers, 17, 43, 60, 64, 93, 131–32, 164, 222–24, 234, 243–45, 249–52, 256, 258, 263, 275, 281–82, 284–85, 301–2, 304, 315, 323, 325, 332, 353, 356, 358, 360–65, 367–68, 371, 374, 378, 381
Newton, Isaac, 29
Nieuw Nederlandsch Biografisch Woordenboek, 327
Nieuwenhuyzen, Jan, 181
Nièvre, 77, 152
Nîmes, 71, 85, 328
Nimrod, 302
Noah, 251
Noël, F.-J.-M., 179
Nonconformist, 353, 372
Norfolk, 302
Normal School, Superior, 48, 267
Normandy, 118
Norris, J. P., 223, 259–60, 367–68
North, Department of (France), 150
Northamptonshire, 302
Northumberland, 283
Notre Dame, 38, 275
Nottingham, 217, 372
Numa Pompilius, 302

"Old Dog Tray," 263
Oratorians, 39
Ordnance Survey, 252–56, 364–66
Oriel College, Oxford, 381
Orleans, 35, 39
Overstone, Samuel, Lord, 244–46, 361–62
Overyssel, 202
Ovid, 268
Oxenstierna, Axel, Count, 263
Oxford, 89, 253, 266, 275, 290, 300, 315, 366, 370, 372, 375–76, 381
Oxford and Cambridge Local Examinations, 288–89, 372
Oxford Companion to French Literature, 327
Oxfordshire, 255, 363

Pakington, Sir John, 154, 305, 372, 378–79
Pall Mall Gazette, 333
Palm, J. H. van der, 181
Palmerston, Henry John, Viscount, 242
Paris, 11, 30, 34, 38, 40–42, 73, 75, 82, 97, 101, 104–24, 131, 134, 148, 163, 254, 265–66, 272–74, 278, 328–29, 344, 366; Academy of, 57, 119, 151; Archbishop of, 274; British school, 132; papal nuncio, 273; police, 42, 273; University of, 36, 38, 47
parish, 34, 38, 65, 71, 73, 86, 98, 120–22, 145–46
Parke, Sir James, 332
Pas-de-Calais, 55
Pascal, Blaise, 36
"Paterfamilias," 369
Pattison, Mark, 328
pedagogy, 40, 57, 80–81, 124, 131–32, 135–36, 175, 185, 187, 216
Peel, Sir Robert, 156
Penzer, N. M., 368

people: *see* populace
Pepin the Little, 272
perfection, 29, 312–14, 317–22, 325
Pericles, 316
Pestalozzi, J. H., 342
Peter the Hermit, 320
Peyrot, M., 266, 268
Phaedrus, 268
Philippe, Frère (Matthieu Bransiet), 41, 71, 77
physics, 48, 90, 152, 269
physiology, 250, 269
Pictet, Armand, 344
Piedmont, 328
Piguet, M., 167
Pindar, 269
Plato, 25, 269, 343, 394
Plautus, 373
Plutarch, 269
Plymouth, 355
political economy, 156, 232, 243, 254, 281–82, 360, 380–81
political parties, 156, 158, 260
Polytechnic School, 48
Pope, Alexander, 160, 252, 336
Pope, papal, 36, 41–42, 273, 334, 369
populace, popular, 6–15, 17–18, 21, 23, 25–26, 44–45, 60, 68, 87, 122, 148, 153–54, 156–59, 161–63, 209–10, 215–16, 219, 221, 223, 226–28, 230, 234, 240–41, 243, 245, 282, 292, 305–7, 310, 315, 324–25, 372, 378, 394
Portugal, 340
practical application, 21, 297, 315
prebend, 35, 39
Prees (Salop), 251
priesthood, 122, 158, 160–62, 331
Prinsen, P. J., 187, 205
prisons, 228, 231, 249, 304
professional class, 87–89, 279, 281, 284
progress, 9, 25, 274, 317
Protestant Dissent, 20, 24, 143, 158, 194, 198, 243, 302, 306, 308, 317, 320–21, 323–24, 332, 339, 353, 371, 373, 381
Protestantism, 34, 38–39, 43, 61, 71–72, 84–85, 118, 129, 133–34, 143, 167, 180, 190–93, 195–97, 199, 205, 267, 334, 338, 367
provincialism, 163, 318, 322
Prussia, 159, 167, 179, 208
Prussianisation, 159, 161
Puritanism, 20, 317–18
Pyrenees, 271
Pyrénées-Orientales, 55

Quélen, H.-L. de, 274
Quimper, 120, 328
Quintilian, 237

race, 6, 135, 162–63, 306
"raindeer," 252, 365
Rapet, J.-J., 30–31, 92, 105, 109, 116, 133, 137, 333
Reading, 367, 375
reading, 41, 44, 48, 51, 57–58, 68, 107, 111, 125–28, 135–36, 138, 151–52, 169, 200, 202, 215–25, 227–28, 235–37, 241, 248, 250, 257, 259, 341–42, 349, 353–55, 360–62
reason, 11, 17, 19, 24, 26, 28–29, 113, 145, 153–59, 164–65, 177, 199, 202, 210–12, 301, 394
Reformation, 38–39, 167
religious education, 142, 157, 193, 197–99
religious skepticism, 194, 198
Rémusat, Charles, comte de, 227

Rendu, Ambroise, 43, 114, 116, 334–37
Rendu, Eugène, 43, 102, 328
Rennes, 328
republican, 48, 57, 292, 339, 394
revolution, 119, 158
Revue germanique, 298, 380
Rheims, 40
Rhin-et-Moselle, 336
Robespierre, Maximilien, 336
Rocher, M., 266
Rocher, Rue du, 113–14, 116–17
Roebuck, J. A., 308, 310, 379–80, 400
Rogers, William, 352
Rohan (family), 162
Roman Catholicism, 34, 36, 43–44, 65, 85, 133, 143–44, 162, 167, 180, 190–92, 194–95, 199, 205, 239, 267, 274, 278, 334, 338–39, 346, 367, 373–75
Roman law, 36–37
Rome, 6, 144, 253, 275, 280, 322, 369, 378
Rotterdam, 190, 329
Rouen, 40
Rouland, Gustave, 30, 82, 101, 105, 123, 131–32
Rousseaud de Lacombe, Guy du, 36
Royer-Collard, P.-P., 43, 62
Rugby, 140, 262, 268, 280–81, 297, 373, 375, 377, 399
Russell, G. W. E.: *see* Arnold, M., *Letters*
Russia, 208

St. Antoine, Faubourg, 42
St. Francis of Assisi, 322
St. Francis of Paola, Order of, 40
St. James's Square, 378
St. Lazare, Rue, 112–13
St. Mark's School, Windsor, 291–92
St. Martin de Touche, 130
St. Martin de Villers, 38
St. Patroclus of Berry, 37
St. Paul, 29, 262
St. Paul's School, 262
St. Peter, 144
St. Vincent de Paul, 373
St. Yon, 40
Salisbury, 252
Sallust, 268
Salvandy, Narcisse, comte de, 75
Saturday Review, 381
Schimmelpenninck, M., 196
Schimmelpenninck, R. J., 181
sciences, 48, 54, 86, 90, 152, 163, 200, 262, 269–70, 341–42, 376
Scotland, 38–39, 143–44, 180, 342, 347, 380
Scott, John, 227
Scott, Walter, *Ivanhoe*, 279
sectarianism, 142–44, 161, 165, 190–92, 194–96, 199, 318, 323, 393
securities, educational, 65, 69, 112, 117–18, 146, 175, 188, 230, 249, 257–59, 271, 276, 282–90, 293–94, 296, 322, 363, 375
Seignette, M., 266, 268
Seine, 76
Seine-et-Marne, 151
Senior, Nassau W., 342–43, 352
Sesostris, 136
Shakspeare, William, 29, 316; *Othello*, 249
Shedd, W. G. T., 356
Sheffield, 308
Shoreham, 287, 375
Shrewsbury, 262, 364
Shropshire, 251, 355

Shuttleworth: *see* Kay-Shuttleworth
simultaneous system, 31, 114
Sinclair, John, 213, 217, 356
Sisters of Charity, 267
slavery, 319
Smith, Goldwin, 321, 352–53
socialism, 178
Société d'Instruction élémentaire, 120
Society for the Public Good, 181, 186, 346
Society of Arts, 290, 376
Socrates, 160
Somerset, 376
Sophocles, 263, 269
Sorbonne, 335
Sorèze, 271–73, 275–82, 284, 298, 328, 371, 374
Sourdière, Rue de la, 110
Southey, Robert, 257
Sparta, 56
Spectator, 234, 371
Spinoza, Benedict de, 160, 331, 365
Spitalfields, 246, 324
Spurlin, P. M., vi
Staffordshire, 355, 364
Stanford, Edward, 254, 256, 365
Stanley, Edward, Lord, 228, 230, 355
State, 3–4, 7, 16–21, 23, 25–29, 33, 35–57, 43, 145, 155–59, 161, 164–65, 188, 199, 211, 253–56, 301–6, 308–9, 313–14, 359, 379–80; definition, 26–27, 294, 300, 302, 310, 377; regulation and support of schools, 21–23, 37, 46–47, 49–51, 55, 64, 69–70, 72–73, 76, 86–89, 94–98, 113, 122, 131, 133, 140, 144–47, 149, 168, 173, 181–82, 197–98, 209–10, 213–19, 225–35, 238–46, 248–49, 257–59, 266, 271, 276, 282–83, 286–87, 290, 294–95, 297–301, 304, 309–11, 322–24, 347–54, 360, 364, 368, 370–72, 379–80, 382, 393; religious establishment, 85, 122, 143, 194–96, 198–99, 210, 244, 308–9
Stephen, Fitzjames, 328
Stewart, R. C., vi
Strand, 254
Strasbourg, 60, 72, 85, 116, 134, 329
Strauss, D. F., 346
Sumner, J. B., 212
"supply and demand": *see* free trade
Sussex, 287, 375
swimming, 50
Switzerland, child labour, 170–72; French Cantons, 30–31, 166–78, 328; German Cantons, 31, 166, 175; government, 167–69, 171, 174, 176–77, 344–45; maps, 254, 256, 366; political and social conditions, 167, 170–71, 173, 176–78, 298, 344–45; population, 167; religion, 167, 345; reviews, 259; Sonderbund, 167, 176
Switzerland, education in, 259; administration, 167–69, 171–72, 175; attendance, 166, 171–72; boys, 168; certification of teachers, 169, 174, 185; clerical influence, 176–77; communes, 168–74, 176; compulsion, 168–72, 176–77; democratic influence, 167–68, 176; domestic, 177; *écoles d'hiver*, 174; endowments, 177; fees, 173–74; free, 168–69, 173, 176; girls, 168; holidays, 166, 170; infant schools, 168; inspectors,

169–70, 175–76; laws, 167, 169–70, 172–77, 209; local control, 170–72, 174–76; normal schools, 166–67, 174; primary, 169–70, 172–73, 175–77; private, 168, 174, 176; public, 168; religious instruction, 168–69, 176; salaries, 169, 173–74, 177; school-books, 173; schools, numbers of, 166, 168; secondary, 169, 279, 298; social influence, 166, 177–78; state support, 168, 173–74, 209; students, numbers of, 172, 174; subjects of instruction, 169, 175, 177; teachers, 166, 168–69, 173–76; taxation, 173

Tabourin, Abbé, 42
Tacitus, 269
Talleyrand-Périgord, C.-M. de, 46, 87
Tarn, 271
taste, 341–42
Taunton Commission, 372
Temple, Frederick, 288, 301–2, 377–78
Terence, 333, 385
Tets van Goudriaan, J. G. H. van, 204
Teutons, 163
Thames, 132, 253, 262
Themistocles, 136
Theodulf, 35
Thierry, Amédée, *History of the Gauls*, 306
Thiers, Louis-Adolphe, 76
Thucydides, 269
Times, 243, 245, 249, 251–52, 256, 258, 263, 281–82, 301–2, 304, 315, 323, 351–68, 372, 374, 378–80
Tiverton, 373
Tobias, R. C., vi, 377
Tocqueville, Alexis de, 9, 62
Toulouse, 129–30, 265–66, 270–72, 275 279–82, 284, 294, 297, 328
Touque, 38
Trent, Council of, 111
Tübingen, 199
Turgot, A.-R.-J., 46

ultramontanism, 122
Uniformity, Act of, 20
United States: *see* America
Univers, 275
University College, Oxford, 375
unction, 40
Unreason, Goddess of, 260
Ursulines, 40, 54
Utrecht, 188, 197, 199, 329

Valais, 167, 170, 173
Vallet de Viriville, Auguste, 35, 41, 334–37
Vatimesnil, A.-F.-H. Lefebvre de, 64
Vaucluse, 58
Vaud, 166–68, 170–75
Vaughan, C. J., 212, 216, 222, 229
Vendée, La, 277, 374
Venetian glass, 260
Versailles, 134
Vevey, 329
Vienna, 254; Treaty of, 123, 167
Villemain, A.-F., 44, 328–29
Vimeiro, 123
Virgil, 15, 268, 280, 303
Visigoths, 271
Vollenhoven, Hendrik, 204
Voltaire, 122, 158, 257, 268–69, 367
Vosges, 70
vulgarisation, 160–61, 163

Walcott, F. G., 327
Wales, 288, 340, 347, 377
Walpole, Spencer, 250, 360, 362–64
Walter, John, 249, 257–61, 363, 367–68
Wapley, 364
Ward, W. R., 200, 204
Warren, Samuel, *Select Extracts from Blackstone*, 237
Warwickshire, 129
Washington, George, 18
Waterloo, 60
Watkins, Frederick, 220
Webster, F. A. M., 377
Wellington, Arthur, Duke of, 340
Wesleyanism, 107, 143, 199, 227, 239, 356, 359
Westminster, 132, 356, 375; School, 262
Westminster Review, 337
Westphalia, Treaty of, 344
Whitridge, Arnold, vi
Wightman, Sir William, 364, 370
William the Silent, 208
Wiltshire, 217
Winchester, 262, 268, 280, 300
Windsor, 291–92, 376
Winkler Prins Encyclopaedie, 327
Wood, Robert, 14
Woodard, Nathaniel, 286–88, 296, 301, 324, 375
Woods, Margaret L., 375
Worcestershire, 378
Wordsworth, William, 162
Wright, I. C., 362
writing, 41, 44, 48, 51, 57–58, 68, 107, 125, 128, 131, 136, 138, 151–52, 169, 200, 202, 215–21, 224–25, 227–28, 235–36, 241, 248, 250, 257, 259, 349, 353–55, 360, 362
Württemberg, 346

Xenophon, 25, 268

Yorkshire, 214, 355, 380
Young, Karl: *see* Arnold, M., *Note-Books*

Zaandam, 328
zoological gardens, 237
zoology, 269